The Evolution of the
Fourth Amendment

The Evolution of the Fourth Amendment

Thomas N. McInnis

LEXINGTON BOOKS

A division of
ROWMAN & LITTLEFIELD PUBLISHERS, INC.
Lanham • Boulder • New York • Toronto • Plymouth, UK

Published by Lexington Books
A division of Rowman & Littlefield Publishers, Inc.
A wholly owned subsidary of The Rowman & Littlefield Publishing Group, Inc.
4501 Forbes Boulevard, Suite 200, Lanham, Maryland 20706
http://www.lexingtonbooks.com

Estover Road, Plymouth PL6 7PY, United Kingdom

British Library Cataloguing in Publication Information Available

Library of Congress Cataloging-in-Publication Data

The hardcover edition of this book was previously cataloged by the Library of Congress
as follows:

McInnis, Thomas N. 1958–
    The evolution of the Fourth Amendment / Thomas N. McInnis.
        p. cm.
    Includes bibliographical references and index.
    1. Searches and seizures—United States. 2. United States. Constitution. 4th
Amendment. I. Title.
    KF9630.M38 2009
    345.73'0522—dc22   2009006239

    ISBN 978-0-7391-2976-0 (cloth : alk. paper)
    ISBN 978-0-7391-2977-7 (pbk. : alk. paper)
    ISBN 978-0-7391-2978-4 (electronic)

Printed in the United States of America

Dedicated to my father, Jerry Duncan McInnis, the true scholar in the family, and my mother, Jolene Mae McInnis, the heart of the family.

Contents

Acknowledgments

I am indebted to a number of people for help in completing this project. The University of Central Arkansas provided a sabbatical leave which was essential in the preparation of this manuscript. My colleagues in the Political Science Department at the University Of Central Arkansas are a great group of people with which to work. Lisa Murphy has been very helpful in bringing in materials from other library collections. Thank you to the anonymous reviewer whose insights made this a stronger work. All mistakes are, however, my own. For the ease of reading, unless otherwise noted all citations and notes have been omitted in the quotations of all court opinions. I am also indebted to a number of people for other reasons. Thanks to my family, friends, the Coal Boys (for serving the public), and the Rolling Stones. Finally, thank you, as always, to Jan for being my best friend.

Chapter 1
Prologue

The fourth amendment is the Supreme Court's tarbaby: a mass of contradictions and obscurities that has ensnared the "Brethern" in such a way that every effort to extract themselves only finds them more profoundly stuck.[1]

A man can still control a small part of his environment, his house; he can retreat thence from outsiders, secure in the knowledge that they cannot get at him without disobeying the Constitution. . . . A sane, decent, civilized society must provide some such oasis, some shelter from public scrutiny, some insulate enclosure, some enclave, some inviolate place which is a man's castle.[2]

All governments have incredible powers to improve the lives of their citizens. Unfortunately, this same power may be used to destroy a person's life. This fact has long been recognized in America. British abuses of power provided one reason that Americans revolted against the British during the American Revolution. It was also one of the reasons that the first Congress proposed and the states ratified the Bill of Rights. The Bill of Rights was an attempt by Americans to place specific limits on the power of the government to interfere in a person's life in an arbitrary manner. Starting in the fall of 2001, the limits on the power of the government to interfere in one's life in an arbitrary manner must have seemed like a cruel joke to Steven Hatfill. That fall the nation was subjected to some of the worst horror in our history. On September 11, the twin towers of the World Trade Center were destroyed as men advancing an al Qaeda plot flew two commercial airliners into the towers. A separate airliner was flown into the Pentagon while a fourth one went down in a field in Pennsylvania. About a week later it was discovered that a number of letters containing the deadly pathogen anthrax had been mailed to various media outlets. On October 9, additional letters were sent to two members of the U.S. Senate. All of the letters had been mailed from Princeton, New Jersey. A total of five people died and a number of others were taken ill as a result of the anthrax attacks. Upon hearing of the anthrax letters the nation was taken into a panic and feared that we were again being subject to terrorist attack.

The initial investigation into the anthrax crime took federal law enforcement agencies to hundreds of scientists in fields related to biological weapons as they looked for clues and suspects. Dr. Steven Hatfill, an expert in virology and a former U.S. Army biodefense researcher, was included in this group of scientists. Over the next several months Dr. Hatfill was questioned by the FBI several times. He took and passed a polygraph that showed he had no involvement with the anthrax letters. Lacking clues, the FBI sent to microbiologists throughout the country posters of the envelopes that the anthrax letters had been mailed in for purposes of handwriting comparisons. The FBI also offered a reward to members of the scientific community to share their suspicions. One of the persons who responded was Dr. Barbara Hatch Rosenberg, who was a professor of environmental sciences in New York. Dr. Rosenberg had a theory that the person responsible for the anthrax letters was opposed to her campaign to get the United States to agree to monitor the Biological Weapons and Toxin Convention and her suspicions settled on Dr. Hatfill who fit her profile.

At first, the FBI ignored Dr. Rosenberg's accusations. They had, after all, already questioned him and he had passed a polygraph. A couple of things changed the FBI's mind. The first was the lack of any suspect and the increasing pressure to make progress in the case. The second was an increase in political pressure to find suspects after Dr. Rosenberg had an audience with the two senators who had received anthrax letters on June 18, 2002 in which she told them of her suspicions. As a result of these forces, Special Agent Van Harp directed all of the FBI's attention to Steven Hatfill. On June 25, 2002 Dr. Hatfill was again interviewed by the FBI and consented to have his home searched. The FBI had conducted a number of consensual searches of the homes of other scientists during the investigation but Hatfill's was different. To Dr. Hatfill's shock, when he arrived at his apartment complex, the media had been tipped off about the search. The complex was surrounded by news media vans and news helicopters filming the unfolding events which were broadcast live on television. Dr. Hatfill then became a focus of national attention.

Despite an offer of further cooperation from Dr. Hatfill which was voiced through his attorney, on August 1, 2002 the FBI decided to obtain and serve a search warrant to go through Dr. Hatfill's apartment a second time. As had happened with the first search, the media was again informed in advance and again showed up to broadcast the search to a national audience. At this time, an employee of the Department of Justice, Daryl Darnell, placed a call to Louisiana State University that Dr. Hatfill was about to start employment in a position that was to pay $150,000 a year there. Darnell told university officials that Hatfill was not to be employed on any job that used Department of Justice funds. Louisiana State University terminated Dr. Hatfill's position because he had been hired to work on projects that were funded by the Department of Justice. Neither the Department of Justice nor Louisiana State University provided any process by which Dr. Hatfill could challenge the basis of his termination.

On August 6, 2002, with no real evidence pointing at Dr. Hatfill nor any charges filed against him, Attorney General John Ashcroft appeared on national television and named Dr. Hatfill as a person of interest in the anthrax investigation. On August 22 he repeated the statement in a press conference. Under incredible pressure caused by Attorney General Ashcraft's remarks, government leaks, and media speculation Dr. Hatfill publicly defended himself on August 11 against the accusations that he was involved in the anthrax letters. Angered by Dr. Hatfill's attempt to clear his name the government sought to discredit him in several ways. First, it leaked to ABC news a copy of an unpublished novel that Dr. Hatfill had authored. The novel's plot involved a biomedical terrorist attack. Second, it told *Newsweek* magazine that a bloodhound's sniff tests had implicated Dr. Hartfill in the anthrax crime. The government also leaked information that Dr. Hatfill had failed three different polygraph tests to Nicholas Kristoff, a *New York Times* columnist.

The government also intensified its surveillance over Dr. Hatfill. The form that the surveillance took differed from most surveillance which attempts to covertly watch a person. The surveillance of Dr. Hatfill lasted 24 hours a day and took the form of harassment. Dr. Hartfill was followed by a caravan of five to seven agents where ever he went. They followed him so closely that Dr. Hatfill volunteered, though the FBI declined the offer, to wear a tracking bracelet to make their job easier. One agent even ran over Dr. Hatfill's foot when he tried to take a picture to show how closely they followed him. The government also continued to interfere with Dr. Hatfill's ability to get employment. In August the Department of Justice approved the FBI putting a wire tap on Dr. Hatfill's home phone. The phone tap was renewed every thirty days despite no evidence being gained through it. In order to renew the warrant for the phone tap the FBI had to swear to a federal judge that there was indeed probable cause to believe that it would result in the overhearing of phone conversations which would implicate Dr. Hatfill in the anthrax letters. During the fall of 2002 the FBI found out that Dr. Hatfill had discovered that his phones were tapped. Despite the fact that this would cause any intelligent criminal not to discuss such things on the phone, the FBI kept the phone tap going. The phone tap, of course, severely limited Dr. Hatfill's ability to have discussions of a private nature with anybody.

The harassment of Dr. Hatfill continued unabated so in the fall of 2003 he filed a federal lawsuit against Attorney General John Ashcroft and other members of the government involved in the investigation. There were four claims in the suit: (1) violation of his Fifth Amendment due process liberty and property rights; (2) violation of his First Amendment rights to free speech and to petition the government for grievances; (3) violation of privacy rights by disclosing records which were harmful to Dr. Hatfill; and (4) violation of Department of Justice rules required by law prohibiting the type of public disclosures that had taken place.[3] After a considerable delay in the case, the discovery process did go forward and when it was finished District Court Judge Reggie Walton ordered the attorneys for the two parties to try to settle the case. After reviewing the documents involved in the case he hinted that the government's efforts to pursue Dr. Hatfill were questionable. In August of 2008 the parties to the case settled and the government, which admitted no liability, agreed to pay Dr. Hatfill a $5.28 million settlement. When the case was settled Judge Walton stated that "There is not a scintilla of evidence that would indicate that Dr. Hatfill had anything to do with this."[4] After its settlement with Dr. Hatfill, the government focused its scrutiny on a new suspect, Bruce Ivins, a government scientist. Ivins committed suicide on July 29, 2008, effectively bringing an end to the government's investigation into the anthrax letters despite lingering questions.[5]

As Dr. Steven Hatfill's story demonstrates, there has, especially in the post-9/11 world, been an increase in the desire of governments to be able to meet all the possible threats to the well-being of the nation's citizens. This presents a challenge to both citizens and governments as they try to balance the need to provide security, yet maintain liberty. The power that a government has to interfere with an individual's privacy reflects upon what type of society a person will live in. Too much power and the government will be able to interfere in the lives of its citizens in arbitrary ways, too little power and the government will fail in its attempts to protect its citizens and stop criminal activities. Not all societies have meaningful limitations on the power of their governments to interfere in the lives of citizens. To help ensure that there will be limits on the power of the American government to arbitrarily interfere in the lives of its citizens the first Congress proposed and in 1791 the states ratified the Fourth Amendment to the Constitution. The Fourth Amendment to the Constitution is a short amendment that addresses the issue of governmental search and seizure. The Fourth Amendment reads:

> The right of the people to be secure in their persons, houses, papers, and effects, against unreasonable searches and seizures, shall not be violated, and no Warrants shall issue, but upon probable cause, supported by Oath or affirmation, and particularly describing the place to be searched, and the persons or things to be seized.

Understanding the Fourth Amendment and its requirements for search and seizure is not an easy task to accomplish. As is often true, things which may not be easy can be extremely important to a society. The principles of the Fourth Amendment are so important that they serve as "*the* centerpiece of a free, democratic society."[6] This is because the Fourth Amendment sets the limits for government intrusion into one's private affairs. If the Fourth Amendment is ignored, the government's actions can quickly become arbitrary and oppressive. This principle was clearly enunciated by Justice Robert Jackson, after his return from the Nuremberg trials, when in his dissent in *Brinegar v. United States* (1949)[7] he wrote:

Uncontrolled search and seizure is one of the first and most effective weapons in the arsenal of every arbitrary government. And one need only briefly to have dwelt and worked among a people possessed of many admirable qualities but deprived of these rights to know that the human personality deteriorates and dignity and self reliance disappear where homes, persons, and possessions are subject at any hour to unheralded search and seizure by the police.[8]

As Justice Jackson and others have recognized, through its ability to give meaning to the Fourth Amendment, the Supreme Court defines in what type of society we will live.

No one can be one hundred percent sure as to how the first Congress believed that the Fourth Amendment would be applied in practice. We can, however, be fairly certain of the primary principle which stood behind the amendment's adoption. It was the view that government power to interfere in the lives of citizens should be limited and that no one's life should be interfered with in an arbitrary manner. Phillip Hubbart has stated that ratification of the amendment "was not a pedantic legal exercise, but [done] to protect an almost sacred right that the colonists felt about their privacy, particularly the privacy of their homes, but also their persons, businesses, and other private premises."[9]

Despite the brevity of the Fourth Amendment and the clarity of its principle that the government not be able to arbitrarily interfere in the lives of its citizens, the courts have struggled to come up with a clear understanding of what constitutes a violation of the amendment. In 1974 Professor Lloyd Weinreb said of the Court's interpretation of the Fourth Amendment that the "body of doctrine . . . is unstable and unconvincing."[10] In 1985 Professor Craig Bradley's review of Fourth Amendment law convinced him that "it is apparent that not only do the police not understand fourth amendment law, but that even the courts, after briefing, argument, and calm reflection, cannot agree as to what police behavior is appropriate in a particular case."[11] Today, the Court still struggles with interpreting the Fourth Amendment. Arguments over whether the two clauses, the provision forbidding unreasonable searches and seizures and the warrant provision, must be read in conjunction with each other or may be interpreted independently of each other persist. Justices and judges are in constant conflict over what might be considered reasonable in light of the Fourth Amendment. Justices and judges debate whether probable cause is always required for a search and seizure to be reasonable. They also disagree as to whether individualized suspicion is necessary prior to a person being searched or seized. The list of potential competing views of what the Fourth Amendment requires seems, at times, as varied as the number of factual situations to which it can be applied.

Adding to the difficulties of interpreting the amendment is the exclusionary rule. The exclusionary rule involves the issue of what happens when the government fails to obey the Fourth Amendment and does engage in an unreasonable search and seizure. The exclusionary rule traditionally disallowed the use of evidence at trial when that evidence was gathered through a constitutional violation. While members of the Court understand that the exclusionary rule plays an important role in enforcing the Fourth Amendment and stopping police from violating the Fourth Amendment, they often dislike the costs of the rule's application. Those costs mean that probative evidence which directly point towards a person's guilt will not be allowed to be entered at trial as evidence and the guilty may go free. Due to this cost, the Court has often tried to avoid the necessity of applying the rule in Fourth Amendment cases. When there is a violation of the Fourth Amendment the Court is put in the position of trying to determine what brings more harm on society, the violation of the law by criminals or the violation of the law by the government. It also brings forth the issue of how society can best stop both types of violations from taking place in the future.

The judicial practice of *stare decisis* can help advance the goal that individuals not have their affairs interfered with in an arbitrary manner. American courts have practiced *stare decisis* since the early days of the republic.[12] *Stare decisis* is Latin for "to stand by that which is decided." It is a general legal principle that when a rule of law has been announced in a case, it forms a precedent which is honored in later decisions. Under the practice of *stare decisis*, judges use earlier precedent or court decisions in deciding a case currently before them. This is done by recognizing that two cases have similar factual situations and applying the rule of law that was announced from the earlier case to the later case.

The advantages that result from *stare decisis* include predictability, reliance, equality, and efficiency. These advantages can help to ensure that individuals won't have their lives arbitrarily interfered with. The first advantage, predictability, results when a judge decides a case based on the rule of law that comes out of earlier decisions. Relying on earlier cases and the rule of law from those decisions develops stability and consistency in the way that individuals are treated under the law. This stability is important because it leads to predictability in the application of the law. The Court has explained the importance of this by stating that *stare decisis* "permits society to presume that bedrock principles are founded in the law rather than in the proclivities of individuals, and thereby contributes to the integrity of our constitutional system of government, both in appearance and in fact."[13] In regards to the Fourth Amendment, predictability would allow law enforcement officials to clearly understand by what legal methods they could gather evidence and make arrests. This helps to ensure that the lives of citizens are not interfered with in arbitrary ways. Once the law becomes predictable another advantage that comes out of the practice of *stare decisis* is that individuals can develop reliance on the law. When predictability in law exists and people come to rely on it, citizens have a strong sense as to what the law allows and can adjust their behavior to conform to the expectations established by the law and avoid government interference in their lives. Likewise, law enforcement officials can also rely on the rules developed by the courts to ensure that the methods by which they gather evidence are legal and the fruits thereof will be admissible at trial. When the courts consistently apply the law it also creates another benefit for the society. That is equality of treatment before the law. Equality of treatment requires that the principles of the Fourth Amendment should be applied across the board in the same way in all cases regardless of who is the defendant, of what they are accused, or to what organizations they may belong. A final advantage that comes from the use of *stare decisis* is that of efficiency in the administration of justice. Because each judge does not have to reach a new and unique decision in each case, once a judge determines the facts of a case and recognizes similar factual patterns in earlier cases a judge can quickly reach a decision in the case currently before the court. Justice Benjamin Cardozo explained the importance of this principle prior to his Supreme Court appointment stating, "the labor of judges would be increased to almost the breaking point if every past decision could be reopened in every case, and one could not lay one's own course of bricks on the secure foundation of the courses laid by others who had gone before him."[14] Proper following of precedent also makes the appeals process less likely, thus helping to bring each case to a close as efficiently as possible. All of the advantages of *stare desisis* bestow on the court system another great benefit. It advances the legitimacy of the court system as citizens come to the belief that they are governed by the rule of law rather than the whims of individual judges. Development of legitimacy within the courts helps, in turn, to maintain political stability for the governmental system.

There are actually two different types of *stare decisis* that exist within the American court system. The first is vertical *stare decisis*. This form of *stare decisis* is built upon the legal principle that lower courts need to follow the precedents and rule of law established by higher courts. Thus, because the United States Supreme Court is the highest court in the land that can rule on questions concerning the United States Constitution, the precedents it establishes for the Fourth Amendment should be followed by all lower courts. Vertical *stare decisis* helps to ensure that the law will be uniform throughout the land. The other type of *stare decisis* is horizontal. Horizontal *stare decisis* is based on the need for courts to not overrule themselves in order to make decisions that will help to develop the advantages, predictability, reliance, equality, and efficiency, that come from the application of *stare decisis*. There are several problems with horizontal *stare decisis*. One is that even though following precedents does create advantages, it is not always easy to determine what was the precedent or rule of law of a case. Even cases which have a number of similarities will also contain some differences. Judges presiding over a case can emphasize the similarities or the differences and come to very different results. On top of that, the Supreme Court is free to overrule earlier decisions when it believes it to be necessary. Doing so changes the direction of the law, but at least it does so with clarity. It is also problematic when a court cites earlier precedent and states that it is following the rule of law coming from that case, but narrows or broadens the law in such a way that it is difficult to see the consistency in how the two cases were decided. This has often been done in Fourth Amendment cases when the Supreme Court has distinguished one case from another causing confusion in what may have seemed like a clear rule of law. The ability to distinguish case results because of the differing fact situations creates judicial freedom of choice because no two cases have the same facts. This freedom of choice may be exercised differently depending on who the justice or judge is that hears the case. Therefore, the result of an individual case may be dependent on a combination of the facts, the law, and the person who decides the case.

All of these variables in determining the protections of the Fourth Amendment and application of the exclusionary rule have resulted in a lack of clarity in Fourth Amendment law as the Court has tried to accomplish multiple goals in each case. One goal that the Court pursues is to establish precedent which creates clear rules for search and seizure that law enforcement will be able to understand and follow. However, because it is hard to lay down clear rules that apply to every situation that law enforcement officials confront, a second goal of the Court is to create flexibility in its Fourth Amendment decisions so that the rules may be applied in a reasonable manner in the real world. In its attempts to accomplish these goals the Fourth Amendment has not been static and meant the same thing throughout American history. The purpose of this book is to demonstrate the evolution of the Fourth Amendment over time.

Chapter 2 develops an historical understanding of the Fourth Amendment. This chapter begins with an explanation of why the amendment was added to the Constitution. The chapter then examines the development of what is known as the traditional approach for what constituted a legal search and seizure prior to 1961. It ends with an examination of the seminal case of *Mapp v. Ohio.*[15] *Mapp* was decided while the Supreme Court was under the leadership of Chief Justice Earl Warren. It is a landmark case because it incorporated the exclusionary rule which stopped the practice of allowing state and local law enforcement officials to violate the Fourth Amendment and use the evidence at trial. Observers of the Supreme Court have long considered the years of the Warren Court to have been a noteworthy period in American history for the protection of civil liberties, especially for the rights of criminal defendants.[16] The support that the Warren Court demonstrated for the rights of criminal defendants covered the spectrum of rights found in the Bill of Rights. Not only did it incorporate the exclusionary rule, it also required the states to provide counsel to indigents in felony criminal cases[17] and ruled that prior to custodial interrogation individuals taken into custody had to be warned of their rights to remain silent and to an attorney.[18] Central to the revolution in the rights of criminal defendants were changes the Warren Court made in Fourth Amendment jurisprudence.

The Warren Court applied what is known as the cardinal principle of the Fourth Amendment. This principle, which reflects the Court's traditional approach to Fourth Amendment jurisprudence, emphasizes the preference for a warrant prior to a search or seizure. For that reason Chapter 3 explains the warrant rule which the Warren Court tried to apply and the warrant process. Included are discussions of affidavits, probable cause standards, and issues related to the execution of warrants.

The reality of law enforcement work is that warrants are not always practical when criminals are on the move. As a result, the Court has always made exceptions to the need for a warrant prior to a legal search and seizure. Chapter 4 examines the exceptions to the warrant rule. The chapter explains that at first, these exceptions were based on the existence of probable cause and an exigent circumstance being present. It then examines how, over time, the exceptions have been broadened to include circumstances which involve neither the existence of probable cause or an exigent circumstance.

Due to the Warren Court's efforts to better protect the rights of criminal defendants, it is often assumed that it had a clear record which advanced civil liberties in the area of search and seizure. This is not, however, necessarily true. Despite the Warren Court's actions to more effectively protect the rights of criminal defendants through such vehicles as better oversight of the techniques by which police gathered evidence, the Warren Court also planted the seeds that would later be used as precedent to bypass the traditional interpretation of the Fourth Amendment. This is because the language the Warren Court used in its opinions created a double-edged sword. As a result, civil libertarians could use the opinions to expand the protections of the amendment, but law and order oriented justices could just as easily rely on the same opinions to limit the protections of the amendment. Because what has happened since the Warren Court is as important as what happened during that Court, the remaining chapters of the book trace how the language of the most important Fourth Amendment cases decided by the Warren Court have been reshaped by later Courts to limit the protections of the amendment.

Chapter 5 examines an alternative approach to the warrant rule of the Fourth Amendment, the reasonableness approach. The Warren Court originally developed a reasonableness approach to the Fourth Amendment in circumstances, such as administrative searches[19] and stop and frisks,[20] where it believed that a balance needed to be reached between the government's interests and the privacy interests protected by the amendment. Under this approach the ultimate question that must be answered as to whether the government's actions violated the Fourth Amendment is, were those actions reasonable under the circumstances. This approach only forbids unreasonable searches and seizures, while reasonable searches are considered constitutional. The reasonableness test is closely connected to a further extension of the Fourth Amendment, the special needs test. Today, the reasonableness approach plays a major role in Fourth Amendment jurisprudence and influences the Court's decisions in a wide variety of circumstances when no warrant preceded governmental efforts to gather evidence.

Chapter 6 explains that post-Warren Courts have not only expanded the power of the government to engage in search and seizure through the reasonableness approach, they have also narrowed the application of the exclusionary rule. Rather than interpreting the exclusionary rule to be a central component of the Fourth Amendment, later Courts have seen the rule as a judicial remedy which requires a balancing of interest to determine if exclusion is necessary. In reaching a balance the Court examines the social costs of exclusion, throwing out probative evidence, against the rules benefits, requiring law enforcement to adhere to the Fourth Amendment. In finding a balance, the rule currently only needs to be applied when it will serve as a deterrent to future police violations of the Fourth Amendment.

Chapter 7 examines how the Warren Court decision of *Katz v United States* (1968)[21] established the potential for greatly expanding the protections of the Fourth Amendment by ruling that the amendment protects persons, not property. Despite this potential, later courts have used the language from the opinions in *Katz* to limit the protections of the Fourth Amendment by finding that not all expectations of privacy are legitimate. This has allowed the Court to limit the protections of the Fourth Amendment by ruling that government activities which do not interfere with legitimate expectations of privacy are not actually searches and do not therefore trigger Fourth Amendment protection.

The final chapter considers what the future of the Fourth Amendment may look like in a post-9/11 world. It discusses the government's reaction to the continuing threats of crime and terrorism and the technologies it may use to combat those threats. It also examines the direction of the Court under the leadership of Chief Justice John Roberts on Fourth Amendment issues. It ends with an assessment what the future of the Fourth Amendment may be and the role that *stare decisis* will continue to play in this area of law.

Notes

1. Craig M. Bradley, "Two Models of the Fourth Amendments," *Michigan Law Review* 83 (1985): 1468.

2. *Silverman v. United States*, 365 U.S. 505, 511-512 n.4 (1961).

3. This discussion is based on the complaint that Steven Hatfill filed on August 26, 2003 in the case of *Hatfill v. Ashcroft, et al.* in the United States District Court for the District of Columbia. The full complaint may be accessed at the following address: http://www.npr.org/documents/2008/aug/hatfillsettlment.pdf (27 October 2008).

4. David Willman, "Anthrax Subject Receives Payment," *Los Angeles Times*, June 28, 2008, 1.

5. USA TODAY, August 7, 2008 Thursday, NEWS; Pg. 1A.

6. Yale Kamisar, "The Fourth Amendment and Its Exclusionary Rule," *The Champion* (Aug. 1991): 2.

7. *Brinegar v. United States*, 338 U.S. 160 (1949).

8. Ibid., 180-81, (1949) (Jackson, J. dissenting).

9. Phillip A. Hubbart, *Making Sense of Search and Seizure Law: A Fourth Amendment Handbook* (Durham: Carolina Academic Press, 2005), 77.

10. Lloyd L. Weinreb, "Generalities of the Fourth Amendment," *University of Chicago Law Review*, 42 (1974): 49.

11. Bradley, "Two Models of the Fourth Amendments," 1468.

12. For an examination of early attitudes concerning the use of *stare decisis* see, Thomas R. Lee, "Stare Decisis in Historical Perspective: From the Founding Era to the Rehnquist Court," *Vanderbilt Law Review* 52 (1999): 647-735.

13. *Vasquez v. Hillary*, 474 U.S. 254, 265-266 (1986).

14. Benjamin N. Cardozo, *The Nature of the Judicial Process* (New Haven, Conn.: Yale University Press, 1921), 149.

15. *Mapp v. Ohio*, 367 U.S. 643 (1961).

16. Omar Saleem, "The Age of Unreason: The Impact of Reasonableness, Increased Police Force, and Colorblindness on *Terry* 'Stop and Frisk,'" *Oklahoma Law Review* 50 (1997): 452; and Bernard Schwartz, *A History of the Supreme Court* (New York: Oxford University Press, 1993), 279.

17. *Gideon v. Wainwright*, 372 U.S. 335 (1963).

18. *Miranda v. Arizona*, 384 U.S. 436 (1966).

19. *Camara v. Municipal Court*, 387 U.S. 523 (1967).

20. *Terry v. Ohio*, 392 U.S. 1 (1968).

21. *Katz v. United States*, 389 U.S. 347 (1967).

Chapter 2
The History of the Fourth Amendment

The poorest man may, in his cottage, bid defiance to all the force of the crown. It may be frail; its roof may shake; the wind may blow through it; the storm may enter; the rain may enter; but the King of England may not enter; all his force dares not cross the threshold of the ruined tenement.[1]

The Fourth Amendment, like the other central provisions of the Bill of Rights that loom large in our modern jurisprudence, was designed, not to prescribe with "precision" permissible and impermissible activities, but to identify a fundamental human liberty that should be shielded forever from government intrusion. . . . We strive, when interpreting these seminal constitutional provisions, to effectuate their purposes to lend them meanings that ensure that the liberties the Framers sought to protect are not undermined by the changing activities of government officials.[2]

Illustrative Case

March 10, 1946 was a Sunday. Despite it being the weekend, Secret Service Agent Greene was at work in his office in Camden, New Jersey. While at work Agent Greene received two phone calls about a possible counterfeiter who was working out of an area hotel room. One of the calls was from the local police and another was from a chamber maid who worked at the hotel. Because the Secret Service is charged with the duty of stopping counterfeit U.S. currency, Agent Greene decided to go to the hotel and investigate. When he arrived at the hotel Agent Greene got the names of the inhabitants of room 402, Lustig and Reynolds, from the registry. Agent Greene went to room 402 and peeked through the keyhole of the lock. Through the keyhole he saw Mr. Lustig, two briefcases, and a large suitcase, but no evidence of criminal behavior. He then talked to the chambermaid whom had called him with the tip. She told him that she became suspicious when she heard noises "like glass hitting against glass or metal hitting against metal" coming from the room.[3] The maid also told Agent Greene that she had seen money lying on the table in the room.

With this knowledge Agent Greene went to the Camden Police Station and reported to Detective Arthur that he had seen no evidence of counterfeiting. Despite this, he also told Detective Arthur that he was confident that "something was going on."[4] Captain Koerner of the Camden Police was then called into the station and given a report on what Agent Greene had seen. The officers thought they recognized the name of one of the men as an individual who was a bookie, a racehorse man, or a tout. Captain Koerner verified the names on the registry and reached the conclusion that the men might be trying to counterfeit racetrack tickets, rather than money. Based on everything he heard Captain Koerner secured arrest warrants for Lustig and Reynolds. The offense which was charged in the warrant was a local ordinance which made it a crime for known criminals to fail to register with the Camden police within 24 hours of arriving in town. Captain Koerner told the officers who went with him to make the arrests that they were going to "get into that room and find out what was in there."[5] Around four o'clock that afternoon the Camden police officers secured a key from the manager of the hotel and used it to gain admission to room 402. When the police arrived at the room, Lustig and Reynolds were gone. Nevertheless, the police used the key to enter the room. Once inside the room the police went through the drawers of the bureau and some bags that were in the room. They found evidence that Mr. Lustig and his roommate were not counterfeiting race track tickets. Instead, they were counterfeiting currency.

Agent Greene had not gone to the hotel for the arrest or the search, but remained at the police headquarters because he was interested in what the Camden police would discover. When the search was completed Captain Koerner contacted Agent Greene and told him what they found. Based on the report, Agent Greene proceeded to go the hotel to examine the evidence. While there Lustig and Reynolds arrived at the hotel and were taken under arrest. They were searched, but no counterfeit currency was found on them. Agent Greene then went up to room 402 with the Camden police and researched it looking for the plates that had been used in the counterfeiting. Some of the evidence was given to Agent Greene before they left the room. Later all the evidence was eventually given to Agent Greene.

The case of *Lustig v. United States* (1949)[6] presented the Supreme Court with a number of issues that had to be resolved to bring a resolution to the case. These included questions such as does the Fourth Amendment require a search warrant prior to a search of a hotel room? Can a search of a person's hotel room be conducted based on an arrest warrant being issued? If this search was illegal, does it matter whether it was conducted by state officials or federal officials? If the search was illegal can the evidence be used anyway? The history of the

Fourth Amendment and its application prior to 1961 helps to explain the traditional approach to the Fourth Amendment which was used to resolve this case. After examining this history, this chapter will explain how the Supreme Court resolved the *Lustig* case.

Creation of the Fourth Amendment

Prior to looking for clarification as to what the Fourth Amendment currently requires, a short history of the amendment and how the Supreme Court interpreted it in earlier cases will help to place the Court's current decisions into perspective. A close examination of history indicates two principal forces helped to create the desire for protection against governmental searches and seizures to be included in the Constitution. The first of these was the history of abuses of personal privacy in Great Britain and the second was a similar history in the American colonies.

It is often forgotten, but in British history the right to be free from unreasonable searches and seizures and freedom of press are integrally related. This was due to the Crown's desire to control all literature thought to be seditious and nonconformist. In 1538 King Henry VIII created a system of censorship which required all publications to be licensed by the government. In 1557 the primary enforcement powers for the licensing system was given to the Stationer's Company, a private guild of publishers, in return for a monopoly in the area of publishing. Included in the guild's power to enforce the licensing program was the authority to search anywhere they believed unlicensed publications could be found and to seize such materials when found. To ensure that citizens of Great Britain did not read materials which were thought to be dangerous, the authority of the Stationer's Company came over time to include all the necessary search and seizure powers to stop materials published in other parts of the world from entering Great Britain. At the same time that the Stationer's Company saw an increase in its powers to stop the publication and distribution of unlicensed literature, the Crown, especially under Charles I, was also establishing broad search and seizure powers to help in the collection of import duties.

Two of the tools that were used to ferret out unlicensed literature or smuggled goods were the general warrant and writs of assistance. General warrants allowed government agents broad discretion in the searches they conducted. This was because they required no oath or affirmation to support their claims, no grounds explaining the basis of suspicion as to why someone had broken the law, and placed no limits on the locations to be searched or the objects which could be seized. Each general warrant, however, was limited to a single specific event that created the cause behind the search. Writs of assistance were similar, but had a longer life span since they continued in operation until six months after the death of the sovereign under whom they were issued. As a result, they were not limited to their use being triggered by a specific event to justify each search. To further justify broad search and seizure powers the Court of the Star Chamber was created and it approved continuing the practice of allowing the King's messengers to search any subject at any time, day or night, to enforce the laws involving sedition, customs, or printing. The decline and fall of the monarchy between 1641 and 1643 resulted in the abolition of the Court of the Star Chamber, but did not permanently end the power of the government to conduct extensive searches and seizures. After the fall of the monarchy, the power to search and seize, including use of general warrants and writs of assistance, transferred from the Crown to Parliament.

Resistance to the government's power to search and seize began to develop in the common law. Common law jurists such as Sir Matthew Hale and Edward Coke started to develop standards that they believed search and arrest warrants had to meet. Among these standards was the belief that general warrants were not enforceable since they allowed those involved in an investigation the sole power to decide when a search should be conducted. The common law, it was argued, required specific warrants to be obtained for each search or seizure. Speaking to the requirements for a warrant Hale stated that warrants "are not to be granted without oath made before the justice of a felony committed, and that the party complaining hath probable cause to suspect they are in such a house or place and do shew his reasons of such suspicion."[7] The influence of the common law jurists was felt in a series of cases which helped develop America's views on search and seizure. The most famous cases involved John Wilkes and John Entick.

The case involving John Wilkes started in 1762 after Wilkes had authored a criticism of the Crown. The Crown found the publication to be very offensive and became determined to apprehend the author and publishers. The Secretary of State, Lord Halifax, George Montagu Dunk, issued a general warrant for the purpose of arresting those responsible and seizing the papers. The warrant was so general that it did not specify the persons who were subject to seizure, the places subject to search, or the object of such searches. Forty-nine people were arrested before it was discovered that John Wilkes had authored the offending publication. When Wilkes was arrested his bureau and personal papers were seized. Several legal suits then followed. The printers sued the messengers sent by Lord Halifax for false imprisonment. The case was presided over by Chief Justice Charles Pratt who informed the jury hearing the case that the use of general warrants to gather evidence was a practice worse than those used in the Spanish Inquisition. The jury found in favor of the publishers and awarded them 300 pounds. Chief Justice Pratt believed the amount was justified in order to send a clear message throughout the kingdom that general warrants were not supported by law. John Wilkes then successfully sued both the undersecretary who executed the warrant and Lord Halifax. In his suit against the undersecretary, Chief Justice Pratt declared that the use of a general warrant "Is totally subversive of the liberty of the subject."[8]

The second case which greatly influenced America's understanding of the power of the government to engage in search and seizure was *Entick v. Carrington* (1765).[9] John Entick, who published materials critical of the government, had been subject to a warrant which specifically named him, but the subject matter of the search was not specifically listed. As a result, all of Entick's papers were seized in the search. The search had taken place prior to the one involving John Wilkes, but the result of the *Wilkes* case gave Entick the incentive to sue the perpetrators of the warrant for trespass. Entick was successful in his suit and on appeal, Chief Justice Pratt, who had been elevated into the peerage as Lord Camden, upheld the decision. Lord Camden grounded his decision in the law of trespass noting, "No man can set his foot upon my ground without my license, . . . If he admits to the [trespass], he is bound to shew by way of justification that some positive law has empowered or excused him."[10] He reasoned that if the power of the government to search under general warrants was sustained, "the secret cabinets and bureaus of every subject in this kingdom will be thrown open to the search and inspection of a messenger, whenever the secretary of state shall think fit to charge, or even to suspect, a person to be the author, printer, or publisher of a seditious libel."[11] Lord Camden explained in his opinion that government agents were subject to the same limitations in search and seizures that private persons had under common law when they believed a person had stolen goods. Before such a search could be conducted, a person first had to swear an oath out to the judge and explain why they believed that stolen goods could be found at a specific location. After the warrant was served, the person who had obtained it would have to go before a neutral officer and demonstrate that the seized items matched those things listed in the warrant. If the person who executed the warrant took items not listed, the neutral officer was to testify against them.

From these early decisions the common law came to support safeguards against searches and seizures which were thought to be unreasonable. In the colonies the development of the common law moved in the same direction. For Americans during the founding era the possible abuses of governmental power concerning search and seizure were not distant or remote fears. Americans had examples of abuses from the colonial era which they could point to in order to justify the need for strong limits on the power of the government to conduct searches and seizures. During the colonial era, Parliament passed the Act of Frauds in 1696. It gave custom officers in America power "to enter, and go into any House, Shop, Cellar, Warehouse, or Room, or other Place, and in Case of Resistance, to break open doors, chests, trunks, and other Package, there to seize, and from thence to bring, any Kind of Goods or Merchandize whatsoever, prohibited and uncustomed."[12]

The extent of the problems caused by abusive searches fluctuated during the colonial period and did not come to a head in America until the mid-1750s. The crisis at the time resulted from three factors. The first was a change in British trade policy which triggered tougher enforcement of custom laws. In 1760, William Pitt, Secretary of State, ordered strict enforcement of the Molasses Act of 1733 which required high duties on molasses entering the colonies. A second factor was the strengthening of vice-admiralty courts and their power of ruling in forfeiture cases. The third was that due to the increased enforcement of the Molasses Act the colonial courts began issuing writs of assistance. By 1760 their use was common.[13] Custom officers made wide usage of writs of assistance to search buildings for various smuggled goods. Writs of assistance commanded all persons to assist officials in searching or seizing property. The writs of assistance were broad in the power they conveyed to the government because unlike the general warrant which expired upon being served, writs of assistance, although mandated by Parliament, continued in force until the death of the sovereign who was living when it was issued.

The colonist's fear of continued abuse of writs of assistance was behind one of the first public demonstrations of the colonies' unhappiness with the mother country. That was James Otis, Jr.'s legal arguments denouncing writs of assistance in 1761. Otis' involvement in the condemnation of writs of assistance began in 1755 when James Paxton, a collector for the Customs House, sought a writ of assistance to aid him in his duties for the Superior Court of Massachusetts. A number of Boston merchants petitioned the Superior Court asking it to deny the writ. In order to represent the interests of the merchants James Otis, Jr. resigned his position within the government.

When the case came to court Otis and his co-counsel, Oxenbridge Thatcher, first questioned the authority of the Superior Court to grant writs of assistance under English law. The second argument put forward by Otis and Thatcher was that the writs themselves violated the law. In Otis' speech before the court he declared that writs were "the worst instrument of arbitrary power, the most destructive of English liberty and the fundamental principles of law, that was ever found in an English law book." Otis went on to discuss the destructive ability of writs to interfere with a person's right to serenity in their home. The problem behind the evil of the writs could be traced to granting government officials too much discretion because the searcher who had a writ had no oversight and answered to no one. As Otis stated it, "It is a power that places the liberty of every man in the hands of every petty officer." This created a problem because "Every one with this writ may be a tyrant; if this commission be legal, a tyrant in a legal manner, also, may control, imprison, or murder any one within the realm." The result of granting this type of power was that although under English law "A man's house is his castle; and whilst he is quiet, he is as well guarded as a prince in his castle. This writ, if it should be declared legal, would totally annihilate this privilege."[14]

On top of that, the writs lacked particularity in describing the location which could be searched and the items which were the subject of the search. After delaying a ruling to give the Superior Court time to study comparable practices in Great Britain, Judge Thomas Hutchinson, who spoke for the court, ruled that there needed to be consistency in practice between America and Britain and the prevailing practice was to allow the Superior Court to issue writs of assistance. Paxton was then granted his writ.

Otis and Thatcher may have lost the day, but their arguments against writs of assistance reverberated across America and would shortly win the hearts of Americans. As colonial opposition to use of writs became prevalent, customs officers turned away from their use to protect their own safety. Increasingly, American courts found that writs were not authorized by the law and by 1772 American courts were uniform on this position.

After declaring independence, despite writs no longer being in fashion, Americans took steps to ensure that writs and other abusive search and seizure tactics would not work their way back into accepted legal practice. This helps to explain why after declaring themselves independent eight states included provisions in their state constitutions to protect against abusive search and seizure practices.[15] In 1787 the inability of the Constitution to limit the power of the government to conduct search and seizures was widely seen as a flaw which was addressed by the Anit-Federalists who were opposed to the Constitution. An example can be found in one of Richard Henry Lee's "Letters from the Federal Farmer" where he explained

> [T]hat all persons shall have a right to be secure from all unreasonable searches and seizures of their persons, house, papers, or possessions; and that all warrants shall be deemed contrary to this right, if the foundation of them be not previously supported by oath, and there be not in them a special designation of persons or objects of search, arrest, or seizure; . . . These rights are not necessarily reserved, they are established, or enjoyed in few countries: they are stipulated rights, almost peculiar to British and American laws. In the execution of those laws, individuals, by long custom, by magna charta, bills of rights & c. have become entitled to them.[16]

During the ratification debates over the Constitution, the ratifying conventions in five states were so worried about the need to protect citizens against abusive searches they proposed amendments barring unreasonable searches and seizures.[17]

Continued concerns with the lack of a bill of rights caused James Madison to submit proposed amendments to the Constitution during the first Congress in 1789. Those proposed amendments included one to limit the search and seizure powers of the government. Madison warned members of the House of Representatives that if they didn't protect citizens against the use of general warrants

Congress could pass legislation authorizing their use in the collection of revenues through Congress' necessary and proper powers. Madison's original draft for the amendment which he submitted to the House of Representatives read:

> The rights of the people to be secured in their persons, houses, papers, and their other property, from all unreasonable searches and seizures, shall not be violated by warrants issued without probable cause, supported by oath or affirmation, or not particularly describing the places to be searched, and the persons or things to be seized.[18]

In the House the language that Madison submitted was referred to the Committee of Eleven on July 31, 1789. The Committee revised the proposal to read:

> The right of the people to be secured in their persons, houses, papers, and effects, shall not be violated by warrants issuing without probable cause, supported by oath or affirmation, and not particularly describing the place to be searched, and the persons or things to be seized.[19]

The House Committee of the Whole then met on August 13 to consider the language of the proposal. Elbridge Gerry successfully convinced the House to replace "secured" with "secure" and to bring back the "against unreasonable searches and seizures" phrase. The Committee of the whole rejected an attempt by Congressman Egbert Benson to replace the phrase "by warrants issuing" with "and no warrants shall issue." Despite the defeat of Benson's proposal he used his position as chair of the Committee of Three, which had been appointed to arrange the amendments, to reinsert his preferred language which was accepted by the House and sent to the Senate for approval. Benson's change is important because the preexisting language could be interpreted to simply be a prohibition against general warrants. The final language makes it clear that the purpose of the amendment was to provide a general protection against all unreasonable searches and seizures. Because the Senate did not have public debate until 1794 there is no record of the debate over the amendment within the Senate. The amendment was then sent to the states and was ratified in 1791.

Development of the Traditional Approach to the Fourth Amendment

The interpretation of the Fourth Amendment and the use of *stare decisis* have presented the Court with a variety of problems through the years. As pointed out in Chapter 1 the amendment has been said to be wrought with confusion and inconsistencies, but this has not necessarily been true throughout American history. Prior to the incorporation of the Fourth Amendment and exclusionary rule, the Supreme Court developed a coherent rule of law, in most regards, for applying the Fourth Amendment to the actions of the national government.

Two important facets of American law did delay the development of the Fourth Amendment and the exclusionary rule. The first was the American judicial system's, including the Supreme Court's, deep commitment to the provisions of British common law. For more than a century after the American Revolution, American courts used the same common law rule of evidence as had English courts. This rule allowed evidence which was obtained through an illegal search and seizure to be admissible at trial.[20] Thus, as long as the rules of evidence were derived from common law, rather than constitutional interpretation, illegalities in obtaining evidence were overlooked. The second reason behind the delay of the Supreme Court to enunciate clear rules for the Fourth Amendment can be found by examining its appellate jurisdiction. Fourth Amendment jurisprudence was slow to develop in America because criminal law was primarily a state activity and due to the decision in *Barron v. Baltimore* (1833),[21] which held that states were not bound by the Bill of Rights, the Supreme Court had few early chances to review possible violations of the Fourth Amendment. On top of this, Congress did not grant the Supreme Court appellate jurisdiction in all criminal cases until March 3, 1911.[22] While lacking jurisdiction the Court did not, in most instances, have the ability to rule whether evidence was gained through a violation of the Fourth Amendment. Lacking leadership from the Supreme Court, lower courts continued to use the common law rule of evidence allowing tainted evidence to be used at trial.

Due to the above reasons the Supreme Court heard only five Fourth Amendment cases in the nineteenth century. Despite the Court hearing so few Fourth Amendment cases, it was able to develop a consistent approach to interpreting the amendment. That approach required a warrant prior to a governmental search and seizure. One of the first cases in which the Supreme Court did address the heart of the Fourth Amendment was *Ex Parte Jackson* (1877).[23] Government officials suspected Jackson of mailing lottery advertisements and opened up one of his pieces of mail he sent without a warrant. They found a lottery advertisement and used it to gain a conviction. Jackson filed a writ of *habeas corpus* and the Court granted review. The Court ruled in favor of Jackson stating:

> The constitutional guaranty of the right of the people to be secure in their papers against unreasonable searches and seizures extends to their papers, thus closed against inspection, wherever they may be. Whilst in the mail, they can only be opened and examined under like warrant, issued upon similar oath or

affirmation, particularly describing the thing to be seized, as is required when papers are subject to search in one's own household.[24]

The most important early case that made it to the Supreme Court concerning the use of evidence gained in violation of the Constitution prior to the Court being granted appellate jurisdiction in criminal cases was *Boyd v. United States* (1886).[25] The *Boyd* case, which was a civil case, involved a charge that George and Edward Boyd, New York City merchants, had committed fraud by importing thirty-five cases of glass into the United States without paying the required duty. In order to ascertain how much glass the Boyds had imported the government subpoenaed an old invoice from the Boyds' import business. The Boyds then challenged the admissibility of the invoice claiming that by being forced to produce the invoice they were being compelled to give evidence against themselves in violation of the Fourth and Fifth Amendments.

After the district court allowed the invoice to be received into evidence the case was appealed to the United States Supreme Court which reversed. The reason for the Court's reversal as announced in Justice Joseph Bradley's opinion was the Court's belief that private papers were immune from search and seizure since they were not contraband items. Justice Bradley stated that the protections of the Fourth Amendment were broad and "apply to all invasions on the part of the government and its employees of the sanctity of a man's home and the privacies of life."[26] Any invasions of such privacy required a warrant even if the evidence was compelled rather than gained through a search and seizure. Furthermore, one of the purposes of the Fourth Amendment provision against unreasonable searches was to protect the broader Fifth Amendment right against self-incrimination. The Court reasoned that forcing the production of private papers was too close to requiring compelled testimony. Justice Bradley also noted that constitutional provisions that were meant to protect the security of persons and property should be liberally construed. Therefore, the Court found that Fourth Amendment violations could be enforced through the Fifth Amendment. This made the use of the invoice gained from the Boyds' business inadmissible as evidence in court since it violated the right against self-incrimination. The *Boyd* case made it a matter of record that in civil cases evidence which was gained in violation of individual rights protected by the Constitution would not be admissible at trial. It did not explain what would happen to similar evidence in criminal cases.

The first criminal case in which the United States Supreme Court found evidence to be illegally admitted at trial was *Weeks v. United States* (1914).[27] In this case Fremont Weeks was sentenced to jail after his conviction for making illegal use of the United States postal system to distribute lottery tickets. The evidence obtained against Weeks was a result of the work of police in Kansas City, Missouri. The police arrested Weeks at Union Station in Kansas City. While this was happening, other police went to his home without a warrant. A neighbor told them where Weeks kept a key. Police then used the key to enter the home and gather evidence. The police then gave the evidence to U.S. marshals. Prior to a federal trial, Weeks filed a motion to regain possession of all the evidence which had been gathered in violation of the Fourth Amendment. The district court judge in charge of Weeks' trial ordered the return of all the seized articles not a part of the prosecution's case against Weeks, but allowed the government to retain all the evidence which it planned to use in the trial. After his conviction for illegal gambling, Weeks appealed claiming that the evidence used against him was obtained in violation of the Fourth Amendment and should not have been admissible at trial.

In a unanimous decision, written by Justice William Day, the Supreme Court for the first time enunciated the rationale for an exclusionary rule under the Fourth Amendment. The Court first held that the search had indeed violated the Fourth Amendment because police entered Weeks' home without a warrant. It went on to explain that when the trial court allowed illegally gathered evidence to be used it had made a reversible error in the trial forcing the case to be remanded for a new trial in which the evidence would have to be suppressed. The Court based its reasoning on several principles. The first was that the Fourth Amendment was meant to act as a restraint on both the police and courts so both were obligated to enforce it. Second, Fourth Amendment rights continued to exist at trial and use of illegally obtained evidence at this stage amounted to a continued governmental invasion of constitutionally protected privacy. Third, the integrity of justice in the federal system would be compromised if federal courts allowed illegally seized evidence to be used. Justice Day summarized his view of the exclusionary rule stating:

> If letters and private documents can thus be seized and held and used in evidence against a citizen accused of an offense, the protection of the Fourth Amendment, declaring his right to be secure against such searches and seizures is of no value, and, so far as those thus placed are concerned, might as well be stricken from the Constitution. The efforts of the courts and their officials to bring the guilty to punishment, praiseworthy as they are, are not to be aided by the sacrifice of those great principles established by years of endeavor and suffering which have resulted in their embodiment in the fundamental law of the land.[28]

The opinion in *Weeks* adopted a unitary model of government concerning the role of the exclusionary rule. According to this model, an unconstitutional search is only the first stage in a constitutional violation. The violation is made complete by admitting the evidence into trial in order to convict the perpetrator of the crime. Proponents of the unitary model believe that not only should the government not engage in constitutional violations, it should also not benefit from them. Thus, they believe that courts have a duty to suppress illegally gathered evidence to ensure not only that defendants have a fair trial, but also that the government is fair in its prosecution of the defendant. Any gain by the government which was the result of constitutional violation is unacceptable in the unitary model. It is also important to note that in *Weeks* the exclusionary rule was seen as a constitutional requirement and therefore relied on a principled basis that all violations of the Fourth Amendment by the federal government should result in the suppression of evidence. The principle was to avoid the ratification or rewarding of unconstitutional behavior on the part of the government, to avoid judicial complicity in the violation and to force the government to take the Fourth Amendment seriously. Under this principle there was to be no balancing of the cost versus the benefits of the rule.

As the Court was struggling with fleshing out the scope of the exclusionary rule, it was developing what has become known as the traditional approach to the Fourth Amendment. This approach joins the two clauses of the amendment and finds that searches and seizures are unreasonable when police lack a warrant. This approach infers a preference for the existence of a warrant prior to a search and seizure taking place. This approach was enunciated in *Agnello v. United States* (1925)[29] when the Court stated, "searches conducted outside the judicial process, without prior approval by judge or magistrate are *per se* unreasonable under the Fourth Amendment—subject only to a few specifically established and well-delineated exceptions."[30] The traditional approach to the Fourth Amendment was also well illustrated by Justice Frank Murphy in *Trupiano v. United States* (1948) when he announced

> It is a cardinal rule that, in seizing goods and articles, law enforcement agents must secure and use search warrants wherever reasonably practicable. . . . To provide the necessary security against unreasonable intrusions upon the private lives of individuals, the framers of the Fourth Amendment required adherence to judicial processes wherever possible.[31]

In *Burdeau v. McDowell* (1921)[32] the Court made it clear that the Fourth Amendment only applied to governmental actions. *Burdeau* involved evidence in a criminal case which was collected by a private detective in a way that would have violated the Fourth Amendment if he had been a government official. The Court ruled that the words of the Fourth Amendment are directed only at limiting the power of the government to engage in unreasonable search and seizures. When non-governmental actors engage in searches or seizures that are unreasonable it does not create a constitutional violation and the evidence gathered through such a search is admissible in Court. An example would be when a person goes through the drawers of a roommate and gathers evidence that incriminates the room mate in criminal activity and gives it to the police. If a private person was instructed by a government official to conduct a search, then the Fourth Amendment does come into play and any evidence which is gathered must fall within the Fourth Amendment's accepted procedures to be admissible in court.

Once the Court proclaimed a preference for the requirement that warrants precede searches and seizures, despite the creation of a few exceptions to the warrant requirement, Fourth Amendment jurisprudence went through few major doctrinal changes until after *Mapp v. Ohio* (1961) when the Court incorporated the exclusionary rule. The opinion in *Weeks v. United States* had, however, failed to discuss the scope of the exclusionary rule. Clarification of the ramifications of the exclusionary rule was therefore needed. The Court in *Weeks* also made no distinction between the two types of illegally obtained evidence which could exist, primary and derivative. Primary evidence is found as a direct result of illegal conduct. An example would be finding a map in a home which was illegally entered. Derivative evidence is obtained through information gained due to the primary illegality of law enforcement officials, such as using the map to direct officials to a place marked "drugs" on the map to locate a stash of narcotics.

Clarification concerning the scope of the exclusionary rule came in 1920 in the case of *Silverthorne Lumber Co. v. United States*.[33] The factual situation of the *Silverthorne* case is as follows. The Silverthornes, a father and son, owned the Silverthorne Lumber Company when they were taken into custody after being indicted for failing to obey subpoenas to produce books and documents concerning their business for a grand jury. While in custody, federal law enforcement officials, acting without a search warrant, entered the company's offices and seized all the books, papers, and documents they could find. These documents were then copied and studied for evidence of wrongdoing, resulting in a new indictment. In the meantime, in reaction to a pretrial application of the defendants, the district court ordered all the documents that were seized in violation of the Fourth Amendment to be returned to the defendants. Based on the knowledge that the government gained from the copies it had made of the documents it was forced to return, the government sought and received subpoenas ordering the defendants to produce the original documents before the grand jury. The Silverthornes refused to comply with the subpoenas which resulted in the company being fined and the younger Silverthorne being jailed for contempt.

On appeal the Supreme Court reversed the contempt judgement and helped to clarify the scope of the exclusionary rule. The Court, in an opinion written by Justice Oliver Wendell Holmes, held that the exclusionary rule rejects not only the use of direct evidence which was illegally seized, but also the use of evidence or knowledge derived from or found as a result of constitutional violations. To allow the government to make use of evidence gained through illegal activities Holmes believed, "reduces the Fourth Amendment to a form of words."[34] This was an important milestone in the history of the Fourth Amendment because it meant that the ability for a defendant to object to the use of evidence which was gathered illegally would not be contingent on whether the evidence had been personal property of theirs. Defendants, instead, could seek suppression merely based on the method of acquisition of the evidence. The opinion clearly reinforces the unitary model of government for application of the exclusionary rule first enunciated in *Weeks*. This is clearly demonstrated by Justice Holmes who wrote: "The essence of a provision forbidding the acquisition of evidence in a certain way is that not merely evidence so acquired shall not be used before the Court, but that the facts thus obtained become sacred and inaccessible."[35] In this particular case the conviction was overturned because the subpoena didn't need to be honored since the information that it was based upon was too directly connected to the illegal search which had earlier taken place. Despite adding the derivative evidence rule, the Court went on and ruled that derivative evidence of this type could, under certain conditions, still be used. This, according to Holmes, was true "if knowledge of them is gained from an independent source" as long as "the knowledge gained by the Government's own wrong cannot be used by it."[36]

Silverthorne thus contains two important constitutional doctrines. The first is the inadmissibility of derivative evidence gained through Fourth Amendment violations. The second is the independent source exception to the exclusionary rule which allows illegally seized evidence to be used if law enforcement officials can show knowledge of it through a source independent of constitutional violation. The key to the independent source exception was that the evidence had to come from a source that was not mixed with the police illegality. An example of how the independent source exception works would be if the police had violated a suspect's right to counsel and convinced him to tell police the location of a body, but he did not lead them to the body. In the meantime, if a separate group of police conducting a legal search for the body found it without communicating with the police involved with the violation, the body would be admissible because it was found through an independent source. The independent source exception rewards honest police work while taking away the incentive for police to violate the law.

Nineteen years later in *Nardone v. United States* (*Nardone II*),[37] Justice Felix Frankfurter coined the term "fruit of the poisonous tree" to describe the relationship between primary and derivative evidence in the application of the exclusionary rule.[38] The "tree" refers to primary evidence obtained through constitutional violation and thus inadmissible while the "fruit" refers to derivative evidence also obtained through constitutional violation and also inadmissible in court. *Nardone* involved a tax fraud case that twice made it to the Supreme Court. In the first case, *Nardone I* (1937)[39] the Supreme Court reversed Nardone's tax fraud conviction because the prosecution had gained primary evidence through illegal wiretaps which were used to help convict Nardone. In the second trial of Nardone the conversations from the wiretaps were not themselves admitted, but information gained from the conversations was admitted. Nardone was again convicted, again appealed, and the Supreme Court again reversed. In *Nardone II* the Court reaffirmed the holding in *Silverthorne* that derivative evidence could not be used unless it was also discovered from a source independent of the legal violation. The Court believed allowing illegally gathered evidence would encourage law enforcement officers to continue to violate the law. The second *Nardone* case then added another exception to the blanket provision that all derivative evidence which had been originally discovered through a constitutional violation was inadmissible at trial. This new exception was the attenuation exception. The attenuation exception to the exclusionary rule applies to derivative evidence. According to its provisions, such evidence can be admitted at trial if the prosecution can show that the connection between the initial constitutional violation and the derived evidence had become "so attenuated as to dissipate the taint."[40] Primary evidence, however, can never be attenuated. The derivative evidence in *Nardone II* was not found to be attenuated. In later cases, the attenuation exception has been used to allow evidence to be admitted when the connection between the illegal action and the discovery of the evidence is shown to be too remote to serve as a remedy to deter the actions of law enforcement officials from violating the law.

By 1946, the traditional approach of the warrant rule and the exclusionary rule were considered by the Supreme Court to be a settled enough rule of law within the federal court system that the Court could declare that illegally obtained "evidence is suppressed on the theory that the government may not profit from its own wrongdoing."[41] The Supreme Court had, however, not examined the issue of whether the exclusionary rule applied to violations of the Constitution that resulted from state, not federal, governmental action.

Early Exceptions to the Warrant Rule

During the period in which the Court was developing the traditional approach to the Fourth Amendment and fleshing out the meaning of the exclusionary rule there were periods in which considerable pressure existed to aid law enforcement in its goal of apprehending and gaining convictions of criminals. Such periods included the era of Prohibition and, due to fraud involving war rations or other war activities, the period of World War II. During these periods, the Court felt increased pressure to narrowly interpret the protections of the Fourth Amendment. Responding to this pressure the Court ruled that two broad areas of searches were not, in fact, searches under the Fourth Amendment. These included searches of open fields and wire taps. Another way the Court responded to law enforcement pressures was by creating two exceptions to the warrant requirement.

The first narrowing of what constituted a search under the Fourth Amendment came in what is known as the open fields doctrine in the case of *Hester v. United States* (1924).[42] *Hester* came to the Court as a result of Hester's conviction for his moonshining activities. Revenue agents suspected Hester of moonshining and had Hester's father's farmhouse under surveillance when they saw Hester come out and hand a suspected bottle of whiskey to his partner. When the agents announced their presence Hester went to his car, grabbed a gallon jug and then with his partner tried to outrun the police. After an agent fired a shot, Hester and his partner dropped containers containing moonshine whiskey. Agents found another container of whiskey in the yard outside of the house, but found nothing in the house. At trial all the whiskey was used as evidence over Hester's objection that the agents lacked a warrant and were trespassing when they conducted their raid.

On appeal the Court ruled in *Hester* that despite trespassing on Hester's property in order to gather evidence, there had been no constitutional violation. That was because the land involved was an open field and did not deserve the protection of the Fourth Amendment. Justice Holmes, speaking for the Court, traced the ability to search open fields without a warrant back to the common law. Due to this history, the Court ruled there was no need to obtain a warrant prior to law enforcement officers searching an open field.

The Court also narrowed the protections of the Fourth Amendment by ruling in *Olmstead v. United States* (1928)[43] that wire tapping was not a violation of the Fourth Amendment. The *Olmstead* case involved a violation of the National Prohibition Act. Chief Justice William Howard Taft in the majority opinion approached the Fourth Amendment very literally and stated that it only protected persons, papers and effects. He also reasoned that since wiretapping did not require a physical trespass onto the property of a person, it could not be a violation of the amendment.

Early in its handling of Fourth Amendment issues the Court created two exceptions to the warrant requirement, one for automobiles and one for searches incident to a lawful arrest. Prior to the incorporation of the exclusionary rule, these were the only exceptions to the warrant rule that the Court accepted. Both exceptions rested on a practical understanding of law enforcement and a common theoretical foundation which justified bypassing the need for a warrant. That foundation was the existence of the probable cause necessary to justify a warrant and an exigent circumstance which made obtaining a warrant difficult. With both warrant exceptions the Court was worried about possible losses of evidence due to the difficulties of protecting the evidence until such time that a warrant could be obtained.

The warrant exception for automobiles was announced in 1925 when the Court decided *Carroll v. United States*.[44] In *Carroll v. United States* the defendants, Carroll and Kiro, drove past federal prohibition agents on a highway between Detroit and Grand Rapids, Michigan. The agents suspected that they were transporting whiskey, stopped the vehicle, and then searched it finding 68 bottles of whiskey behind the upholstery of the backseat. Carroll was convicted of violating the National Prohibition Act. On review after conviction the Supreme Court rejected the defendant's argument that the lack of a warrant meant the search was in violation of the Fourth Amendment. The Court held in an opinion by Chief Justice William Howard Taft, that the search was reasonable because, due to a number of factors, the agents had probable cause to believe that the vehicle was transporting alcohol.

According to the opinion, the National Prohibition Act stated that there could be no property rights in liquor. On top of this, a supplemental act penalized agents enforcing the law who did not get a warrant to search private property. Based on its reading of the law, the Court decided that Congress clearly intended to "make a distinction between the necessity for a search warrant in the searching of private dwellings and in that of automobiles and other road vehicles in the enforcement of the Prohibition Act."[45] The Court reasoned that Congress' differing treatment of private property such as a dwelling and a vehicle was acceptable as long as it did not lead to unreasonable searches. The Court concluded that a warrantless search of an automobile was reasonable "where it is not practicable to secure a warrant, because the vehicle can be quickly moved out of the locality or jurisdiction in which the warrant must be sought."[46] The Court also noted that due to the mobility of the vehicle "seizure [was] impossible except without warrant."[47] Chief Justice Taft's majority opinion said that the Fourth Amendment was to be interpreted according to the understanding of those who wrote it. If this was done, it was clear that the provision against unreasonable searches "has been construed, practically since the beginning of Government, as recognizing a necessary difference between a search of a store, dwelling, house, or other structure" which require warrants, and the search of a "ship, motor boat, wagon, or automobile, for contraband goods, where it is not practicable to secure a warrant because the vehicle can quickly be moved out of the locality or jurisdiction."[48] To support his position, Chief Justice Taft noted that the First, Second, and Fourth Congresses passed legislation which allowed custom agents to enter vessels without a warrant, conduct searches, and seize materials if the duty tax had not been paid, or the goods had been illegally brought into the country.

Due to the precedent of *Carroll*, if probable cause existed to search a motor vehicle, the validity of a search was not dependent on whether a warrant had been issued. However, as in cases involving a warrant the final determination as to whether probable cause existed was to be made by the reviewing judge, not the officers on the scene. The emphasis the Court placed on the mobility of automobiles clearly places the auto exception under the rubric of the exigent circumstances which make warrants impractical and unnecessary. It was the first time the Court announced the exigent circumstances exception.[49] The Court in *Carroll* was so focused on the mobility of the vehicle that it did not consider the ability of police to detain a vehicle while they sought a warrant. *Carroll* serves however, to demonstrate the Court's view that probable cause by itself was not an exception to the warrant requirement. The exception was justified by the existence of both probable cause and an exigent circumstance. The Court applied the precedent of *Carroll* in *United States v. Lee* (1927)[50] to allow for warrantless searches of other self-propelled vehicles when they were mobile and probable cause existed.

The exception to the Fourth Amendment that the Court struggled the most with prior to the incorporation of the exclusionary rule was that of search incident to a lawful arrest. American jurisprudence has long recognized an exception to the warrant rule when a search was incident to a lawful arrest. The ability to engage in such searches had existed in British common law. In 1914 the Supreme Court gave its support to such searches stating the right had always been recognized under both British and American law "to discover and seize the fruits or evidences of crime."[51] These searches were also seen as acceptable in order to protect the safety of government agents. It was believed that the ability of the arrestee to either destroy evidence or threaten the safety of the officer if they weren't searched created an exigency which made a search without a warrant acceptable. The fact that the standard for a lawful arrest is probable cause meant that this exception was also based on probable cause and an exigent circumstance. Having established that a right to search incident to a lawful arrest existed, the Court had difficulty determining what should be the proper scope of such searches. The years leading up to *Mapp v. Ohio* (1961) would see Court doctrine swinging back and forth between allowing a narrow and wide scope in searches incident to a lawful arrest.

Traditionally, under common law, searches incident to a lawful arrest were strictly limited in scope to the body of the person arrested or items subject to seizure that were in clear view of the arresting officer. The Supreme Court backed away from this limited scope for such searches in *Agnello v. United States* (1925).[52] There the Court stated that when a person is lawfully arrested their person can be searched, but the government could also "search the place where the arrest is made in order to find and seize things connected with the crime as its fruits, or as the means by which it was committed, as well as weapons and other things to effect an escape from custody."[53] Despite broadening the common law rule, the Court did place a limit on the scope of the search undertaken in *Agnello* by ruling that evidence gathered in a warrantless search of Agnello's house which was located blocks away from where he was arrested could not be admitted. The Court not only believed that such searches should be limited to that area under the physical control of the person arrested, it also established the primacy of the home as a place protected by the Fourth Amendment. It stated, "The search of a private dwelling without a warrant is in itself unreasonable and abhorrent to our laws."[54]

The Court reaffirmed the existence of a broad scope in *Harris v. United States* (1947).[55] Harris was arrested in his home on a valid arrest warrant for forgery of checks, but police had no search warrant. Nevertheless, after Harris was arrested and handcuffed, five FBI agents searched all four rooms of his apartment in hopes of finding forged checks. They found no evidence related to the forged checks, but they did find some unrelated evidence which was used to convict Harris of illegal possession of selective service documents. Chief Justice Fred Vinson wrote a majority opinion upholding Harris' conviction. The opinion emphasized several factors. The first was that the FBI agents had entered the apartment legally since they had a valid arrest warrant. Furthermore, once the agents had made the arrest they could conduct a search incident to that arrest. The entire apartment fit into an acceptable scope for the search. This was true due to the nature of the items sought which could easily be concealed anywhere in the apartment. Another consideration was the fact that the search was not exploratory. It was done to find particular evidence to connect Harris to the crime for which he was arrested. Finally, even though the items which were found were not what the agents were looking for, the articles were contraband and could, thus, properly be seized.

As is often true of Supreme Court rulings, the decision in *Harris* was quickly moderated when Justice William Douglas changed his mind about supporting such a broad scope for searches incident to a lawful arrest. This change took place in *Trupiano v. United States* (1948)[56] when the majority of the Court held that the admission of evidence seized as a result of a search incident to a lawful arrest would hinge upon the reasonableness with which a warrant could have been obtained prior to the arrest. Also in 1948 in *United States v. Di Re*[57] the Court clarified that a lawful arrest had to precede any search. In speaking for the Court, Justice Robert Jackson stated, "a search is not to be made legal by what it turns up. In law it is good or bad when it starts and does not change character from its success."[58]

The Court's adherence to the *Trupiano* precedent quickly faded when Justices Frank Murphy and Wiley Rutledge, who had been strong supporters of a limited scope in searches incident to a lawful arrest, died. They were replaced by Justices Tom Clark and Sherman Minton, who supported broader governmental powers. The change became apparent in *United States v. Rabinowitz* (1950).[59] *Rabinowitz* came to the Court after an undercover agent bought some stamps bearing overprints which proved to be forgeries. Officers then secured an arrest warrant and proceeded to arrest Rabinowitz in his one room office. The officers then conducted an hour and a half search of the entire office including the desk, safe, and cabinets which resulted in finding additional stamps with forged overprints. Rabinowitz unsuccessfully objected to any admission of the fruits of the search from being admitted at trial. He then appealed after conviction.

In a majority opinion which had the potential for completely rewriting the Court's approach in Fourth Amendment cases Justice Minton began by examining what constituted a reasonable search. He then argued that the reasonableness of a search was a separate issue from whether a warrant existed. Justice Minton wrote that unreasonableness was not defined in the Constitution. Therefore, to discover if a search was unreasonable, the facts and circumstances of each case would have to be examined. Furthermore, he added that unlike the *Trupiano* precedent "The relevant test is not whether it is reasonable to procure a search warrant, but whether the search was reasonable."[60] Justice Minton argued that the rejection of the traditional approach linking reasonableness to the existence of a warrant was necessary in order that "[s]ome flexibility be accorded law officers engaged in daily battle with criminals."[61] In examining all of the facts and circumstances of the *Rabinowitz* case the Court found that the search was indeed reasonable and thus not a violation of the Fourth Amendment.

State Court Oversight and the Exclusionary Rule

The decision in *Barron v. Baltimore* (1833) that states were free to ignore the Bill of Rights effectively limited the Supreme Court's oversight of possible state violations of the Fourth Amendment. The first time that the Court confronted the question as to whether the Fourth Amendment and exclusionary rule applied to actions of the states as a part of the Due Process Clause of the Fourteenth Amendment was in the 1949 case of *Wolf v. Colorado*.[62] The case entered the judicial system when the Denver, Colorado district attorney heard that Julius Wolf, an obstetrician, was performing illegal abortions. The district attorney searched Dr. Wolf's office without a warrant and removed records for 1943 and 1944. From the office records the district attorney gained enough information to charge and convict Dr. Wolf with conspiracy to commit abortions. Wolf then appealed the conviction claiming that the Fourteenth Amendment's Due Process Clause prohibited searches that were in violation of the Fourth Amendment and that the evidence gathered from such searches was inadmissible in state courts just as it was in federal courts.

In resolving the issues presented in *Wolf*, Justice Felix Frankfurter's majority opinion did not hesitate to incorporate the Fourth Amendment through the Fourteenth Amendment since it was "implicit in the concept of ordered liberty."[63] Justice Frankfurter explained that "a search without authority of law, but solely on authority of the police . . . [was] inconsistent with the conception of human rights enshrined in the history and the basic constitutional documents of English-speaking peoples."[64] In a gesture meant to convey respect for the principles of federalism Justice Frankfurter did not, however, incorporate the exclusionary rule along with the Fourth Amendment. Unfortunately for Wolf, the Court found that his Fourth Amendment rights had been violated, but his conviction was still upheld because the Court allowed the states to continue to admit illegally seized evidence at trial. The Court's opinion distinguished between the federal rights protected under the Fourth Amendment and the federal remedy, the exclusionary rule, which the Court had created to protect those rights. For the first time, the Court stated that the exclusionary rule was a judicially created remedy which was "not derived from the explicit requirements of the Fourth

Amendment" and not "an essential ingredient of the rights" contained in the Fourth Amendment.[65]

The view that the exclusionary rule is a Court created remedy meant to further the protections of the Fourth Amendment as part of the Court's supervisory power over the federal courts was a new idea when presented in Frankfurter's opinion. For Justice Frankfurter and the majority, the exclusionary rule as a remedy was meant to act as a deterrent to future police misconduct. Such an approach to the exclusionary rule had the potential for changing the role of the exclusionary rule. Justice Frankfurter reasoned that rather than automatically excluding evidence the states were free to develop other remedies "which, if consistently enforced would be equally effective"[66] in protecting the rights of the Fourth Amendment. The other remedies that Frankfurter alluded to included: (1) common law action for damages against officers or judges who improperly are involved in illegal searches; (2) an individual resisting an unlawful search with force and not being liable for the consequences; and (3) statutes that could punish those who maliciously procure or execute illegal warrants.

In *Wolf* the Court incorporated the Fourth Amendment and ruled that state governments were indeed bound by the amendment. While this ruling would have seemingly placed the Court in a position of exercising considerable oversight on state actions involving search and seizure, such activity was limited by the Court's unwillingness to incorporate the exclusionary rule at the same time. The decision not to incorporate the exclusionary rule did great damage to the principle of *stare decisis* by allowing precedents established by the Supreme Court which explained when the Fourth Amendment was violated to be ignored in state courts. The Court believed that states would develop their own exclusionary rules or other alternative remedies to ensure that their activities did not violate the Fourth Amendment. This left individuals who believed that a state government had violated their Fourth Amendment rights little reason to seek enforcement of the Fourth Amendment by the Supreme Court since evidence gathered through its violation could still be used at trial.

Ever since the Court's declaration in *Wolf* that the exclusionary rule was a judicially created remedy rather than a constitutionally required rule, scholars have criticized the Court's handling of the exclusionary rule for not clearly articulating the principles upon which the rule has been founded.[67] The opinions enunciating the exclusionary rule have lead to a continuing debate about the true source and reasoning behind the exclusionary rule. Another debate exists between those who believe that the Court should adhere to a unitary model of government in regards to application of the exclusionary rule and not allow the government to benefit in any way when it has violated the law and those who believe that the Court should accept the fragmented model of government that Justice Frankfurter seemed to suggest in *Wolf*. According to the fragmented model, the courts should serve as a neutral forum for evidence to be brought forward at trial. The judge should, therefore, not consider the source of the evidence, even when gained through a violation of the law, because a fair trial can only be held by considering all available evidence. The fragmented model sees the constitutional violation as a distinct and separate stage from the admission of the evidence at trial and believes that suppression of the evidence cannot correct the government's constitutional violation of a person's right.

Regardless of the continuing debate, due to the decision in *Wolf* states did not have to follow the traditional approach of the Fourth Amendment which the Supreme Court had developed requiring warrants to be used in most circumstances. Without incorporation of the exclusionary rule, the one strategy that remained open to individuals who objected to the use of evidence that was gathered when a state government violated the Fourth Amendment was to argue that the government's actions violated the Due Process Clause of the Fourteenth Amendment. To win such an argument the defendant would have to demonstrate to the Court's satisfaction that the method by which the government gathered evidence had failed the test of fundamental fairness that our legal system is built upon. The most famous example of such a case is *Rochin v. California* (1952).[68] *Rochin* began when police received information that Rochin had been selling narcotics. Three police officers went to his home. Upon finding the front door open they walked in, went up to the second floor, forced open a bedroom door, and found Rochin on the bed. The officers noticed two capsules on a nightstand next to the bed and began questioning Rochin about them when he reached over and swallowed them. The officers then tried to force Rochin's mouth open so they could extract the capsules. Having failed to do so, they handcuffed Rochin and took him to a hospital where they had doctors administer an emetic causing him to vomit. Police then seized the capsules which proved to contain morphine. When the capsules were admitted at trial over his objections, Rochin was convicted.

The *Rochin* case required the Court to decide whether the actions of the police officers had denied Rochin due process of law. In a unanimous opinion the Court ruled that due process had been denied. Justice Frankfurter wrote the opinion of the Court. Justice Frankfurter noted that considerations of due process had to be determined on a case by case basis, but there was an overarching theme that had to be applied. That was that "convictions cannot be brought about by methods that offend 'a sense of justice.'"[69] In this case the Court believed that such a sense was violated. After explaining the extremes the state went through to gather evidence in this case, Justice Frankfurter wrote "This is conduct that shocks the conscience. . . . They are methods too close to the rack and screw."[70]

Rather than being indicative of the mainstream within the Court's Fourth Amendment cases *Rochin* should be seen as an anomaly case. In most due process cases the Court allowed illegally gathered evidence to be used in state prosecutions because the Court did not believe that the methods used to gather the evidence had failed the fundamental fairness test. Even the Warren Court of which Anthony Lewis has commented "wrote what amounted to a new constitutional code of criminal justice, one restraining the whole process of law enforcement from investigation through arrest and trial" had a difficult time in its first year finding that evidence which had been gathered through clearly illegal means should be excluded.[71] An example may be found in *Irvine v. California* (1954),[72] where the police were so adamant about gathering evidence against Patrick Irvine, whom they suspected of bookmaking activities, that they secretly had a locksmith make a key to his house. The police entered his home three times with the key for a variety of purposes which included concealing microphones, even in the bedroom, and punching a hole through the roof and stringing wires to a nearby garage where they had a listening post. The police eavesdropped on conversations for a period of more than three weeks. The conversations they heard helped to secure a conviction despite Irvine's claim that the state's activities denied him due process of law.

In a 5-4 decision the Court upheld Irvine's conviction with no single opinion being supported by a majority. Justice Jackson's opinion which announced the decision found that, "Few police measures have come to our attention that more flagrantly, deliberately, and persistently violated the fundamental principle declared by the Fourth Amendment."[73] Despite this, he emphasized that there could not be a denial of due process without an element of physical coercion as had existed in *Rochin*. Justice Jackson desired to advance the possibility of remedies other than exclusion and ended his opinion with a paragraph which was joined by Chief Justice Warren. In it he pointed out that under federal law "whoever, under color of any law, statute, ordinance, regulation or custom, willfully subjects any inhabitant of any state to the deprivation of any rights, privileges or immunities secured or protected by the Constitution of the United States shall be fined or imprisoned." The opinion continued "the Clerk of this Court should be directed to forward a copy of the record in this case, together with a copy of this opinion, for attention of the Attorney General of the United States."[74] Despite this recommendation by two justices, when the case file arrived at the Department of Justice, the Attorney General did not open an investigation much less initiate proceedings against the offending officers. In later years Chief Justice Warren explained that this sent a clear message to him that the Court could not count on other branches of the government to enforce remedies other than exclusion when the Fourth Amendment was violated.[75]

Justice Clark's concurring opinion in *Irvine* showed he was unhappy with the failure of *Wolf* to incorporate the exclusionary rule, but believed it was necessary to apply it consistently and allow illegally gathered evidence to be used in hope that others would see the necessity of the exclusionary rule. Despite voting to uphold *Wolf*, Justice Clark complained that the fundamental fairness standard of determining if there was a violation of the Fourteenth Amendment's Due Process Clause created unpredictability in the resolution of cases. He further complained that this unpredictability as to what constituted a violation of due process would not send an appropriate signal to police and prosecutors that it was unacceptable to violate the Fourth Amendment's provisions against unreasonable search and seizure.

One other case, *Breithaupt v. Abram* (1957),[76] also helps to demonstrate how the Court oversaw state search and seizure cases through the Due Process Clause of the Fourteenth Amendment. Like *Rochin, Breithaupt* also involved the question of bodily integrity. Breithaupt was involved in an auto accident in which three people were killed. At the scene of the accident police found an almost empty bottle of whiskey in the glove box of Breithaupt's truck. Police also noticed the smell of alcohol coming from Breithaupt's breath, so, despite his unconscious state, they had doctors take a blood sample which indicated that Breithaupt had been intoxicated at the time of his accident. The results of the blood tests were used over Breithaupt's objection to gain a conviction for involuntary manslaughter.

On appeal Breithaupt argued that drawing blood without his permission violated the due process clause for reasons similar to those in *Rochin*. The Court disagreed and confirmed the conviction. Justice Clark wrote the Court's opinion and emphasized that due process was lacking when procedures used against an individual were below standards that were morally accepted by the community. The procedures questioned in this case did not fall into that category for several reasons. The first was that every state but one accepted use of blood tests or other chemical tests in cases involving driving while intoxicated. A second was that the drawing of blood was done by a qualified physician under procedures that were routine. When the Court balanced the level of intrusion necessary to draw blood against the interest of the community to keep drunk drivers off the road, the community interests were thought to carry more weight.

Wolf v. Colorado was also responsible for continuing an interesting situation by making the provisions against unreasonable search and seizure of the Fourth Amendment applicable to both the federal and state governments, but only requiring exclusion of illegally gathered evidence in federal courts when it was obtained through the actions of federal government officials. Not only was illegally gathered evidence admissible in state courts, the decision also continued a loophole in the application of the exclusionary rule known as the "silver platter" doctrine which allowed evidence that was illegally seized by state and local officials to be used in federal courts.

The Court moved to close the silver platter loophole in *Elkins v. United States* (1960).[77] Movement in this direction was possible because of changes in personnel on the Supreme Court. Since *Wolf*, Earl Warren had taken over as Chief Justice. There were also four new associate justices, Potter Stewart, who wrote the *Elkins* opinion, John Harlan (II), William Brennan, and Charles Whittaker. In *Elkins* the defendants in the case had been convicted of illegal wire tapping after evidence which state officials had gathered in violation of the Fourth Amendment was passed on to federal law enforcement officials and used to prosecute in federal district court. On *certiorari*, the defendants asked the Supreme Court to reexamine the silver platter doctrine. In a 5-4 decision the Court closed the silver platter loophole as a source of admissible evidence. The opinion has been influential in later exclusionary rule cases because of the emphasis that Justice Stewart placed on the exclusionary rule not serving as a remedy for past violations of the Fourth Amendment, but instead as a deterrent for future violations. The emphasis on deterrence indicated the Court's primary concern in applying the exclusionary rule was "to prevent, not to repair" constitutional violations.[78] Ending the silver platter loophole took away from state officials some of the incentive to disregard the Fourth Amendment. Justice Stewart also argued that ending the silver platter loophole advanced the principle of federalism by avoiding conflicts between state and federal courts. He further noted that adherence to a strict policy of excluding illegally seized evidence in federal courts would further the goal of preserving judicial integrity by stopping judges from being accomplices to constitutional violations by rewarding law enforcement officials who disobeyed the Constitution. Justice Stewart's opinion ended the silver platter doctrine, but it created questions as to whether the exclusionary rule was necessary because it was an integral component of the Fourth Amendment or merely because it was judicial remedy which helped to promote respect for the Fourth Amendment and deter future constitutional violations.

While *Elkins* shows the unwillingness of the Warren Court to allow any evidence which was gained through Fourth Amendment violations into federal courts, the eagerness of the Warren Court to end the ability of state governments to submit similar evidence within their own courts became apparent in *Mapp v. Ohio* (1961). The record of *Mapp v. Ohio* shows that Dollree Mapp lived on the second floor of a two-family dwelling with her daughter. On May 23, 1957 three police officers knocked on Mapp's door and demanded to be admitted in order to search for a man who was a suspect in a recent bombing. Dollree Mapp called her attorney who advised her not to let the officers in without a search warrant. After informing their headquarters of these events, the officers then established surveillance of the Mapp home. Three hours later four more officers were dispatched to Mapp's home. They then forcibly opened Mapp's door and entered the premises. When Mapp saw that the officers had broken into her house she asked to see their warrant. Police waved a piece of paper which they claimed to be a warrant. Mapp then grabbed the paper and placed it down the front of her blouse. The police then struggled with Mapp as they tried to retrieve the paper. Mapp was then handcuffed for becoming belligerent and the officers removed the paper from her blouse. The original police report did state that there was a warrant which justified the search, but Officer Carl Delau, who was in charge of the investigation, admitted twenty years later that police did not have a warrant, they only had an affidavit.[79] At trial, no warrant was ever produced. In the downstairs apartment, which Mapp rented to another person, the suspect which the police were looking for was found. While all this had taken place, Mapp's attorney had arrived on the scene, but was denied entry into the house or the ability to consult with his client. Mapp was then taken upstairs to her bedroom where police officers started their search. The search of the bedroom included an examination of a chest of drawers, a closet, and suitcases. The search then proceeded to include a look at her private papers and a photo album. The search moved on to the daughter's bedroom and the rest of the second floor. The search moved to the basement where a trunk was located. Inside the trunk the officers found four books and a hand-drawn picture deemed to be obscene. As a result of this evidence, Mapp was tried and convicted under Ohio law for possession of obscene materials. Her conviction was upheld by the Supreme Court of Ohio and Mapp was granted *certiorari* by the United States Supreme Court.

The interesting thing about the Supreme Court's history of *Mapp v. Ohio* was that neither the Fourth Amendment nor the exclusionary rule were issues briefed or argued before the Court. Instead, it was appealed as a First Amendment case. Virtually all of the legal briefs and oral argument before the Court were directed at the issue of whether the Ohio obscenity law was vague and overbroad and, therefore, in violation of the First and Fourteenth Amendments. In fact, in the brief submitted by Mapp's counsel there was no request that the exclusionary rule be incorporated. Furthermore, when asked at oral argument whether he was seeking to have *Wolf* overruled and thus to exclude the evidence which had been seized in violation of the Fourth Amendment, Mapp's counsel answered that he had never heard of the *Wolf* case.[80] The only group to mention that this would be a good case to overrule *Wolf* and to incorporate the exclusionary rule was the American Civil Liberties Union in the *amicus curiae* brief that it submitted. Even the American Civil Liberties Union did not dwell on overruling *Wolf*, covering the issue in a three sentence paragraph out of a twenty page brief.

In the Court conference which followed the arguments for *Mapp v. Ohio* Justice Douglas suggested that the case could be used to overturn *Wolf v. Colorado* but his suggestion only received the support of Chief Justice Warren and Justice Brennan. Instead of deciding the case based on incorporating the exclusionary rule the Court unanimously agreed that the conviction would be overturned because the Ohio obscenity statute violated the First and Fourteenth Amendment.

The opinion was then assigned to Justice Tom Clark. During the writing of the opinion, the reasoning for overturning the conviction of Mapp switched from First to Fourth Amendment grounds including incorporation of the exclusionary rule to the states through the Fourteenth Amendment's Due Process Clause. Justice Potter Stewart, who objected to resolving the case on an issue which was not briefed or argued before the Court, speculated that the justices who made up the *Mapp* majority met in secret to discuss using the Fourth and Fourteenth Amendments as grounds for overturning the conviction.[81] In actuality, there was not one particular meeting that caused Justice Clark to change his approach to the case.

Historically, Justice Clark had disagreed with *Wolf* which was demonstrated both in his published concurring opinion in *Irvine v. California* and in a draft opinion in the same case which was only sent to Justice Jackson which called for overturning *Wolf*.[82] After the case conference, Justice Clark approached Justices Brennan and Black and asked if this would be a good case to overturn *Wolf*. Despite this inquiry, Justice Clark's uncirculated first draft upheld *Wolf*. Justice Clark then instructed his law clerks to research exclusionary rule cases since *Weeks v. United States*. Despite the less than persuasive research uncovered by his clerks, Justice Clark shifted to Justice Douglas' conference position and was now determined to write an opinion which overruled *Wolf*. His change of heart gave that position four votes and Justice Clark focused on getting Justice Black's vote. After sending a draft of his opinion only to Justice Black, Justice Black made some suggestions regarding the constitutional foundations of the exclusionary rule. Prodded by more input by Justice Black concerning the relationship between the Fourth and Fifth Amendments and whether the exclusionary rule was a rule of evidence or a constitutional requirement a third draft was for the first time circulated to the entire Court. After dissenting memorandums from Justices Stewart and Harlan were received, Justice Clark revised his opinion one more time and circulated it again to the whole court. Only then did Justice Black announce that he would be writing a concurring opinion, giving Justice Clark the crucial fifth vote he needed for a result that overruled *Wolf*.[83]

The *Mapp* decision is monumental for holding that the exclusionary rule is constitutionally required in all criminal courts. It did not, however, build this monument on the firmest foundation since the decision did not clarify the exact source of the exclusionary rule. As a result, debate has continued both on and off the Court as to where the justification for excluding evidence comes from and when it is appropriate.[84]

Justice Clark's opinion in *Mapp* began with the facts of the case. It then quickly moved on to discuss the history of the exclusionary rule. In doing so it provided the first justification supporting the exclusionary rule which holds that the Constitution itself forbids the introduction of illegally seized evidence. Justice Clark's majority opinion emphasized a constitutional basis for the exclusionary rule stating that "the exclusionary rule is an essential part of both the Fourth and Fourteenth Amendment."[85] Justice Clark believed that the lack of an exclusionary rule would reduce the Fourth Amendment to a form of words. According to Justice Clark, *Wolf* had to be overruled and the exclusionary rule incorporated since "without that rule the freedom from state invasions of privacy would be so ephemeral and so nearly severed from its conceptual nexus with the freedom from all brutish means of coercing evidence as not to merit this Court's high regard as a freedom 'implicit in the concept of ordered liberty.'"[86] Justice Clark also made it clear that the decision in *Wolf* which had changed the foundational

basis of the exclusionary rule to that of a judicially created rule had left the constitutional foundations of the rule coming from *Weeks* "entirely undisturbed."[87]

A second justification expressed in Justice Clark's opinion finds the exclusionary rule necessary in order to preserve the integrity of the government and
court system. This foundation of the exclusionary rule can be traced back to the
majority opinion in *Weeks v. United States*. The application of the exclusionary
rule was necessary to preserve judicial integrity because in Justice Clark's
words: "Nothing can destroy a government more quickly than its failure to observe its own laws, or worse, its disregard of the charter of its own existence. As
Mr. Justice Brandeis, dissenting, said . . . 'If the Government becomes a law-
breaker, it breeds contempt for law; it invites every man to become a law unto
himself; it invites anarchy.'"[88] Justice Clark also believed that application of the
exclusionary rule gave to the courts, "that judicial integrity so necessary in the
true administration of justice."[89]

The third justification for the exclusionary rule that found its way into Justice Clark's opinion in *Mapp* was that the exclusionary rule was required as a
remedy for constitutional violations. The primary purpose of the exclusionary
rule as remedy was to prevent future constitutional violations by providing a
deterrent to such abuses. The exclusionary rule as remedy also provided the majority in *Mapp* with a practical reason for overruling *Wolf v. Colorado* which is
often seen as essential when a precedent is overruled. That reason being that the
precedent was unworkable. In *Wolf* the Court had rejected applying the exclusionary rule to the states because it believed that the states could satisfy the requirements of the Fourth Amendment through other remedies. The states, however, had failed to develop other effective remedies to ensure that the Fourth
Amendment would not be violated. This caused Justice Clark to call remedies
other than the exclusionary rule "worthless and futile."[90] When reviewing why in
the *Wolf* case the Court had failed to incorporate the exclusionary rule Justice
Clark explained:

> The Court's reasons for not considering [the exclusionary rule] essential to the
> right to privacy, as a curb imposed upon the States by the Due Process Clause,
> that which decades before had been posited as part and parcel of the Fourth
> Amendment's limitation upon federal encroachment of individual privacy, were
> bottomed on factual considerations.[91]

Justice Clark noted the facts now demonstrated that since *Wolf* had been decided
a majority of the states had adopted the exclusionary rule. The exclusionary rule
was, therefore, seen as the only effective remedy which deterred Fourth Amendment violations by "removing the incentive to disregard it."[92]

Justice Clark ended his opinion with a pragmatic summary stating:

> The ignoble shortcut to conviction left open [by *Wolf*] to the State tends to de-
> stroy the entire system of constitutional restraints on which the liberties of the

people rest. Having once recognized that the right to privacy embodied in the Fourth Amendment is enforceable against the States, and that the right to be secure against rude invasions of privacy by state officers is, therefore, constitutional in origin, we can no longer permit that right to remain an empty promise. Because it is enforceable in the same manner and to like effect as other basic rights secured by the Due Process Clause, we can no longer permit it to be revocable at the whim of any police officer who, in the name of law enforcement itself, chooses to suspend its enjoyment. Our decision, founded on reason and truth, gives to the individual no more than that which the Constitution guarantees him, to the police officer no less than that to which honest law enforcement is entitled, and, to the courts, that judicial integrity so necessary in the true administration of justice.[93]

The ruling in *Mapp* was clear as Justice Clark wrote: "We hold that all evidence obtained by searches and seizures in violation of the Constitution is, by that same authority, inadmissible in a state court."[94]

In his concurring opinion, Justice Hugo Black explained that although he had agreed with *Wolf* when it was decided he now believed that the exclusionary rule was a constitutional requirement. However, instead of finding it solely in the Fourth Amendment he also found support for it in the Fifth Amendment's right against self-incrimination. He traced this view back to the decision in *Boyd v. United States*. He also had pragmatic concerns about the need for clarity in the law stating:

> The Court's opinion, in my judgment, dissipates the doubt and uncertainty in this field of constitutional law and I am persuaded, for this and other reasons stated, to depart from my prior views, to accept the Boyd doctrine as controlling in this state case and to join the Court's judgment and opinion which are in accordance with that constitutional doctrine.[95]

Justice William Douglas wrote a concurring opinion in which he argued that the incorporation of the exclusionary rule was properly before the Court because all the issues regarding the illegality of the search of Mapp's home had been raised in the state courts and on appeal. He further made it clear that he believed that the decision in *Wolf* "was not the voice of reason or principle."[96] That was because the failure to incorporate the exclusionary rule undercut the Fourth Amendment in the states and led to shabby law enforcement practices.

Justice Potter Stewart in a memorandum explained that he supported overruling Mapp's conviction on First Amendment grounds, but, because it wasn't properly before the Court, that he was expressing no position in regard to the incorporation of the exclusionary rule.

In a dissent written by Justice John Harlan and supported by Felix Frankfurter and Charles Whittaker, Harlan first criticized the way that the majority had used a First Amendment case to overrule *Wolf*. He then went on to express doubt that the exclusionary rule should be imposed on the states. Instead, he thought the imposition of the rule on the states would be destructive of the principles of federalism by denying to the states the ability to develop their own methods of dealing with unlawful searches.

Many scholars have helped to explain why the Warren Court decided to incorporate the exclusionary rule and enforce other provisions of the Constitution regarding the rights of criminal defendants. We can certainly point to the determination of the majority of the Court to rid the legal system of the deceit of granting specific protections in the criminal justice process, but not providing any means of making them a reality. Years after the decision Justice Clark explained in his pragmatic manner why he thought it was necessary to make the decision that the Court made in *Mapp*. He said, "I Couldn't understand why *Wolf v. Colorado* said that the fourth amendment applied to the states, but it just didn't seem to go all the way. . . . In fact, it was just an empty gesture . . . unless you really live by it and enforce it."[97] The scholar, A. Kenneth Pyle provides another reason for the *Mapp* decision. He argued that "The Court's concern with criminal procedure can only be understood in the context of the struggle for civil rights."[98] In this regard, the Court's decisions which protected the rights of criminal defendants must be seen in the larger struggle to stop discrimination against minorities. Minorities, such as Dollree Mapp, had often been subject to police abuses. Carolyn Long points to a couple of other reasons which help to explain the Court's motivation. One was the Court's realization that any hope of making the Bill of Rights meaningful for criminal defendants had to come from the Court because state legislatures would not provide relief for people who were abused by the state governments. A second was the justices, through their own experiences, understood that police abuses would not stop until strong leadership was provided by the Court.[99]

Mapp has contributed a number of benefits that went beyond simple incorporation of the exclusionary rule. One group that reaped dramatic benefits from the decision has been minority communities who had traditionally been subject to illegal police practices. As noted, the abuse which this community had been subjected in American society was often targeted by the Warren Court. Much to the surprise of the law enforcement community, its members also became one of the beneficiaries of *Mapp*. Law enforcement felt the benefits through the advanced professionalization of the vocation and by officers receiving greater training. The largest possible benefit of *Mapp* was that through application of clear Fourth Amendment precedents *Mapp's* implementation could bring about uniform treatment throughout the country in the area of search and seizure.

Conclusion

The protections provided by the Fourth Amendment have been subject to change throughout American history. The Supreme Court has, at times, expanded the protections of the amendment while, at others, those protections have been curtailed. For the first 100 plus years of the American Republic the Supreme Court was basically inactive in trying to set the limitations on governmental power to search and seize. This was due to the fact that most criminal investigations were conducted by state governments, who, at the time, were not bound by the Fourth Amendment. This limited the Court to only interpreting the Fourth Amendment in federal cases. Despite the paucity of cases that the Court had resolved concerning the Fourth Amendment prior to the Prohibition Era, the Court had by then established some important precedents. The most important of which was the primacy of the warrant requirement in determinations as to whether a search or seizure violated the Fourth Amendment.[100] The Court has called the warrant requirement the cardinal principle of the Fourth Amendment and it is the Court's traditional approach to Fourth Amendment jurisprudence.[101] This approach to the Fourth Amendment reads the two clauses of the amendment, the provision to be secure against unreasonable search and seizure and the warrant provision, as being interconnected. Thus, a search is seen as unreasonable, if it did not involve a warrant. Accordingly, early Fourth Amendment analysis involved a series of questions that had to be examined by the Court to determine if there was a constitutional violation. These questions included: (1) was the search or seizure of a person or area protected by the Fourth Amendment and (2) was there a warrant based on probable cause which described the things to be searched for or seized with particularity. If there was no warrant, another inquiry was made necessary by the practical realities of criminal investigations: given that there was no warrant, did probable cause exist and did the search or seizure fall within one of the recognized exceptions to the warrant requirement? The only exception that the Court had recognized was searches incident to a lawful arrest.[102] Equal in importance for the development of the Fourth Amendment prior to the Prohibition Era was the Court's declaration that due to the exclusionary rule, which was considered to be a part of the Fourth Amendment, the federal government could not use evidence which it had gathered through constitutional violations.[103]

The Prohibition Era was a period in our history in which a renewed emphasis on law and order was seen as necessary by the Court. As has often been true of such eras, the Court strengthened the power of the government to search and seize. By the end of the Prohibition Era, although the Court continued to apply the traditional approach to the Fourth Amendment, the power of the government to search and seize was broadened by growth in the number of areas which were declared not to be protected by the amendment including open fields[104] and

Prohibition Era

phone conversations heard through tapped phone lines.[105] The protections of the Fourth Amendment were also weakened by a new exception to the warrant requirement, the search of automobiles.[106] The Court also created exceptions to the exclusionary rule. These included the independent source exception[107] and the attenuation exception.[108]

Once the Prohibition Era was over, the decision to incorporate the Fourth Amendment in *Wolf v. Colorado* (1949)[109] did not greatly facilitate the Supreme Court's development of Fourth Amendment jurisprudence. This was due to the Court's failure to also incorporate the exclusionary rule. This made state violations of the Fourth Amendment insignificant since the states could continue to use at trial evidence that was illegally gathered. The only oversight the Supreme Court provided to state interpretations of the Fourth Amendment was through the infrequent use of the fundamental fairness standard of the Fourteenth Amendment's due process clause. An example is *Rochin v. California* (1952)[110] when the Court found the particular police behavior of forcing a suspect to vomit to gather evidence had shocked the conscience of the Court.

Mapp v. Ohio ended the period in which the Supreme Court applied the fundamental fairness standard of the Fourteenth Amendment to determine if evidence which was found in violation of the Fourth Amendment had to be suppressed. However, the lack of clarity as to the foundation supporting the exclusionary rule also created confusion as to which model of government, unitary or fragmented, was accepted in the *Mapp* decision. This would create problems for later courts which had to decide if the government could ever make use of constitutionally tainted evidence. Despite the lack of clarity over the source of the exclusionary rule in *Mapp v. Ohio*, after 1961 the Warren Court continued to be firmly committed to the application of the rule at both the federal and state levels when governmental officials violated the Fourth Amendment. It is only with the decision in *Mapp* that we can talk about a modern Fourth Amendment jurisprudence. This case also initiated the Warren Court's revolution in criminal procedure for which it has become known. Although the Court had broken with horizontal *stare decisis* and decided not to follow its own precedent established in *Wolf*, the decision in *Mapp v. Ohio* created the possibility that with Supreme Court oversight and the practice of vertical *stare decisis* the protections of the Fourth Amendment could become a reality in the streets at the state level where most law enforcement decisions were made. If the decision was properly implemented it would remove from our legal system the hypocrisy that had existed since *Wolf* was decided in which the Fourth Amendment was declared to be a fundamental right within our legal system, but states were free to ignore it. Under *Mapp* it seemed that the traditional approach to the Fourth Amendment requiring the warrant rule would now have to be followed in all courts.

One would think that incorporation of the exclusionary rule and the uniformity it would bring in the application of the Fourth Amendment at the state and national levels would be the last chapter in Fourth Amendment jurisprudence. The problem that has developed is that *Mapp* can only be implemented properly by lower courts when Fourth Amendment law is clearly understood. Since *Mapp,* however, there have been many changes in Fourth Amendment jurisprudence which have made creating uniformity in the application of the Fourth Amendment difficult. With the growing importance of Fourth Amendment cases caused by *Mapp,* the Court became more aware of the social costs that its decisions would have on society. The largest social cost of the exclusionary rule is its propensity for throwing out probative evidence and releasing the guilty. After *Mapp* it became clear that unless there were changes in police behavior large numbers of cases would fail due to the suppression of evidence. Faced with this possibility even the Warren Court balked.

What may seem odd is that although the Warren Court, the champions of civil liberties, remained dedicated to the traditional approach to the Fourth Amendment and usually sought to expand its protection, after *Mapp* its decisions took on a more pragmatic flavor and the language used in its later opinions set the stage for later Courts to limit the protections of the Fourth Amendment. Later changes in the Fourth Amendment were not brought about by overruling the decisions of the Warren Court. Instead, the broad, flexible language used by the Warren Court gave later courts the opportunity when practicing *stare decisis* to emphasize different aspects of Fourth Amendment doctrine or distinguish the facts to justify a different result. Adding to the constantly evolving interpretation of the Fourth Amendment in post-Warren years, the Court has also changed its interpretation of the exclusionary rule. Yale Kamisar has commented about the line of cases following *Mapp,* "Whether or not the Warren Court intended this . . . *Mapp* and its progeny have brought about a great clarification and simplification of the law of search and seizure—almost always in favor of the police."[111] George C. Thomas, III, writing in 2001, agreed with this and said that one of the unforeseen results of incorporation of the Bill of Rights including the Fourth Amendment and the exclusionary rule, has been a tendency for the Court to rewrite the Bill of Rights and lessen its protections for the rights of criminal defendants.[112]

It is the evolution of these changes in the interpretation of the Fourth Amendment and the exclusionary rule from the Warren Court's attempts to broaden the Fourth Amendment to those of later Courts which have limited the amendment's protections that will be the focus of the rest of this book. Because the Warren Court stated that it is a "cardinal principle that 'searches conducted outside the judicial process, without prior approval by judge or magistrate, are *per se* unreasonable under the Fourth Amendment—subject only to a few specifically established and well-delineated exceptions'" in the next chapter we will examine the warrant process.[113]

Illustrative Case Reprise

In the case of *Lustig v. United States* (1949) which we examined at the beginning of the chapter the Court used many of the rules for the traditional application of the Fourth Amendment that have been covered in this chapter to bring it to a resolution. The Court ruled that the search of Lustig and Reynold's hotel room was indeed a constitutional violation because law enforcement officials lacked a search warrant. Furthermore, the police lacked two things that might have allowed them to overcome the need to have a warrant, probable cause and an exigent circumstance which could have allowed police to make an exception to the need to have a warrant. Likewise, the search could not fall under the incident to a lawful arrest exception, because the search came before, not after, the arrest. Despite the fact that the search violated the Fourth Amendment when the Supreme Court heard this case in 1949 all of the evidence could have still been used in state courts. This was because the exclusionary rule had not been incorporated so states could ignore the Fourth Amendment without suppression of the evidence. However, because the case was heard in federal court, a central issue of the case was whether Agent Greene had a hand in the illegal search. If he did not, the silver platter doctrine would come into effect and the U.S. government would be free to use the evidence which was illegally gathered by state officials. The Court believed that Agent Greene did play a role in this search. It ruled that even though the idea and original entry into the room was an action of the Camden police, Agent Greene was called in before the illegal search was concluded. At that point he used his expertise in combating counterfeiters to direct the searchers as to what type of evidence they should be trying to discover. This activity made Agent Greene an integral part of the Fourth Amendment violation and the exclusionary rule had to be applied. Thus, because the evidence had been gathered by a federal officer through a violation of the Fourth Amendment it should not have been used in a trial at which Lustig and Reynolds were prosecuted by the federal government for counterfeiting. Their convictions were therefore overturned.

Notes

1. Nelson B. Lasson, *The History and Development of the Fourth Amendment to the United States Constitution* (Baltimore: The Johns Hopkins Press, 1937) 49-50 n.1 (1937).

2. Oliver v. United States, 466 U.S. 170, 186-87 (1984) (Marshall, J., dissenting).

3. *Lustig v. United States,* 338 U.S. 74, 76 (1946).

4. *Lustig,* 338 U.S. at 76.

5. *Lustig,* 338 U.S. at 76.

6. *Lustig*, 338 U.S. 74 (1946).

7. Jacob W. Landynski, *Search and Seizure and the Supreme Court* (Baltimore: John Hopkins Press, 1966), 27.

8. *Wilkes v. Wood*, 19 Howell's State Trials 1153, 1167 (1763).

9. *Entick v. Carrington*, 19 Howell's State Trials 1029 (1765).

10. *Entick*, 19 Howells' State Trials at 1066.

11. *Entick*, 19 Howells' State Trials at 1063.

12. William J. Stuntz, "The Substantive Origins of Criminal Procedure," *Yale Law Journal* 105 (1995): 404.

13. Stuntz, "The Substantive Origins," 405.

14. Otis'completepeechmaybefoundathtttp://www.constitution.org/bor/otis_against_writs.htm (28 Oct. 2008).

15. The states in order of adoption include Virginia (1776), Delaware (1776), Pennsylvania (1776), Maryland (1776), North Carolina (1776), Vermont (1777), Massachusetts (1780), and New Hampshire (1784).

16. Herbert J. Storing, ed., *The Complete Anti-Federalist, vol. 2* (Chicago: University of Chicago Press, 1981), 328.

17. Edward Dumbauld, *The Bill of Rights: And What It Means Today* (Norman: University of Oklahoma Press, 1957), 33.

18. Lasson, *The History and Development of the Fourth*, 100 n. 77.

19. Lasson, *The History and Development of the Fourth*, 101.

20. Bradford Wilson, "The Origins and Development of the Federal Rule of Exclusion," *Wake Forrest Law Review* 18 (1982): 1074.

21. *Barron v. Baltimore*, 32 U.S. 243 (1833).

22. Brent D. Stratton, "The Attenuation Exception to the Exclusionary Rule: A Study in Attenuated Principle and Dissipated Logic," *Journal of Criminal Law and Criminology* 75 (1984): 139 n. 1.

23. *Ex Parte Jackson*, 96 U.S. 727 (1877).

24. *Ex Parte Jackson*, 96 U.S. at 728.

25. *Boyd v. United States*, 116 U.S. 616 (1886).

26. *Boyd*, 116 U.S. at 630.

27. *Weeks v. United States*, 232 U.S. 383 (1914).

28. *Weeks*, 232 U.S. at 393.

29. *Agnello v. United States*, 269 U.S. 20 (1925).

30. *Agnello*, 269 U.S. at 33.

31. *Trupiano v. United States*, 334 U.S. 699, 705 (1948).

32. *Burdeau v. McDowell*, 256 U.S. 465 (1921).

33. *Silverthorne Lumber Co. v. United States*, 251 U.S. 385 (1920).

34. *Silverthorne Lumber Co.*, 251 U.S. at 391.

35. *Silverthorne Lumber Co.*, 251 U.S. at 392.

36. *Silverthorne Lumber Co.*, 251 U.S. at 392.

37. *Nardone v. United States*, 308 U.S. 338 (1939).

38. *Nardone*, 308 U.S. at 341.

39. *Nardone v. United States*, 302 U.S. 379 (1937).

40. *Nardone*, 308 U.S. at 341 (1939).

41. *Zap v. United States*, 328 U.S. 624, 630 (1946).

42. *Hester v. United States*, 265 U.S. 57 (1924).

43. *Olmstead v. United States*, 277 U.S. 438 (1928).

44. *Carroll v. United States*, 267 U.S. 132 (1925).

45. *Carroll*, 267 U.S. at 151.

46. *Carroll*, 267 U.S. at 153.

47. *Carroll*, 267 U.S. at 156.

48. *Carroll*, 267 U.S. at 153.

49. Cynthia R. Mabry, "The Supreme Court Opens a Pandora's Box in the Law of Warrantless Automobile Searches and Seizures—*United States v. Ross*," *Howard Law Journal* 26 (1983): 1243.

50. *United States v. Lee*, 274 U.S. 559 (1927).

51. *Weeks v. United States*, 232 U.S. 383, 392 (1914).

52. *Agnello v. United States*, 269 U.S. 20 (1925).

53. *Agnello*, 269 U.S. at 30.

54. *Agnello*, 269 U.S. at 32.

55. *Harris v. United States,* 331 U.S. 145 (1947).

56. *Trupiano v. United States*, 334 U.S. 699 (1948).

57. *United States v. Di Re*, 332 U.S. 581 (1948).

58. *United States v. Di Re*, 332 U.S. at 595.

59. *United States v. Rabinowitz*, 339 U.S. 56 (1950).

60. *United States v. Rabinowitz*, 339 U.S. at 66.

61. *United States v. Rabinowitz*, 339 U.S. at 65.

62. *Wolf v. Colorado*, 338 U.S. 25 (1949).

63. *Wolf*, 338 U.S. at 27.

64. *Wolf*, 338 U.S. at 28.

65. *Wolf*, 338 U.S. at 28.

66. *Wolf*, 338 U.S. at 31.

67. Silas Wasserstrom and William J. Mertens, "The Exclusionary Rule on the Scaffold: But was it a Fair Trial?," *American Criminal Law Review* 22 (1984): 85.

68. *Rochin v. California*, 342 U.S. 165 (1952).

69. *Rochin*, 342 U.S. at 173.

70. *Rochin*, 342 U.S. at 172.

71. Anthony Lewis, "Earl Warren," in *The Warren Court: A Critical Analysis,* ed. Richard H. Sayler, Barry B. Boyer, and Robert E. Gooding (New York: Chelsea House, 1969), 1.

72. *Irvine v. California*, 347 U.S. 128 (1954).

73. *Irvine*, 347 U.S. at 132.

74. *Irvine v. California*, 347 U.S. 128, 137-38 (1954).

75. Edward G. White, *Earl Warren: A Public Life* (New York: Oxford University Press, 1982): 266.

76. *Breithaupt v. Abram*, 352 U.S. 432 (1957).

77. *Elkins v. United States*, 364 U.S. 206 (1960).

78. *Elkins*, 364 U.S. at 217.

79. Carolyn Long, *Mapp v. Ohio: Guarding against Unreasonable Searches and Seizures* (Lawrence, Kansas: University of Kansas Press, 2006), 13.

80. Potter Stewart, "The Road to Mapp v. Ohio and Beyond: The Origins, Development and Future of the Exclusionary Rule in Search-and-Seizure Cases," *Columbia Law Review* 83 (1983): 1367.

81. Stewart, "The Road to Mapp v. Ohio and Beyond," 1368.

82. Long, *Mapp v. Ohio: Guarding against Unreasonable Searches and Seizures,* 53.

83. Long, *Mapp v. Ohio: Guarding against Unreasonable Searches and Seizures,* 82-104.

84. See Bradley C. Canon, "Ideology and Reality in the Debate Over the Exclusionary Rule: A Conservative Argument for its Retention," *South Texas Law Review* 23 (1982): 559-582; Charles McC. Mathias, Jr., "The Exclusionary Rule Revisited," *Loyola Law Review* 28 (1982): 7-12; Bradford Wilson, "The Origins and Development of the Federal Rule of Exclusion," *Wake Forest Law Review* 18 (1982): 1073-1109; Yale Kamisar, "Does (Did) (Should) the Exclusionary Rule Rest on a 'Principled Basis' Rather than an 'Empirical Proposition'?," *Creighton Law Review* 16 (1983): 565-667; and John M. Burkhoff, "The Court that Devoured the Fourth Amendment: The Triumph of an Inconsistent Doctrine," *Oregon Law Review* 58 (1979): 151-192.

85. *Mapp v. Ohio,* 367 U.S. 643, 657 (1961).

86. *Mapp,* 367 U.S. at 655.

87. *Mapp,* 367 U.S. at 649.

88. *Mapp,* 367 U.S. at 659 (quoting *Olmstead v. United States,* 277 U.S. 438, 485 [1928]).

89. *Mapp,* 367 U.S. at 660.

90. *Mapp,* 367 U.S. at 652.

91. *Mapp,* 367 U.S. at, 650-651.

92. *Mapp,* 367 U.S. at 656.

93. *Mapp,* 367 U.S. at 660.

94. *Mapp,* 367 U.S. at 655.

95. *Mapp,* 367 U.S. at 666 (Black, J., concurring).

96. *Mapp,* 367 U.S. at 669 (Douglas, J., concurring).

97. Long, *Mapp v. Ohio: Guarding against Unreasonable Searches and Seizures,* 104.

98. A. Kenneth Pye, "The Warren Court and Criminal Procedure," *Michigan Law Review* 67 (1968): 256.

99. Long, *Mapp v. Ohio: Guarding against Unreasonable Searches and Seizures,* 150.

100. *Ex Parte Jackson,* 96 U.S. 727 (1877).

101. *Trupiano v. United States,* 334 U.S. 699, 705 (1948).

102. *Weeks v. United States,* 232 U.S. 383, 392 (1914).

103. *Boyd v. United States,* 116 U.S. 616 (1886) and *Weeks v. United States,* 232 U.S. 383 (1914).

104. *Hester v. United States,* 265 U.S. 57 (1924).

105. *Olmstead v. United States,* 277 U.S. 438 (1928).

106. *Carroll v. United States,* 267 U.S. 132 (1925).

107. *Silverthorne Lumber Co. v. United States,* 251 U.S. 385 (1920).

108. *Nardone v. United States,* 308 U.S. 338 (1939)

109. *Wolf v. Colorado,* 38 U.S. 25 (1949).

110. *Rochin v. California,* 342 U.S. 165 (1952).

111. Yale Kamisar, "The Warren Court and Criminal Justice," in *The Warren Court: A Retrospective*, ed. Bernard Schwartz (New York: Oxford University Press, 1996), 137.

112. George C. Thomas III, "When Constitutional Worlds Collide: Resurrecting the Framers' Bill of Rights and Criminal Procedure," *Michigan Law Review* 100 (2001): 151.

113. *Mincey v. Arizona*, 437 U.S. 385, 390 (1978) (quoting *Katz v. United States*, 389 U.S. 347, 357 [1967]).

Chapter 3
The Cardinal Principle of Search and Seizure

Let's face it—cops hate to mess with search warrants. It's a genuine hassle. It's inconvenient. It's time-consuming. And some cops think it's downright demeaning for a grown, professional lawman to have to go get a "note from Mama" before he can do his job. Just when you're hot on the trail and you want to swoop down on some hood and round up all the evidence while you know its still there, you have to put your detective impulses into neutral, sit down at a typewriter and fill out a bunch of forms, and then go over to the courthouse and cool your heels until you can get a judge to spare you a few minutes of his valuable time. And if you've made a mistake or left something out in all the paperwork, you have to start all over. In the meantime, you just know that sneaky little crook has found out that you've found out, and he's disposing of all the evidence. No doubt about it, it's a hassle.[1]

While Government has a responsibility to detect and deter illegal activity, unreasonable governmental searches and seizures must be viewed every bit as illegal as individual illegal activity.[2]

Illustrative Case

In February of 1997 Jeff Groh, a special agent for the Bureau of Alcohol, Tobacco and Firearms, received a tip from a concerned citizen that Joseph Ramirez was storing a large stock of weapons which included an automatic rifle, grenade launchers and grenades, as well as a rocket launcher at his ranch. The citizen who provided the tip said that he had seen the weapons on a number of visits to the ranch. Based on this information Agent Groh filled out and signed an application for a search warrant for the ranch. According to the application the search was for "any automatic firearms or parts to automatic weapons, destructive devices to include but not limited to grenades, grenade launchers, rocket launchers, and any and all receipts pertaining to the purchase or manufacture of automatic weapons or explosive devices or launchers."[3] Along with the warrant application Agent Groh provided a detailed affidavit which he also wrote that explained his reasons for believing that the items which were listed could be found on the ranch. He then gave the warrant application and supporting documents to a magistrate who signed the application.

The next day, Agent Groh and a team of law enforcement officers under his leadership searched Ramirez's ranch. At the time Joseph Ramirez was not at home, but his wife and children were. Agent Groh described the items that were the focus of the search to Mrs. Ramirez as an explosive device in a box and repeated the description to Mr. Ramirez in a phone call. When the search was completed no illegal weapons or explosives were found and no charges were ever filed against Mr. Ramirez. Agent Groh left a copy of the search warrant with Mrs. Ramirez when the search was over. The application for the warrant had been sealed, but was released to Mr. Ramirez the next day.

Mr. Ramirez was angry about the search and examined the search warrant and its application in detail. In doing so he discovered that although the application for the warrant clearly described the place to be searched and the items that Agent Groh expected to find and seize, the warrant was not as clear. In fact, the warrant failed to identify any of the items for which Agent Groh was searching. In the part of the warrant which asked for a description of the person or property to be seized the warrant stated: "[T]here is now concealed [on the specified premises] a certain person or property, namely [a] single dwelling residence two story in height which is blue in color and has two additions attached to the east. The front entrance to the residence faces in a southerly direction."[4] The warrant did not contain a description of the stockpile of weapons that was the focus of the search. The warrant did contain verification that the magistrate was satisfied that the affidavit which supported the warrant application did indeed create probable cause to believe that Joseph was hiding contraband on his ranch. Because he believed the warrant to be fatally flawed and the search to therefore be a violation of the Fourth Amendment, Joseph Ramirez sued Agent Groh for violating his constitutional rights under Title 42 U.S.C., chapter 21, subchapter 1, section 1983. According to this law, "Every person who, under color of any statute, ordinance, regulation, custom, or usage, of any State or Territory or the District of Columbia, subjects, or causes to be subjected, any citizen of the United States or other person within the jurisdiction thereof to the deprivation of any rights, privileges, or immunities secured by the Constitution and laws, shall be liable to the party injured in an action at law, suit in equity, or other proper proceeding for redress."[5]

The *Ramirez* case presents some interesting issues. Under what conditions is a search warrant valid? How specific do warrants need to be in naming the location to be searched and the items to be seized? If an officer has a warrant when he conducts a search, is he protected from civil suits? The purpose of this chapter is to examine the warrant process. In doing so it will help to clarify how officers get warrants and why it is advisable.

The Warrant Rule

By incorporating the exclusionary rule the Supreme Court under Chief Justice Earl Warren put itself in a position of overseeing the application of the Fourth Amendment throughout the American judicial system. This constituted a dramatic change from the approach the Court had used from 1949 when it incorporated the Fourth Amendment in *Wolf v. Colorado*[6] up to 1961 when it incorporated the exclusionary rule in *Mapp v. Ohio*.[7] From 1949 until 1961 the Court used a due process approach to Fourth Amendment violations in the states. In doing so, it would only overturn the use of evidence gathered through a violation of the Fourth Amendment when there was also a violation of the Fourteenth Amendment's Due Process Clause. Finding a due process violation required the majority of the Court to agree that the questioned method of gathering evidence had violated the fundamental fairness implicit in our system of justice. Between 1949 and 1961 evidence gathered by state officials through a violation of the Fourth Amendment which did not shock the conscience of the Court was admissible at trial.

If followed, the language of *Mapp* established a precedent which would require, "that all evidence obtained by searches and seizures in violation of the Constitution [be] . . . inadmissible in a state court."[8] It gave the Supreme Court the primary responsibility within the American judicial system of deciding exactly what constituted a violation of the Fourth Amendment. In assuming this responsibility the Supreme Court took control of this controversial legal issue from the state courts which had up to that point more or less been given freedom to ignore the Fourth Amendment. Incorporation of the exclusionary rule required the development of a uniform understanding of the Fourth Amendment that could be applied throughout the entire country at all levels of government. Two years after *Mapp* the Court ruled in *Ker v. California* (1963)[9] that the federal standards the Court had developed would govern what was considered to be a reasonable search and seizure in both state and federal courts.

The cases that the Supreme Court had resolved prior to *Mapp* established what has been known as the traditional approach to Fourth Amendment jurisprudence.[10] The traditional approach demonstrates a preference for warrants. The decision in *Mapp* and a continued adherence to the traditional approach to the Fourth Amendment by the Warren Court helped to establish what has been referred to by Anthony Lewis as the "consensus approach" to viewing the Warren Court. Scholars who adhere to this group, include Lewis, Martin Shapiro, G. Edward White, Bernard Schwartz, and Archibald Cox. These scholars see the Warren Court's legacy as one of advancing a commitment to humanitarian goals such as equality of law for underrepresented groups in society, including criminal defendants.[11]

In the years since *Mapp*, the Supreme Court has continued to indicate a preference for the traditional approach regardless of whose leadership it was under.[12] The traditional approach to the Fourth Amendment reads the two clauses of the amendment, the provision to be secure against unreasonable search and seizure and the warrant provision, as being interdependent. Thus, searches and seizures are seen as unreasonable, if they did not involve a warrant. According to the practical application of this approach, Fourth Amendment analysis involved a series of questions that had to be asked by the Court to determine if there was a Fourth Amendment violation. These questions included the following: (1) did the government engage in a search or seizure of a person or area protected by the Fourth Amendment; (2) was there a warrant based on probable cause which described the things to be searched for or seized with particularity; and (3) if there was no warrant, was there probable cause and did the search or seizure fall within one of the delineated exceptions to the warrant requirement. The only two exceptions of areas protected by the Fourth Amendment that existed at the time of the *Mapp* decision were based on the existence of probable cause and an exigent circumstance which made the warrant process difficult. They were for automobiles[13] and searches incident to a lawful arrest.[14] Since *Mapp* was decided there has been an increase in the number of exceptions to the warrant requirement. These are covered in the next chapter.

Despite the Court's support for the traditional application of the warrant rule, there has in recent years been an increasing willingness on the Court to accept a reasonableness approach to the Fourth Amendment. There has been a lively debate among scholars as to the wisdom of this approach to Fourth Amendment jurisprudence.[15] Under the reasonableness approach to the Fourth Amendment, the warrant clause and the reasonableness clause are not interconnected. When the Court uses this approach it asks itself whether in light of all the facts, the government acted in a reasonable manner. If it did, there is no violation of the Fourth Amendment. For greater coverage of this approach to the Fourth Amendment, see Chapter 5.

The Supreme Court has consistently affirmed its belief that the traditional approach to the Fourth Amendment should be followed in determining if there has been a violation of the Fourth Amendment. The traditional approach to the Fourth Amendment was well illustrated by Justice Frank Murphy in *Trupiano v. United States* (1948) when he declared

> It is a cardinal rule that, in seizing goods and articles, law enforcement agents must secure and use search warrants wherever reasonably practicable. . . . To provide the necessary security against unreasonable intrusions upon the private lives of individuals, the framers of the Fourth Amendment required adherence to judicial processes wherever possible.[16]

Thirty years later, the Court steadfastly declared that in Fourth Amendment cases it follows, the "cardinal principle that 'searches conducted outside the judicial process, without prior approval by judge or magistrate, are *per se* unreasonable under the Fourth Amendment—subject only to a few specifically established and well-delineated exceptions.'"[17] This cardinal principle clearly states the Supreme Court's preference for searches and seizures that take place only after the warrant process has been followed. Due to the importance of warrants in the traditional approach to the Fourth Amendment, the focus of this chapter is to explain the warrant process. The warrant process today is similar to what it was under the Warren Court when *Mapp* was decided. Later Courts have, however, relaxed the standard necessary to demonstrate probable cause. The importance of following the warrant process is clear. If the process is adhered to, all evidence gathered through search and seizure is admissible in court.

Prior to presenting the factual circumstances in which the Fourth Amendment applies, it should be clarified when the Fourth Amendment does not apply. Due to the wording of the amendment and the process of incorporation, it only protects persons against actions of government officials. The actions of private individuals are not of concern to the Fourth Amendment.[18] As a result, searches that would clearly be unconstitutional if conducted by a government official do not raise constitutional issues when conducted by a private individual. In such cases, when a private individual provides the evidence to law enforcement officials the evidence may be used at trial without fear of its being suppressed.

Despite the Court's belief in the cardinal principle that all searches should follow the warrant process, most searches and seizures, including arrests, actually take place without a warrant. This is primarily due to the nature of police work which often makes the warrant process impractical due to the need to act quickly to combat crime. As Chapter 4 reveals many of the exceptions to the warrant rule are based on the existence of an exigent circumstance which makes the warrant process impractical. The ability to act without a warrant in cases of arrests was approved by the Court's decision in *United States v. Watson* (1976).[19] In that case the Court ruled that police may arrest suspects in a public place during daytime without a warrant as long as they have probable cause. Arrests must be reasonable in the amount of force exerted and an officer may only use deadly force if it is necessary to prevent the suspect's escape and the suspect presents a serious threat of physical injury or death to the officers or others.[20] If an arrest is to take place in a suspect's home without consent, then a warrant is required.[21] When an arrest takes place without a warrant there must be judicial review of the arrest within a reasonable period to determine if there was probable cause for the arrest. A reasonable period has been interpreted by the Court to mean within 48 hours.[22]

The Court's approval of some searches and seizures without a warrant should not be taken by law enforcement officials as a green light to conduct such searches. Whenever possible, police should obtain a warrant because of the advantages that result. The first advantage is that whenever a warrant has been issued there is a presumption that probable cause did indeed exist and the search or seizure is therefore assumed to be valid. That presumption places the burden of proving that the seizure violated the law on the defendant and with a warrant in place this will be a difficult burden to meet. This provides police with incentive to follow the cardinal principle. Taking the time to obtain a warrant may save an officer the need to appear at a suppression hearing when the trial process begins. A second advantage is that in cases where probable cause is doubtful or marginal the Supreme Court has said that searches under a warrant may be upheld, whereas those without warrants may not.[23] A third advantage of procuring a warrant is that it provides a solid defense in a civil case should an officer be sued for violating an individual's civil rights. The only exception to a warrant providing such a defense is when the warrant was clearly facially flawed and the officer should have recognized the flaw.

Warrant Requirements

The Court maintains a preference for the warrant process due to its view that the privacy of citizens may be better protected if information which might justify a search or seizure is judged by a magistrate. As Justice Robert Jackson stated in *Johnson v. United States* (1948):[24]

> The point of the Fourth Amendment, which often is not grasped by zealous officers, is not that it denies law enforcement the support of the usual inferences which reasonable men draw from evidence. Its protection consists in requiring that those inferences be drawn by a neutral and detached magistrate instead of being judged by the officer engaged in the often competitive enterprise of ferreting out crime. Any assumption that evidence is sufficient to support a magistrate's disinterested determination to issue a warrant would reduce the Amendment to a nullity and leave the right of officers to thrust themselves into a home is also a grave concern, not only to the individual but to a society which chooses to dwell in reasonable security and freedom from surveillance. When the right of privacy must reasonably yield to the right of search is, as a rule, to be decided by a judicial officer, not by a policeman or government enforcement agent.[25]

A search warrant is "a written order, issued by a magistrate, directing a peace officer to search for property connected with a crime and bring it before the court."[26] An arrest warrant is a written order that allows the officer who serves it to take the person named in the warrant into custody and bring them before the court to answer to the offense they have been charged with committing. Warrants generally require four components in order to be valid. These requirements are: (1) a statement of probable cause in the affidavit, (2) a supporting oath or affirmation that the probable cause is true, (3) a particular description of the place to be searched and the items sought, and (4) the signature of the issuing magistrate or judge. Rather than requiring a specific description of the place to be searched, an arrest warrant must specifically name the person subject to arrest or in cases in which the specific name is unknown provide a specific description of the person to be arrested.

The most important role of the judge or magistrate that oversees the issuance of a warrant is to make an independent determination of whether all the requirements of a warrant exist to allow a governmental intrusion into an individual's personal or business activity. A search warrant can generally be issued to search and seize four types of materials. These items include: (1) the fruits of crime, such as the proceeds from a robbery; (2) the instrumentalities of the crime, such as the equipment at a meth lab; (3) contraband items which under normal circumstances are illegal for anyone to possess, such as illicit drugs; and (4) evidence of the crime, such as a ski mask worn in a robbery.

Probable Cause and the Affidavit

Prior to issuing a warrant a magistrate must examine the affidavit submitted by police within the warrant application to determine if the police do have probable cause to search or seize. Probable cause is a universal standard under the Fourth Amendment which is required by the language of the amendment which states "no warrants shall issue, but upon probable cause." All American courts are expected to follow the mandates of probable cause before issuing warrants. Even in warrantless searches or seizures, probable cause is still the standard by which governmental actions will normally be judged. In such cases, the initial decision that a law enforcement officer made that probable cause did exist to search and/ or seize will be subject to judicial overview at subsequent judicial hearings and trial. In cases involving warrants, judges are not to rest their decision that probable cause did exist solely on the conclusions of the police. Instead, there must be enough information in the affidavit for the magistrate to reach his or her own conclusion as to the existence of probable cause.

Central to the concept of the Fourth Amendment is the assumption that searches and seizures will only happen as a result of probable cause, not suspicion. Police officers do not have the lawful authority to search or arrest based on hunches, feelings, guesses, or suspicions. As far back as 1933 and the decision of *Nathanson v. United States*[27] the Supreme Court ruled as fatally defective a warrant application that was issued "upon a mere affirmation of suspicion and belief without any statement of adequate supporting facts."[28] In the case of arrest, this means that police cannot arrest without a specific charge to file. Attempts to arrest without charge through such tools as dragnet arrests, arrest on suspicion, investigatory arrests, and arrests on open charges will all lack constitutional authority. Denial of power to arrest on suspicion means that police will not be able arrest a person and then at a later time try to find a crime with which to charge them. The fact that suspicion does not allow an officer to conduct a search or make an arrest does not, however, mean that investigating a suspicion cannot enlarge a situation to the point in which the officer will be able to develop the probable cause necessary to justify a search or seizure. For example, if a police officer observed a car swerve over the middle line that in itself would not justify a search of the car. The officer might have suspicions that the driver was drunk, but no probable cause. If, however, he stopped the car on the suspicion and then saw drugs in the glove box when the driver got the registration papers, the officer would then have the probable cause necessary to seize the drugs and to make an arrest.

For all law enforcement officers, recognition of what constitutes probable cause is essential for their actions to be legal. An early explanation of what constituted probable cause was given in *Carroll v. United States* (1925).[29] According to *Carroll*, probable cause exists where "the facts and circumstances within [the officials'] knowledge and of which they had reasonably trustworthy information were sufficient in themselves to warrant a man of reasonable caution in the belief" that a criminal offense had occurred and the evidence would be found in the suspected place.[30] Traditionally, the degree of certainty necessary for a finding of probable cause was the preponderance of evidence burden of proof. The preponderance of the evidence burden required a degree of certainty greater than fifty percent. In other words a magistrate would have to believe it was more likely than not that should a search be done the evidence described in the affidavit would be found. This is a substantially easier burden of proof to meet than absolute certainty which would take 100 percent certainty or the beyond a reasonable doubt standard used to convict in a criminal trial which requires a 95 percent degree of certainty. Preponderance of the evidence is, however, a much tougher level of proof than the reasonable suspicion burden which is needed to justify a stop and frisk.

The Court under the leadership of Chief Justice Warren Burger weakened the degree of certainty necessary for a finding of probable cause. In the 1983 case of *Texas v. Brown*[31] the Court replaced the more likely than not standard for probable cause and defined probable cause in the following way:

> Probable cause is a flexible, common-sense standard. It merely requires that the facts available to the officer would "warrant a man of reasonable caution in the belief," . . . that certain items may be contraband or stolen property or useful as evidence of a crime; it does not demand any showing that such a belief be correct or more likely true than false. A "practical, nontechnical" probability that incriminating evidence is involved is all that is required.[32]

In *Illinois v. Gates* (1983)[33] the Court clarified that a finding of fair probability was sufficient to demonstrate probable cause. The Court explained that probable cause is a "fluid concept . . . not readily, or even usefully, reduced to a neat set of legal rules."[34] The Court also came out in favor of a totality of the circumstances test for probable cause. It instructed lower court judges that, "The task of the issuing magistrate is simply to make a practical common-sense decision whether, given all the circumstances set forth in the affidavit before him . . . there is a fair probability that contraband or evidence of a crime will be found in a particular place."[35] The word "fair" implies that in issuing warrants magistrates may use a balancing approach in which the degree of intrusion can be weighed against other governmental concerns. Yale Kamisr has noted that "After *Gates*, it does not require very much to issue a warrant, but it takes even less to uphold one on review."[36]   *Arrest   Warrants*

In cases involving arrest warrants, probable cause "exists if the facts and circumstances known to the officer warrant a prudent man in believing that the offense has been committed."[37] Probable cause for arrest warrants can be the result of a combination of facts, or apparent facts, seen through the eyes of an experienced police officer, which would allow a reasonable, cautious individual to conclude that a specific person is committing or has committed a crime. Probable cause for issuance of a search warrant requires a set of facts or apparent facts which when viewed by an experienced officer would lead a reasonably cautious person to believe that if a location was to be searched, something would be found there which could be connected with a violation of the law. The information necessary to provide probable cause for the purposes of a warrant can come directly from an officer's own knowledge, information given the officer by a reliable informant, or information given by someone without proven reliability which has been corroborated. A finding of probable cause is so crucial in making a determination that governmental action was legitimate that its existence often provides the legal answer as to whether a case will go forward, evidence gathered, and be prosecuted. Therefore, the establishment of probable cause is central to the efforts of police and prosecutors. For this reason, prosecutors in some jurisdictions like to give their approval to affidavits prior to police presenting them to a magistrate.

It should be noted that the probable cause necessary to obtain a search warrant is different than that necessary to secure an arrest warrant. The probable cause that needs to exist in order to obtain a search warrant requires that those things sought must be connected to criminal activity and can be found in the location to be searched. The central concern of a search warrant is the location of evidence. Arrest warrants, on the other hand, must demonstrate probable cause that show either that a crime has been attempted or committed in the presence of an officer, or that evidence exists which reasonably lead the officer to believe that the person named in the warrant has committed a crime. The central concern of an arrest warrant is with the guilt or duplicity of the individual named in the commission of a crime. Due to their different focuses one warrant cannot be used for both purposes. In other words, the probable cause necessary to secure a search warrant, does not justify the arrest of the person who controls the location of the search. Likewise, the probable cause necessary to justify an arrest warrant does not justify a search of the home or business of the person named in the warrant.

When magistrates review probable cause prior to issuing warrants they examine the information through the eyes of an experienced officer. The professional training of law enforcement officers allows them to make connections and reach conclusions as to whether criminal activity has taken place that the lay person may not. In the affidavit, officers may therefore explain their reasoning why they believe seemingly innocent behavior may create probable cause of criminal activity. For example, while the layperson may simply see an aluminum can in a vehicle, an officer based upon their experience, may see that the dents and holes in the can make it an appropriate tool for smoking hashish. Judges reviewing the probable cause that police officers submit in an affidavit for warrants will give officers the benefit of relying on their experience.

In trying to get a search warrant police officers can rely on a wide variety of facts in presenting their probable cause. Officers can rely upon information that they directly gain using any of their five senses. There are no limitations on the types of facts upon which police officers may rely on in their presentation of probable cause. While not being exhaustive, the list of factors that officers can use to demonstrate probable cause include: (1) the fact that a crime or felony has been committed, (2) highly suspicious or unusual conduct on the part of the suspect, (3) the suspect's flight from or attempts to hide from or avoid the police, (4) the presence of incriminating evidence such as fingerprints, ballistics, hairs, DNA, fabric, and handwriting comparisons, (5) identification by a witness or a physical resemblance to the perpetrator, (6) the suspect's attempt to destroy evidence, (7) a prior criminal record, (8) incriminating statements made by the suspect, (9) evasive answers or unbelievable explanations by the suspect, and (10) the suspect's presence in a high-crime area.

In considering the facts supporting an affirmation of probable cause, the courts have allowed police to include ambiguous facts. They have held, however, that such facts are not strong enough in and of themselves to create the reasonable suspicion of guilt needed to justify the granting of a warrant. In those instances in which a warrant is applied for, it is the duty of the magistrate reviewing the application to determine if there are enough other incriminating facts to overcome the presence of ambiguous facts which would not clearly allow a reasonable person to make a conclusion concerning the probable guilt of the suspect. The officer who conducts a search or seizure without a warrant and who relies on ambiguous facts runs a serious risk of having his actions affect the outcome of the case during any subsequent suppression hearing.

Any and all facts accepted in good faith by an officer may be used to present probable cause for a search or seizure. There are some limited rules of evidence that guide which facts are legally allowed to be presented in the affidavit and which are not. One rule that does exist is the government may not rely on information gathered through a constitutional violation to serve as the basis of its probable cause. A finding of probable cause may, however, rest upon evidence which is not legally allowed at trial.[38] For example, unlike a trial, officers can use their knowledge that a suspect has a prior criminal record as one fact in trying to determine whether it is reasonable to believe that they are currently involved in criminal activity. The officer can rely on any type of fact and facts from any source in making his or her case for probable cause. An officer can use information that is received from other officers, members of the public, informants and even anonymous individuals. Officers can even use facts if they have no personal knowledge of a crime being committed and come upon the information second hand. Such information is known as hearsay. As far back as 1959 in the case of *Draper v. United States*[39] the Court ruled that hearsay information could be used as one factor in determining if there was probable cause for a warrantless search. In *Jones v. United States* (1960)[40] the Court ruled that hearsay information from a police informant could also help to demonstrate probable cause in warrant cases "so long as there [is] a substantial basis for crediting the hearsay."[41]

The truth of hearsay statements is dependent not on the officers' personal observations, but those of the person who provided him with the information. Often this presents no difficulties because the person who provides the information is known, assumed to be truthful, and will be available to provide testimony at trial. For example, when a victim of a robbery gives the officer a description of the person who committed the crime the victim is assumed to be credible. Information given by one police officer to another is also assumed to be reliable. Other times, hearsay evidence does present a problem in probable cause determinations because it is more difficult to determine its reliability. This is often the case when the individual who provides the information is a police informant. Police informants are often themselves involved in criminal activity and the reliability of their information may be questionable resulting in a lack of credibility with the courts. Another problem with police informants is that they often choose to stay anonymous which creates further problems with reliability.

In informant cases, as in all cases, the truthfulness of the information provided for the affidavit is only as honest as the individual who provided it. To provide guidance for magistrates and judges in the determination of probable cause in cases involving informants the Supreme Court under Chief Justice Earl Warren developed two separate and distinct tests in the 1964 case of *Aguilar v. Texas*.[42] Both tests had to be passed before a magistrate could find the information provided by an informant credible and thereby issue a warrant. One prong of the *Aguilar* test was the veracity prong. In this prong the affidavit had to provide the facts necessary to cause the magistrate to conclude that either the informant was reliable or that the information was reliable. This prong could normally be met by the officers' sworn statement that they had used the informant in the past and found the information passed on to be credible or by corroborating the information. The second prong coming from *Aguilar* was the basis of knowledge prong. Under it there also had to be present in the affidavit a statement which demonstrated that the informant gained his or her information through personal observation or some other equally dependable manner. This prong was meant to help stop rumors from becoming the basis of the probable cause for a warrant to be issued. Because each of these two prongs had to be satisfied independently of each other, before a warrant could be issued, the magistrate had to be convinced that the informant or information was reliable and that the information was based on a reliable source. Police may have found demonstrating these two prongs to be onerous, but the Warren Court did allow police to continue to use information gained from confidential informants in their affidavits.

In the 1969 case of *Spinelli v. United States*[43] the Burger Court refined the two prong approach coming out of *Aguilar*. After recognizing the difficulty police had of trying to satisfy both prongs of the *Aguilar* test, the Court found that the inability to meet one of the two prongs could be overcome with additional information on the other prong. The basis of knowledge prong, for example, could be used to overcome a weakness in the veracity prong if the tip was very detailed and would permit a magistrate to make an inference that the information was not only gained in a reliable manner but that the information itself was also credible. The veracity prong, on the other hand, could be strengthened so there was no need to meet the basis of knowledge prong if the police could provide individual corroboration of the tip provided by the informant and thus demonstrate the reliability of the information.

These two cases combined created the *Aguilar-Spinelli* test. Under this test the basis of knowledge prong could be satisfied by the informant's personal knowledge of the information contained in the tip or by self-verifying details. The most common method of satisfying the "veracity" prong was to point to the informant's track record and demonstrate that the informant had provided credible information in the past. The veracity prong of the test could also be satisfied by use of hearsay evidence from someone who would presumptively be telling the truth, such as an informant who had been demonstrated as reliable, or by sufficient police corroboration of the details provided by the informant. The best method of meeting the "knowledge" prong was for the informant to claim that he or she had personally observed the facts included in the affidavit.

Whenever police use information provided by an informant one method of determining the truthfulness of the material in a way which will allow a magistrate to make a finding that probable cause does exist is corroboration. By gathering corroborating evidence the police can either confirm the information in an informant's tip or make more certain it is reliable. The more evidence that can be found which confirms the tip, the easier it will be for an officer to convince a magistrate to find that probable cause does exist even if it is in part dependent on an anonymous tip.

The Court found the *Aguilar-Spinelli* test to be workable until it rejected it in 1983 in the case of *Illinois v. Gates*.[44] In *Gates*, the Court rejected the separate and independent interpretation of the two prong approach of *Aguilar-Spinelli* as being too rigid and too technical. To the Court the two prongs of *Aguilar-Spinelli*, while being relevant to the determination of probable cause, should best be understood as "closely intertwined issues that may usefully illuminate the common-sense practical question whether there is 'probable cause.'"[45] The Court ruled that a more balanced approach to determining if an informant's tip was reliable would be an examination of the totality of the circumstances rather than requiring an independent finding of both of the prongs of the *Aguilar-Spinelli* test. According to Justice Rehnquist's majority opinion, "The task of the issuing magistrate is simply to make a practical, common-sense decision, whether given all the circumstances set forth in the affidavit before him, including the 'veracity' and 'basis of knowledge' of persons supplying hearsay information, there is a fair probability that contraband or evidence of a crime will be found in a particular place."[46] Justice Rehnquist then instructed reviewing courts that their task was "simply to ensure that the magistrate had a 'substantial basis for . . . [concluding]' that probable cause existed."[47] In determining if the totality of the circumstances demonstrate probable cause, the Court reasoned that anonymous informants could be considered reliable if the information could be corroborated by the police. As a result, under the test currently applied, a warrant can be issued when a neutral and detached magistrate concludes that probable cause does exist based on an informant's information and all other available facts.

Another concern of magistrates as they review the probable cause presented in a warrant application is the freshness of the information. Since the purpose of the warrant application is to make a claim that if a particular area is searched particular evidence of criminal activity will be found, the information provided must be fresh enough to allow a reasonable person to conclude that the evidence will still be at the location where the warrant is served. Fresh information is required because events change quickly and contraband or evidence can often be moved with great ease causing information that has grown stale to no longer be accurate. The Court has not stated with precision how much time can elapse before information grows stale and no longer provides probable cause for a search. In *United States v. Leon* (1984)[48] it found that information about a drug sale that had taken place five months earlier at an address had become too stale to provide probable cause to believe that drugs still existed at the same address. In other cases the Court has preserved a more flexible approach that will allow magistrates who issue warrants to take into consideration the type of evidence sought in a warrant and the likelihood that it has been moved. The *Leon* case is even more famous for creating the good faith exception to the exclusionary rule. Under that exception, which is covered in more detail in Chapter 6, if police had a warrant which should not have been issued, but they in good faith believed that it was a legal warrant, the evidence is admissible. This exception demonstrates the importance that the Court places on police following the warrant procedure of the Fourth Amendment.

In determining whether probable cause exists the Court realizes that affidavits are often quickly prepared in the rush of an ongoing investigation. One result is that officers may not always take the time to clearly enunciate all the technical requirements for a demonstration of probable cause. In such cases, the Court ruled in *United States v. Ventresca* (1965)[49] that magistrates should use a common-sense approach to reading affidavits rather than being sticklers for technical details and to rule in favor of issuing the warrant in close cases. To try to give officers incentive to follow the cardinal principle the Court explained to magistrates that a "grudging or negative attitude toward warrants will tend to discourage police officers from submitting their evidence to judicial officers before acting."[50]

Oath or Affirmation

The language of the Fourth Amendment requires that warrants shall only be issued "supported by Oath or affirmation." The oath or affirmation is a part of the affidavit for the warrant. The affidavit includes the officer's statement of why probable cause exists for the warrant to be issued. The key to the affidavit meeting the requirements of the Fourth Amendment is that the officer must swear that the information provided to constitute probable cause is to the best of his or her knowledge accurate and truthful.

There are three standard ways for an officer to provide a sworn statement that the materials included in the affidavit are truthful to the best knowledge of the officer. The best method is through a written affidavit which explains how the officer came to have knowledge of the information contained in the affidavit. This method is preferable because putting the material in writing allows the officer to review the material prior to presenting it to the magistrate. This gives the officer opportunities to correct errors before they present a problem which stops the warrant from being issued. In situations which require quicker action on the part of officers, affidavits can be given and sworn to either over the phone, or in person to the magistrate. Telephone warrants are allowed and involve a taped conference call between the officer seeking a warrant and the magistrate. Telephone warrants require the officer and the magistrate to identify themselves and for the officer to read a completed warrant application and affidavit to the judge. If the judge is convinced that the affidavit does present probable cause, the warrant will be issued and the date and time will be noted. At the earliest opportunity a transcription of the conversation will be made, certified by the judge, and filed with the court clerk. If it was not possible for the magistrate to record the conversations, he or she will create a verbatim record of the conversation. When an officer appears in person before a magistrate he or she will verbally cover the material in the affidavit, swear to its honesty, and explain why probable cause is thought to exist. In both telephone and personal appearances, police can be at a disadvantage because they may slip in their comments leaving out pertinent information and not be able to correct the mistake before a magistrate makes a decision on the issuance of a warrant.

Due to the oath or affirmation it is assumed that all of the information contained in the affidavit will be true. At times, however, this does not prove to be the case and false information may lay the foundation for probable cause. When that happens it does not necessarily lead to the warrant being found to have been issued in violation of the Fourth Amendment. Instead, the Supreme Court has instructed reviewing courts to uphold searches if they determine that the false information reasonably appeared to be accurate and reliable at the time in which the warrant was issued.[51] If false information was deliberately and recklessly placed into the affidavit, the person whose property was searched can challenge the legality of the warrant. They must, however, follow a strict procedure. First, the person challenging a warrant must demonstrate that statements contained in the affidavit were not only false, but they were knowingly or recklessly included in the warrant application. Second, they must also demonstrate that the false statements were necessary to the magistrate's finding of probable cause. The person challenging the warrant at an evidentiary hearing must then be able to, through a preponderance of the evidence, establish that the officer who applied for the warrant knowingly or recklessly disregarded the truth. Finally, if the burden of proof has been met, the warrant will only be quashed if after the removal of the false statements, there is no probable cause for the issuance of the warrant.[52]

Particularity

The Fourth Amendment also states that the constitutionality of a warrant depends on it "particularly describing the place to be searched, and the persons or things to be seized." The particularity requirement limits the scope of a search or seizure. A warrant needs to describe several things with particularity. In *Marron v. United States* (1927)[53] the Court ruled that the particularity requirement is meant to stop law enforcement officials from having discretion regarding the scope of a search or seizure. The particularity requirement has meant that a warrant must include an exact address for the location to be searched. Such a requirement limits the use of a warrant to only one location and prevents the warrant from being used in a manner which would infringe on the rights of individuals who are not suspected of criminal activity. If the warrant is for a residence there should be an exact address and a description of the residence, which will help the officer serving the warrant to identify the proper place to be searched. For example, it is better to clearly state the warrant is for the house at 210040 Pine Cone Drive rather than the last house on the east side of the road before the curve. The warrant should describe things to be searched or seized with enough particularity so that any officer serving the warrant will know exactly what the purpose of the warrant is. For example, if the warrant is an arrest warrant, it must name the individual who is to be arrested. Stating that there is probable cause to allow the arrest of the residents at 244 North Sixth, is not particular enough to allow the warrant to be issued. If the warrant is an arrest warrant for a person, it is in the interest of the officer to include not only the name of the person, say, Randy Williams, but also any aliases they may use, such as, Rawhide Willi Washington, as well as a detailed physical description of the person. If the warrant is for a vehicle, it is best to include the color, year, make model, license number, the VIN number, and the vehicle's probable location.

Historically, use of a warrant at the wrong address would lead to suppression of any evidence since there had been no probable cause to justify a governmental intrusion into the privacy of the individual whose property was invaded. In 1987 this approach was altered in *Maryland v. Garrison*.[54] In *Garrison* police had a valid warrant for a third floor apartment at 2036 Park Avenue which was rented by a man named McWebb. The police served the warrant not knowing that there were two apartments on the third floor and they found evidence in the wrong apartment that was rented by Garrison. At trial Garrison unsuccessfully objected to the use of the drugs found in the search of his apartment since the warrant was for a different residence. On *certiorari*, the Supreme Court ruled that the actions of the officers who served the warrant had to be judged in light of the best information available to them at the time they served the warrant. Based on the officers' understanding that there was only one apartment on the third floor and that they were in it, the warrant had properly been issued and served. The precedent in *Garrison* therefore widens the latitude of the particularity requirement of the Fourth Amendment. Now, if a warrant is overly broad in describing the location to be searched, it will be upheld if its issuance was based on an affidavit which was based on reasonable, but mistaken, information. The information in the affidavit still must pass the good faith requirements of all probable cause information. If police provide mistaken information on purpose in order to enlarge the parameters of a search, the warrant will still be considered fatally flawed and the evidence gathered will be suppressed.

Not only must the location of the search be described with particularity, so must the items to be seized. A general description of items such as "stolen goods" would not be sufficiently particular because it would allow police to engage in a fishing expedition by providing those who served the warrant no real guidance for what they were searching. To be valid the warrant application needs to list the stolen goods which are being sought. Contraband items do not have to be described in as much detail because of the illegal nature of their possession. The Court has ruled that even when the affidavit contains a particular list of items to be searched or seized, if the actual warrant lacks a similar description, it violates the Fourth Amendment's particularity requirement.[55]

A final thing that should be described with particularity is the identity of the officer applying for the warrant. The identification of the officer should include a statement explaining the officer's experience in law enforcement and in investigating the type of crime involved in that particular warrant request. Alluding to the expertise of the officer is especially important when the affidavit is in part based on conclusions that the officer has drawn on from his or her experience. This is because the role of the magistrate is to take the experience of the officer into account in reaching a decision as to whether there is probable cause.

Following the particulars of the warrant when it is being executed is essential to the police. This is because if they stay within the scope of the limits established by the warrants particulars, those items which are named in the warrant will be allowed as evidence. Police will also be allowed to seize and use as evidence any other evidence which was found within the allowable scope of the warrant if they have probable cause to believe the property is contraband, the fruits or instrumentalities of crime, or evidence of crime. This is due to the plain view rule which will be discussed in more detail in Chapter 4.

One instance in which the strict particularity requirement is not necessary is in cases of anticipatory warrants. Unlike regular warrants, anticipatory warrants are not supported by probable cause that a particular piece of evidence will be found if a search is done. Instead, anticipatory warrants are issued when there is probable cause to indicate that particular evidence will be found at a particular place in the future. Anticipatory warrants are especially useful when police believe that evidence will soon be delivered to an address and then moved shortly thereafter. In *United States v. Grubbs* (2006)[56] the Supreme Court unanimously ruled that anticipatory warrants are acceptable and found that they need not contain an explanation of the triggering event under which the warrant can be served to be constitutional.

Signature of the Magistrate

The final requirement for a valid warrant to be issued is that it must bear the signature of the neutral and detached magistrate who has concluded that the affidavit does present probable cause for a search and seizure. The magistrate need not be a lawyer.[57] The need for the magistrate who signs and issues the warrant to be neutral and detached caused the Court in *Coolidge v. New Hampshire* (1971)[58] to rule that a state attorney general involved in a criminal investigation and prosecution is not in a neutral position to issue a search warrant. Likewise, a magistrate who receives a fee when issuing a warrant also has lost the ability to remain neutral and detached when judging the merits of a warrant, so such warrants are not allowed.[59] In *Lo-Ji Sales, Inc. v. New York* (1979)[60] the Court also ruled that a magistrate that accompanies police as they serve a warrant to help determine the proper scope of the search also violates the need for a magistrate to be neutral and with detachment make a reasoned decision about probable cause.

Service of Warrant

The rules for serving a warrant are generally contained in a state's criminal code. This said, there are some uniform procedures. These procedures include that the warrant must state the grounds for its issuance and contain the names of those individuals who swore to the affidavits included in the warrant. The warrant needs to name the judge or magistrate to whom it is to be returned after its issuance. The warrant also needs to tell the officers the number of days for which the warrant is valid. The warrant need not be served by the officer who applied for it. Instead, it may be served by any officer working for the department to which it was granted. The warrant under normal circumstances will only be valid within the jurisdictional boundaries of the magistrate who issued it. If officers are waiting at a location for a warrant they expect to be issued, they can restrict access to the location for a reasonable time.[61] Most search warrants must be served during the daytime in order to limit the increased possibility of mistaking officers for other individuals who might be entering a property without permission. Search warrants can be issued allowing for nighttime service if there are special circumstances which are pointed out in the affidavit. Chief among these circumstances are the protection of evidence against destruction, expected movement of property, or crimes that are committed at night. Arrest warrants, especially for felony arrests, may be served at any time of the day or night.

The American legal tradition has long favored a knock and announce rule by law enforcement officers while warrants are being served. This tradition may be traced back to British common law when in 1603 in *Semayne's Case*[62] the King's Bench ruled in favor of a requirement that officers knock and request voluntary compliance with a warrant prior to doors being broken down. The knock and announce rule was adopted by ten states prior to the time of the Constitutional Convention.[63] There are several purposes behind the knock and announce rule. One purpose is to allow the individual against whom it is served to voluntarily comply and thereby avoiding having their property damaged by officers having to break into the property. The announcement that police have a warrant also serves the function of legitimizing the actions of the police. Announcement also helps to cut down on needless violence which might result as a reaction to a forced, unannounced entry of a person's property. Under such circumstances property owners may react with force to protect their property from what they believe to be a break-in. After announcing themselves and their purpose, officers must wait a reasonable amount of time to allow a voluntary response. If there is no compliance, then police may forcibly enter and execute the warrant. When officers are fearful that announcement would cause individuals to fail to answer the door, they can use a trick to get the residents to answer the door. If such a trick is used, prior to entering the premises, police need to identify themselves, state their purpose, and provide a copy of the warrant.

If there are exigent circumstances, officers can avoid any announcement that they are there to serve a warrant. There are three exceptions to knock and announce rules that have been developed for exigent circumstances. The first and oldest is apprehension of peril. This exception applies when officers have a reasonable basis to be fearful that announcement of their presence will make the situation more dangerous for themselves or others. The mere fact that a suspect may be armed is not enough to allow police to bypass announcement. Instead, there also needs to be present additional facts which point to increased danger such as a past history of violence or a threat to use violence. A second exception is the useless gesture exception. This exception applies when the occupants of a place for which the warrant is to be served already understand the officer's purpose or police know that they are not present at the location. For example, if police were in hot pursuit of a suspect for which they had an outstanding warrant and the suspect ran into his residence, it would be a useless gesture to announce their purpose for entering. A final exception to the knock-and-announce rule is to stop the destruction of evidence. Under this exception if police have a reasonable belief that evidence will be destroyed if they announce themselves prior to entry, they may bypass announcement. In the application of this exception, the courts have differed widely on what type of burden of proof must be demonstrated to show that there is a serious threat that evidence is at risk. The Supreme Court was slow to indicate its support for the knock and announce rule.[64] The Court clarified its position on the knock and announce rule in *Wilson v. Arkansas* (1995).[65] *Wilson* came to the Court after state police in Arkansas had several times used an informant to buy drugs from Wilson and the person with whom she lived. During the last purchase, Wilson threatened the informant with a gun. State police then got a search warrant for Wilson's residence. When they served it, the police walked through the door way and only announced their purpose once they were inside the house. Wilson unsuccessfully moved to have the evidence that was found suppressed at trial. Eventually, the Supreme Court granted *certiorari* to determine if the knock and announce rule forms a part of the Fourth Amendment reasonableness inquiry. In a unanimous decision the Court, in an opinion written by Justice Clarence Thomas, ruled that the knock-and-announce rule is one consideration that must be examined in determining whether a search is reasonable under the Fourth Amendment. Thomas' opinion pointed to the long history of acceptance of the rule in both common law and within American law prior to ratification of the Constitution. The Court believed that the "Framers of the Fourth Amendment thought that the method of an officer's entry into a dwelling was among the factors to be considered in assessing the reasonableness of a seizure."[66] Ruling that knocking and announcing their presence was only one factor to be considered in the determination of whether a search was reasonable did leave open the ability of lower courts to determine when exigent circumstances would allow police not to knock and announce prior to entering a residence. Despite ruling that the Fourth Amendment requires officers to follow the knock and announce rule prior to executing a warrant, the Court in *Hudson v. Michigan* (2006)[67] decided that evidence gathered through violation of the rule did not have to be suppressed at trial.

In *Richards v. Wisconsin* (1997),[68] the Supreme Court overruled a decision by the Wisconsin Supreme Court which found no-knock warrants were always allowed in drug cases due to how closely intertwined were drug trafficking and guns. The majority opinion by Justice John Paul Stevens failed to support the Wisconsin ruling because "not every drug investigation will pose these risks [of danger to officers and loss of evidence] to a substantial degree," this was because "a search could be conducted at a time when the only individuals present in a residence have no connection with the drug activity and thus will be unlikely to threaten officers or destroy evidence."[69] Justice Stevens clarified that in order to conduct a no-knock warrant police needed reasonable suspicion to believe that officers would be in danger or that evidence would be destroyed. The burden to allow a no-knock warrant in Stevens' words was "not high, but the police should be required to make it whenever the reasonableness of a no-knock entry is challenged."[70] In 2003 the Court clarified that the reasonableness of an entry under the knock and announce rule was to be determined not by the length of time between the knock and announcement of a warrant and subsequent breaking into the premise, but instead by the totality of the circumstances.[71]

When a warrant is served, a copy of the warrant must be given to those individuals against whom it is served. The description of those items which may be seized in the warrant establishes the parameters of the scope of the search. For example, if the warrant states that police are looking for a 50-inch Sanyo television set, the search is limited to only those places where such an item may actually be hidden. Thus, a search for the television would not allow police to open drawers within a bureau since a person could not logically conceal the television there. On the other hand, if the same search warrant included authorization to seize records of sales from other stolen television sets, the scope of the search allows officers to look any place where such records may be found. This would not only allow officers to open all the drawers in a bureau, but to also examine jewelry boxes, a computer's hard disk or anywhere else where the records of illegal sales could be recorded or hidden. In such circumstances, no additional warrant is needed to enter containers such as locked drawers, cabinets, or suitcases. When an arrest warrant is served in a home police are allowed to conduct a protective sweep of the home to determine if there is anyone in the home who may present a threat to the safety of the officers.[72] No wider search may be conducted.

Any contraband items that are found but not listed on the warrant during the search may be seized and used as evidence since they will fall under the plain view exception to the warrant requirement. All items which are found in plain view within an area that the police have a right to observe may be seized and used as evidence. One limitation on the ability of police to seize materials both through plain view and through searching is the time sequence in which evidence is seized. Once the items listed on the search warrant are found, the reason for the warrant being issued is gone and the search needs to end. Any items found after the items for which the warrant was issued will be suppressed. Failure to suppress such articles would allow police to use warrants to engage in fishing expeditions to find evidence that was not related to the purpose of the warrant. During a search for contraband based on a warrant, police may detain any person who is at the location.[73]

If any property is seized as a result of a warrant, it must be listed on an inventory and a receipt must be given to the individual who was in charge of the premises. If no one was home at the time of the search, a copy of the warrant and an inventory list of materials confiscated in the search need to be left in a place where they will easily be noticed when someone enters the premise. When the search is completed, the officers who served the warrant also need to provide an inventory list and an officer's report to the magistrate who issued the warrant.

It should be noted that in no place does the Court take the warrant requirement more seriously than in invasions of a person's home. As the Court stated in *Silverman v. United States* (1961),[74] "The Fourth Amendment, and the personal rights which it secures, have a long history. At the very core stands the right of man to retreat into his own home and there be free from unreasonable governmental intrusion."[75] The Court added in 1990 that "physical entry of the home is the chief evil against which the wording of the Fourth Amendment is directed."[76] Due to the high value the Court places on the sanctity of the home, it ruled in *Wilson v. Layne* (1999)[77] that it exceeds the scope of a warrant for law enforcement officers to allow members of the media to accompany them when they serve warrants in an individual's home.

Illustrative Case Reprise

To recap the case at the beginning of the chapter, the Supreme Court in *Groh v. Ramirez* (2004)[78] ruled that the search warrant which was served by Agent Groh did not meet Fourth Amendment standards. The Court in an opinion by Justice John Paul Stevens said:

> This warrant did not simply omit a few items from a list of many to be seized, or misdescribe a few of several items. Nor did it make what fairly could be characterized as a mere technical mistake or typographical error. Rather, in the space set aside for a description of the items to be seized, the warrant stated that the items consisted of a "single dwelling residence . . . blue in color." In other words, the warrant did not describe the items to be seized at all. In this respect the warrant was so obviously deficient that we must regard the search as "warrantless" within the meaning of our case law.[79]

The Court added that Agent Groh's oral description of the items to be seized did not make up for the constitutional defect and was not enough to make the search reasonable under the Fourth Amendment.

The Court then moved on to determine if Agent Groh was eligible for qualified immunity from the suit. The Court noted that if an officer could in good faith have believed that a faulty warrant was facially valid it did indeed provide cover for the officer and give him immunity. The problem here was that because the particularity requirement is clearly set forth in the Fourth Amendment and a long standing rule of law, no officer could believe that a warrant which lacked a specific description of those items to be seized complied with the Constitution. On top of this, in this case, Agent Groh had prepared the invalid warrant so the problem could not be blamed on an error of the magistrate. The Court concluded that, "No reasonable officer could claim to be unaware of the basic rule, well established by our cases, that, absent consent or exigency, a warrantless search of the home is presumptively unconstitutional."[80] Due to this belief, the Court ruled that Agent Groh lacked qualified immunity for his violation of Joseph Ramirez's Fourth Amendment rights.

Even though the Court in cases like *Groh v. Ramirez* (2004) has been adamant that searches must be accompanied by a valid warrant, not all searches are based on warrants. Now that the warrant process is understood, the rest of this book examines situations in which warrants are not the norm which includes the majority of searches and seizures which are conducted in the United States. We start that discussion with the next chapter which examines the numerous exceptions to the warrant rule that the Court has recognized.

Notes

1. Devallis Rutledge, *The Search and Seizure Handbook For Law Officers* (Flagstaff, AZ: Flag Publishing Company, 1980), 141-142.

2. Ken Nuger, "The Special Needs Rationale: Creating a Chasm in Fourth Amendment Analysis," *Santa Clara Law Review* 32 (1992): 96.

3. *Groh v. Ramirez*, 540 U.S. 551 (2004).

4. *Groh*, 540 U.S. at 554 n.2.

5. Title 41 U.S.C., chapter 21, subchapter 1, section 1983.

6. *Wolf v. Colorado*, 338 U.S. 25 (1949).

7. *Mapp v. Ohio*, 367 U.S. 643 (1961).

8. *Mapp*, 367 U.S. at 655.

9. *Ker v. California*, 374 U.S. 23 (1963).

10. Cases in which the Court had indicated its preference for search warrants prior to *Mapp* include: *Agnello v. United States,* 269 U.S. 20 (1925); *United States v. Lefkowitz,* 285 U.S. 452 (1932); *McDonald v. United States*, 335 U.S. 451 (1948); *Trupiano v. United States*, 334 U.S. 699 (1948); and *United States v. Jeffers*, 342 U.S. 48 (1951).

11. Anthony Lewis, "The Warren Court in Historical Perspective," in *The Warren Court: A Retrospective,* ed. Bernard Schwartz (New York: Oxford University Press, 1996), 293.

12. Since *Mapp* was decided in 1961 the Court has favorably asserted the warrant rule at least 40 times. For a listing of cases see Phillip A. Hubbart, *Making Sense of Search and Seizure Law: A Fourth Amendment Handbook* (Durham: Carolina Academic Press, 2005), chapter 11, notes 1-3.

13. *Carroll v. United States*, 267 U.S. 132 (1925).

14. *Chimel v. California*, 395 U.S. 752 (1969).

15. For examples in this debate which support the traditional approach see, Carol S. Steiker, "Second Thoughts About First Principles," *Harvard Law Review* 107 (1994): 820-857 and William W. Greenhaigh and Mark J. Yost, "In Defense of the 'Per Se' Rule: Justice Stewart's Struggle to Preserve the Fourth Amendment's Warrant Clause," *American Criminal Law Review* 31 (1994): 1013-1098. For examples arguing against the traditional approach see, Akhil Reed Amar, "Fourth Amendment and First Principles," *Harvard Law Review* 107 (1994): 757-819 and H. Richard Uviller, "Reasonability and the Fourth Amendment: A (Belated) Farewell to Justice Potter Stewart," *Criminal Law Bulletin* 25 (1989): 29-50.

16. *Trupiano v. United States*, 334 U.S. 699, 705 (1948).

17. *Mincey v. Arizona*, 437 U.S. 385, 390 (1978) (quoting *Katz v. United States*, 389 U.S. 347, 357 [1967]).

18. *Burdeau v. McDowell*, 256 U.S. 465 (1921).

19. *United States v. Watson*, 423 U.S. 411 (1976).

20. *Tennessee v. Garner*, 471 U.S. 1 (1985).

21. *Payton v. New York*, 445 U.S. 573 (1980).

22. *County of Riverside v. McLaughlin*, 500 U.S. 44 (1991).

23. *Jones v. United States*, 362 U.S. 257, 270 (1960).
24. *Johnson v. United States*, 333 U.S. 10 (1948).
25. *Johnson*, 333 U.S. at 13-14.
26. Rolando Del Carmen, *Criminal Procedure: Law and Practice*, 2nd ed. (Pacific Grove, CA: Brooks\Cole, 1987), 164.
27. *Nathanson v. United States*, 290 U.S. 41 (1933).
28. *Nathanson*, 290 U.S. at 46.
29. *Carroll v. United States*, 267 U.S. 132 (1925).
30. *Carroll*, 267 U.S. at 162.
31. *Texas v. Brown*, 460 U.S. 730 (1983).
32. *Texas v. Brown*, 460 U.S. at 742.
33. *Illinois v. Gates*, 462 U.S. 213 (1983).
34. *Illinois v. Gates*, 462 U.S. at 238.
35. *Illinois v. Gates*, 462 U.S. at 238.
36. Yale Kamisar, "The 'Police Practice' Phases of the Criminal Process and the Three Phases of the Burger Court," in *The Burger Years: Rights and Wrongs in the Supreme Court 1969-1986*, ed. Herman Schwartz (New York: Viking Penguin, 1987), 160.
37. *Henry v. United States*, 361 U.S. 98, 102 (1959).
38. *Brinegar v. United States*, 338 U.S. 160, 172-173 (1949).
39. *Draper v. United States*, 358 U.S. 307 (1959).
40. *Jones v. United States*, 362 U.S. 257 (1960).
41. *Jones*, 362 U.S. at 272.
42. *Aguilar v. Texas*, 378 U.S. 108 (1964).
43. *Spinelli v. United States*, 393 U.S. 410 (1969).
44. *Illinois v. Gates*, 462 U.S. 213 (1983).
45. *Illinois v. Gates*, 462 U.S. at 230.
46. *Illinois v. Gates*, 462 U.S. at 238.
47. *Illinois v. Gates*, 462 U.S. at 238-239.
48. *United States v. Leon*, 468 U.S. 897 (1984).
49. *United States v. Ventresca*, 380 U.S. 102 (1965).
50. *United States v. Ventresca*, 380 U.S. at 108.
51. *Illinois v. Rodriguez*, 497 U.S. 177 (1990).
52. *Franks v. Delaware*, 438 U.S. 154 (1978).
53. *Marron v. United States*, 275 U.S. 192 (1927).
54. *Maryland v. Garrison*, 480 U.S. 213 (1987).
55. *Groh v. Ramirez*, 540 U.S. 551 (2004).
56. *United States v. Grubbs*, 547 U.S. 90 (2006).
57. *Shadwick v. City of Tampa*, 407 U.S. 345 (1972).
58. *Coolidge v. New Hampshire*, 403 U.S. 443 (1971).
59. *Connally v. Georgia*, 429 U.S. 245 (1975).
60. *Lo-Ji Sales, Inc. v. New York*, 442 U.S. 319 (1979).
61. *Illinois v. McArthur*, 531 U.S. 326 (2001).
62. *Semayne's Case*, 77 Eng. Rep. 194 (K.B. 1603).
63. Mark Josephson, "Supreme Court Review: Fourth Amendment—Must Police Knock and Announce Themselves Before Kicking in the Door of a House? Wilson v. Arkansas, 115 S. Ct. 1914 (1995)," *Journal of Criminal Law and Criminology* 86 (1996): 1237.
64. Jennifer M. Goddard, "Note, The Destruction of Evidence Exception to the Knock-and-Announce Rule: A Call for the Protection of Fourth Amendment Rights," *Boston University Law Review* 75 (1995): 458-459.

65. *Wilson v. Arkansas*, 514 U.S. 927 (1995).
66. *Wilson*, 514 U.S. at 934.
67. *Hudson v. Michigan*, 547 U.S. 586 (2006).
68. *Richards v. Wisconsin*, 520 U.S. 385 (1997).
69. *Richards*, 520 U.S. at 393.
70. *Richards*, 520 U.S. at 393-94.
71. *United State v. Banks*, 540 U.S. 31 (2003).
72. *Maryland v. Buie*, 494 U.S. 325 (1990).
73. *Michigan v. Summers*, 452 U.S. 692 (1981).
74. *Silverman v. United States,* 365 U.S. 505 (1961).
75. *Silverman,* 365 U.S. at 511.
76. *New York v. Harris*, 495 U.S. 14, 18 (1990).
77. *Wilson v. Layne*, 526 U.S. 603 (1999).
78. *Groh v. Ramirez*, 540 U.S. 551 (2004).
79. *Groh*, 540 U.S. at 558.
80. *Groh*, 540 U.S. at 564.

Chapter 4
Exceptions to the Cardinal Principle

The Supreme Court's Fourth Amendment jurisprudence, as tattered and full of holes as a beggar's winter coat, calls into question whether the remaining protection it offers to citizens against searches and seizures has any value. In no area is this question presented more sharply than in cases involving cars, their drivers, and their different passengers. Indeed it is no exaggeration to say that in cases involving cars, the Fourth Amendment is all but dead.[1]

It may be that it is the obnoxious thing in its mildest and least repulsive form; but illegitimate and unconstitutional practices get their first footing in that way, namely, by silent approaches and slight deviations. . . . It is the duty of the courts to be watchful for the constitutional rights of the citizen, and against any stealthy encroachment thereon.[2]

Illustrative Case

The case of *Whren v. United States* (1996)[3] started out like many other cases involving vehicle stops. Officer Ephriam Soto and his partner were patrolling a neighborhood in the District of Columbia on the evening of June 10, 1993. They were plain clothes officers in an unmarked car. The neighborhood was a high drug area so the officers were watching things closely. While patrolling they saw a dark colored Pathfinder truck that was tagged with temporary license plates. There were two young African-American men in the truck. The officer's suspicions were raised when the truck stopped at a stop sign longer than normal, more than 20 seconds, during which the driver was looking down into the lap of the passenger on his right. When the police pulled a U-turn to investigate, the

Pathfinder made a sudden right turn, without signaling, and took off at a high rate of speed. The officers followed the truck until it soon became trapped in other traffic at a stop light. When the officers pulled along the Pathfinder, Officer Soto stepped out and walked to the driver's door and identified himself as a police officer. He told the driver to put the vehicle into park. He next looked into the vehicle and saw two large plastic bags of what appeared to be crack cocaine in the hands of the passenger, Whren. Whren and the driver, Brown, were then arrested and the vehicle was searched resulting in a quantity of several types of drugs being found.

What happened next in the *Whren* case was unusual. When Whren and Brown challenged the admissibility of the drugs at their trial they admitted that Officer Soto had probable cause to believe that they had violated a number of traffic ordinances such as failure to give full time and attention to the operation of the vehicle, failure to use turn signals, and driving beyond a speed that was reasonable and prudent for conditions. They argued, however, that "in the unique context of civil traffic regulations" the officers should have been required to have had more than probable cause to stop their vehicle.[4] This was because they believed that Officer Soto's claim that he wanted to warn them about possible traffic violations was merely a pretext for stopping them to investigate drug related crimes for which the police lacked both reasonable suspicion and probable cause. This was especially true in this case because Whren's attorney argued that undercover police rarely involve themselves in violations of traffic ordinances. Furthermore, they argued that because automobiles are so heavily regulated in minute ways that it is next to impossible for any driver, no matter how careful, to avoid technical violations of the law. This allows police to decide in an arbitrary manner which drivers to stop. The decision to stop a motorist for a technical violation of traffic laws may then be used as an excuse for further investigation of an unrelated activity. The real problem with this they argued was that it created a temptation for officers to decide to use traffic stops as a pretext for further investigation based on unacceptable criteria such as the race of the car's occupants. To stop this situation they ended their argument by stating that the Fourth Amendment standard for traffic stops should not be the presence of probable cause, but whether an officer that was acting reasonably would have made the stop for the reason given.

The case of *Whren v. United States* raises some interesting questions about the Fourth Amendment. One is if there are going to be exceptions to the warrant rule, when are warrants necessary? A second is if there are going to be exceptions to requirement that a warrant exist prior to a search, what conditions must be present to ignore the warrant rule? A third is does the exception to the warrant rule apply to vehicles and if so, when and why? A fourth is whether exceptions to the warrant rule always require probable cause to investigate for a particular crime? Finally, can probable cause that a person has committed one crime be used as a pretext to investigate another crime? The purpose of this chapter is to examine and explain the exceptions the Court has found acceptable to the warrant rule of the Fourth Amendment.

Exceptions to the Warrant Rule

Six years after *Mapp v. Ohio* (1961)[5] incorporated the exclusionary rule the Supreme Court, led by Chief Justice Earl Warren, tried to explain with finality the requirements of the Fourth Amendment in search and seizure cases. It did so in *Katz v. United States* (1967)[6] and again used the traditional approach of tying together the two clauses of the Fourth Amendment and found that "searches conducted outside the judicial process, without prior approval by judge or magistrate, are *per se* unreasonable under the Fourth Amendment—subject only to a few specifically established and well-delineated exceptions."[7] It further announced that probable cause itself did not justify search and seizures. The Court clearly came out in favor of making warrants a necessity prior to government intrusion on a person's privacy. This demonstrated the Court's preference for a judicial officer, who would be neutral and detached from any police investigation, rather than a police officer, to determine if it was appropriate to invade the privacy of citizens. Although the Court's cardinal principle of the Fourth Amendment states that searches without warrants are per se unreasonable, the Court has also recognized that the realities of law enforcement do not allow the police to get prior approval in all circumstances while investigating crime and gathering evidence. In effect, while emphasizing the interconnectedness of the two clauses of the Fourth Amendment, the Court has recognized that in some circumstances the lack of a warrant does not make government efforts unreasonable. The willingness of the Court to find that not all warrantless searches are unreasonable does, despite the Court's statements otherwise, disconnect the two clauses of the Fourth Amendment and force the Court to examine the broader question of under what conditions should a warrantless search be considered reasonable under the Fourth Amendment.

At the time that *Mapp* and *Katz* were decided the exceptions to the warrant requirement that had been recognized were categorical rather than ones that required a case-by-case analysis of individual facts. These categorical exceptions applied to all cases which appropriately fit into that category. By relying on categorical exceptions, the Supreme Court sought to fashion rules that law enforcement could easily follow without giving officers the individual discretion to determine what was reasonable under the Fourth Amendment. If a case didn't fit into any of the specified exceptions that existed, it gave police notice that it would be necessary to go before a magistrate and obtain a warrant prior to search and seizure. At the time of *Mapp* and *Katz* the only two exceptions to the warrant rule of areas protected by the Fourth Amendment were based on the presence of probable cause and an exigent circumstance which made the warrant process difficult. These exceptions were for automobiles[8] and searches incident to a lawful arrest.[9] The Court also allowed people to waive their rights and consent to a search. The Court's willingness to accept the existence of exigent circumstances to bypass the warrant requirement is its admission that sometimes practicality and time do not permit procurement of a warrant. In these circumstances it is reasonable for officers to secure evidence first and then, if it is challenged, have the independent judiciary make a decision as to whether it was gathered in accordance with the Constitution. This situation still begs the question as to what constitutes an exigent circumstance. In *Minnesota v. Olson* (1990)[10] the Court tried to clarify its position on what constituted an exigent circumstance. The Court found that for an exigent circumstance to exist law enforcement needed probable cause to believe at least one of the following scenarios existed: (1) the need to prevent a suspect from escaping, (2) the need to stop imminent destruction of evidence, or (3) the risk of danger to police or others in or around a dwelling which is the subject of a search. Furthermore, the Court added "that in assessing the risk of danger, the gravity of the crime and the likelihood that the suspect is armed should be considered."[11]

Starting under the leadership of Chief Justice Warren Burger and continuing through today the Court has relied much more heavily on the reasonableness clause of the Fourth Amendment than the warrant clause. For greater understanding of this evolution of the Fourth Amendment see the next chapter. When the Court relies on the reasonableness clause it uses a balancing test to determine if an exception to the warrant requirement can be justified due to the reasonableness of government behavior. In the balancing test, the Court weighs the citizen's expectation of privacy against the governmental interest to search and seize. This has constituted an important shift in Fourth Amendment jurisprudence. While the Warren Court did not use the balancing approach to expand the number of exceptions to the warrant requirement, its decisions which advanced a balancing approach to the Fourth Amendment such as *Camara v. Municipal Court* (1967)[12] and *Terry v. Ohio* (1968),[13] which will be discussed in detail in the next chapter, did establish a framework by which later courts could use a reasonableness approach to expand the exceptions to the warrant requirement.

The exceptions to the warrant requirement that are derived from a balancing approach often do not involve the existence of exigent circumstances that make use of the warrant process difficult or impossible. The Burger and Rehnquist Courts were willing to drop the exigency requirement especially in cases where the Court didn't believe that the governmental interest was primarily criminal investigation. In these cases the Court moved even farther from the traditional exceptions to the warrant requirement to also allow exceptions that do not require probable cause before a search without a warrant may be justified. The Court believed this change was acceptable because when the government was involved in functions other than law enforcement, such as community caretaking, it was not unreasonable to increase the government's power to search and seize. Application of the balancing test also increased the number of exceptions to the warrant requirement. Any real understanding of how the Fourth Amendment actually operates must take into consideration the numerous exceptions to the warrant requirement. We will first examine those exceptions that require the existence of an exigent circumstance. The chapter will then examine exceptions that don't require an exigent circumstance.

Exigent Circumstances Exceptions

Automobiles

In 1967 when the Warren Court announced that the warrant rule was the cardinal principle of the Fourth Amendment the automobile exception to the warrant requirement was one of the few established exceptions that was well delineated. Throughout the Warren Court era the automobile exception was well delineated and based on two essential features being present. Those were probable cause and an exigent circumstance. The foundations of this exception can be traced back to *Carroll v. United States* (1925).[14] *Carroll* demonstrates the Court's view that probable cause in itself was not an exception to the warrant requirement. The emphasis the Court placed on the mobility of automobiles in *Carroll* clearly places the auto exception under the rubric of the exigent circumstances which make warrants impractical and unnecessary. In fact, the auto exception was the first time the Court made note of exigent circumstances.[15] Due to *Carroll* it was clear that if probable cause existed in a moving vehicle, the vehicle could be searched for contraband, the fruits or instrumentalities of crime and after the 1967 case of *Warden v. Hayden*[16] for evidence of crime. As with all challenged warrantless searches the final determination as to whether probable cause existed will be made by the reviewing judge, not the officers on the scene.

After the exclusionary rule was incorporated, one indication that the Warren Court took the warrant preference seriously is that it never used the *Carroll* doctrine to uphold a warrantless search of a vehicle. For example, in *Preston v. United States* (1964)[17] the Warren Court unanimously rejected the idea that *Carroll* allowed the police to search a car after its occupants had been arrested and the car was impounded and subjected to a search several hours later. The Court ruled that with the arrest of the occupants the search of the vehicle was too remote to be incident to the arrest.

In the years following the Warren Court the automobile exception became less well delineated and, temporarily, lost its clarity, as the Burger Court changed the focus of the exception from one based on actual exigent circumstances to one based on expediency in the gathering of evidence. Over time, the Burger and Rehnquist Courts have again provided clarity in the auto exception, but have emphasized police expediency over exigency.

Movement in favor of expediency first came in *Chambers v. Maroney* (1970).[18] The *Chambers* case came to the Supreme Court after Chambers' conviction for armed robbery. Police had received a description of a car involved in a robbery and were told that there were four men in it and that one of them was wearing a green sweater. An hour later police found a car matching the description which contained four men in it, one of which was Chambers, who was wearing a green sweater. The police arrested the men and seized the car taking it to the police station. While the car was at the police station it was subjected to a warrantless search in which the police found evidence connected to the robbery.

Chambers did not raise the Fourth Amendment question at trial, but he did on a unsuccessful writ of *habeas corpus*.

When the Supreme Court reviewed *Chambers* it found that the search of the vehicle could not be justified as incident to a lawful arrest. Therefore, for the evidence to be admissible another justification for the search would have to be forwarded. The Court found that the case was similar enough to *Carroll* to apply the automobile exception to the warrant requirement. The primary reason why *Carroll* could be applied, according to Justice Byron White's majority opinion, was that the police had probable cause at the time of the vehicle's impoundment to believe that if the car was searched evidence connecting the men to the robbery would be found. The existence of probable cause meant that there was "no difference between on the one hand seizing and holding a car before presenting the probable cause issue to a magistrate and on the other hand carrying out an immediate search without a warrant."[19] In the Court's mind the only difference between *Carroll* and *Chambers* was that the search in *Carroll* took place on the highway, whereas the one in *Chambers* took place elsewhere. The Court further reasoned that since police had probable cause to search the vehicle on the highway, but would have had difficulties due to the darkness of the hour, the same probable cause justified the search at the police station which was well lighted.

The decision in *Chambers* changed and enlarged the notion of what constituted an exigent circumstance. The Court's reasoning from *Carroll* leads one to believe that in cases where there was probable cause a warrantless search of vehicles was justified only because of the vehicle's actual mobility and the ease by which it could flee thereby causing the police to lose evidence. In *Chambers* we learn that due to the generic or inherent mobility of all automobiles a warrantless search is possible when probable cause exists, even if there is no chance of that particular vehicle fleeing and police thus losing valuable evidence. The widening of the automobile exception to allow the admission of evidence despite the lack of an exigent circumstance would over time become a pattern for the Burger Court.

Complicating the work of police and courts in determining the proper scope of vehicle searches has been the question as to whether containers found in a car may be searched. It wasn't until 1977 and the case of *United States v. Chadwick*[20] that the Supreme Court first provided an answer. *Chadwick* came to the Court after federal agents in San Diego contacted agents in Boston that two suspected drug dealers were taking a train to Boston with a footlocker they believed to be filled with marijuana. When the pair reached Boston they were met by Chadwick and the footlocker was placed in the trunk of his car. Before the suspects could get in and start the car, the three were arrested and the footlocker was confiscated. Over an hour later the locker, which had been both locked and padlocked, was opened without a warrant or any of the suspect's consent. The trial court suppressed the marijuana which was found in the locker. The government was eventually granted *certiorari*.

Upon review the Supreme Court refused to accept the government's argument that this was a search incident to a lawful arrest. Chief Justice Warren

Burger, speaking for the Court, reasoned that since the officers had gained control of the locker at the time of arrest and did not open it for over an hour, the search did not properly fit the reasons the Court had accepted for warrantless searches incident to a lawful arrest. The Court did agree with the government's position that due to the differences between automobiles and other types of property there was a diminished expectation of privacy in automobiles. This was because the main function of automobiles is to provide transportation. On top of that autos are subject to licensing and registration which further lessen expectations of privacy. Finally, autos are rarely a residence or the main repository of a person's effects. The Court held, however, that despite the lessened expectation of privacy in automobiles "a person's expectations of privacy in personal luggage . . . [are] substantially greater than in the automobile" and deserve the extra protections that the warrant process requires.[21] Furthermore, just because luggage and other containers are subject to mobility does not mean that they do not qualify for protection under the Fourth Amendment. The Court upheld the lower court's decision because even though the seizure of the footlocker was valid, police custody of the suspects took away any exigency that may have existed and made the footlocker immobile. As a result, there was no longer a chance that the evidence would be subject to flight so opening the footlocker without a warrant was unreasonable and thus violated the Fourth Amendment.

Chadwick is important because it helps explain an additional reason beyond the inherent mobility of automobiles which justifies the warrantless search of autos. That reason being the diminished expectation of privacy that a person has in their car. Over time, this diminished expectation of privacy, not the presence of exigent circumstances, would become the primary logic supporting the automobile exception to the warrant requirement.

Due to its peculiar facts, what *Chadwick* did not decide was whether luggage would remain protected from warrantless searches when it was discovered during a vehicle search that fell within the automobile exception to the warrant requirement. The Supreme Court was confronted with this issue in *Arkansas v. Sanders* (1979).[22] *Sanders* arrived at the Supreme Court after an informant told police that Sanders would be flying into the Little Rock airport with a green suitcase containing marijuana. Sanders arrived in Little Rock with a green suitcase, met an accomplice, and then placed the suitcase in the trunk of a taxi. The police stopped the taxi and asked the driver to open the trunk. Police then confiscated the unlocked suitcase and upon opening it discovered 9.3 pounds of marijuana. Over his objections the marijuana was used at trial and Sanders was convicted, but the Arkansas Supreme Court, relying in part on *Chadwick*, reversed.

The United States Supreme Court affirmed the decision of the Arkansas Supreme Court in an opinion by Justice Lewis Powell. It held that, unless there were exigent circumstances, luggage that was seized during a search which was justified by *Carroll*'s automobile exception to the warrant requirement cannot be searched without a warrant. A search of the luggage did not fit into either of the reasons which justified the automobile exception. Those being, that "the inherent mobility of automobiles often makes it impractical to obtain a warrant. In addition, the configuration, use, and regulation of automobiles often may dilute the reasonable expectation of privacy that exists with respect to differently situated property."[23] Since neither of these justifications was true of luggage found in a vehicle, the Court refused to extend the ruling of *Carroll* to include luggage simply because it was located in a car lawfully stopped by the police.

The Court continued and reasoned that due to heavy administrative burdens warrantless vehicle searches would be treated differently than warrantless searches of containers seized in a warrantless vehicle search. Containers seized in a vehicle, the Court reasoned, could more easily be impounded than entire vehicles due to their more manageable size. Justice Powell's opinion refused to allow the mobility which had existed in the vehicle to also justify a search of the luggage. He reasoned that because the police had firm possession of the suitcase at the time of the search, the exigencies which allowed warrantless searches of automobiles, mobility and possible loss of evidence, were no longer a consideration. While the precedent coming from *Sanders*, that luggage seized from an automobile cannot be searched without a warrant pursuant to the automobile exception, seems to be clearly delineated, the Court then muddied the waters. This was because the Court stated:

> Not all containers and packages found by police during the course of a search will deserve the full protection of the Fourth Amendment. Thus, some containers (for example a kit of burglar tools or a gun case) by their very nature cannot support any reasonable expectation of privacy because their contents can be inferred from their outward appearance.[24]

This last quote from *Sanders* had the potential to confuse police departments as they tried to determine exactly what types of containers could and could not be searched. The uncertainty of the situation is illustrated by the case of *Robbins v. California* (1981).[25] Robbins was pulled over by California highway patrolmen after his station wagon was observed to be meandering down the road. When Robbins got out of his vehicle, the officers smelled marijuana. The patrolmen then initiated a search of the passenger compartment of the vehicle and found marijuana and drug paraphernalia. Robbins was then arrested and placed in the highway patrol car. The patrolmen then continued with the search of Robbins' vehicle. In a recessed luggage compartment the officers found two sealed packages wrapped in green opaque plastic. Upon opening these packages the officers discovered fifteen pounds of marijuana in each.

In its decision in *Robbins* a plurality of the Court in an opinion by Justice Potter Stewart ruled that the Fourth Amendment does not distinguish between personal effects, such as luggage, which are worthy of Fourth Amendment protection and impersonal effects, such as the packages of Robbins, which would be unworthy of protection. There were two reasons given by the plurality as to why they were unwilling to make such a division. The first was that the language of the Constitution did not distinguish between worthy and unworthy effects that were protected by the Fourth Amendment. The second was that "it is difficult if not impossible to perceive any objective criteria by which" police could determine between worthy and unworthy containers.[26] The Court clarified that only two types of containers were exceptions to the ban on searching containers mentioned in *Sanders*. Those were containers which were already open and those which were so distinctive that the police could reasonably predict the contents. In *Robbins* the Court was not convinced that the marijuana which had been wrapped in green plastic was so distinguishable that officers could infer the contents. Furthermore, the wrapping indicated that Robbins wished to maintain an expectation of privacy in the contents of the packages. This case helped to demonstrate that violations of the *Chadwick-Sanders* rule that warrantless searches of closed containers found in vehicles would not be tolerated. This ruling, which should have been easily understandable by law enforcement officers, respects the expectation of privacy that people have when they store effects in a container inside of their vehicle. This decision also respects the cardinal principle of the Fourth Amendment that a warrant is needed prior to searching any object which does not in and of itself fall into one of the warrant exceptions.

Having provided a series of consistent decisions, three cases in five years, in which the Court upheld the automobile exception, but limited the opening of closed containers, the Burger Court abruptly changed directions in its 1982 decision in *United States v. Ross.*[27] In this case police had information from an informant that a man was selling narcotics from the trunk of his car. The informant also gave police a description of the car. Upon seeing the described car, police stopped Ross, searched the car, and found a bullet on the front seat and a gun in the glove compartment. Police then took Ross' keys and opened up the trunk. Inside the trunk they found a brown paper sack that resembled a lunch sack which was closed, but not sealed. They opened the sack and found glassine bags of heroin. The car was then taken to police headquarters where it was again searched without a warrant. In the second search the police found a red leather pouch that was zipped shut. When they looked inside they found $3,200 in cash. The trial court accepted all the evidence and Ross was convicted.

On review, the Supreme Court upheld the decision of the lower court. Justice John Paul Stevens, writing for the majority, relied on a two-prong analysis to support the Court's decision. The first prong was an analysis of the scope of searches allowed under the warrant clause. Stevens pointed out that the scope of any legitimate search is as wide as could be authorized by a magistrate based on the probable cause. Any limitation on the scope of a search is defined not by the containers which police may come across, but by the object of the search. To support this line of reasoning Justice Stevens used an analogy comparing the scope of a car search to the scope of a home search. In doing so, he pointed out that if police had a warrant to search for evidence in a person's home, they would not have to secure a separate warrant for every container found in the home in which the sought after evidence might be placed. In both a person's home and in their automobile it only made sense that the purpose of the search should take priority. Thus, in the case of *Ross*, there was probable cause to search any container in which drugs could be hidden.

A second line of analysis that Justice Stevens used was by relying on precedent. *Carroll* and *Ross* were consistent, Justice Stevens pointed out, because the police in both cases had probable cause and continued to search all the places where the evidence could be concealed. In *Carroll* they took the upholstery out of the back seat and in *Ross* they opened a brown paper sack and a leather pouch. In both cases the evidence they were searching for could be logically found in the locations searched. To interpret *Carroll* to disallow police to have authority to search those places where contraband evidence could be concealed in an automobile would nullify its effect since contraband evidence is normally hidden from the prying eyes of others. Consistency in precedent required that if police have probable cause to believe that evidence is in a vehicle, they may search the car and its contents for the evidence. Based on this reasoning, the Court concluded that the scope of a search conducted pursuant to the automobile exception to the warrant requirement "is not defined by the nature of the container in which the contraband is secreted. Rather, it is defined by the object of the search and the places in which there is probable cause to believe it will be found."[28]

The decision in *Ross* did place two limits on the ability of officers to search containers found in a warrantless search of a car. The first limitation was based on the holding in *Sanders* and limited the ability of the police to search a container when it is the focus of the interest to the police, not the vehicle. The second limitation was based on the nature of the object sought by the probable cause which established the justifiable scope of the search. For example, if police had probable cause to believe the suspect had a shotgun, a purse could not be searched.

The holding of the Court in *Ross* lessened the protections of the Fourth Amendment when compared to *Chadwick* and *Sanders*. The *Ross* rule is far less supportive of the cardinal principle of the Fourth Amendment that searches without a warrant violate the Constitution. This is because in allowing all containers which might contain the evidence police are searching for to be opened without a warrant, the freedom of police rather than magistrates to make the initial determination of probable cause is widened allowing for more searches to be conducted that might not fulfill Fourth Amendment requirements. As had the *Chadwick-Sanders* rule, *Ross* created a new bright-line rule which is easy for police to understand and apply in the field. The Court clearly announced this rule stating:

> We hold that the scope of the warrantless search authorized by [the automobile] exception is no broader and no narrower than a magistrate could legitimately authorize by a warrant. If probable cause justifies the search of a lawfully stopped vehicle, it justifies the search of every part of the vehicle and its contents that may conceal the object of the search.[29]

As demonstrated by *Ross*, for the Burger Court the automobile exception became increasingly removed from its exigency requirements. This movement was driven by several factors. The first was the Court's dislike of the costs of the exclusionary rule.[30] A second was the Court's desire to develop a bright-line rule for auto searches which would be easily understood by law enforcement.[31] By relying on the inherent mobility of automobiles, declaring that people have a diminished expectation of privacy in their vehicles, assuming that police departments didn't have the ability to seize and hold vehicles until warrants could be issued, and treating automobiles and the containers found in them the same, the Court developed a blanket rule that applied to all auto searches when probable cause was present. In so doing the exigency requirement was replaced by a rule that placed the expediency of gathering evidence above the factual realities that had previously justified the vehicle exception in some auto searches.

The Rehnquist Court continued down this path of broadening the auto exception. The holding in *Ross* was applied by the Rehnquist Court to searches when an individual is in a car at the time they give consent to a search. In *Florida v. Jimeno* (1991)[32] the Court ruled that when an individual gives consent to police to conduct a search of a vehicle, the police have a right to search all closed containers which may conceal the object of the search. The Court held that there was no Fourth Amendment violation as long as it was reasonable for the officer to believe that "the scope of the suspect's consent permitted him to open [the] particular container within the automobile."[33]

As broad and relatively clear as the holding from *Ross* was, the Rehnquist Court thought that it was too confusing for police. The confusion came about because the key to whether there had been a violation of the Fourth Amendment in an automobile search was found in where the probable cause justifying a search was located. If the probable cause was for an item possibly in the car in general, then *Carroll/Ross* would apply and all of its contents could be searched. If the probable cause was focused on a specific container in the vehicle, then *Chadwick-Sanders* would apply and only that specific container could be seized and would be subject to warrant requirements before it could be opened.

The Court corrected this perceived problem in *California v. Acevedo* (1991).[34] The facts to *Acevedo* were simple. Police intercepted and examined a package of marijuana that had been sent through Federal Express. Police made arrangements for the package to be delivered and trailed the person who picked it up at a Federal Express office back to his apartment. While one officer went to get a warrant other officers saw Acevedo arrive at the apartment and ten minutes later he left the apartment. When Acevedo left he had a small brown paper bag which was the appropriate size to carry one of the packages of marijuana police had observed in the delivery they had opened. Acevedo placed the package in his car trunk and drove away. Police stopped the car, opened the trunk, took the bag out, and found marijuana in it. Acevedo pleaded guilty when the marijuana was admitted as evidence, but reserved the right to appeal the decision. When he did the California Court of Appeals reversed and then the California Supreme

Court refused to hear the case. The State's petition for *certiorari* was then granted by the Supreme Court.

The Supreme Court's decision held that police may conduct warrantless searches of all containers found in a car regardless of whether they have probable cause to search a specific container, or just the car in general. The Court reviewed the history of vehicle searches and found that it had "provided only minimal protection for privacy and have impeded effective law enforcement."[35] In an interesting line of reasoning the Court widened the authority of police to search containers without a warrant in order to better protect the privacy interests of citizens. Speaking for the Court, Justice Harry Blackmun reasoned, "[t]he line between probable cause to search a vehicle and probable cause to search a package in the vehicle is not always clear, and separate rules . . . may enable the police to broaden their power to make warrantless searches and disservice privacy interests."[36] This was because "if police know that they may open a bag only if they are actually searching the entire car, they may search more extensively than they otherwise would in order to establish the general probable cause required by *Ross*."[37] Furthermore, the Court explained that even if police were not allowed to search a container through an expansion of the automobile exception, they could seize it until they got a warrant to search and since police had probable cause to seize the container a warrant would be issued in the overwhelming majority of cases. Therefore, the ability to legally search the container was just a matter of timing. Another justification given for the ruling was that the search of containers, such as Acevedo's paper bag, was much less intrusive on individual privacy than taking out the upholstery of the car in *Carroll*. The Court also pointed out, without taking note of its own inconsistencies, that police and the lower courts had difficulty applying the *Chadwick-Sanders* rule, due to the lack of a clear guideline, and this resulted in the need for the Supreme Court to resolve twenty-nine Fourth Amendment cases since *Ross* had been decided in 1982. Due to these problems, the Court believed that it was time to create a clear rule and it held: "We conclude that it is better to adopt one clear-cut rule to govern automobile searches and . . . the Carroll doctrine set forth in Ross now applies to all searches of containers found in an automobile."[38] In other words, the police may search everything in a vehicle without a warrant if their search is supported by any probable cause.

Ohio v. Robinette (1996)[39] is an example of a vehicle case which builds on a separate exception, covered later in the chapter, to the warrant rule, consent. The case came to the Court after Robert Robinette was stopped for speeding. The officer who stopped Robinette gave him a verbal warning and returned his driver's license. The officer then asked Robinette if he had any illegal contraband, weapons, or drugs in the vehicle. Robinette answered "no" and the officer then asked and was given permission to do a search. He found a small amount of marijuana and methamphetamine. It was introduced over Robinette's objections at trial resulting in his conviction. The conviction was overturned by the Supreme Court of Ohio which ruled that the consent was not voluntary because the officer had illegally detained Robinette. This was because he did not inform

Robinette of his right to leave before asking for consent to search, when the officer had no articulable basis for continuing the original stop. On *certiorari* to the Supreme Court, the Court found no Fourth Amendment violation. According to the Court, the Fourth Amendment does not require an officer to inform individuals who have been lawfully seized, in this case for the speeding violation, that they are free to go in order for their consent to be voluntary. The Court believed that in examining the totality of the circumstances, the facts showed that the officer's actions were reasonable. Furthermore, the Court did not believe that it was appropriate to create a bright line rule which would require officers to instruct individuals about their options in these cases.

In *Wyoming v. Houghton* (1999)[40] the Supreme Court expanded the rulings from *Ross* and *Acevedo* to include searches of the property of passengers who are in a car even when the probable cause that exists for the auto search is directed toward the driver/owner of the vehicle. According to Justice Antonin Scalia's majority opinion, the crucial question that had to be answered to resolve the case was whether the item for which probable cause existed could be concealed in the searched container. Ownership of the container was not important. Furthermore, the Court believed that passengers in cars had a reduced interest in privacy that when balanced against the substantial state interests could not carry the day. The Court clearly believed that efficiency in law enforcement took priority by explaining that effective law enforcement would be "impaired without the ability to search a passenger's personal belongings when there is reason to believe contraband or evidence of criminal wrongdoing is hidden in the car."[41] The Court also noted that continuation of a bright-line rule for all car cases would advance the governmental interest in effective law enforcement. The impact of this case is that police may justify a search of each and every piece of property belonging to passengers, even innocent ones, based on the misconduct of only the driver. In 2003 the Court made it even easier to search a vehicle by ruling that an officer's observation of large amounts of cash permits a warrantless arrest on probable cause of commission of a felony.[42] Vehicles can, of course also be searched incident to a lawful arrest.

Incident to a Lawful Arrest

The Supreme Court allows searches that are incident to a lawful arrest to be conducted without the necessity of a warrant. Acceptable under common law, searches incident to a lawful arrest have been allowed throughout American history. The existence of a lawful arrest means that such searches have met a probable cause standard since that is the standard required for a lawful arrest. Once a person is arrested the Supreme Court ruled in *United States v. Rabinowitz* (1950)[43] that police are allowed to conduct searches for two purposes. To advance concerns with public safety, weapons may be the subject of a search. Searches for contraband and other forms of evidence are also allowed in order to stop it from being destroyed after the suspect's apprehension. The search allowed under this exception is a full blown search, rather than just a frisk of the individual who was arrested. Both of these reasons are said to constitute an exigent circumstance which when coupled with probable cause justify the exception to the warrant rule. The exception can only be used when police take a person into full custody at the time of arrest.[44] Crucial to a valid search incident to a lawful arrest is the timing of the arrest. A search that takes place a substantial time after a lawful arrest may also be upheld as reasonable.[45] A search just prior to arrest will be upheld, if there was probable cause to arrest prior to the search.[46] In *Smith v. Ohio* (1990)[47] the Court stated that searches that take place prior to arrest will not be upheld when the fruits of the search provide police the probable cause to make the arrest.

One of the big issues that the Court has been asked to resolve in relation to searches incident to a lawful arrest, has been what is the proper scope of such a search? Originally, the exception allowed police to conduct searches of the person and the premises where a person was arrested as long as the scope of the search was consistent with the nature of the objects which were being sought.[48] In one of the last Warren Court cases, *Chimel v. California* (1969),[49] the Court narrowed the scope of searches incident to a lawful arrest. *Chimel* came to the Court after Chimel was arrested in his home on a warrant related to the burglary of a coin shop. After his arrest, police conducted a search of the home which lasted about an hour. The search turned up several items and coins which were introduced at trial over Chimel's objections. After a conviction which was affirmed by the California Supreme Court, Chimel's case was reviewed by the Supreme Court.

In an opinion by Justice Potter Stewart, the Court stated that in reliance on the primary precedent in this area, *United States v. Rabinowitz*, the police searched an area that was too broad by including not only the person of the arrestee, but also the place where the person was arrested. This gave "law enforcement officers the opportunity to engage in searches not justified by probable cause, by the simple expedient of arranging to arrest suspects at home rather than elsewhere."[50] The Court then clearly reaffirmed the purposes behind searches incident to a lawful arrest that had been announced in *Rabinowitz*. As to the scope of such a search Justice Stewart explained:

> A gun on a table or in a drawer in front of one who is arrested can be as dangerous to the arresting officer as one concealed in the clothing of the person arrested. There is ample justification, therefore, for a search of the arrestee's person and the area "within his immediate control"—construing that phrase to mean the area from within which he might gain possession of a weapon or destructible evidence.
>
> There is no comparable justification, however, for routinely searching any room other than that in which an arrest occurs—or, for that matter, for searching through all the desk drawers or other closed or concealed areas in that room itself.[51]

To search beyond the area within the immediate control of the arrestee, police would be required to get a warrant unless the situation fit into one of the other exceptions to the warrant requirement.

Since *Chimel*, the Court has allowed for a broader search incident to a lawful arrest in one circumstance. That is to allow officers to conduct protective sweeps of the premise in which a person is arrested in order to ensure that there are no other persons on the property who may be able to endanger the officers. Police may conduct such a sweep when they have a "reasonable belief based on specific and articulable facts that the area to be swept harbors an individual posing a danger to those on the arrest scene."[52] Protective sweeps are not to last any longer than necessary to determine if any danger is present. The sweep is to involve no more than a cursory inspection of the premises for victims or suspects, but other items may be seized if they are in plain view. This precedent was established in *Maryland v. Buie* (1990).[53]

The need to stop an arrestee from bringing harm on individuals or destroying evidence shows that as first rationalized the incident to a lawful arrest exception was based on exigent circumstances. As with the development of the automobile exception, the Burger Court's decisions helped to remove the exception away from its foundation in exigency. In *United States v. Robinson* (1973)[54] the Court made it clear that searches incident to a lawful arrest were not contingent on a showing that the arrested person might be dangerous or have on their person evidence which could be destroyed. The Court believed that searches conducted incident to a lawful arrest were *per se* reasonable and did not need further justification. In *Robinson* the Court authorized searches of individuals arrested for traffic violations.

Prior to *Chimel*, it was accepted practice for police to search the entire vehicle and the trunk when a person was arrested in their car. After *Chimel*, the Court had to determine what the scope of searches incident to a lawful arrest would be when the individual was arrested in a car. The Court considered this issue in *New York v. Belton* (1981).[55] In *Belton* a New York State Trooper stopped a vehicle for speeding and then observed an envelope on the floor marked "Supergold."[56] The trooper ordered all four occupants of the car to get out and separated them from each other and the vehicle. When he found marijuana in the envelope he arrested all four men and proceeded to search the passenger compartment including a leather jacket which belonged to Belton. Cocaine was found in the jacket. After the trial court ruled to admit the evidence, Belton pleaded guilty to the possession of the cocaine, but reserved the right to appeal the ruling. When it was heard by the New York Court of Appeals it reversed the trial court and ruled that because Belton and his associates had been isolated from the vehicle and his jacket, they were outside the *Chimel* zone of being under their immediate control and no longer were subject to search.

When the Supreme Court granted *certiorari* it decided the *Chimel* precedent applies to arrests which are made when a person is in an automobile. Justice Stewart, writing for the majority, explained that although the lower courts clearly understood the principles behind *Chimel*, protecting the safety of officers and

stopping the destruction of evidence, the lower courts had a difficult time applying these principles to specific factual situations. Stewart went on and clarified
in applying the principles of *Chimel* to vehicles that articles inside "the passenger compartment of an automobile are generally, even if not inevitably," within
the area covered by *Chimel*.[57] Rather than explaining exactly how the principles
of *Chimel* were still being served when the arrestee was isolated from the object
of the search and was no longer in a position to have access to a possible weapon or to destroy evidence, the Court believed it necessary to adopt a
straightforward rule, easily applied and predictably enforced. The Court therefore created a bright-line rule that police may search the person, the passenger
compartment of the vehicle, and any containers within the passenger compartment even after police have removed the ability of the arrestee to access the vehicle. Police are not, however, allowed to search the trunk incident to lawful
arrest.

As a result of *Belton,* when a person is arrested in their vehicle, the police
do not need the probable cause to search the vehicle that would be necessary
under the automobile exception to the warrant requirement. Instead, the only
justification that is needed for the search is that a lawful arrest was made. If the
search is conducted under the incident to a lawful arrest exception, however, the
scope of the search will be narrower. Police will only be able to search the passenger compartment and containers found therein, whereas if they were searching under the automobile exception, they could also search the trunk if the object
of the search could be found there. Once again an exception to the warrant requirement that was based on exigent circumstances has morphed into an exception that expedites the gathering of evidence even when the original exigency is
no longer present.

The Rehnquist Court refused to expand *Robinson* and *Belton* to allow
searches when a person was given a traffic citation, but not arrested in 1998
when it heard *Knowles v. Iowa*.[58] Knowles had been stopped for speeding and
after the citation was written the officer, following the provisions of a state statute, conducted a full blown search of the vehicle and found some marijuana and
a pipe. Knowles moved to have the evidence suppressed arguing that the search
incident to a lawful arrest did not cover situations in which was no arrest.
After his conviction he appealed and the case eventually came to the Supreme
Court on *certiorari*. The Court ruled neither of the historical reasons which supported searches incident to a lawful arrest, to protect the safety of the officer and
stop destruction of evidence, existed when there was no arrest. Furthermore, the
need to discover evidence of a crime, such as speeding, did not exist in traffic
stops. The Court noted that traffic stops could place officers in danger of their
safety and clarified that when officers suspected individuals of presenting a danger, they could still act to protect themselves with a frisk for weapons. The
Court's decision in *Atwater v. Lago Vista* (2001)[59] does, however, open the door
for police to search anyone pulled over for a traffic stop. It does this by upholding the power of the police to arrest anyone for traffic violations. Once an arrest

is made, a search incident to a lawful arrest following the ruling of *Belton* will allow a search of everything in the passenger compartment of the vehicle.

Hot Pursuit

The Warren Court added to the warrant exceptions with the hot pursuit exception for warrants in the case of *Warden v. Hayden* (1967).[60] The hot pursuit exception was based on the presence of both probable cause and an exigent circumstance. *Warden* came to the Court as result of an armed robbery at the Diamond Cab Company in Baltimore, Maryland. Several cab drivers saw the perpetrator, Hayden, running from the scene of the crime and followed him to a house. One of the cabbies radioed the dispatcher the location of the suspect, who in turn relayed the information to the police who were reacting to the robbery call. The cab driver also provided a description of the suspect and the clothes he was wearing. The police then proceeded to the address and arrived at the residence within minutes. The police entered without having secured a warrant and quickly set about searching the three floors of the building. They found Hayden in an upstairs bedroom pretending to be asleep. They continued the search for evidence and found two guns and clothes matching the description given by the cab driver. All of the evidence was used over Hayden's objections resulting in a conviction. In his majority opinion, Justice William Brennan reasoned that in hot pursuit cases time was of the essence. He stated "The Fourth Amendment does not require police officers to delay in the course of an investigation if to do so would gravely endanger their lives or the lives of others. Speed here was essential, and only a thorough search of the house for person and weapons could have insured . . . that the police had control of all weapons which could be used against them or to effect an escape."[61] The Court has subsequently ruled that if the presence of a felon is traced to a particular home, but there is not hot pursuit, the home cannot be entered for the purposes of an arrest without a warrant.[62]

Another important rule of law that came out of *Warden* and demonstrated that law enforcement did have some important victories during the Warren Court was that the Court abolished the "mere evidence" rule. Under that rule, law enforcement could only seize personal property that was contraband, or the fruits or instrumentalities of crime. They could not seize a person's personal property, even when it was incriminating, if it was mere evidence. The "mere evidence" rule had been an extension of the Fifth Amendment right against self-incrimination and the view that property which a person lawfully possessed could not be used against them in court. In *Warden* the mere evidence rule would have forbidden police from confiscating the clothes that Warden had worn during the robbery. According to the Court, there was no rational distinction between a search for mere evidence and one for an instrumentality of a crime in terms of the privacy which is safeguarded by the Fourth Amendment.

By overruling the mere evidence rule the Court made it much easier for the government to collect corroborating evidence that had great probative value.

Exigent Circumstances

Law enforcement officers may conduct a search without a warrant when there is probable cause for the search and there are exigent circumstances. The Court recognized this exception as early as 1948 when in *Johnson v. United States*[63] it said that there sometimes exists "exceptional circumstances in which, on balancing the need for effective law enforcement against the right of privacy, it may be contended that a magistrate's warrant may be disposed with."[64] Over time the Court has clarified what constitutes exigent circumstances. Elements of the exigent circumstances exception include when probable cause exists and evidence is in imminent danger of destruction, the safety of the public or officers is threatened, or the suspect is likely to flee before officers can obtain a warrant. Although the hot pursuit exception would seem to be based on exigent circumstances, the Court in *United States v. Santana* (1976)[65] distinguished hot pursuit cases from those involving exigent circumstances. It noted that hot pursuit cases have a component that does not exist in exigency cases. That being that hot pursuit cases involve "some element of chase" whereas in exigency cases the danger to evidence or police normally already exists on the premises searched.[66] In trying to determine whether an exigency exists and thus justifies a warrantless search, the Court examines the totality of the circumstances which existed immediately prior to the search. It has also held that a police officer is justified in a warrantless entry of a residence as long as there is an objective basis for the officer believing that an exigency exists.[67]

The Warren Court in *Schmerber v. California* (1966)[68] used exigent circumstances to allow police to take a blood sample in a driving under intoxication case. Schmerber was arrested, for suspicion of driving under intoxication. He was taken to a hospital for treatment made necessary by an automobile wreck that he had caused. Under advice of counsel, Schmerber declined to give a blood sample. Police then ordered the attending physician to take a sample anyway. The positive results were entered at trial over Schmerber's objection and resulted in his conviction. On review the Supreme Court allowed use of the blood. The majority opinion by Justice Brennan found that blood samples were admissible since they were physical evidence, not testimonial evidence, and were not taken in violation of the Fourth Amendment. There was no Fourth Amendment violation because police had probable cause, due to his drunken appearance, to believe that Schmerber had been driving intoxicated. There was an exigent circumstance, making a warrant unnecessary, created by the need to get a blood sample before the alcohol worked itself out of Schmerber's system. Furthermore, Justice Brennan explained that the procedure used to take the blood sample was reasonable since it had been taken using an accepted medical practice by a trained physician.

To help preserve evidence that could be destroyed while they wait for a warrant, the Supreme Court in *Segura v. United States* (1984)[69] gave police the ability to protect evidence from being destroyed. To stop an exigent circumstance from developing that would justify a warrantless search, the Court allowed police to secure the premises and stop outsiders from entering preventing the destruction or removal of evidence before police could serve a warrant. To further stop destruction of evidence, in the 2002 case of *Illinois v. McArthur*[70] the Court ruled that when police are actively in the process of getting a warrant they may prevent the owner of a home from entering the residence.

Not every crime scene in which a violent crime has occurred creates a situation in which the exigency exception is satisfied. In *Mincey v. Arizona* (1978),[71] for example, the Court held that there was no murder scene exception to the Fourth Amendment warrant requirement which could be justified based on the exigencies. In *Mincey* there had been a drug raid on Mincey's apartment and an undercover officer was shot. Mincey was wounded in the gun exchange and taken to the hospital. After all this had transgressed, the police searched Mincey's apartment without a warrant and gathered evidence which was used to gain a conviction against Mincey. The Arizona Supreme Court upheld the conviction ruling that there was a murder scene exception to the warrant rule. On *certiorari*, the Supreme Court believed that not every murder scene automatically created some type of exigency which would permit police to immediately enter a premise without a warrant. The Court was concerned that even though Mincey was under arrest and had a lesser expectation of privacy, his home retained the same expectation of privacy that homes had always had under the Fourth Amendment. The Court further reasoned that since there was no longer a life threatening situation at the apartment, there was no emergency situation to justify the search. On top of that, the seriousness of the offense did not create an exigency when there was no threat that police would lose evidence if they followed the warrant procedure. Overall, the Court believed that a general murder scene exception to the warrant rule gave officers too much discretion to determine the scope of what constituted a reasonable search. The Court added, however, that the exigency exception did apply when at a murder scene, as with any crime scene, police "reasonably believe that a person within it is in need of immediate aid."[72]

Plain View

The plain view exception to the warrant requirement allows police to seize evidence which is in plain view despite the lack of warrant. The legitimacy of plain view searches goes back to common law which did not consider such observations to be a search. As Lord Camden pointed out, "the eye cannot by the laws of England be guilty of a trespass."[73] The Supreme Court has explained, "It has long been settled that objects falling in the plain view of an officer who has a right to be in the position to have that view are subject to seizure and may be introduced into evidence."[74] Seizure of items left in plain view make sense because there can be no privacy expectation in such items. Furthermore, a person cannot make a legitimate claim that they have a right to possess an item which is readily observable as contraband. The reason why the plain view exception is based on exigent circumstances is that due to the public nature of the evidence, if police were to wait to seize it until a warrant was obtained, it would often result in a loss of evidence.

In an early discussion of the plain view exception, Justice Stewart wrote a plurality opinion in *Coolidge v. New Hampshire* (1971)[75] that stated that plain view seizures were not adverse to the two functions of the Fourth Amendment. The first function of the Fourth Amendment was that searches only be conducted pursuant to probable cause. The second function was to deny the government the power to conduct general exploratory searches. To help ensure that the plain view exception did not lead to exploratory searches, thus violating the amendment, Justice Stewart stated that the exception had three limitations. The first was the need for police to have lawful access to the location where the evidence is located in plain view and seized. This limitation helped to ensure that police could not use the plain view exception to initiate a search. The second limitation was that while conducting a legal search the police could only seize materials which were inadvertently found in plain view. This limitation disallowed police to use evidence seized in plain view when its discovery was anticipated. Stewart explained that evidence which was anticipated needed to be in a warrant in order to preserve the ability for magistrates to check police discretion. The third requirement was that the incriminating nature of the evidence has to be immediately apparent. If these criteria were met, Justice Stewart argued that plain view searches would present little threat to the purposes behind the Fourth Amendment. In addition, he believed:

> [T]here is a major gain in effective law enforcement. Where once an otherwise lawful search is in progress, the police inadvertently come upon a piece of evidence, it would often be a needless inconvenience, and sometimes dangerous— to the evidence or to the police themselves—to require them to ignore it until they have obtained a warrant particularly describing it.[76]

In *Horton v. California* (1990)[77] a majority of the Court rejected the inadvertence limitation that had been accepted by the *Coolidge* plurality. It found the goals of the limitation to be adequately protected through other means. The Court had a hard time believing that police would knowingly leave items out of a warrant application due to their knowledge that if they found additional evidence in plain view it could be admitted as evidence anyway. Furthermore, the Court believed that the goal of stopping general searches was already met by the particularity requirement for warrants so adding an inadvertence requirement granted little extra protection. The result for the defendant is the same whether or not the inadvertency limitation is in place, the invasion of the suspect's privacy is not enlarged, it remains limited by the scope of the search allowed by the warrant.

With the removal of the inadvertence requirement the plain view exception requirements are as follows. First, the police must have lawful access to the location from which the item seized can be plainly visible. Lawful access can be gained through a search or arrest warrant or by any of the recognized exceptions to the warrant requirement. Second, the item must actually be in plain view. Finally, the incriminating nature of the evidence must be immediately apparent to the police when it is discovered.

With the inadvertence requirement dropped, the Court has concentrated its effort in clarifying the plain view exception on determining when the incriminating nature of an object is immediately apparent. In *Texas v. Brown* (1983)[78] the Court ruled that it was acceptable for a police officer to use a flashlight and shift his position in order to better examine the interior of a vehicle. The Court believed that such efforts by an officer was not enlarging a search, but merely increasing the ability of the officer to inspect something that was already in view. Furthermore, the Court said that in their desire to better view an object thought to be contraband and to then seize it police need not be certain that the object is incriminating, probable cause was the standard to be applied. The Court has also ruled that the exterior of a vehicle is considered to be plain view.[79] Individuals, as a result, cannot be said to have an expectation of privacy that can stop police from examining the outer appearance of their vehicle when parked in a public place.

In *Arizona v. Hicks* (1987)[80] the Court had to determine whether a secondary search which was an extension of a plain view search for the purpose of determining the incriminating nature of evidence should be allowed. This case came to the attention of the police after a gunshot traveled through the floor of one apartment in a building into a lower apartment, struck a person, and caused their death. When police, without a warrant due to the exigent circumstances, entered the upper apartment to investigate the gunshot, there were guns strewn about, a ski mask was in plain sight, and the apartment was described as squalid in its furnishings with the exception of two sets of expensive stereo equipment. Suspecting that the equipment was stolen, one of the officers moved some of the equipment so that he could write down the serial numbers to determine if they had been reported stolen. After calling in the serial numbers, it was confirmed that the equipment was stolen and it was seized. After conviction, Hicks appealed and the case worked its way up to the U.S. Supreme Court which granted *certiorari* to determine if the plain view doctrine may be invoked when the police can see an item in plain view, but lack probable cause to believe it is evidence of a crime or contraband.

The Court, in a majority opinion by Justice Scalia, held that the incriminating nature of the stereo was not immediately apparent. Furthermore, whether the stereo was stolen was unrelated to the exigent circumstances that allowed the officers to enter the apartment in the first place. Therefore, any movement of the stereo in order to get the serial numbers could not be justified by the plain view exception. Moving the stereo constituted a new search and therefore had to be based on probable cause. In this case the Court did not believe that probable cause existed. Justice Scalia provided guidance for other courts in their determination of whether the immediately apparent contraband requirement would be met in future cases:

> The "distinction between 'looking' at a suspicious object in plain view and 'moving' it even a few inches" is much more than trivial for purposes of the Fourth Amendment. It matters not that the search uncovered nothing of any great personal value to respondent—serial numbers rather than (what might conceivably have been hidden behind or under the equipment) letters or photographs. A search is a search, even if it happens to disclose nothing but the bottom of a turntable.[81]

The significance of the *Hicks* ruling is that it instructs lower courts that in order for an object in plain view to be seized police must have probable cause to believe that it is evidence of crime or contraband. It also instructs police and lower courts that any extra step beyond simply viewing an object and being able to tell its incriminating nature will not fall within the plain view exception and must be justified by probable cause. The Court has noted one exception to this general rule. That exception is the search of documents. When serving a warrant for documents, the Court has noted that innocuous documents will have to be examined in order to determine if they fall under the warrant. Just seeing a document will not indicate if it holds the sought after evidence, or any other incriminating evidence. Therefore, an initial inspection of any document will be necessary and if it indicates incriminating evidence not covered by the warrant, the documents will be admissible.[82]

The Supreme Court added an interesting extension onto the plain view exception in *Minnesota v. Dickerson* (1993).[83] *Dickerson* came to the Court after Dickerson was arrested for possession of crack cocaine. Dickerson came to the attention of police when they saw him leave a reputed crack house. When Dickerson saw the police car, he turned and started walking in the opposite direction entering an alley. The police followed Dickerson into the alley and then ordered him to stop and subjected him to a frisk. The frisk revealed no weapon, but the officer who conducted it felt a small lump in Dickerson's front pocket which he thought was a lump of crack cocaine wrapped in cellophane. The officer then reached into the pocket and seized a rock of crack cocaine. The trial court allowed use of the cocaine at trial and Dickerson was convicted. The conviction was overturned by the Minnesota Court of Appeals and its decision was upheld by the Minnesota State Supreme Court. The State of Minnesota then was granted *certiorari* by the United States Supreme Court.

The Court found that the officer did legally have a right to subject Dickerson to a frisk. The Court relied on *Terry v. Ohio* (1967) to demonstrate that based on Dickerson's actions of leaving a crack house and trying to avoid the police, there were articulable suspicions for stopping Dickerson. Furthermore, due to the close association between the drug trade and violence, police were justified in suspecting that Dickerson may be armed and dangerous. Therefore, the initial frisk did not violate the Fourth Amendment. The Court continued and held that within the context of the plain view exception to the warrant requirement of the Fourth Amendment there was a plain feel corollary. As with plain view, the ability of police to rely on the plain feel exception to justify use of evidence gained without a warrant was dependent on several things. First, whether the officer was in a lawful position to be able to feel the object. Second, whether the object's incriminating nature was immediately apparent. On the question as to whether the incriminating nature of the object was readily apparent, the Court found that in Dickerson's case it had not been and ruled the seizure of the cocaine to be unlawful. The reason behind this decision was the officer's testimony that he had to manipulate the object to be able to determine that it was a rock of crack. The Court determined that this went beyond the scope of search permitted under *Terry v. Ohio* since it became an evidentiary search rather than a frisk for a weapon. As a result, even though both the initial stop and the frisk were lawful, when the purpose for the stop was enlarged to a general search for evidence, the Fourth Amendment was violated and the evidence had to be suppressed.

Nonexigent Searches

In the past few decades the Supreme Court has been moving away from an exigency requirement for exceptions to the warrant requirement in favor of a balancing approach. This approach balances the privacy expectations of citizens with various governmental interests. When the warrant requirement is seen as placing too large of a burden on the ability of the government to achieve its goals, the Court has been willing to carve out additional exceptions to the warrant requirement.

An explanation for why the Court has been willing to open new exceptions to the warrant rule may come from changes in public views and personnel on the Court. Many people, especially those who worked in law enforcement, believed that *Mapp v. Ohio* (1961) and other decisions by the Warren Court had tilted the playing field in favor of criminals. Barry Goldwater, a Republican, was the first presidential candidate to draw the public's attention to the issue in his failed 1964 contest. His claim that the Democrats where soft on crime registered with many voters. The fears of the law enforcement community and citizens seemed to be coming true when between 1964 and 1968 the incidences of reported crime in the United States doubled and concerns about crime became one of the biggest domestic issues according to public opinion polls.[84]

These concerns caused Lyndon Johnson, who defeated Goldwater in the presidential election of 1964, to address the issue of crime in America. After taking office, Johnson's first speech to Congress was titled "Message on Law Enforcement on the Administration of Justice." He also created a commission to investigate the causes of crime and delinquency in America. The commission was also given the task of making recommendations to improve the administration of justice. In 1967 the commission's report recommended two hundred ways that the rising crime rates could be addressed. Many of these recommendations were made a part of the Omnibus Crime Control and Safe Streets Act which President Johnson sent to Congress in 1967 and became law in 1968.

In 1968 Richard Nixon, the Republican nominee for president, decided that the issue of crime control was still potent and was a political issue of which he could take advantage. Nixon's line of attack was different than Goldwater's had been in 1964 because he blamed the Democrats and a new target, the Supreme Court. He promised that if he were elected president he would appoint justices who were strict constructionists and would only interpret the Constitution as it was written, rather than substituting their own values. Furthermore, his justices would stop coddling criminal elements within our society. Enough people agreed with Nixon's views that he was elected president in 1968. Nixon quickly got the opportunity to start to recast the Supreme Court since Chief Justice Warren had announced his intention to retire before the election and the Senate had failed to confirm President Johnson's nominee, Associate Justice Abe Fortas. President Nixon set out to fulfill his campaign pledge by nominating Warren Burger to be the Chief Justice. Warren Burger had a record of being a law and order judge while serving on the U.S. Court of Appeals, District of Columbia Circuit. He also had a public record of being opposed to the automatic application of the exclusionary rule. When other vacancies came open on the Court, President Nixon continued to appoint people who would be tougher on criminals. Altogether President Nixon would get four appointments to the Supreme Court, Warren Burger, Harry Blackmun, Lewis Powell, and William Rehnquist. A similar law and order approach by President Ronald Reagan, who made three appointments to the Court, Sandra Day O'Connor, Antonin Scalia, and Anthony Kennedy and also elevated William Rehnquist to the position of Chief Justice firmly stacked the Court with justices who did not desire to see expansion of the protections of the Fourth Amendment. One way that these justices found to be tougher on crime was to allow more and broader exceptions to the warrant rule.

Consent

The Court first upheld the constitutionality of a person voluntarily waiving their Fourth Amendment rights in *Zap v. United States* (1946).[85] Searches based on consent have never required the existence of exigent circumstances. Police officers will seek a person's consent to conduct a search because consent searches have several advantages over warrant searches. The first is that an officer is subjected to less paperwork since the warrant application does not have to be filled out, nor will the officer be required to submit a report to the magistrate who signed the warrant. Another advantage is that if consent was given for the search, the officer avoids the risks of having the evidence suppressed due to a legal snafu which had not been recognized and acted upon. An added advantage of a consent search for an officer is that it may be done when the officer lacks the probable cause necessary to otherwise carry out a search. Perhaps, due to these advantages police secure consent in ninety-eight percent of the searches they conduct without a warrant.[86]

The Supreme Court has been forced to resolve several issues concerning consent searches. The first is what constitutes voluntariness. The Warren Court expressed its view concerning the importance of voluntariness in consent searches in *Bumper v. North Carolina* (1968)[87] when it declared, "where there is coercion there cannot be consent."[88] In *Bumper* the Court found coercion exists when police falsely told an individual that they had a warrant to search a place and then asked for permission to get consent.

The Burger Court in *Schneckloth v. Bustamonte* (1973)[89] also decided that consent must be given voluntarily. *Schneckloth* came to the legal system after a police officer on a routine patrol stopped a car with a broken headlight and license plate light. When the driver could not produce a driver's license the officer asked a passenger who said the car belonged to his brother for permission to search the vehicle. The passenger, Robert Bustamonte, gave permission and helped the officer by opening the glove box and trunk. Under the left rear seat the officer found three stolen checks. He then arrested Bustamonte for theft. Bustamonte claimed that since he had not been informed of his rights, his consent could not have been voluntary so the evidence needed to be suppressed. Bustamonte's argument was not persuasive to the trial court and he was convicted. On collateral review in the federal courts the Ninth Circuit ruled that a voluntary waiver of a person's constitutional rights required knowledge by the person as to what were their rights.

On review the Supreme Court found that the determination of what constituted a voluntary waiver should balance the need for effective law enforcement with "society's belief that the criminal law cannot be used as an instrument of unfairness."[90] In reaching a balance the Court determined that requiring police to give Miranda-type warnings prior to gaining consent to search would be impractical due to the difference in the protections of the Fourth Amendment compared with those of the Fifth and Sixth Amendments. The Supreme Court therefore adopted a totality of the circumstances test for determinations of voluntariness in consent search cases. The Court also found that consent may be either express or implied. The crucial question was not whether a person was warned of their rights, it was whether the suspect's consent was voluntary under the totality of the circumstances. The Court's opinion was sensitive to the coerciveness inherent in police stops and explained:

In examining all the surrounding circumstances to determine if in fact the consent to search was coerced, account must be taken of subtly coercive police questions, as well as the possibly vulnerable subjective state of the person who consents. Those searches that are the product of police coercion can thus be filtered out without undermining the continuing validity of consent searches.[91]

Factors which have been examined under the totality of circumstances to determine if consent was voluntary include, the person's age, education, intelligence, level of cooperation with the police, length of questioning or detention prior to consent being given, and police misbehavior.

In later decisions such as *Florida v. Bostick* (1991)[92] the Court has helped to clarify that one thing which must be examined in the totality of the circumstances is whether the person who gave consent for a search thought they were free to leave if they didn't grant consent. In making such a determination the Court held that if a reasonable person in view of all the circumstances had thought they were no longer free to leave the consent could not be voluntary. The Court in *Bostick* ruled that a police sweep of a public transit bus in which police entered and asked for consent to search luggage did not create a situation in which individuals would feel that they were not free to leave, and thus their consent for a search was considered voluntary.

The Court reviewed the use of consent searches in bus sweeps in *United States v. Drayton* (2002).[93] It again upheld their use and reinforced its line of consent searches going back to *Bumpers v. North Carolina* and *Schneckloth v. Bustamonte*. The Court first found that the police tactics of boarding a bus and asking all passengers for consent to search was not coercive. The Court again stated that police were not required to warn people that they could refuse consent and that the determination of whether consent was voluntary was dependent on the totality of circumstances. By the time that *Drayton* was decided the Court's sensitivity to the inherent coerciveness of police stops had somewhat faded. In his majority opinion Justice Kennedy clarified that the "proper inquiry is 'whether a reasonable person would feel free to decline the officers' requests or otherwise terminate the encounter."[94]

Normally, when law enforcement officers use deception, such as telling a lie to an individual that they might as well consent to a search because a warrant is on the way, the consent is not seen as voluntary.[95] This is not, however, always true. Police can use deception in order to get consent in cases involving undercover agents. The Court has found it acceptable for undercover agents to use deception to gain access to a location for the purpose of buying contraband articles.[96] The Court has reasoned that not allowing undercover agents to use deception would undermine the ability to use such agents and get results.

The Court has not only had to resolve cases in which the party which is the subject of a search has given consent for a search, it has also had to resolve whether third parties can give consent. The results have been mixed, dependent on who was the third party. In *Stoner v. California* (1964)[97] the Court ruled that because the Fourth Amendment is a personal right, hotel clerks could not give consent to search the rooms of clients. In *United States v. Matlock* (1974)[98] the Court clarified that third parties could give consent for a search when the person giving consent had common authority over the area searched. In *Matlock* the Court recognized the right of an adult daughter to consent to a search for those parts of the house she shared with her parents, despite their absence. The Court reasoned "that it is reasonable to recognize that any of the co-habitants has the right to permit the inspection in his own right and that the others have assumed the risk that one of their number might permit a common area to be searched."[99] *Matlock* thus established a clear rule for third party consent. To have the authority to give consent for a search, a third party had to co-habitat the residence and exercise common control over those areas to which consent to search is granted. Thus, a roommate could give consent to search common living quarters, but not a private bedroom.

Recently, the Court has muddied the clear rule established in *Matlock*. This is because it changed the focus in its determinations of whether there was consent to search from an objective determination as to whether a third party had authority to give consent to a subjective examination as to whether the police officer who conducted the search believed that consent had been given. This change came about in *Illinois v. Rodriguez* (1990).[100] In *Rodriguez* a girlfriend of Edward Rodriguez, Gail Fischer, claimed that he had beat her up in his apartment. She then went to her mother's home where she and her kids were living. Her mother called the police and reported the incident. The police met Fischer at her mom's home where she told them she wanted Rodriguez arrested. One of the officers recognized Rodriguez's name as that of a person suspected of drug dealing. Fischer then told police that Rodriguez was probably at home sleeping. Without getting an arrest warrant, police then took Fischer to the apartment which she referred to as "ours" and with a key she possessed she let the police in for the purpose of arresting Rodriguez. Once the police were inside the apartment they saw cocaine scattered in various rooms in plain view. Upon finding Rodriguez sleeping, he was arrested. At a suppression hearing, it was discovered that Fischer did not live with Rodriguez and did not have common authority over the apartment. Furthermore, the key she used had been borrowed without Rodriguez's knowledge. For these reasons the cocaine was suppressed at trial and Illinois initiated the appeals process.

After the Supreme Court granted *certiorari* in *Rodriguez* the Court agreed that Fischer did not have the authority to give consent for the entry into Rodriguez's apartment. Nevertheless, the Court in a 6-3 decision in which Justice Scalia wrote the majority opinion ruled the cocaine could be admissible. This was because the Court found that it didn't matter that Rodriguez had not given consent for the search, since the Fourth Amendment does not state "that no government search of [a person's] house will not occur unless [a resident] consents; but that no such search will occur that is 'unreasonable.'"[101] In resolving whether the search was unreasonable, Justice Scalia argued that searches were reasonable when police had consent to conduct a search. He went on to point out that the critical issue to examine was the officer's assessment of the situation when the search began. If the officer believed that a consenting third party had common authority and it was reasonable belief, then facts which later demonstrated that the situation was not as the officer believed will be ignored and the search will be found to be reasonable. In the case of Rodriguez the Court remanded to allow the trial court to determine whether the officer's reliance on a third party for consent was reasonable.[102]

In *Georgia v. Randolph* (2006)[103] the Court ruled that the consent of all cohabitants of a property who are present must be given in order for police to conduct a consent search. The case came about when police responded to a domestic dispute call at the home of Scott Randolph and his estranged wife, Janet. At the heart of the domestic dispute was the custody of the Randolph's son. On the morning in which the events leading to the case began, Janet Randolph complained to the police that her husband took their son away. When officers arrived at the Randolph's residence Janet told them that her husband was a cocaine user whose habit had caused financial troubles. Shortly after the police arrived, Scott Randolph returned and explained that he had removed the child to a neighbor's house to stop his wife from again taking the boy out of the country. He also denied using drugs. Police asked for permission to search for evidence of drug use which was granted by the wife, but expressly denied by Scott. Police, nevertheless, searched the home and found cocaine which was introduced over Randolph's objections at trial. After his conviction, Randolph appealed to the state courts and won. The state was then granted *certiorari*. The Supreme Court ruled that although police may enter a residence without a warrant when the inhabitant grants consent, when multiple people are co-tenants over a common dwelling and one had steadfastly refused to give permission the Fourth Amendment makes it clear that the government may not search the residence. The Court hinted that there could be exceptions to the blanket rule if there was an indication of the need for protection inside the house or if the entry of the house could be justified under the rubric of an exigent circumstance, but neither of these scenarios existed in this case.

In consent searches the Court has stated "A suspect may of course delimit as he chooses the scope of the search to which he consents."[104] When limiting the scope of a search, the true limitations will, however, be gauged by the understanding of an objectively reasonable officer who witnessed the giving of consent and the officer's view of the scope.[105] Thus, consent to search a car will normally be taken by an officer to mean consent has also been given to search containers within the car. In a similar manner, if a suspect gives permission to officers to search for a gun, they may look anywhere in which a gun could be concealed. In a consent search the person granting consent may limit the scope of the search by setting specific parameters. Should officers find evidence which was not related to the purpose of the search it will fall under the plain view exception. Whenever a person objects to the use of evidence and claims that they did not give consent, the burden of proof is on the prosecution to demonstrate that there was consent. The decision at trial as to whether there was consent is a question of fact that will be upheld on appeal unless the lower court's ruling is clearly erroneous.

Community Caretaking

In *Cady v. Dombrowski* (1973)[106] the Supreme Court first examined the community caretaking exception to the warrant requirement. The *Cady* case came to the Court after a defendant, who was intoxicated, wrecked his car disabling it in the process. When police arrived, the vehicle presented a nuisance along the highway so they had it towed to a private garage since the suspect was at first too drunk and then comatose and thus unable to make arrangements to move the vehicle himself. The police then found out that the defendant was a Chicago police officer who was required to carry his weapon at all times. There was no gun on the suspect's person, so, out of concern for the public safety, an officer searched the vehicle. During the search, which was described as standard procedure for impounded vehicles within the department, evidence tying the suspect to a murder was found. In deciding that the evidence found in the search was not in violation of the Fourth Amendment the Court explained, "Local police officers, unlike federal officers, frequently . . . engage in what, for want of a better term may be described as community caretaking functions, totally divorced from the detection, investigation, or acquisition of evidence relating to the violation of a criminal statute.[107] The caretaking function is based on the view that the police exist not only to solve crimes, they also help to ensure both the safety and the welfare of the community. In this particular case the police had acted reasonably in trying to assure that if the car had a gun in it, the gun was not "vulnerable to intrusion by vandals."[108]

Since its recognition, the community caretaking exception has branched into three different caretaking functions which allow police to bypass warrant requirements. Those are the functions of being a public servant, providing emergency aid, and conducting inventory searches. Despite the Court's willingness to enunciate a community caretaking exception to the warrant requirement, it has not done a satisfactory job explaining the scope and limits of the exception. This has left lower courts with no uniform standards. The one exception to this general statement is in regards to inventory searches.

In *Cady* the Court recognized that police often act not as investigators of crime, but as public servants. The variety of circumstances in which police act as public servants is wide. It can include police checking on parked cars when the driver appears to be lost, sick, or having car problems, and helping pedestrians who look lost, sick, or drunk. Acting as a public servant can also involve police checking on homes of people who are on vacation, elderly, or infirm. Under such circumstances the Court has reasoned that the Fourth Amendment's reasonableness approach is the proper standard to determine if there is a constitutional violation.

The emergency aid aspect of community caretaking was endorsed by the Supreme Court in *Michigan v. Tyler* (1978).[109] In *Tyler* the Court gave approval to firefighters entering a burning building without getting a warrant or consent. It also approved use of evidence found by firefighters which pointed toward arson being submitted at trial as long as it was found during the emergency. The warrant exception coming out of this aspect of community caretaking was justified by the belief that government officials should be able to act quickly, without a warrant, when they reasonably believe that someone or some situation needs attention immediately. The nature of the emergency places a limit on the scope of any actions on the part of the government. Once the emergency is over, the exception ends. In *Tyler* the Court did not allow additional evidence that was found at the arson scene to be admitted at trial when it was found in searches which took place after the emergency was over. The emergency aid component of the community caretaking exception should not be confused with the exigent circumstances exception. The exigent circumstances exception is based on the existence of an ongoing investigation being present. It is meant to allow evidence to be gathered prior to its destruction or an arrest to be made prior to flight. The emergency aid component of the community caretaking exception ends when police start to engage in an investigation.

The most extensive component of the community caretaking exception involves inventory searches. The Court has sanctioned use of inventory searches by law enforcement agencies and these searches are an exception to the warrant requirement. This exception was announced in *South Dakota v. Opperman* (1976).[110] In *Opperman*, Donald Opperman had his car impounded for overtime parking. After the impoundment, a police officer saw a watch on the dashboard of the car and decided to inventory the vehicle's contents using an inventory form following standardized departmental procedures. The procedures did not require a warrant to be gained to have authority to search an impounded vehicle. During the inventory search, police found a bag of marijuana inside the unlocked glovebox. Opperman was arrested and convicted for possession of marijuana. Opperman was granted *certiorari* by the Supreme Court.

In the majority opinion, Chief Justice Burger found three important governmental interests were advanced by inventory searches: (1) protection of the owner's property while it remained in police custody; (2) protection of police against claims of stolen, lost, or vandalized property; (3) protection of police from possible dangers.[111] The opinion went on and balanced these governmental interests against the relatively low expectation of privacy that citizens have in their vehicles. The Court also pointed out that inventory searches are conducted within the caretaker role of police and not for the purpose of investigation. Since the purposes behind inventory searches are not investigation the Court reasoned that a warrant supported by probable cause was not necessary. The Court found that inventory searches would be reasonable if a vehicle was lawfully impounded, standardized procedures existed that governed how searches were conducted, (thereby guarding against such searches being used for the purpose of investigation) and the procedures were followed.

In *Illinois v. Lafayette* (1983)[112] the Court enlarged the inventory search exception to allow police to also conduct inventory searches of articles in the possession of a person at the time of arrest. In this case the arrestee, Ralph Lafayette, had a shoulder bag on him when he was arrested for disturbing the peace. The officer confiscated the bag and following departmental procedures, conducted an inventory search during which he found some amphetamine pills in a cigarette package in the bag. When it came to the Supreme Court on *certiorari* the Court relied on *Opperman* in upholding the search because the purpose was not investigative. The Court also reasoned that the search was acceptable because police who make arrests need to be able to efficiently complete inventories without having to worry about the legality of the scope of their search. Furthermore, the Court expressed concern about the necessity of searching arrestees to be able to protect jail security.

In 1987 in *Colorado v. Bertine*[113] the Court again enlarged the inventory search exception. In this case police in Boulder, Colorado arrested Steve Bertine for driving while under the influence. The Boulder Municipal code authorized police officers to impound vehicles when the driver was arrested or allow the driver to park and lock the car. The police made arrangements to tow Bertine's vehicle to an impoundment lot. Before the tow truck arrived, the police, following departmental procedures, conducted an inventory search of the vehicle. While conducting the inventory search police found a closed backpack behind the front seat. The officer opened the back pack and found several nylon bags. These bags were then opened and the officer found cans which contained a variety of drugs and cash. The trial court suppressed the evidence because the inventory search violated the Colorado Constitution. The Colorado Supreme Court did not rule on whether there was a violation of the Colorado Constitution, but did hold that the inventory search of closed containers in a vehicle violated the Fourth Amendment. The case was then brought to the United States Supreme Court on a writ of *certiorari* by Colorado.

The Supreme Court in a majority opinion written by Chief Justice William Rehnquist ruled that containers found in inventory searches could be opened and searched without a warrant. The Court began its opinion by relying on *Opperman* and *Lafayette* noting that the inventory search exception to the warrant requirement was well established. The Court emphasized that "there was no showing that the police, who were following standardized procedures, acted in bad faith or for the sole purpose of investigation."[114] The Court again reiterated the lesser expectations people have in cars and the need to protect impounded property from theft, false claims of loss, and presenting a danger to police. The Court further ruled that police were not required to use the least intrusive means possible to protect property. Police also did not have to exercise the option of allowing Bertine to park and lock his vehicle. The Court believed that it was reasonable and thus not a violation of the Fourth Amendment to give police the latitude allowed in standard departmental procedures to determine what course of action was best in each situation. Rather than weighing Bertine's privacy interest in the closed containers in his vehicle, the Court believed that it would be more helpful for police if it created a bright-line rule that containers found in an inventory search also fit into the warrant exception and may be opened.

One other issue involved in inventory searches that seemed to be settled in *Colorado v. Bertine* concerned the amount of discretion police had to pick and choose which containers might be opened in an inventory search. Five justices, three in a concurrence written by Justice Harry Blackmun, and the two dissenters, Thurgood Marshall and William Brennan, all indicated that they would only support inventory searches in which the procedures left no discretion for police officers to pick and choose which containers would be opened and searched. In practice this would mean that police would either open all containers or no containers. This limit on police discretion was overruled in *Florida v. Wells* (1990).[115] In *Wells* the Court found that the particular inventory search involved was a violation of the Fourth Amendment since the Florida Highway Patrol had no standardized inventory search policy. The Court went on, however, and stated that when standardized procedures did exist those procedures did not preclude officers from using their discretion to determine both the scope and propriety of the inventory search. This ruling puts police in a position to ignore the all containers or no containers standard supported by a majority in *Bertine*.

Brent Rogers has pointed out that by authorizing police the discretion to decide which containers will and won't be opened in an inventory search the Court has effectively cut the inventory search exception from its original justification. That justification being, the noninvestigative nature of inventory searches.[116] Allowing officers to decide which containers to open lets the officer's investigative hunches, rather than their concern with protection of a suspect's property or any of the other justifications which gave rise to the exception, to be the guiding force behind the search. The small change in the rules for inventory searches coming out of *Florida v. Wells* makes the use of pretextual inventory searches to gather evidence an expedient way for police to gather evidence without a warrant. Furthermore, the Court made it clear in *Arkansas v. Sullivan* (2001)[117] that it will not examine the actual motivations of individual officers who make arrests which provide the legal foundation for conducting an inventory search of a vehicle. The Court's decision in *Atwater v. Lago Vista* (2001),[118] which gave the police authority to arrest individuals for all traffic violations opens the door for many opportunities for police to conduct pretextual inventory searches when probable cause or consent is lacking and police desire to search vehicles beyond the scope allowed incident to a lawful search.

Open Fields

One of the oldest exceptions to the Fourth Amendment is the open fields exception. The Supreme Court first announced the exception in *Hester v. United States* (1924).[119] This case came to the Court when revenue officers put a field under surveillance near the home of Hester's father. When the officers saw Hester give a bottle of moonshine to a customer, he was arrested and the bottle was confiscated. Hester tried to get the bottle of moonshine suppressed as evidence because he claimed that the search and the surveillance of the field violated the Fourth Amendment. In a unanimous decision with the opinion written by Justice Oliver Wendell Holmes, the Court ruled that no illegal search had been conducted. The reason being, "The special protection accorded by the fourth amendment to the people in their 'persons, houses, papers, and effects' is not extended to the open fields. The distinction between the latter and the house is as old as the common law."[120] Simply put, open fields are not protected by the Fourth Amendment.

The opinion in *Hester* did not define what constituted an open field. Three years later in *Olmstead v. United States* (1927)[121] the Court provided a definition. In *Olmstead* the Court decided that use of wiretaps did not constitute a Fourth Amendment violation. In his majority opinion Chief Justice William Howard Taft explained that a Fourth Amendment violation could not take place unless there was a physical violation of the defendant's house or its curtilage. Applying this principle to the open fields doctrine meant that any area outside of the curtilage of a house or business was not protected by the Fourth Amendment and could be searched without a warrant. In subsequent cases, courts have found a variety of situations which are deemed open fields and thus not protected by the Fourth Amendment. These include fenced land, open waters, vacant lots in urban areas, wooded areas, deserts, and reservoirs. The Court has had opportunities to overrule *Hester* and end the open fields exception, but has refused to do so because it believes that society does not find claims of privacy in open fields to be reasonable.[122]

Border Searches

Persons and property entering or leaving the United States may be routinely searched without a warrant because the government, as sovereign, has the right to protect itself. Such border searches may be conducted without probable cause or reasonable articulable suspicions. Detention beyond that necessary to conduct such a stop does require reasonable suspicion of wrongdoing. The border search exception extends beyond the actual borders of the country. These searches may be conducted at the "functional equivalent" of the border which is the first practical point in which inspections can be done at a border crossing or a port of entry.

In *United States v. Martinez-Fuerte* (1976)[123] the Supreme Court ruled that warrantless border searches for illegal aliens were acceptable under the Fourth Amendment. Under the procedures approved by the Court, vehicles may be initially stopped at permanent check points and the occupants questioned without reasonable suspicion. Vehicles and occupants may also be selectively referred to a second checkpoint, for further questioning even when there is no reasonable suspicion of there being any illegal aliens. Further detention, however, requires either probable cause or consent.

To protect the country from illegal aliens the Court has also allowed roving border patrols. The power of roving border patrols to conduct suspicionless stops of vehicles fluctuates depending on the location of the stop. The Court ruled in *Almedia-Sanchez v. United States* (1973)[124] that warrantless searches conducted by roving border patrols twenty miles from the border required probable cause or consent. Roving border patrols located along the border or its functional equivalent may, however, stop vehicles and ask questions of the occupants without suspicion. According to *United States v. Brignoni-Ponce* (1975),[125] roving border patrols that are not at the border, may only stop vehicles if they have reasonable articulable suspicions of illegal aliens entering the country. Furthermore, while Mexican ancestry may be taken into consideration it alone does not establish reasonable suspicion.

In a case involving the power of border guards to conduct searches after the terrorist attacks of 9/11 the Court in *United States v. Flores-Montano* (2004)[126] ruled that border patrol agents can conduct routine searches of vehicles crossing the border without reasonable suspicion to trigger the search. Chief Justice Rehnquist's majority opinion explained that when a person crosses a border they have a lesser expectation of privacy and are thus subject to search. Furthermore, the scope of the particular search in this case, removal and inspection of the gas tank, was not an unacceptable deprivation of property given that a border crossing was involved.

Searches at Sea

Vessels on the high seas, within 12 miles of the United States Coast, or in the territorial waters of the United States are subject to routine document and safety inspections. Inspections of this type may be done pursuant to statute and require no warrant or articulable suspicion of criminal activity. The scope of such searches is limited to the ship's documents and its public area including the cargo hold in order to obtain the main beam number. The scope of these limited stops may, of course, be enlarged if probable cause develops. That is what happened in *United States v. Villamonte-Marquez* (1983).[127] In this case the *Henry Morgan II* was boarded for purposes of an inspection of the vessel's documents when officers smelled marijuana and then enlarged their search to find a large quantity of marijuana hidden on the boat. In *Villamonte-Marquez* the Court used a balancing approach to weigh the seriousness of intrusions on Fourth Amendment rights compared to the value of allowing the practice of boarding boats without warrants to satisfy law enforcement concerns. In doing so, the Court found that the government interest carried greater weight. It reasoned that such limited inspections may be done without a warrant since the First Congress authorized the suspicionless boarding of vessels which indicated that the Framers of the Fourth Amendment did not mean to limit this activity. The Court also found that a number of important governmental interests including federal regulation of maritime commerce, border security, maritime safety, and protection of the marine environment were advanced by suspicionless stops. While it did find that there were important Fourth Amendment interests involved, they were "limited" since it only involved a document inspection unless other probable cause developed. In balancing the competing interests, the Court decided that on-land situations of a similar nature which do not approve of this type of suspicionless intrusion into the lives of citizens were not applicable. Instead, the Court found that state interests were dominant and ruled in favor of such searches. A limited search that goes beyond this scope and enters areas on a vessel where there is a reasonable expectation of privacy requires reasonable suspicion of criminal activity. An even more intrusive stem to stern inspection requires probable cause, although it does not require a search warrant due to the exigent circumstances caused by possible flight.

Pervasively Regulated Industries

The view that pervasively regulated industries could be subject to warrantless searches and seizures was mentioned in *United States v. Biswell* (1972).[128] *Biswell* involved the constitutionality of a provision of the Gun Control Act of 1968 which allowed warrantless searches of the inventory of gun dealers during business hours. The Court upheld the provision on three grounds. The first part of its reasoning was its conclusion that the government had a substantial interest in such inspections due to the connection between gun traffic and federal efforts to prevent violent crime. A second reason for upholding the law was that its proper enforcement required flexibility as to the time, scope, and frequency of inspections for violations to be discovered and any protections provided by a warrant issued based on these needs would be negligible. A third reason was that due to the pervasiveness of the regulation in this business, gun dealers did not have justifiably high expectations of privacy. This was because individuals who sold guns did so with knowledge that the records of the business, the firearms, and ammunition were subject to inspection.

Having established the ability of the government to search pervasively regulated business and industries without a warrant, the Court in *New York v. Burger* (1987)[129] sought to clarify when an inspection scheme for a business or industry was so pervasive that it nullified the need for a warrant to conduct a search. The Court held that only businesses which affected a public interest fit into this category. It then came up with a multiple part test for determining if a warrantless search violated the Fourth Amendment. First, there has to be a substantial governmental interest in regulation of the business. Second, the inspections must be necessary to further the governmental interests. Third, the law establishing the regulatory scheme must provide an adequate alternative to the warrant requirement of the Fourth Amendment by limiting both the scope of the inspections and the discretion of the officers conducting the inspection and informing individuals within the industry about the lawfulness of the warrantless inspections. Finally, the government may not use the fact that warrants are not required to track industry actions as a pretext to gather evidence of criminal violations. In *Burger* the Court ruled that the auto salvage industry falls under the pervasively regulated industry exception to the warrant requirement. The Court has also to date ruled that the liquor and coal mining industries are also pervasively regulated.[130]

Individuals on Parole

The Roberts Court recently added a new exception to the warrant rule in *Samson v. California* (2006).[131] In *Samson*, the Court found that states may allow parole and law enforcement officers to bypass Fourth Amendment protections for individuals on parole. California required parolees to sign a form waiving their Fourth Amendment rights and after Samson was searched solely for being a parolee and found with drugs on him, he challenged the law. Justice Clarence Thomas reasoned in the majority opinion that individuals on parole had no legitimate expectation of privacy due to their status. For this reason the Court found that persons on parole could be searched by government officials even when they lacked any individualized suspicions of wrong doing.

Conclusion

The Court's approach to exceptions to the warrant rule has evolved over time. The first exceptions to the rule all required the presence of both probable cause and an exigent circumstance which made obtaining a warrant difficult due to the likelihood of loss of a suspect or evidence. At the time that *Mapp v. Ohio* (1961) was decided there were only two exceptions for areas protected by the Fourth Amendment. They were for automobiles and searches incident to a lawful arrest. The Warren Court added one exception, hot pursuit. The hot pursuit exception did not dramatically change the Fourth Amendment jurisprudence. This was because the hot pursuit exception, as had all previous exceptions, was based on the existence of both probable cause and an exigent circumstance being present.

All the post-Warren Courts have expressed a preference for the traditional approach to the Fourth Amendment and the warrant rule, but they have not been shy about creating further exceptions.[132] What has been different in their approach has been that their exceptions did not require the existence of probable cause and an exigent circumstance as required by previous Courts. Examples of exceptions added by the Burger and Rehnquist Courts include searches involving community caretaking and pervasively regulated industries. Rather than requiring the existence of probable cause and an exigent circumstance which made the warrant process impractical, these Courts favored a balancing approach to the Fourth Amendment. The use of a balancing approach did not require judicial creativity from the Burger or Rehnquist Courts since the Warren Court had created the framework in cases like *Camara v. Municipal Court* (1967)[133] and *Terry v. Ohio*. In the next chapter we examine these cases and the balancing of the reasonableness approach to which they gave rise. Over time, it has become increasingly clear that the reasonableness to which the Fourth Amendment refers has been refocused on the ability of law enforcement to expediently do its job. One type of search where this desire to aid effective law enforcement is clearly seen involves consent searches. In consent searches law enforcement has been aided by the Court's decisions that individuals do not have to be informed of their ability not to grant consent to a search. The Court has also allowed use of evidence in consent searches when police believe the party giving consent has authority to consent, but the party doesn't have legal authority to do so. The Roberts Court added another exception which allows individuals on parole to be searched at any time.

Not only has the Court created new exceptions to the warrant requirement, it has also broadened old exceptions. This broadening is most apparent when it comes to searches of automobiles. The automobile exception to the warrant requirement has been well established since *Carroll v. United States* (1925). When established the Court found that automobiles were subject to search without a warrant only when there was probable cause to do so and the existence of an exigent circumstance caused by the mobility of the vehicle. The Burger Court removed the need for an exigent circumstance in *Chambers v. Maroney* (1970) and ruled that even vehicles which no longer had a chance of mobility could be searched with no warrant when probable cause existed.

To facilitate effective law enforcement the Court has sought to develop bright-line rules regarding the search of automobiles which would make the rules more understandable to police. With the development of each new bright-line rule, the Court has simplified the requirements of the Fourth Amendment to allow police to more easily understand their powers by placing fewer limitations on those powers. Each time the Court sought to help clarify the rules for vehicle searches, it expanded the power of the state to search without a warrant. This is well illustrated by comparing the evolution of the bright-line rules developed in *Robbins v California* (1981), *United States v. Ross* (1982), and *California v. Acevedo* (1991). The *Robbins* decision followed the cardinal principle by allowing a warrantless search of an automobile if probable cause was present together with an exigent circumstance. Reasoning that containers found in autos have substantial privacy interests of their own that is not lost simply because the container is placed in a vehicle, the Court did not allow a warrantless search of containers found in a vehicle. To search such containers police were required to obtain a warrant based upon probable cause for the container. Clearly, in *Robbins* the Court placed its emphasis on the reasonableness of waiting to open a container until a warrant was obtained.

In *Ross* the Court found that police had a hard time applying the *Robbins* rule so it created a new bright-line rule that allowed containers to be searched incident to a warrantless automobile search. All containers in a vehicle could be searched even if there was no specific probable cause concerning the container. This was true as long as there was probable cause to believe that a search of the vehicle would reveal specific evidence of criminal behavior and the evidence sought could fit into a container that was in the vehicle. The Court in *Ross* emphasized the reasonableness of the search itself due to the existence of probable cause, rather than the reasonableness of waiting until a warrant was obtained to search a container.

In *Acevedo* the Court found its *Ross* bright-line rule confusing so it created another one which further enhanced the expediency by which evidence can be gathered. Under the new rule, containers in a vehicle can be searched without a warrant incident to a car search under the warrant exception *or* based on probable cause concerning a container itself. This bright-line rule allows a container that police could not search without a warrant if a person was carrying it down the street to be searched, if it is placed in a car.

The ability to search either a person in a vehicle, or the vehicle, goes beyond even these relaxed bright-line rules. This is because the automobile exception to the warrant requirement dovetails with a number of other exceptions making it possible to search most vehicles even when probable cause does not exist. For example, if a person is stopped in their vehicle for violating any traffic ordinance, police can ask for consent to search. Police, of course, do not have to tell a person that they have the right not to grant consent. If consent is not granted and police want to conduct a search anyway, the Court has said that individuals can be arrested for all traffic violations. Once arrested, they can be searched incident to a lawful arrest. In *New York v. Belton* (1981) the Court ruled that when a person is arrested in their vehicle, the entire passenger compartment and all its containers can be searched incident to the arrest. Furthermore, if police desire to search the trunk of the vehicle and all of its contents, they may impound the vehicle for safety reasons and then subject it to an inventory search as long as it is a part of the department's standardized procedures. The final result of these exceptions is that if you are in a vehicle and have been stopped for a traffic violation, if police want to, they may search your vehicle whether or not probable cause exists and whether or not you desire it.

More recently the Court has developed exceptions which have dropped the need for probable cause and an exigent circumstance. The areas where the Court has been most willing to drop the need for the presence of probable cause and an exigent circumstance is when the Court believes that government agents are engaged in behavior which is not predominately related to law enforcement and criminal investigation. In these areas, such as community caretaking, the regulation of pervasively regulated industries, and border crossings, the Court has preferred a balancing approach to the Fourth Amendment which weighs privacy interests against government goals. In reaching a balance, it has become increasingly clear that the Court believes that the ability of the government to expediently advance its goals carries greater weight than an individual's privacy interests.

Over time, the Court has provided so many bright-line rules for different exceptions that it has clouded its first bright-line rule, that searches without warrants are *per se* unreasonable. Perhaps this is why, due to the dramatic growth in the number of exceptions to the warrant requirement, Justice Scalia commented in *California v. Acevedo* (1991) that the warrant requirement has "become so riddled with exceptions that it [is] basically unrecognizable."[134] Justice Scalia went on and urged the Court to drop the warrant rule in favor of a reasonableness approach to the Fourth Amendment. Although the Court has not rejected the traditional approach to the Fourth Amendment in a written opinion, it now competes with a reasonableness approach to the Fourth Amendment. It is to the reasonableness approach and its increasing influence that we turn our attention to in the next chapter.

Illustrative Case Reprise

In *Whren v. United States* (1996), the case discussed at the start of this chapter, the Court gave its approval to pretextual traffic stops. Pretextual traffic stops are ones in which a police officer sees a traffic violation and stops the individual to investigate a crime which is unrelated to the traffic violation. For example, police pull over a person for failing to signal a turn in order to investigate whether they may have drugs in the vehicle. In *Whren*, Justice Scalia wrote the Court's opinion and ruled that the probable cause which was created by the traffic violation created an initial justification for all of Officer Soto's actions which followed. As this chapter has shown, if police have a right to be somewhere and they see evidence of criminal activity, they need not turn their back on the evidence. Thus, when Officer Soto saw drugs in Whren's hands he had a right to confiscate those drugs. Furthermore, when the drugs were seen, Whren and Brown were taken into custody. At that point the passenger compartment of the vehicle was subject to a search incident to a lawful arrest. Another aspect of Justice Scalia's opinion in *Whren* examined whether the officer had acted in a reasonable manner. In examining the reasonableness of the officer's actions Justice Scalia explained that when a person was stopped for a traffic violation if it raised other reasonable suspicions on the part of the officer, the officer could engage in all subsequent searches and seizures permissible under *Terry v. Ohio* (1967). The Court refused to rule that the reasonableness provision of the Fourth Amendment required judges to determine whether officers would have stopped a vehicle for a traffic violation if the officers had not also been interested in the occupants for another offense for which the police lacked reasonable suspicion to justify a *Terry* stop. The Court also found it unnecessary for judges to determine if other reasonable officers would have made the traffic stop given the nature of the violation. Instead, the Court ruled that the beginning and end of the

Fourth Amendment inquiry is whether the initial probable cause for the stop existed, not the true motives of the officer who may have desired to make the stop for activity unrelated to the traffic violation for which reasonable suspicion did not exist. After an initial stop based on probable cause, police, under *Terry*, are free to conduct further investigation to determine if other laws have been violated.

Notes

1. David A. Harris, "Car Wars: The Fourth Amendment's Death on the Highway," *George Washington Law Review* 66 (1998): 556.
2. *Boyd v. United States*, 116 U.S. 616, 635 (1886).
3. *Whren v. United States*, 517 U.S. 806 (1996).
4. *Whren*, 517 U.S. at 810.
5. *Mapp v. Ohio*, 367 U.S. 643 (1961).
6. *Katz v. United States*, 389 U.S. 347 (1967). For a full description of *Katz* see Chapter 7.
7. *Katz*, 389 U.S. at 357.
8. *Carroll v. United States*, 267 U.S. 132 (1925).
9. *Chimel v. California*, 395 U.S. 752 (1969).
10. *Minnesota v. Olson*, 495 U.S. 91 (1990).
11. *Minnesota v. Olson*, 495 U.S. at 97.
12. *Camara v. Municipal Court*, 387 U.S. 523 (1967).
13. *Terry v. Ohio*, 392 U.S. 1 (1968).
14. *Carroll v. United States*, 267 U.S. 132 (1925). For a discussion of *Carroll* see Chapter 2.
15. Cynthia R. Mabry, "The Supreme Court Opens a Pandora's Box in the Law of Warrantless Automobile Searches and Seizures—*United States v. Ross*," *Howard Law Journal* 26 (1983): 1243.
16. *Warden v. Hayden*, 387 U.S. 294 (1967).
17. *Preston v. United States*, 376 U.S. 364 (1964).
18. *Chambers v. Maroney*, 399 U.S. 42 (1970).
19. *Chambers*, 399 U.S. at 52.
20. *United States v. Chadwick*, 433 U.S. 1 (1977).
21. *United States v. Chadwick*, 433 U.S. at 13.
22. *Arkansas v. Sanders*, 442 U.S. 753 (1979).
23. *Arkansas*, 442 U.S. at 761.
24. *Arkansas*, 442 U.S. at 764 n. 13.
25. *Robbins v. California*, 453 U.S. 420 (1981).
26. *Robbins*, 453 U.S. at 426.
27. *United States v. Ross*, 456 U.S. 798 (1982).
28. *United States v. Ross*, 456 U.S. at 824.
29. *United States v. Ross*, 456 U.S. at 825.
30. Timothy E. Gammon, "The Exclusionary Rule and the 1983-1984 Term," *Marquette Law Review* 68 (1984): 1-25.

31. Steven D. Clymer, "Warrantless Vehicle Searches and the Fourth Amendment: The Burger Court Attacks the Exclusionary Rule," *Cornell Law Review* 68 (1982): 106.

32. *Florida v. Jimeno*, 500 U.S. 248 (1991).

33. *Florida v. Jimeno*, 500 U.S. at 249.

34. *California v. Acevedo*, 500 U.S. 565 (1991).

35. *California v. Acevedo*, 500 U.S. at 574.

36. *California v. Acevedo*, 500 U.S. at 574.

37. *California v. Acevedo*, 500 U.S. at 574-575.

38. *California v. Acevedo*, 500 U.S. at 579.

39. *Ohio v. Robinette*, 519 U.S. 33 (1996).

40. *Wyoming v. Houghton*, 526 U.S. 295 (1999).

41. *Wyoming v. Houghton*, 526 U.S. at 304.

42. *Maryland v. Pringle*, 540 U.S. 366 (2003).

43. *United States v. Rabinowitz*, 339 U.S. 56 (1950).

44. *United States v. Robinson*, 414 U.S. 218, 235 (1973).

45. *Michigan v. Defillippo*, 443 U.S. 31, 35 (1979).

46. *Rawlings v. Kentucky*, 448 U.S. 98, 111 (1980).

47. *Smith v. Ohio*, 494 U.S. 541, 543 (1990).

48. *Harris v. United States*, 331 U.S. 145, 152 (1947).

49. *Chimel v. California*, 395 U.S. 752 (1969).

50. *Chimel*, 395 U.S. at 767.

51. *Chimel*, 395 U.S. at 763.

52. *Maryland v. Buie*, 494 U.S. at 337.

53. *Maryland v. Buie*, 494 U.S. 325 (1990).

54. *United States v. Robinson*, 414 U.S. 218 (1973).

55. *New York v. Belton*, 453 U.S. 454 (1981).

56. *New York v. Belton*, 453 U.S. at 456.

57. *New York v. Belton*, 453 U.S. at 460.

58. *Knowles v. Iowa*, 525 U.S. 113 (1998).

59. *Atwater v. Lago Vista*, 532 U.S. 318 (2001).

60. *Warden v. Hayden*, 387 U.S. 295 (1967).

61. *Warden*, 387 U.S. at 299.

62. *Minnesota v. Olson*, 495 U.S. 91 (1990).

63. *Johnson v. United States*, 333 U.S. 10 (1948).

64. *Johnson*, 333 U.S. at 14-15.

65. *United States v. Santana*, 427 U.S. 38 (1976).

66. *United States v. Santana*, 427 U.S. at 43 n. 3.

67. *Brigham City, Utah v. Stuart*, 547 U.S. 398 (2006).

68. *Schmerber v. California*, 384 U.S. 757 (1966).

69. *Segura v. United States*, 468 U.S. 796 (1984).

70. *Illinois v. McArthur*, 531 U.S. 326 (2001).

71. *Mincey v. Arizona*, 437 U.S. 385 (1978).

72. *Mincey*, 437 U.S. at 392.

73. *Entick v. Carrington,* 19 How. St. Tr. 1029, 1066 (1765).

74. *Harris v. United States*, 390 U.S. 128, 136-67 (1990).

75. *Coolidge v. New Hampshire*, 403 U.S. 443 (1971).

76. *Coolidge*, 403 U.S. at 467-468.

77. *Horton v. California,* 496 U.S. 128 (1990).

78. *Texas v. Brown*, 460 U.S. 730 (1983).

79. *New York v. Class*, 475 U.S. 106 (1986).

80. *Arizona v. Hicks*, 480 U.S. 321 (1987).

81. *Arizona v. Hicks*, 480 U.S. at 325 (quoting Justice Powell in dissent).

82. *Andresen v. Maryland*, 427 U.S. 463 (1976).

83. *Minnesota v. Dickerson*, 508 U.S. 366 (1993).

84. Carolyn Long, *Mapp v. Ohio: Guarding Against Unreasonable Searches and Seizures* (Lawrence, KS: University Press of Kansas, 2006), 155.

85. *Zap v. United States*, 328 U.S. 624 (1946).

86. Richard Van Duizend, et. al., *The Search Warrant Process: Preconceptions, Perceptions, and Practices* (National Center for State Courts, 1984), 21.

87. *Bumper v. North Carolina*, 391 U.S. 543 (1968).

88. *Bumper*, 391 U.S. at 550.

89. *Schneckloth v. Bustamonte*, 412 U.S. 218 (1973).

90. *Schneckloth*, 412 U.S. at 224-225.

91. *Schneckloth*, 412 U.S. at 229.

92. *Florida v. Bostick*, 501 U.S. 429 (1991).

93. *United States v. Drayton*, 536 U.S. 194 (2002).

94. *United States v. Drayton*, 536 U.S. at 201-202 (quoting *Florida v. Bostick*, 501 U.S. 429, 436 (1991)).

95. *Bumper v. North Carolina*, 391 U.S. 543 (1968).

96. *Lewis v. United States*, 385 U.S. 206 (1966).

97. *Stoner v. California*, 376 U.S. 483 (1964).

98. *United States v. Matlock*, 415 U.S. 164 (1974).

99. *United States v. Matlock*, 415 U.S. at 171 n. 7.

100. *Illinois v. Rodriguez*, 497 U.S. 177 (1990).

101. *Illinois v. Rodriguez*, 497 U.S. at 183.

102. For an interesting critique of *Illinois v. Rodriguez* by the counsel who represented the defendant see, Thomas Y. Davies, "Denying a Right by Disregarding Doctrine: How *Illinois v. Rodriguez* Demeans Consent, Trivializes Fourth Amendment Reasonableness, and Exaggerates the Excusability of Police Error," *Tennessee Law Review* 59 (1991), 1-100.

103. *Georgia v. Randolph*, 126 S. Ct. 1515 (2006).

104. *Florida v. Jimeno*, 500 U.S. 248, 252 (1991).

105. *Florida v. Jimeno*, 500 U.S. at 251.

106. *Cady v. Dombrowski*, 413 U.S. 433 (1973).

107. *Cady*, 413 U.S. at 441.

108. *Cady*, 413 U.S. at 448.

109. *Michigan v. Tyler*, 436 U.S. 499 (1978).

110. *South Dakota v. Opperman*, 428 U.S. 364 (1976).

111. *South Dakota v. Opperman*, 428 U.S. at 367-368.

112. *Illinois v. Lafayette*, 462 U.S. 640 (1983)

113. *Colorado v. Bertine*, 479 U.S. 367 (1987).

114. *Colorado*, 479 U.S. at 376.

115. *Florida v. Wells*, 495 U.S. 1 (1990).

116. Brent A. Rogers, "*Florida v. Wells*: The Supreme Court bypasses an Opportunity to Protect Motorists from Abuses of Police Discretion," *Iowa Law Review* 77 (1991): 365.

117. *Arkansas v. Sullivan*, 532 U.S. 769 (2001).

118. *Atwater v. Lago Vista*, 533 U.S. 294 (2001).

119. *Hester v. United States*, 265 U.S. 57 (1924).

120. *Hester*, 265 U.S. at 59.

121. *Olmstead v. United States*, 277 U.S. 438 (1927).

122. *Oliver v. United States*, 466 U.S. 170 (1984).

123. *United States v. Martinez-Fuerte*, 428 U.S. 543 (1976).

124. *Almedia-Sanchez v. United States*, 413 U.S. 266 (1973)

125. *United States v. Brignoni-Ponce*, 422 U.S. 873 (1975).

126. *United States v. Flores-Montano*, 541 U.S. 149 (2004).

127. *United States v. Villamonte-Marquez*, 462 U.S. 579 (1983).

128. *United States v. Biswell*, 406 U.S. 311 (1972).

129. *New York v. Burger*, 482 U.S. 691 (1987).

130. Liquor was so ruled in *Colonnade Catering Corp. v. United States*, 397 U.S. 72 (1970) and coal mining in *Donovan v. Dewey*, 452 U.S. 594 (1981).

131. *Samson v. California*, 547 U.S. 843 (2006).

132. Burger Court examples of invoking the primacy of the warrant rule include: *Franks v. Delaware*, 438 U.S. 154, 164 (1978); *Robbins v. California*, 453 U.S. 420, 423 (1981); and *California v. Carney*, 471 U.S. 386, 390-391 (1985). Rehnquist Court examples include: *National Treasury Employees Union v. Von Raab*, 489 U.S. 656, 665 (1989); *Vernonia School District 47J v. Acton*, 515 U.S. 646, 653 (1999); and *Flippo v. West Virginia*, 528 U.S.11, 14 (1999). The Roberts Court quoted the warrant rule in *Brigham City, Utah v. Stuart*, 547 U.S. 398, 403 (2006) but the case only applied to home searches.

133. *Camara v. Municipal Court*, 387 U.S. 523 (1967).

134. *California v. Acevedo*, 500 U.S. 565, 582 (1991).

Chapter 5
Reasonableness and the Fourth Amendment

It flies in the face of common sense and logic to say that the framers in effect wrote two Fourth Amendments, allowing the reasonableness approach to be used whenever the police do not wish to get a warrant. There is no incentive whatsoever to get a warrant if a search can be reasonable in the absence of a warrant. To add a warrant requirement after having stated that a search is reasonable on different criteria seems to negate the warrant requirement itself.[1]

Nowhere in the text of the Fourth Amendment is there any mention of "special needs." The Court cut "special needs" balancing out of whole cloth. Such a dubious origin means the doctrine is vulnerable to the Court's shifting values; without an anchor in the Amendment or in common law, it can be manipulated to meet any end.[2]

Illustrative Case

From September to December of 2001 Los Angeles County Sheriff's Deputy Dennis Watters was actively investigating a group of four people for fraud and identity-theft. On December 11, Deputy Watters obtained a search warrant for two separate houses in Lancaster, California where it was believed that the suspects were living. The warrant was supported by an affidavit that included several items, such as an internet phone directory, Department of Motor Vehicle reports, an outstanding warrant, and mailing address listings, which seemed to indicate that the suspects lived in the houses named in the warrant. The warrant allowed the sheriff's office to search the homes and three of the suspects for documents and computer files related to fraud and identity-theft. Prior to executing the warrant, Deputy Watters briefed the six other officers involved that they were searching for three African-American suspects and that one of them had a registered handgun, a nine-millimeter Glock.

119

Even though there was a possibility that one of the suspects could be armed, Deputy Watters had not received special permission to serve the warrant at night so it was served at 7:15 a.m. When the warrant was served the door at one of the residencies was answered by Chase Hall, who was a Caucasian and not a suspect in the case. The deputies ordered Hall to lie on the ground with his face down. The deputies then swept through the house with their guns drawn. They entered a bedroom and found Max Rettele and his girlfriend Judy Sadler in bed. Neither of them were African-American. They were ordered to get out of bed and show their hands, but objected because they didn't have on any clothes. The officers, with guns still drawn, forced them out of bed. Rettele stood up and tried to put on some sweatpants, but was stopped by officers. Sadler also stood up and unsuccessfully tried to cover herself with a sheet. Rettele and Sadler were held at gunpoint for a couple of minutes before Rettele was allowed to get a robe for Sadler and he was allowed to dress. The two were then taken into the living room and told to sit on the couch. At that time deputies took an assessment of the situation and realized that something was wrong with their location. They then apologized to Rettele and Sadler for not getting angry and left within five minutes. The deputies then proceeded to the other house on the warrant where they found the three suspects named in the warrant who were then arrested and later convicted.

An investigation as to what went wrong at the first house searched under the warrant revealed that in September, which was months before the search, the first house named in the warrant had been sold to Max Rettele. Since the sale of the house, he and his girlfriend, Judy Sadler, and her 17-year-old son, Chase Hall, all lived in the house. Deputy Watters had failed to find out this crucial bit of information in his investigation of the crime. Angered at their treatment by the Los Angeles County Sheriff's Department Rettele, Sadler, and her son brought a Title 42 U.S.C., section 1983 suit against the department. In their suit they claimed that the department had violated their Fourth Amendment rights by obtaining a warrant in a reckless manner and conducting an unreasonable search and detention.

The case of *Los Angeles County, California v. Rettele* (2007)[3] brings up a number of questions. For instance, does a search of a house named in a warrant, but which turns out not to be the focus of the investigation, violate the Fourth Amendment? Is it reasonable for officers who have been conducting an intensive investigation to catch a fraud ring, not to know that the suspects haven't been living in a house for over three months? Is it reasonable for officers to detain people in a search who do not match the description of the suspects? Is it reasonable for officers to require people to stand naked in front of them during a search? What is the appropriate standard under the Fourth Amendment to determine if individuals who have mistakenly had their liberties interfered with have any legal recourse? To provide answers to questions like these this chapter examines the reasonableness approach to the Fourth Amendment.

Development and Application of the Reasonableness Approach

The Court under the leadership of Chief Justice Earl Warren has often been noted for upholding civil liberties in America.[4] A less well known fact is that the Warren Court also opened the door for interpretations of the Fourth Amendment which have broadened the power of the government to engage in search and seizures. The seeds which were planted by the Warren Court may not have been conscious attempts to weaken the Fourth Amendment, but the effects cannot be ignored. This and the following chapters examine several ways in which the reasoning used by the Warren Court has allowed later Courts to broaden the search and seizure powers of the state. This chapter examines how the Court broadened the powers to search and seize using a reasonableness approach to the Fourth Amendment.

Interpreting the Fourth Amendment as a general test of reasonableness has created a lively debate within the academic community over the appropriateness of this approach to Fourth Amendment jurisprudence. Advocates of this approach to the Fourth Amendment include Telford Taylor[5] and Akhil Reed Amar.[6] After an extensive examination of British common law and colonial law to determine the original intent of the Framers these scholars have reached the conclusion that the Supreme Court's traditional approach to Fourth Amendment jurisprudence cannot be supported by history. Taylor, for example, concluded that the Framers of the Constitution feared use of warrants by governmental officials since warrants provided officials with legal protection for their actions. According to Taylor, the Framers did not consider "the warrant as a protection against unreasonable searches," instead it was seen "as an authority for unreasonable and oppressive searches," so they sought to limit their use.[7] Building on Taylor's conclusion that the Framers were not concerned about warrantless searches, Amar extends the reasoning to argue that the Framers meant for the clause of the Fourth Amendment denying the government to conduct unreasonable searches and seizures to be the first principle of the amendment creating a freestanding reasonableness standard.

Supporters of the reasonableness approach to the Fourth Amendment believe that governmental actions supported by judicial determination of probable cause through the warrant process may be the test of reasonableness in instances when a warrant is used, but not in other searches and seizures. They argue that reasonableness itself is the heart of any inquiry into whether a search or seizure falls within the Fourth Amendment.[8] They emphasize the need to interpret the Fourth Amendment literally and argue that the words "do not require warrants, probable cause, or exclusion of evidence, but they do require that all searches and seizures be reasonable."[9] According to Debra Livingston, "Reasonableness is thus generally associated with highly contextual evaluations of whether intrusions on privacy are sensible, appropriate, and constitutionally tolerable, considering all the circumstances."[10]

The view of the proponents of the reasonableness approach has not gone unchallenged. A number of scholars have examined the same material and reached different conclusions concerning what the original intent of the Framers was concerning the Fourth Amendment.[11] These scholars support the Court's traditional approach to the Fourth Amendment. What unites most of this research is the conclusion that the denial of government power to engage in unreasonable searches must be considered in context with the warrant provisions of the Fourth Amendment. Some scholars such as Jacob Landynski believe that the term "reasonable" may only be understood in context with the warrant clause and therefore conclude that what is reasonable is dependent on whether police have secured a warrant.[12] After an extensive review of historical sources to recover the Framer's understanding of the Fourth Amendment, Thomas Davies concluded that the primary danger the Framers were concerned with was the use of general warrants because this had been the major method by which the government had intruded upon the lives of citizens. Accordingly, due to past abuses, the Framers did not consider the possibility of warrantless searches because they expected warrants to be used and their real fear was warrants which were unreasonable. Davis argues that determinations as to the reasonableness of a search conducted without a warrant were unthinkable to the Framers because "they did not perceive the warrantless officer as being capable of posing a significant threat to the security of person or house."[13] Martin Grayson has also argued that it is "unlikely that the drafters envisioned a search which could be both reasonable and without a warrant."[14] For this group of scholars, the determination of what was an unreasonable search by the Framers had to be made in context with the provisions of a warrant and there was no consideration given to the view that searches might be considered reasonable if there had been no warrant.

A third group of scholars have reviewed the debate concerning the Framers' original intent for the Fourth Amendment and warned against attempting to use this method for giving meaning to the amendment. Craig Lerner, for example, points out that there is little agreement among scholars as to what the common law required in determinations of basic Fourth Amendment issues such as probable cause.[15] Carol Steiker goes even further in her arguments against relying on original intent. Not only does she find it difficult to verify what the Framers' intent may have been, she also finds the desire to do so unhelpful. This is because she argues that contemporary events such as the development of modern law enforcement agencies and the continuation of racial conflict need to be taken into consideration and influence how we interpret the Fourth Amendment.[16]

Regardless of the unsettled academic debate concerning the Framers' intent and the reasonableness approach of interpreting the Fourth Amendment, it has become increasingly accepted by the Supreme Court. This is especially true in regards to government activity which is not directly tied into criminal investigations, but also true in a growing number of criminal situations.

Initial steps toward accepting a reasonableness approach had been taken in the 1950 decision of *United States v. Rabinowitz*.[17] The legal issue involved in

Rabinowitz was the proper scope of a search incident to a lawful arrest. Rabinowitz was arrested in his place of business with an arrest warrant. The business was then searched without a warrant. While searching the business, 573 forged stamps were found. Rabinowitz was unsuccessful in keeping the stamps from being admitted at trial as evidence and was convicted. He appealed the conviction arguing that the search of his business required a warrant.

Justice Sherman Minton wrote the majority opinion for the Court in *Rabinowitz*. In the opinion Justice Minton boldly asserted, "It is unreasonable searches that are prohibited by the Fourth Amendment. It was recognized by the framers of the Constitution that there were reasonable searches for which no warrant was required."[18] Justice Minton went on to state:

> The mandate of the Fourth Amendment is that the people shall be secure against unreasonable searches. . . . The relevant test is not whether it is reasonable to procure a search warrant, but whether the search was reasonable. That criterion in turn depends upon the facts and circumstances—the total atmosphere of the case. It is a sufficient precaution that law officers must justify their conduct before the courts which have always been, and must be, jealous of the individual's right of privacy within the broad sweep of the Fourth Amendment.[19]

In examining the relevant facts of the case the Court found the search to be reasonable. It first pointed out that no one questioned the ability of police to conduct a search incident to a lawful arrest. The Court also noted that the search happened in a place of business to which the public was invited. The business was a small room under the immediate and complete control of Rabinowitz. The Court then pointed out that the search was limited to the room used for criminal activity and that possession of forged stamps was indeed a criminal activity. Taking all those facts into consideration the Court had no problem ruling this search to be reasonable under the Fourth Amendment.

Justice Felix Frankfurter wrote a dissent in which he strongly criticized the majority's approach to the Fourth Amendment. He believed that the majority's approach left no guide to determine what constituted an unreasonable search. This would leave judges, juries, and police in a precarious position when trying to determine whether a search would be acceptable under the Fourth Amendment. Justice Frankfurter argued that the amendment did provide a guide if one read the words while taking into consideration the experiences of the Framers. If one did so, Justice Frankfurter stated:

> When the Fourth Amendment outlawed "unreasonable searches" and then went on to define the very restricted authority that even a search warrant issued by a magistrate could give, the framers said with all the clarity of the gloss of history that a search is "unreasonable" unless a warrant authorizes it, barring only exceptions justified by absolute necessity. Even a warrant cannot authorize it except when it is issued "upon probable cause . . . and particularly describing the place to be searched, and the person or things to be seized.[20]

As time passed the Warren Court increasingly seemed to be committed to the cardinal principle of the traditional approach to the Fourth Amendment; searches without warrants were considered to be *per se* unreasonable unless probable cause existed and the facts fit into one of the well delineated exceptions to the warrant requirement. The traditional approach was resurgent enough that in 1969 the Supreme Court in *Chimel v. California*[21] overruled *Rabinowitz* and limited searches incident to a lawful arrest to the area under the direct control of the detainee.

A case which illustrates how quickly the Court dropped the reasonableness approach to the Fourth Amendment is *Henry v. United States* (1959).[22] *Henry* came to the Court after Henry unsuccessfully challenged the admission of some evidence used against him resulting in his conviction for unlawfully possessing some radios that were stolen from interstate commerce. His arrest came about after an investigation into a theft of interstate whiskey in Chicago. The day after the theft, the FBI received a tip that a friend of Henry's, by the name of Pierotti, might be involved in some way with the interstate goods. The tip was not real clear and never went as far as to accuse Pierotti of the theft. Based on the tip, the FBI placed Pierotti under surveillance. When FBI agents saw Pierotti and Henry leave a tavern and get into a car together, they followed the two suspects. The suspects parked in an alley and went into a house and brought out some cartons. They then went back to the tavern. Later, the two suspects again got in the car and repeated their earlier behavior. The FBI observed the men from around 300 feet and could not determine what was in the cartons. When the men drove off they were stopped and arrested by the FBI. The FBI took the cartons, which had the word "Admiral" stamped on them and had out of state addresses, and placed them into their vehicle. The men and the cartoons were then held at the FBI for two hours until the FBI learned that the cartons contained stolen radios. Henry objected to the use of the evidence against him because he argued that there was no probable cause for the arrest that took place prior to the search in which the evidence was discovered. The Supreme Court granted *certiorari* to determine if there was probable cause for the arrest and search.

In *Henry,* Justice William Douglas wrote a majority opinion that emphasized the importance of the probable cause standard throughout American history. He clarified that "Probable cause exists if the facts and circumstances known to the officer warrant a prudent man in believing that the offense has been committed."[23] In this case, there had been no probable cause prior to the arrest. Even though the FBI had suspicions of Pierotti based on the tips and what they observed, two men riding in a car, stopping in an alley, loading cartons into the car and driving away are all things which could be perfectly innocent. At no place in his opinion did Justice Douglas attempt to ask whether the FBI had acted reasonably. Instead, he stated "Under our system suspicion is not enough for an officer to lay hands on a citizen."[24]

Despite the Warren Court's stated commitment to warrants under the Fourth Amendment, its opinions opened the door for a resurgence of the reasonableness approach. One thing that may have impacted the Supreme Court's unwavering support for the warrant requirement in Fourth Amendment cases may have been the incorporation of the exclusionary rule in 1961 in *Mapp v. Ohio*.[25] Incorporating the exclusionary rule helped to make the protections of the Fourth Amendment a reality on the streets. No longer could law enforcement officers ignore the requirements of the Fourth Amendment and continue to use the evidence. Incorporation also meant that the Warren Court would find it necessary to provide better oversight of how the Fourth Amendment was applied at the state and local levels. The attempt to apply the Fourth Amendment in a consistent manner across the country created added pressure from law and order proponents to limit the effects of the exclusionary rule. As the Warren Court ruled that even though a growing number of governmental activities did invoke the Fourth Amendment, it was difficult to apply the traditional approach to Fourth Amendment jurisprudence to them. As a result, it started to change its stance on the requirements of the Fourth Amendment.

In its largest disturbance of the traditional approach of Fourth Amendment jurisprudence, the Warren Court established and applied a framework by which the probable cause and warrant requirement could be written out of the Fourth Amendment. The ripple effect of this disturbance would lead future courts to develop a full blown reasonableness approach to the Fourth Amendment.[26] Movement toward the acceptance of the reasonableness standard was made possible by three decisions of the Warren Court, *Camara v. Municipal Court* (1967),[27] its companion case *See v. City of Seattle* (1967),[28] and *Terry v. Ohio* (1968).[29] In all of these cases it was not the intent of the Warren Court to weaken the protections of the Fourth Amendment. Instead, the Warren Court meant to enlarge the protections of the Fourth Amendment to cover governmental actions that had previously been unregulated by the Fourth Amendment. In *Camara* and *See* the Court overruled a decision made eight years earlier in *Frank v. Maryland* (1959)[30] that administrative searches did not violate the Due Process Clause of the Fourteenth Amendment. In a similar fashion, in *Terry v. Ohio* the Court placed investigative stop and frisk situations under Fourth Amendment protection.

Camara came to the Court after Camara was charged with violation of the San Francisco Housing Code by not allowing inspectors to inspect his residence without a warrant. While awaiting trial Camara filed for a writ of prohibition due to his belief that the ordinance which allowed warrantless inspections was on its face unconstitutional. The lower courts ruled against Camara and the Supreme Court then granted *certiorari*. The *See* case involved the issue as to whether a fire inspector could conduct a warrantless inspection of a commercial warehouse. Justice Byron White, who would later become a strong voice for the reasonableness approach to the Fourth Amendment, wrote the opinion in *Camara*. He made it clear that both the Fourth Amendment and warrant requirement were applicable in administrative inspection cases because "administrative searches of the kind at issue here are significant intrusions upon the interests protected by the Fourth Amendment."[31]

The Court, however, found the governmental interest of stopping code violations to be weighty and difficult to accomplish by the traditional application of the Fourth Amendment. Justice White stated, "the public interest demands that all dangerous conditions be prevented or abated, yet it is doubtful that any other canvassing technique [besides general searches] would achieve acceptable results."[32] The Court went on to note that routine inspections of property were generally less intrusive than searches for evidence of criminal activity. In its attempt to provide members of the public with protection from arbitrary searches and at the same time ensure that the goals of code enforcement would not be stymied by the Fourth Amendment, the Court found the traditional requirement of probable cause unworkable. Therefore, administrative inspections would have to be justified in terms of their reasonableness. The Court believed that the reasonableness of a search should be determined by balancing the purpose of the legislation requiring administrative searches against the invasion of privacy. In reaching this balance Justice White declared:

> The warrant procedure is designed to guarantee that a decision to search private property is justified by a reasonable governmental interest. But reasonableness is still the ultimate standard. If a valid public interest justifies the intrusion contemplated, then there is probable cause to issue a suitably restricted warrant. [33]

Justice White clarified that administrative search warrants would not require particularity and probable cause. Justice White then went on and found that even though the warrant requirement would apply to administrative searches, "the inspections are neither personal in nature nor aimed at the discovery of evidence of crime, they involve a relatively limited invasion of the urban citizen's privacy."[34] As a result, administrative warrants could be issued based upon the advancement of the governmental interest as established in the standards of legislation which sought to protect the interests. For example, warrants could be issued based on the nature of the building or business, the passage of time since last inspected, or the condition of the entire area. The purpose of the warrant was to explain the foundation and scope of a search to the individual when property was being inspected.

Justice White also argued that this decision,

> [N]either endangers time-honored doctrines applicable to criminal investigations nor makes a nullity of the probable cause requirement in this area. It merely gives full recognition to the competing public and private interest here at stake and, in so doing, best fulfills the historic purpose behind the constitutional right to be free from unreasonable government invasions of privacy.[35]

Contrary to Justice White's belief, the reasoning in *Camara* did dramatically change the nature of the Fourth Amendment. In reality, it set Fourth Amendment jurisprudence on its head by replacing probable cause as the standard for a reasonable search with an understanding that a lower standard of reasonableness, as determined by a balancing test, would now be determinative of whether there was a constitutional violation. The *Camara* case accomplished this in several ways. First, it allowed warrants to be served with no probable cause. Second, it allowed warrants to be served when there was no individualized suspicion. Third, it rejected the particularity requirement for warrants under the Fourth Amendment. Finally, it allowed searches to be declared reasonable if the governmental interest outweighed the invasion upon an individual's privacy.

Commenting on the changes brought about by the Court's decision in *Camara* Scott Sundby has noted:

> After *Camara*, . . . the government could base probable cause on completely innocent activities. As a result the fourth amendment no longer revolved around a concept that unambiguously emphasized both nonintrusion by the government and an individual's right to privacy. Changing probable cause's definition by eliminating its responsive nature subtly shifted the fourth amendment's orientation toward government intrusions.[36]

Once established these changes in Fourth Amendment jurisprudence would not be an isolated event.[37] In fact, in the Court's next term it would expand the reasonableness approach to the Fourth Amendment. In 1968 the Warren Court decided *Terry v. Ohio*. *Terry* came to the Court after a police officer observed two men acting in a suspicious manner, as if they were casing a store for a robbery. When a third man showed up and the suspicious behavior continued the officer approached the men, identified himself as an officer, and asked for their names. When he received a mumbled response the officer grabbed Terry and patted down the outside of his clothing and felt a gun. He also found a gun on one of the other men. The men were arrested for carrying a concealed weapon. Terry unsuccessfully objected to the admission of the gun as evidence and upon conviction appealed. Unlike the stop in *Henry v. United States* which involved a full arrest and search, *Terry* involved an investigative stop and a frisk which was a Fourth Amendment issue the Court had not resolved. The Supreme Court eventually granted *certiorari*.

The Court's primary concern may have been to bring "stop and frisk" situations under the umbrella of the Fourth Amendment. Had the Court not resolved *Terry* as it did, the application of the exclusionary rule coming out of *Mapp* would have placed increasing pressure on the Court for two other outcomes. The first would be to weaken the Fourth Amendment requirements, like the need for probable cause, for making arrests for investigative reasons. The second would be to hold that the Fourth Amendment was not triggered during investigative stops that did not lead to arrest. Scholars have been mixed on their views of the successfulness of Terry.[38] Despite its good intentions in *Terry*, the Court disturbed the traditional approach to Fourth Amendment jurisprudence by, for the first time, upholding warrantless *criminal* searches based on a standard of less than probable cause in "stop and frisk" situations.

Chief Justice Warren, who wrote the opinion, clarified that the Fourth Amendment did play a role in "stop and frisk" situations because whenever "a police officer accosts an individual and restrains his freedom to walk away, he has 'seized' that person."[39] He also clarified that when police explored the outer surfaces of a person's clothes in an attempt to find weapons, a search has taken place. Despite the fact that stop and frisk situations did involve the Fourth Amendment, Chief Justice Warren explained that such cases would not be treated by the traditional approach to the Fourth Amendment:

> If this case involved police conduct subject to the Warrant Clause of the Fourth Amendment, we would have to ascertain whether "probable cause" existed to justify the search and seizure which took place. However, that is not the case. We do not retreat from our holdings that the police must, whenever practicable, obtain advance judicial approval of searches and seizures through the warrant procedure, . . . or that in most instances failure to comply with the warrant requirement can only be excused by exigent circumstances. . . . But we deal here with an entire rubric of police conduct—necessarily swift action predicated upon the on-the-spot observations of the officer on the beat—which historically has not been, and as practical matter, could not be subjected to the warrant procedure. Instead, the conduct involved in this case must be tested by the Fourth Amendment's general proscription against unreasonable searches and seizures.[40]

Since the traditional approach to the Fourth Amendment seemed impractical for stop and frisk situations, the Court decided that police conduct should be judged by a standard of reasonableness based on the balancing of the interests involved. The Court weighed the Fourth Amendment liberty interest of individuals to be unimpeded by governmental actions against the general governmental interests of crime prevention and detection and insuring the safety of law enforcement officers. In reaching a balance between these competing interests the Court found that the brief on the street seizures involved in stop and frisk situations were not as serious of an intrusion on the person as full blown arrests and searches which required probable cause. However, they were still serious enough to invoke the Fourth Amendment. In order to balance the interests involved the Court developed a two part framework. The first prong examined whether the initial stop was reasonable at its inception. *Terry* emphasized the need for police to develop specific, articulable facts prior to making a stop. This was meant to provide a check on police discretion. Police not only had to pay attention to all the reasons which would justify a stop they also had to be able to articulate those reasons during any subsequent judicial review. The second step in the *Terry* framework was a determination that the scope of the search did not exceed the basis for the stop. Therefore, prior to a frisk an officer would also need to have a reasonable basis that the individual was armed. Only after reaching a decision that there was a reasonable basis for an officer to conclude that an individual who was encountered may present a danger, could the officer proceed with a frisk. Chief Justice Warren warned that these encounters were not to be turned into general searches to advance crime detection or to stop the destruction of evidence. Chief Justice Warren's view that the reasonableness of a stop and frisk would be dependent on the facts available to the officer at the time, favored a case-by-case analysis for future cases.

Chief Justice Warren further made it clear in *Terry* that not all police-citizen encounters triggered the Fourth Amendment. The Fourth Amendment came into play only "when the officer, by means of physical force or show of authority, has in some way restrained the liberty of the citizen."[41] This left police free to seek the voluntary help of citizens in any number of scenarios where they could be of assistance.

In making its decision the Court did not establish a bright-line rule to determine when a *Terry* stop had changed over to become an arrest. It did, however, establish four basic foundations which were meant to provide limitations on the ultimate reach of the decision. The first was that it restricted the types of searches and seizures that *Terry* would support. Stops had to be brief for the purpose of allowing a police officer to satisfy his or her concerns. The frisk could only be conducted if the crime involved was inherently violent or there was some indication that the individual was armed and could then only be a pat down of the individual's clothing necessary to determine if there was a weapon. The second foundation was that prior to a stop being made it was necessary for police to have a reasonable basis that a crime had been or was about to be committed, and that those suspicions had to be articulable. Third, the suspicions had to be particularlized. They had to be focused on an individual suspect and could not be generalized observations about a neighborhood or individual. Finally, the purpose of the stop and possible ensuing frisk was the protection of the officer during the encounter. These encounters were not to be used as a pretext for evidentiary searches. The Court clarified that stop and frisks not based on these foundations were *per se* unreasonable. The impact of the decisions, according to Stephen Saltzburg, is that "[m]ost *Terry* stops can be understood as 'freezing the scene' so that an officer can make a determination as to whether probable cause to arrest or search exists, or whether some other permissible action should be taken. A *Terry* stop enables the police to ascertain whether what looks like criminal activity, actually is."[42]

Both Justices John Harlan and Byron White wrote separate concurring opinions to emphasize the need to maintain a balance between the interests of law enforcement and the liberty of citizens. Justice Harlan insisted that until the point that an officer had a reasonable basis for a stop he or she would have no authority to stop a citizen and thereby intrude on their liberty. If the officer did not have the composite reasonable basis to justify a stop, any citizen had the "right to ignore [the] interrogator and walk away."[43] Justice White also noted that a citizen had the right to walk away and not cooperate with an officer if a reasonable basis against the citizen had not previously existed.[44]

Justice Douglas was the only justice who dissented in *Terry v. Ohio*. He complained that prior to *Terry* the only way that police searches or seizures without a warrant were justified was if probable cause was present. He wondered how under circumstances in which there was no probable cause police could constitutionally conduct stop and frisks. Justice Douglas' opinion went on and coined what has probably been the most famous phrase which came out of *Terry v. Ohio*, "reasonable suspicion." He did so by stating that he believed in the need to stick to the probable cause standard because the "term 'probable cause' rings a bell of certainty that is not sounded by phrases such as 'reasonable suspicion.'"[45]

The intent of the Warren Court in *Terry* was similar to its intent in *Camara* in that it meant to enlarge the protections of the Fourth Amendment to a situation which had previously been unregulated by the amendment. Due to its reliance on a reasonableness approach, *Terry* had the same effect as *Camara* and allowed later courts to further upset the traditional approach to the Fourth Amendment by broadening the situations that would separate reasonableness from either the warrant or probable cause requirements.[46] This was because *Terry* further extended the balancing test to cases not covered by the warrant and probable cause requirements of the Fourth Amendment. In perhaps the greatest weakness of the majority opinion, despite stating that the decision should be interpreted narrowly, the opinion gave no hints as to how to limit the wide array of situations to which use of a reasonableness balancing test might be extended. This opening up of an alternative option to the traditional approach to the Fourth Amendment which lacked clear direction or limitations for later courts caused Scott Sundby to comment:

> Although commentators have advanced many explanations as to why current fourth amendment analysis is in disarray, they have overlooked the primary cause. The Court in *Camara* and *Terry* embraced the reasonableness balancing test in a manner that conceptually weakened probable cause and failed to provide any long-term guidance or limits for the future role of reasonableness.[47]

One could ask why wasn't the Warren Court capable of foreseeing the troubles that might evolve out of the decision in *Terry* to read the probable cause standard out of the Fourth Amendment. Answering this is difficult, but one must remember that the Court does not resolve cases in a vacuum. When *Terry* was decided the country was going through a period of unrest and turbulence. The nation had suffered some of the worst urban riots in the nation's history. There were student led demonstrations against the war in Vietnam. Both Martin Luther King and Bobby Kennedy had been assassinated while *Terry* was on the Court's docket. The Court was perceived by many people as coddling criminals by handcuffing the police in their efforts to apprehend and gain convictions over criminals. On top of this, the Court itself became a political issue as two presidential candidates, Richard Nixon and George Wallace, openly attacked the Court for being soft on crime and exacerbating the nation's problems. This compilation of facts may have caused the Court to feel the pressure necessary to help redraw the balance of power between police and criminal suspects by using language that would be more favorable to the police. Yale Kamisar has written that the Warren Court "was a good deal less exuberant about the exclusionary rule in 1968 when it upheld the police practice of 'stopping' and 'frisking' persons on less than probable cause to believe they were engaged in criminal activity."[48]

Despite the rulings in *Camara*, *See*, and *Terry* the Burger Court inherited a tradition of Fourth Amendment jurisprudence from the Warren Court which primarily emphasized the warrant requirement. The Burger Court initially continued to pay homage to the traditional approach to the Fourth Amendment. For example, in *Mincey v. Arizona* (1978)[49] it favorably quoted *Katz v. United States* (1967)[50] and stated "The Fourth Amendment proscribes all unreasonable searches and seizures, and it is a cardinal principle that 'searches conducted outside the judicial process, without prior approval by judge or magistrates, are *per se* unreasonable under the Fourth Amendment—subject only to a few specifically established and well-delineated exceptions.'"[51] Even as late as 1981 as it discussed searches incident to a lawful arrest the Burger Court declared in *New York v. Belton,*[52] that "It is a first principle of Fourth Amendment jurisprudence that the police may not conduct a search unless they first convince a neutral magistrate that there is a probable cause to do so."[53]

Despite the Burger Court's stated preference for warrants, there were forces on the Court which caused the application of the rule to be eroded. One of the most noted of these forces was the Burger Court's great dislike for the exclusionary rule. This dislike, which has been well documented, often caused the Burger Court to interpret the Fourth Amendment in a way which limited the amount of evidence that would be excluded at trial.[54] Another force which brought a change in the method by which the Fourth Amendment was interpreted was the changing personnel on the Court. Richard Nixon promised that if he was elected president he would appoint justices who believed in "law and order." The justices he selected who were confirmed by the Senate acted in a way which demonstrates that President Nixon fulfilled this campaign promise. Of the four appointments which Richard Nixon made, Chief Justice Warren Burger and Associate Justices Harry Blackmun, Lewis Powell, and William Rehnquist, all would come favor a reasonableness approach to the Fourth Amendment.[55]

These new justices did not have to invent new approaches to Fourth Amendment jurisprudence to weaken the protections of the amendment. The opinions of the Warren Court had opened the door for a new balancing approach which could operate to the advantage of law enforcement if a group of justices were so inclined. This was because *Camara* and *Terry* did not place any meaningful limitations on the reasonableness approach to the Fourth Amendment. Anthony Amsterdam has criticized the reasonableness approach stating that without generally applicable rules which police can follow "appellate courts defer to trial courts and trial courts defer to police" thus it will be the police who determine what is reasonable under the Fourth Amendment.[56] Under the Warren Court *Camara* had replaced the probable cause standard with a balancing test which rested on the reasonableness of the governmental action. *Terry* then extended that balancing test to criminal cases which the Court believed were not adequately covered by the warrant and probable cause requirements. As a result of these cases, the stage had been set for use of a reasonableness approach that would be flexible enough to allow the government to engage in a wider variety of searches and seizures. The reasonableness approach's flexibility to tip the balance in favor of law enforcement became increasingly evident as the Burger Court matured.[57] Using this approach, a reasonable search would be one in which the benefits, which would increasingly be defined as more effective law enforcement, outweighed the costs, infringement on a person's liberty.

The Evolution of *Terry* Stops

The ability to apply a reasonableness approach has become evident in several different types of cases. The first that will be examined is investigative stop cases. One of the problems from *Terry* was the announcement by Chief Justice Warren that future stop and frisk cases would have to be settled on a case-by-case basis. This has allowed lower courts to take the language used in *Terry* and enlarge the number of instances in which such stops and frisks may legitimately be conducted. This has also created latitude for later courts to alter *Terry*'s intent to limit the use of stop and frisks to a search for weapons.

The framework for investigative stops which had been established in *Terry v. Ohio* and its companion cases was left undisturbed by the Warren Court which did not revisit the area of law.[58] This left the Burger Court in a position to further develop stop and frisk law. The first area of stop and frisk law that the Burger Court helped to clarify concerned when a stop was appropriate. It did this in the case of *Adams v. Williams* (1972).[59] The facts to *Adams* were that a police officer in Bridgeport, Connecticut had received a tip at 2:15 a.m. from an individual considered to be trustworthy that a man, Robert Williams, sitting in his car had a weapon and narcotics in his possession. The officer approached the car and asked the man to get out. When the man instead rolled down his window the officer reached in and removed a fully loaded pistol from the waist of the man's pants. The man was then arrested and a full search revealed heroin on Williams, a machete under his seat, and another pistol in his trunk. Williams was convicted despite his attempt to have the evidence suppressed. The conviction was upheld by a panel of the Second Circuit, but when the court reheard it en banc it overruled the conviction. It reasoned that Connecticut law allowed people to carry concealed weapons and did not allow officers to routinely frisk for them. Tips about persons carrying weapons did not, therefore, necessarily involve criminal activity. Furthermore, unsubstantiated tips about narcotics do not give rise to reasonable suspicion. Allowing frisks to be done when there is an unsubstantiated tip about narcotics and possession of what might be a lawful gun would allow police to use the gun tip as a pretext to conduct an unjustified search for narcotics. The Supreme Court then granted *certiorari*.

Speaking for a 6-3 Court, Justice Rehnquist wrote the majority opinion in *Adams v. Williams*. He reiterated what he believed were the main points of *Terry*. First, that under appropriate circumstances an officer may approach a person for purposes of investigating the possibility of criminal behavior even when probable cause does not exist. Second, that the officers could do those things necessary to protect themselves against attack. Justice Rehnquist also noted that according to *Terry*, whether the officer acted appropriately in these situations must be judged "in light of the facts known to the officer at the time."[60] Justice Rehnquist then found that in applying these principles to this case that the officer's action had been justifiable and that he had acted reasonably. *Adams* goes beyond *Terry* in describing the types of information that can be taken into consideration by an officer in justifying when an investigatory stop is acceptable. It makes it clear that an officer need not have directly observed the suspicious behavior. If sufficient circumstances exist to make the officer fearful of his safety as there were here where the officer had a tip that there was gun, the hour was late, the neighborhood was a high crime area, and the defendant did not follow the orders of the officer, a frisk for a weapon is reasonable. The Court also made it clear that in encounters with possible criminals, no officer should be expected to conduct an investigatory stop of an individual who is suspected of having a weapon without checking for and, if found, securing the weapon, regardless of the gun laws for that jurisdiction.

Initially, the Supreme Court consistently upheld the principle that stop and frisks are only meant to protect the officer and public by determining if an individual has weapons and were only legitimate when officers had reasonable particularized suspicion. For example, in *Ybarra v. Illinois* (1979)[61] the Court in an opinion by Justice Potter Stewart ruled that an Illinois law which allowed police to detain and search all people present in a location when a search warrant was issued was unconstitutional. *Ybarra* came to the Court after police served a warrant to search a tavern and its bartender. In pursuance of the Illinois law, the police detained and searched all the customers. Ybarra, a customer, was searched and police found narcotics on him. He was convicted over his objections that the search had violated the Fourth Amendment. When the conviction was upheld on appeal, Ybarra sought *certiorari*, which was granted.

The Court found the Illinois law to violate the Fourth Amendment. The Court explained that searches of individuals in a place where a search warrant was issued was not allowed by the framework of stop and frisk cases under *Terry v. Ohio*. Justice Stewart noted that *Terry* had created an exception to the warrant requirement that only allowed for a very narrow frisk, for weapons. Justice Stewart pointed out nothing in *Terry* "can be understood to allow a generalized 'cursory search for weapons' or indeed, any search whatever for anything but weapons."[62] Furthermore, Justice Stewart pointed out that before the *Terry* precedent allowed narrow searches for weapons the police needed reasonable suspicion which was directed at a particular person who was the subject of the search. This was regardless of the fact that the "person happens to be on the premises where an authorized narcotics search is taking place."[63]

Chief Justice Burger, Justice Rehnquist and Justice Blackmun all dissented. Justice Rehnquist pressed the Court to apply a broader interpretation of the reasonableness test. He argued:

Because the police were aware that heroin was being offered for sale in the tavern, it was quite reasonable to assume that any one or more of the persons at
the bar could have been involved in drug trafficking. . . . the police also were
quite conscious of the possibility that one or more of the patrons could be
armed in preparation for just such an intrusion. In the narcotics business, "firearms are as much 'tools of the trade' as are most commonly recognized articles
of narcotics paraphernalia." The potential danger to the police executing the
warrant and to innocent individuals in this dimly lit tavern cannot be minimized. By conducting an immediate frisk of those persons at the bar, the police
eliminated this danger and "froze" the area in preparation for the search of the
premises.[64]

Terry and Vehicle Stops

The Court has been asked to determine if investigatory stops could be conducted
when individuals are in their vehicles. The first cases in this area involved possible illegal aliens crossing America's borders. Initially, the Court refused to allow *Terry* stops of vehicles and applied the traditional approach to the Fourth
Amendment in these cases. *Almeida-Sanchez v. United States* (1973),[65] for example, involved the power of roving border patrols to stop vehicles and subject
the occupants to a search for illegal aliens. In it the Court ruled that unless the
search was preceded by probable cause or consent there was a Fourth Amendment violation. The Court was bothered by the amount of discretion border patrol agents had in deciding which vehicles to search stating the searches "embodied precisely the evil the Court saw in *Camara* when it insisted that the
'discretion of the official in the field' be circumscribed by obtaining a warrant
prior to the inspection."[66]

In *United States v. Brignoni-Ponce* (1975)[67] the Court reversed direction
and expanded the types of investigatory stops which could be conducted to include inquiries into whether illegal aliens were crossing America's borders. Unlike *Almeida-Sanchez v. United States*, this case did not involve a roving border
patrol or require the Court to decide if a search conducted pursuant to the stop
would be acceptable. It only examined the issue as to whether a stop at a stationary border station that wasn't at the actual border passed constitutional scrutiny. In such instances, the Court, through Justice Powell's majority opinion, reasoned that both *Terry* and *Adams* made it clear that in appropriate circumstances
the Fourth Amendment allows a properly limited search or seizure even when
the facts do not create probable cause. Such investigatory stops were acceptable
when meant to protect the public or prevent crime. In this case, there was a further important governmental interest, securing borders, which allowed such
stops to be made if agents have reasonable suspicion and specific and articulable
facts which indicate that a vehicle may contain illegal aliens. When such reasonable suspicions did exist an agent "may question the driver and passengers about

their citizenship and immigration status, and he may ask them to explain suspicious circumstances, but any further detention or search must be based on consent or probable cause."[68] The Court also made it clear that Mexican ancestry alone could not give rise to the reasonable suspicions necessary for an investigatory stop. In *United States v. Ortiz* (1975)[69] the Court, again concerned with the government discretion, relied on *Almeida-Sanchez v. United States* and ruled that a search which followed an investigatory stop at a stationary border patrol station not located on the border must be based on either consent or probable cause.

In *United States v. Martinez-Fuerte* (1976)[70] the Court distinguished between investigative stops at temporary and permanent border patrol stations. This case came to the Court when the border patrol established a permanent immigration checkpoint to detect illegal immigrants sixty-six miles north of the border between San Diego and Los Angles. Along the highway, one mile prior to the check point, large flashing road signs were posted warning motorists of the stop. The border patrol agents stopped vehicles, questioned inhabitants, and visually inspected them. Agents then selected a number of vehicles for secondary inspections, at times using apparent Mexican ancestry as a cue, to determine who to subject to a secondary inspection which more thoroughly investigated the residence status of the occupants of the vehicle. Even though the traffic flow was so heavy that it did not allow particularized study of individual vehicles as they went by, the Court found that the practice was acceptable. The Court did so by balancing the invasion that the stops had on a person's privacy against the governmental goals. The Court noted that even though the "objective intrusion," the actual stopping of vehicles, was the same as in cases involving roving border patrol inspections the "subjective intrusion" to individuals was minimal because drivers had forewarning about the location of the stop and were not singled out among other motorists. The Court also pointed out that immigration roadblocks such as this were an effective method of detecting illegal immigrants and played an important role in enforcing the country's immigration policy. The Court also believed that since there was no less intrusive means to stop illegal immigration the practice should be allowed to continue.

Another indication that the Burger Court was at first hesitant to enlarge the purpose or scope of stop and frisks coming out of *Terry v. Ohio* came in *Delaware v. Prouse* (1979).[71] *Prouse* came to the Court after a police officer randomly pulled Prouse over to check his license and vehicle registration. The officer smelled marijuana coming from Prouse's car and then saw marijuana in plain view on the floor of the car. During the suppression hearing, the officer admitted that he had observed no traffic violations or any other suspicious activities before he pulled Prouse over. Instead, the officer stated that he was not busy at the time and decided to simply stop Prouse to ensure that he had a driver's license and that his vehicle was registered. When the trial judge suppressed the evidence the state appealed and the decision was affirmed by the Delaware Supreme Court. The state sought *certiorari* and it was granted.

In Justice White's majority opinion he noted that the *Terry* framework had already been applied in *United States v. Brignoni-Ponce* to vehicle stops. In *Prouse*, however, the reason for the stop was traffic safety not control of illegal immigration. Despite the difference in the reasons for the stop, as in *Brignoni-Ponce*, the critical question confronted by the Court focused on the amount of discretion that officers should have under the Fourth Amendment to conduct such stops. In determining the answer to this question the Court stated that "[t]he essential purpose of the proscriptions in the Fourth Amendment is to impose a standard of 'reasonableness' upon the exercise of discretion by government officials, including law enforcement agents, in order to 'safeguard the privacy and security of individuals against arbitrary invasions.'"[72] Taking this into consideration the Court ruled that it was inappropriate to allow officers to indiscriminately stop cars for safety checks when there is no reasonable basis for believing that there is a violation. In applying the balancing approach from *Martinez-Fuerte* the Court also noted that even though there may have been an important governmental interest at stake in *Prouse*, the effectiveness of random stops was questionable. Justice White reasoned:

> The marginal contribution to roadway safety possibly resulting from a system of spot checks cannot justify subjecting every occupant of every vehicle on the roads to a seizure—limited in magnitude compared to other intrusions but nonetheless constitutionally cognizable—at the unbridled discretion of law enforcement officials. To insist neither upon an appropriate factual basis for suspicion directed at a particular automobile nor upon some other substantial and objective standard or rule to govern the exercise of discretion "would invite intrusions upon constitutionally guaranteed rights based on nothing more substantial than inarticulate hunches."[73]

The language which Justice White used presents strong evidence that the presence of individualized suspicion will be an important consideration in determining the reasonableness of a police officer's actions in investigative stops. Allowing officers to stop individuals without individualized suspicion permits the discretion of police officer to be unchecked. Despite this strong statement limiting the power of the government to interfere with a person in their vehicle unless there were particularized suspicions that they had broken the law, Justice White went on and substantially weakened the principle by ending the opinion by stating:

> This holding does not preclude the State of Delaware or other States from developing methods for spot checks that involve less intrusion or that do not involve unconstrained exercise of discretion. Questioning of all oncoming traffic at roadblock-type stops is one possible alternative.[74]

Despite the language in *Prouse* which hinted that states could develop methods by which spot checks of all vehicles could pass constitutional scrutiny, the Court in *Brown v. Texas* (1979)[75] was unwilling to accept a state law that allowed police officers to stop all individuals and hold them for the purpose of identification. Brown was observed in an alley known for drug trafficking. Police had no basis for suspecting him of drug trafficking or being armed, but asked Brown to identify himself. When he refused to give his name and address as required by state law he was arrested and convicted. When it came to the Supreme Court, the Court examined the history of *Terry* and its progeny. Chief Justice Burger, writing for a unanimous Court, said that the history demonstrated that the Court had been trying to protect the expectation that individuals have from the unfettered discretion of police officers to interfere with their privacy. In determining the reasonableness of the law the Court balanced the importance of the governmental interest and the effectiveness of the law in advancing that interest against the interference the law had with individual liberty. In reaching a balance the Court was hesitant to give police unlimited discretion to require all citizens to identify themselves. Instead, the Court held that a "seizure must be based on specific, objective facts indicating that society's legitimate interests require the seizure of the particular individual, or that the seizure must be carried out pursuant to a plan embodying explicit, neutral limitations on the conduct of individual officers."[76] *Brown* can be seen as the apex of the Court's unwillingness to allow police to stop citizens unless reasonable suspicion existed prior to the stop.

In subsequent cases, the Rehnquist Court weakened the Court's commitment to an individualized suspicion requirement. The best example is *Michigan Department of State Police v. Sitz* (1990).[77] *Sitz* involved the constitutionality of a sobriety checkpoint established by the Michigan State Police. The checkpoint followed departmental guidelines concerning both site selection and publicity concerning the checkpoint. At the checkpoint each driver was stopped and examined for signs of intoxication. If there was no suspicion of intoxication, drivers were immediately released. If the initial stop created suspicions, the driver would be directed to pull over out of the traffic and was subjected to sobriety tests. When a driver failed the tests, the examining officer had full discretion to arrest the driver for driving under the influence. The particular checkpoint which was challenged lasted one hour and fifteen minutes. In that time 126 vehicles were stopped an average of twenty-six seconds each, two drivers were subjected to sobriety tests and one of those was arrested and charged with driving while intoxicated. One other driver who did not stop at the checkpoint was caught, arrested and also charged with driving while under the influence. The legality of the sobriety checkpoint was challenged by Sitz, a licensed Michigan driver. Both the trial court and the Michigan Court of Appeals found the law unconstitutional, and the Michigan Supreme Court refused to hear the case. At that point the Michigan State Police petitioned the Supreme Court and was granted *certiorari*.

In a 6-3 decision with the majority opinion written by Chief Justice William Rehnquist the Court overruled the lower courts. The Court limited its decision to a determination as to whether the original stop and questioning of each motorist was reasonable under the Fourth Amendment. In doing so it applied the balancing of interest test from *United States v. Martinez-Fuerte* and *Brown v. Texas*. In reaching a balance of the competing interest the Court emphasized the government's interest in eradicating drunk-driving. It rejected a plea by the state police to find that deterring drunk driving was a special need beyond normal law enforcement stating the special needs rationale was not meant to overrule *Martinez-Fuerte* and other precedents involving "police stops of motorists on public highways."[78] After identifying the importance of the governmental interest and emphasizing the severity of the drunk-driving problem in the country, the Court moved on and found the objective intrusiveness of the checkpoints to be minimal. This was because guidelines developed by the state police for sobriety checkpoints limited the discretion of participating officers, the seizures were of brief duration, the intensity of the questioning was low, and the fact that the checkpoints were less likely to create fear and surprise on the part of motorists than being pulled over by a roving patrol where police exercised discretion.

After finding that the governmental interest outweighed the intrusion on privacy in sobriety checkpoints, the Court found that the 1.5% success rate for catching drunk drivers demonstrated that the program was effective. The Court then announced that it would defer to legislative bodies in questions concerning the efficiency of law enforcement methods by stating *"Brown* was not meant to transfer from politically accountable officials to the courts the decision as to which among reasonable alternative law enforcement techniques should be employed to deal with a serious public danger."[79] The Court explained *Brown* was only designed to examine the degree to which a method of seizure advances the public interest.

Justice William Brennan and Justice John Paul Stevens filed separate dissents. Justice Brennan reminded the Court that police normally must show probable cause for a search without a warrant to be reasonable. He also believed that the Court should have continued its analysis of whether the checkpoints were reasonable beyond the initial stop. Justice Stevens believed that the Court understated the intrusiveness of the stops and believed there was a large difference between the permanent checkpoints the Court had accepted in previous cases and these temporary checkpoints. He also believed the Court overstated the effectiveness of the checkpoints explaining that he thought roving patrols which did not infringe on privacy expectations might be more effective at catching drunk drivers.

In *City of Indianapolis v. Edmond* (2000)[80] the Supreme Court balked at the opportunity to enlarge the situations in which law enforcement agencies could use highway checkpoints. The case came to the Court after police in Indianapolis established a checkpoint program. With no individualized suspicion, the police stopped a predetermined number of vehicles at various locations for the primary purpose of discovery and interdiction of illegal drugs. Under the program, when vehicles were stopped officers would advise the driver that the purpose of the stop was a drug checkpoint. Drivers were then asked for their operator's license and vehicle registration. Officers observed drivers for signs of impairment while they surveyed the interior compartment of the vehicle from the outside. Finally, a narcotics-detection dog would walk around the outside of each stopped vehicle. Two motorists who had been stopped brought suit claiming that the checkpoints violated the Fourth Amendment. The district court found no violations, but was overturned by the court of appeals, the Supreme Court granted then *certiorari*.

In a 6-3 decision, with the majority opinion by Justice Sandra Day O'Connor, the Court found the checkpoint to be a violation of the Fourth Amendment. Justice O'Connor reasoned that this checkpoint was not acceptable under the Fourth Amendment because its primary purpose was general crime-control. Under such situations, law enforcement must have some quantum of individualized suspicion before a seizure can be made. The lack of any individualized suspicion prior to the stop could not be overlooked even though the program was designed to combat the severe illegal drug problem that existed in America. Likewise, the checkpoints could not be justified by a highway safety concern or the secondary purpose of discovering impaired motorists or drivers without proper registration or operators licenses.

Chief Justice William Rehnquist wrote a dissent supported by Justices Antonin Scalia and Clarence Thomas which argued that there was no Fourth Amendment violation because the roadblocks were objectively reasonable. This was because the roadblock did serve the substantial interest of preventing drunk driving and checking for licenses and registration documents. They believed that the expectations of law enforcement officers that drugs would also be found were irrelevant since the program would advance these other substantial interests.

Four years later in *Illinois v. Lidster* (2004)[81] the Court upheld the use of a roadblock to help in the investigation of a hit-and-run accident in which a bicyclist had been killed. The road block took place at the same time and place, but a week later than the accident. Police were hoping to find witnesses who could provide the identity of the driver or a description of the vehicle by systematically stopping vehicles at the road block. In doing so, Robert Lidster was stopped and police smelled alcohol on his breath. He subsequently failed a field sobriety test and was then arrested for driving under the influence. Over his objections that the roadblock violated the Fourth Amendment Lidster was convicted. His conviction was overturned in the state appellate system and the Supreme Court granted *certiorari* to the State.

Justice Stephen Breyer wrote for the Court and stated that *Indianapolis v. Edmond* did not rule the case. This case was distinguished because the primary purpose of the roadblock was not to determine if a vehicle's occupants were engaged in criminal behavior. Instead, the purpose of this roadblock was to ask occupants for cooperation in identifying the perpetrator of a crime that in all likelihood was committed by someone else. The Court also noted that police had long been permitted to approach members of the public to try to gather information. The lack of individualized suspicion was to be expected under such circumstances and did not raise constitutional concerns because such stops were unlikely to provoke anxiety. Not only was the stop constitutional, the Court also found it to be reasonable because police were investigating a grave crime that had caused a person's death and their actions only minimally interfered with the privacy interest of those stopped.

Police Inquiry, *Terry* Stop, or Seizure?

One of the difficult points the Court has confronted coming out of cases involving *Terry* stops has been in determining at what point mere police contact turns into a seizure of the person being investigated. The Court shed some light on this issue in *United States v. Mendenhall* (1980).[82] This case came to the Court after Drug Enforcement Agency (DEA) agents approached Mendenhall at the Detroit Metropolitan Airport and requested that she show her identification to the agents. The agents then asked her to go with them to the DEA office for further questioning. When they arrived at the office the agents asked for and received permission to search Mendenhall. The search resulted in the discovery of two small packages of heroin. Mendenhall was then convicted despite her claim that the heroin should be suppressed because the stop constituted a seizure of her. The Court granted *certiorari* and ruled against Mendenhall's claims.

Justice Potter Stewart wrote for a plurality of the Court and found that Mendenhall had not been seized. Justice Stewart noted that even though citizens had the right to refuse to cooperate with police, the police had the liberty to address questions to people on the streets and that when they did so no seizure takes place. Justice Stewart's opinion then enunciated what has become known as the "reasonable person test." In his opinion he instructed courts to examine the suspect's perspective when deciding if a seizure had indeed taken place during a *Terry* stop. Justice Stewart wrote:

> We adhere to the view that a person is seized only when, by means of physical force or a show of authority, his freedom of movement is restrained. Only when such a restraint is imposed is there any foundation whatever for invoking constitutional safeguards. . . . As long as the person to whom questions are put remains free to disregard the questions and walk away, there has been no intrusion upon that person's liberty or privacy as would under the Constitution require some particularized and objective justification.[83]

The opinion explained that if a reasonable person would have considered themselves free to walk away from police and no longer cooperate with the investigation thereby bringing their involvement to a halt, there can be no seizure. No seizure, no violation of the Fourth Amendment. Justice Stewart further pointed out that requiring reasonable suspicion to justify police questioning would have a chilling effect upon "a wide variety of legitimate law enforcement practices."[84] Justice Stewart believed that the Fourth Amendment was only meant to regulate interaction between citizens and the government which was oppressive and arbitrary, but other interactions, such as police questioning where a reasonable person would believe they were free to leave, were not guided by the Fourth Amendment. The opinion instructed judges to consider a wide range of factors to determine if a reasonable person would have considered themselves to be seized. These included the display of weapons, the officer's tone of voice and language used, the number of officers present, and the level of physical contact, if any, between the individual and officers. In the case at hand the Court found that Mendenhall had not been seized when she gave consent for the search which lead to her arrest.

Due to the decision in *Mendenhall*, judges have a number of things they must take into consideration when determining if Fourth Amendment protections were breeched in a police-citizen encounter. The first consideration is whether the officer used physical force or required the individual to submit to an assertion of the officer's authority. A second issue is whether the person's liberty was restrained by the physical force or assertion of authority to the point that a reasonable person would have believed that they were not free to go about their business. If neither of these events are not shown in the factual record, the Fourth Amendment is not implicated and any evidence gathered would be admissible. If the officer's actions through either physical force or an assertion of authority would have caused a reasonable person to believe that they were not free to go, then, as in *Terry*, the officer's action must be justified by reasonable suspicion. If no reasonable suspicion existed prior to the seizure of the citizen, any evidence gathered would normally be suppressed under the exclusionary rule.

In 1983 *Florida v. Royer*,[85] which involved a suspected drug smuggler, helped to clarify when a legitimate investigatory stop crossed the line and became an arrest. Royer, who fit a drug courier profile, was in the Miami International Airport when he came to the attention of police. He was approached by two undercover officers who requested his flight ticket and driver's license. After explaining that they suspected him of drug smuggling the officers requested that Royer accompany them to a private room. His luggage was then brought into the room and searched. The police found marijuana in his luggage.

On review the Supreme Court ruled that the marijuana was inadmissible. Justice White, speaking for a plurality of four, found that police did have enough articulated suspicions to justify a *Terry* investigative stop. The opinion then applied Justice Stewart's reasonable person standard from *Mendenhall* to determine if Royer had been seized. It reasoned that at the point in which the police took Royer to the private room and kept his belongings, including his flight ticket, he was under arrest since the police actions were more intrusive than necessary for an investigative stop. The Court believed that such an arrest must be based upon better facts than the police had in this case. The Court stated: "We cannot . . . agree that every nervous young man paying cash for a ticket to New York under an assumed name and carrying two heavy American Tourister bags may be arrested and held to answer for a serious felony charge."[86] Furthermore, evidence gathered through such an arrest could not be admitted on the theory that Royer had voluntarily consented to a search of his luggage. Justice Blackmun dissented reaching the opposite result in the case, but approved of the reasonable person standard for determining if a seizure of a person has taken place. This standard is often referred to as *Mendenhall-Royer* standard.

The Court in *United States v. Sokolow* (1989),[87] which also involved a drug courier profile, enlarged the basis for *Terry* stops beyond the traditional standard of reasonable suspicion by ruling that when considered together on a case-by-case basis a number of innocent activities, in this case attributes of personal appearance and habits, could create a reasonable suspicion. The Court's opinion by Chief Justice Rehnquist clarified that the "relevant inquiry is not whether conduct is 'innocent' or 'guilty,' but the degree of suspicion that attaches to particular types of noncriminal acts."[88] Central to the question whether there has been a Fourth Amendment violation is the common sense of the police. The Court's decision found that the Fourth Amendment does not stop police from intruding on a citizen's activity if the officer reasonably believes that it is necessary to advance law enforcement concerns. In this case, the Court found that the specific facts which matched a drug courier profile which provided the foundation for a stop were acceptable. A drug courier profile consists of a number of factors established over a period of time by law enforcement officials which helps them to predict which individuals might be involved in the drug trade. The profile in question was found acceptable even though there was no correlation between the officer's observation of a number of factors which showed up on the drug courier profile and the suspected crime. Those factors which matched the profile included: (1) Sokolow paid $2,100 in cash for tickets; (2) his name didn't match with the phone number he listed; (3) he flew to Miami, a drug distribution center; (4) he only stayed in Miami 48 hours despite it being a 20 hour flight from Honolulu; (5) he appeared nervous; and (6) he didn't check any luggage. The Court found the law enforcement concerns outweighed the privacy expectations of the individual involved. In doing so, the Court allowed the police to seize individuals in investigative stops based upon their assumptions that certain innocent behavior is indicative of guilt.

Although the Court in *Sokolow* did find that there were enough articulable facts to create reasonable suspicion to stop Sokolow, the Court has not provided a definitive answer as to whether it approves of drug courier profiles alone as a basis for determining if reasonable suspicion exists for investigatory stops. It is generally supportive of drug courier profiles, but has found that not all are acceptable when they are too general or target such a broad array of behavior that it would also apply to many individuals who were not involved in the illegal drug trade.[89] The lower courts have also been largely supportive of the use of drug courier profiles. Roger Hanson has documented 28 different elements that have been included in various drug courier profiles. Some of the most common characteristics accepted by lower courts as indicative of drug couriers include: (1) arrival from or departure from a city identified as a drug distribution point; (2) excessive travel to cities which are considered drug distribution centers; (3) carrying either little to no luggage, or carrying a number of empty suitcases; (4) immediately making a telephone call after deplaning; (5) purchasing plane tickets with a lot of small denomination bills; (6) having an unusual itinerary, such as a quick return after a long flight; (7) almost exclusive use of public transportation, especially cabs, to leave the airport; (8) use of an alias; (9) carrying unusually large amounts of currency; (10) leaving a fictitious telephone number with airlines; and (11) unusual nervousness. Some of the characteristics seem to be in conflict with others. For example, being the first to leave the plane, leaving in the middle of other passengers, and leaving last have all been said to be indicative of a person being a drug courier.[90]

The need for police to have preexisting reasonable suspicion prior to stopping a citizen became fuzzier as a result of *Illinois v. Wardlow* (2000).[91] Both Justices John Harlan and Byron White had said in their concurring opinions in *Terry* that if there was no reasonable suspicion to stop a citizen, citizens would be free to walk away from police who sought to ask questions of them. *Wardlow* made it clear that running away would not be acceptable, at least if an individual is in a high crime neighborhood. *Wardlow* came to the Court after Sam Wardlow was seen observing police and then took off running. Police saw that he had a bag under his arm as he ran away. Police gave chase and when they apprehended Wardlow they patted the bag down and felt a gun which was then removed from the bag. Wardlow was convicted over his objection that there was no basis for a stop, but the conviction was overturned by the Illinois Appellate Court. This judgement was affirmed by the Illinois Supreme Court. The United States Supreme Court then granted *certiorari* to determine if the original stop was supported by reasonable suspicion.

In a 5-4 decision Chief Justice Rehnquist wrote for the majority in *Wardlow*. In his opinion he found that a proper application of the principles of *Terry* found support for the stop of Wardlow. Two things weighed heavily in his analysis. The first was that Wardlow was in a high crime area at the time in which he was spotted fleeing the police. While Chief Justice Rehnquist did not believe that fact alone justified police finding reasonable suspicion to stop Wardlow, it was not barred from consideration since it was among the "relevant contextual considerations in a Terry analysis."[92] The most influential factor in the Court's opinion which justified the reasonableness of the stop was the flight of Wardlow. Chief Justice Rehnquist wrote that flight may not be conclusive of criminal activity, but "headlong flight . . . is the consummate act of evasion," and suggestive of criminal behavior.[93] The opinion went on and said that courts needed to grant deference to the common sense inferences about human behavior that police officers make seeing flight under these circumstances. The Court then found that citizens still had a right to avoid confrontations with police not authorized by reasonable suspicion by refusing to cooperate and going about one's own business. It stated, however, that flight by its very nature is not a part of going about one's business.[94]

In an opinion which concurred in part and dissented in part, Justice Stevens concurred with the belief that there should be no *per se* rule which created reasonable suspicion based on the locality in which flight from police takes place. The opinion dissented, however, because it reasoned that any number of reasons could explain a person's flight from police. Justice Stevens noted, "A pedestrian may break into a run for a variety of reasons," including "to catch up with a friend a block or two away, to seek shelter from an impending storm, to arrive at a bus stop before the bus leaves, to get home in time for dinner, to resume jogging after a pause for rest, to avoid contact with a bore or bully, or simply to answer the call of nature" he then pointed out that any of these reasons "might coincide with the arrival of an officer in the vicinity."[95] As a result, the opinion stated that under these circumstances, the proper test to determine if reasonable suspicion existed at the time of a stop was the totality of the circumstances test and he failed to find the standards of this test met.

The Court's statement in *Terry* that citizens have the right not to participate with the police has been weakened by other decisions of the Court. For example, in both *Michigan v. Chesternut* (1988)[96] and *California v. Hodari D.* (1991)[97] the Court found that uncooperative behavior could be met with police intimidation in order for police to establish reasonable suspicion. In *Chesternut* the Court unanimously believed that police behavior involving a police chase with police driving parallel to an individual running from the police was not so intimidating that it would "have communicated to a reasonable person an attempt to capture or otherwise intrude upon freedom of movement."[98] Justice Blackmun, who wrote for the Court, found a number of factors which made the actions of the police less intimidating to Chesternut. These included, they did not put on the lights or siren, they didn't display their weapons, and they didn't yell at Chesternut to halt. As a result, when the suspect threw out some pills, they were acceptable as evidence since they were abandoned, rather than seized through a violation of the Fourth Amendment.

In *Hodari D.* police saw some youths who scattered when they observed the police. Police gave chase and before Hodari D. was tackled by an officer he threw out some crack cocaine. The Court ruled that during the chase there had been no seizure and therefore the evidence was admissible. In *Hodari D.* the Court retreated from the *Mendenhall-Royer* reasonable person test which had held that if police asserted their authority a seizure had taken place. The Court ruled that determination of whether there is a seizure is dependent on two things: (1) did the police assert their authority in a way that would convey to a reasonable person that he is no longer free to leave and (2) did this show of authority actually produce a stop. The Court ruled in *Hodari D.* that when police gave chase, they asserted their authority. That chase did not, however, constitute police action which initiated Fourth Amendment protections because Hodari D. had not submitted to the authority of the police. The Court went on and ruled that during the chase there was no physical contact between the police and the suspect so any intimidating activity on the part of the police did not constitute a seizure. Without a seizure there couldn't have been an unlawful search involving the crack. The officer's behavior leading up to the discovery of evidence is irrelevant as long as a reasonable person believes they are free to leave. The officer's intimidating behavior need not be supported by reasonable suspicion. When individuals give up evidence under these circumstances, it is fully consensual so there is no Fourth Amendment violation. Amazing as it may seem, according to the Court's opinion, the average person believes that they will be free to leave when they are being chased by the police.

Robert Burnett has carefully examined the cumulative impact of the Court's decisions concerning when police-citizen encounters fall under the protections of the Fourth Amendment and when they do not. He has noted that under the *Mendenhall-Royer* reasonable person test as long as a police officer is "polite, non-accusatory, and calm" a court will find that a reasonable person would feel free to end the encounter at their discretion.[99] As a result, because the encounter would not be guided by Fourth Amendment principles it could be initiated by police without any justification or reasonable suspicion. A larger problem arises when a citizen decides to exercise their right not to cooperate with the police. Burnett points out:

> If the citizen refuses to reply or walks away, the authorities will deem such a refusal to cooperate as justification for a prolonged detention. Conversely, if the citizen answers the initial, generalized questions and no suspicion or criminality is exposed, the officer will often escalate the encounter by asking the individual if he would consent to a luggage or body search. In either scenario, the intrusion is escalated without justification. More importantly, in both situations, the citizen is unlikely to feel that he is free to leave given the suddenly accusatory environment. In reality, the citizen's liberty has been restrained and his freedom of movement curtailed. The courts will assert that no seizure has occurred and the police conduct remains outside the scope of the Fourth Amendment.[100]

What Constitutes Reasonable Suspicion

Application of the Court's decisions in the lower courts as to what facts will create enough reasonable suspicion to justify a *Terry* stop has created some difficulty for police officers and courts. In *United States v. Cortez*[101] (1981) Chief Justice Burger emphasized the need for police to have a sufficient basis for a coercive *Terry* stop which invokes the Fourth Amendment, as opposed to the noncoercive type of stop which took place in *Mendenhall*, and tried to provide guidance. He went on to explain, "the essence of all that has been written is that the totality of the circumstances—the whole picture—must be taken into account. Based upon that whole picture the detaining officers must have a particularized and objective basis for suspecting the particular person stopped of criminal activity."[102] This standard allows the officer involved in a *Terry* stop to use information based on personal observations or information gathered from other sources to develop the rational basis for the stop. Chief Justice Burger instructed lower courts that the information providing the basis to justify a *Terry* stop "must be seen and weighed not in terms of library analysis by scholars, but as understood by those versed in the field of law enforcement."[103]

The courts have allowed a number of items to be taken into consideration when police are determining reasonable suspicion. A number of elements which are related to a person's physical appearance which have been successfully relied on to uphold reasonable suspicion when other factors are present include "mode of dress and haircut, a 'hippie' appearance, race, gender, age, and factors correlated with wealth or poverty."[104] Under normal circumstances, none of these physical characteristics taken alone, without some form of behavioral action constitutes reasonable suspicion. The environment or surrounding in which police observe a person may also have an impact on whether reasonable suspicion exists. The environment which has been most useful to police in establishing reasonable suspicion has been a person's presence in neighborhoods which have been characterized as high crime areas. The strongest element in reaching a determination of reasonable suspicion remains behavioral activity. Conduct which is necessary in the commission or preparation of a crime always creates reasonable suspicion. Another behavior that may create reasonable suspicion is harder to clearly determine because there could be a number of reasons behind the behavior. This is behavior that indicates that someone is seemingly guilty of wrongdoing and trying to evade detection. Such behaviors which have been accepted by courts include "obvious attempts to evade detection by law enforcement officers, paying cash for expensive plane tickets, failure to check luggage, [and] traveling under an assumed name."[105]

Adding to the power of law enforcement agents to engage in investigative stops is the Court's ruling that behavior which is otherwise innocent may create individualized suspicion when all observations are considered as a whole. The Court has made it perfectly clear that "A determination that reasonable suspicion exists . . . need not rule out the possibility of innocent conduct."[106] The Court believes that because innocent conduct may not seem so innocent to a reasonably trained law enforcement officer who has to make quick decisions on the streets, courts should be deferential to the judgment of officers.

The instructions of the Supreme Court to be deferential to the observations of police and a general willingness of police to make a wide number of claims of suspicious behavior has not been without criticism. Sheri Lynn Johnson has noted:

> Law enforcement agencies cite an amazing variety of behavior as indicating consciousness of guilt. Police have inferred an attempt to conceal both from a traffic violator's reach toward the dashboard or floor of a car, and from his alighting from the car and walking toward the police. Drug Enforcement Agency officers have inferred a desire to avoid detection both from a traveler's being the last passenger to get off a plane and from his being the first. Immigration and Naturalization Service agents have argued both that it was suspicious that the occupants of a vehicle reacted nervously when a patrol car passed, and that it was suspicious that the occupants failed to look at the patrol car. Finally, the government has argued in a customs case that "excessive" calmness is suspicious.[107]

David McTaggert has also criticized the cumulative effects of the decisions of the Court in this area:

> The broad range of intrusive police tactics permitted under the Court's Fourth Amendment jurisprudence creates an incentive for an officer to approach innocent citizens in a highly menacing manner, knowing that this will be likely to ensure cooperation. But if the citizen chooses not to submit to the display of authority, under *Wardlow* the uncooperative response may be regarded as "nervous evasive behavior" and thus will justify a stop and frisk. These two rules read together indicate that a citizen approached by the police really has no chance at all: For all practical purposes, the Court has read into the Fourth Amendment a duty to cooperate with police officers.[108]

In *Hiibel v. Sixth Judicial District Court* (2004)[109] the Court brought into doubt the ability for a citizen to refuse to cooperate with the police during an investigative stop. In *Hiibel*, however, the Court made clear that the law could require a person to honor a request for identification if there was a reasonable basis for the stop and the need to know the identity of the person was reasonable related to the basis of the stop.

Length of a *Terry* Stop

In *United States v. Sharpe*[110] (1985) the Burger Court reemphasized that deference should be granted to police to determine the length of a detention needed to complete an investigatory *Terry* stop before it becomes an arrest. In *Sharpe* a DEA agent, Luther Cooke, was patrolling the coast between North Carolina and South Carolina when he came across a pickup truck with a camper on it. It was being followed by a Pontiac Bonneville. The truck was riding low which indicated that it might have a heavy load. The DEA agent became suspicious and he followed both vehicles for twenty miles and then decided to make a stop to investigate the possibility that the vehicles were engaged in drug smuggling. Prior to the stop, the agent requested assistance from the South Carolina Highway Patrol. The request was answered by Kenneth Thrasher and Agent Cooke radioed Officer Thrasher and instructed him to pull over the vehicles. The highway patrol officer pulled up to the Pontiac and motioned to the driver to pull over. When it did, the pickup truck did not stop. At that point Officer Thrasher gave chase while Agent Cooke stayed with the Pontiac. When Thrasher caught up with the pickup a half mile down the road, he searched the driver, Donald Savage, took his license and registration, and informed Savage that he would be held until Agent Cooke arrived. At that time Savage asked for his license to be returned and told the officer he wanted to leave. His requests were denied. While this was happening Agent Cooke, called the local police, who arrived in ten minutes, to take control of the Pontiac. Fifteen minutes after Savage had been pulled over by Thrasher, Cooke arrived on the scene. Cooke examined the driver's license and twice asked if he could search the pickup. The request was denied. Cooke then walked to the back of the truck and put his nose up to the window of the camper. He said that he smelled marijuana and then without Savage's consent took the keys from Savage and searched the camper. He located a number of burlap bags which had been tightly packed that were similar to bales of marijuana that he had seen in other investigations. Savage was then arrested and Agent Cooke then went back to the Pontiac and arrested its driver, Sharpe. Several days later the pickup was again searched without a warrant. When DEA agents unloaded the truck and subjected the bales to a chemical analysis it identified the contents as marijuana.

At trial, Sharpe and Savage entered motions to suppress the marijuana as a product of an unlawful search and seizure. The motion was denied by the trial court and they were both convicted. The Court of Appeals for the Fourth Circuit reversed. The court believed that the time in which the suspects were held prior to arrest, Savage was held for fifteen to twenty minutes before his arrest and Sharpe was held for thirty to forty minutes before his arrest, violated the brevity requirements of *Terry*. Stopping someone for this long constituted a de facto arrest in the view of the court and thus required probable cause. The case was granted *certiorari* by the Supreme Court.

In its decision the majority found that the controlling precedent was *Terry v. Ohio* which divided investigatory stops into two steps. The first was the basis for the stop, which in *Sharpe* the Court found to be acceptable since police had articulable and reasonable suspicion that Sharpe and Savage were involved in drug smuggling. The second step of *Terry* according to the majority, was determining if the scope of the stop was reasonable under the given conditions. In making its determination on this issue, the majority limited itself to examining the detention of Savage. The Court found that Savage's detention did not last long enough to constitute a de facto arrest and that the time he was held was not unreasonable given the circumstances. The Court refused to place a specific time limit on how long a person could be held during an investigatory stop. The Court ruled the detainment reasonable as to the manner, method and purpose of the detainment. The Court did rely on the framework of *Terry*, but while *Terry* emphasized the invasion of personal autonomy and dignity of citizens involved in police stops, *Sharpe* found that law enforcement interests were to be of utmost importance in deciding if the scope of the search was reasonably related to the purpose of the stop. In examining the needs of law enforcement courts were to give police the "time reasonably needed to effectuate those purposes."[111] The majority also emphasized that in diligently conducting an investigation of someone being detained, the police will not be in violation of the Fourth Amendment if they do not follow the least intrusive investigative means available unless the methods selected by law enforcement are in themselves unreasonable.

The time that the investigative stop took in *Sharpe* seems trivial compared to the sixteen hour detention that the Court accepted in *United States v. Montoya de Hernandez* (1985).[112] In *Montoya de Hernandez* the Court accepted the long detention because the government suspected Montoya de Hernandez of being an alimentary canal smuggler who was entering the country, agents could not confirm their suspicions until the suspected balloons of narcotics had been passed. Essential to the Court's opinion was the fact that this detention took place at the border, so the Court's decision provides little guidance for how long an investigative stop not involving a border crossing may legitimately take before it violates the Fourth Amendment.

The Scope of *Terry* Stop Searches

The Court has been generous to police when it comes to providing them with the tools necessary to protect themselves from individuals who might be armed and dangerous. In *Pennsylvania v. Mimms* (1977)[113] Mimms had been stopped because the car he was driving had expired plates. Mimms was ordered out of the vehicle by an officer who then noticed a large bulge under his jacket. The officer then conducted a frisk of Mimms who was found to have a loaded revolver on his person. Mimms was arrested and convicted for possession of a concealed weapon and an unlicensed firearm. Mimms objected to the admission of the gun arguing that the officer's order for Mimms to evacuate the car and the subsequent frisk and search violated the Fourth Amendment.

The Court in a *per curiam* opinion ruled that there was no violation. The Court believed that the reasonableness of the search was dependant on reaching "a balance between the public interest and the individual's right to personal security free from arbitrary interference by law officers."[114] In reaching a decision in *Mimms* the Court found that since the safety of the officer is better protected by asking a driver to get out of a vehicle, the officer's safety had to be balanced with the inconvenience of the person coupled with the fact that they have already been stopped for a traffic violation. As a result of *Mimms*, any officer has a right to ask a driver to get out of a vehicle when stopped for a traffic violation. Once that result was reached, the officer need only have the reasonable suspicion required by *Terry* to justify the frisk and subsequent search. In this case, the bulge in the jacket observed by the officer created reasonable suspicion for the frisk which then created probable cause for the seizure of the gun. In *Maryland v. Wilson* (1997)[115] the Supreme Court in an opinion by Chief Justice Rehnquist used the same line of reasoning to enlarge the *Mimms* precedent to also allow police officers to require all passengers to get out of a vehicle when the driver is pulled over for a traffic violation.

In 1983 in *Michigan v. Long*[116] the Court enlarged the scope of *Terry* searches when an individual who the police had suspicions about was in an automobile. Police had noticed Long driving erratically and pulled him over. Long then got out of his car and met police behind the vehicle. When he was asked for his registration Long walked toward his car in a way that made the police suspect he was under the influence of something. An officer followed him and observed a large hunting knife on the floor of the car on the driver's side. At that point the officers frisked Long and then proceeded to search the car for weapons. While conducting this search, police found some marijuana which Long was convicted of possessing. The conviction was overturned by the state courts ruling that *Terry* did not allow police to conduct a protective search of the vehicle for weapons when Long was outside the car in the custody of an officer. The Supreme Court then granted *certiorari*.

The Supreme Court in a majority opinion by Justice O'Connor reversed. The opinion noted that *Terry* did not restrict preventive searches for weapons to the person of the stopped individual. Relying in part on *New York v. Belton*,[117] a case which dealt with the scope of a search incident to a lawful arrest when the arrest was made of a person in an automobile, the Court found that in a *Terry* situation the entire interior compartment and those containers in which a weapon could be secreted could be searched. Furthermore, even if the suspect was in custody of the police and was no longer in the vehicle, an area search of a vehicle would be declared reasonable because "the balancing required by *Terry* clearly weighs in favor of allowing the police to conduct a search of the passenger compartment to uncover weapons, as long as they possess an articulable and objectively reasonable belief that the suspect is potentially dangerous."[118] The decision in *Long* disturbed the *Terry* precedent in two ways. One is that it enlarges the scope of a search for weapons beyond the suspect themselves. Thus, even though the suspect has been isolated from the potential source of danger to the police, the police are allowed to conduct a vehicle search for weapons. The second way in which *Long* disturbed *Terry* was that it relaxed the standard for the search. *Terry* limited frisks to incidents when the police had reasonable articulable beliefs that a suspect was armed and *presently* dangerous, but *Long* allowed police to search vehicles for weapons whenever they had reasonable articulable beliefs that the suspect was armed and *potentially* dangerous. The Court also used *Long* to help clarify whether police had to use the least intrusive means possible to determine if a person was armed and dangerous. The Court explained "we have never required the police to adopt alternative measures to avoid a legitimate *Terry*-type intrusion."[119]

The decision in *Long* accomplished what the Burger Court desired; it redrew the balancing of interests required by *Terry* in favor of effective law enforcement by allowing broader searches in situations that could be potentially dangerous. Due to judicial declarations by lower courts, the ability to automatically frisk has increased to include many situations even when there has been no personal observation by the officer to believe that a person is armed. The types of offenses which are always considered potentially dangerous now include illegal drugs and burglary. The types of persons and situations which are automatically assumed to be dangerous and justifiably lead to frisks in every encounter include companions of arrestees, persons present when police execute a search warrant, people in illegal gambling establishments, persons placed in a squad car, and situations which are bad for police.[120] The standard required for the particularized articulable suspicion that a crime has been or is about to be committed to justify a stop and frisk has also been weakened by the lower courts.

For example, lower courts generally uphold the power of the police to conduct a stop and frisk when a person seems to be in a neighborhood or area in which they don't seemingly "fit." Stop and frisks are also generally upheld if a person is observed in a "high crime" area. Another scenario in which stop and frisks are normally upheld is when police believe that a person tried to avoid contact with police when observed.[121] These later applications of *Terry* have changed it from a technique that protected the safety of police whenever an officer could verify an articulable particularized suspicion of possible criminal activity and a present danger from the suspect, to a blanket doctrine which allows police to automatically frisk an increasing number of categories of people.

Anthony Amsterdam has criticized such an approach stating that without generally applicable rules which police can follow "appellate courts defer to trial courts and trial courts defer to police" thus it will be the police who determine what is reasonable under the Fourth Amendment.[122] *United States v. Place* (1983)[123] provides such an example. *Place* also forced the Court to consider the time limitations of a *Terry* stop. While at the Miami airport, Place came under suspicion of police officers who suspected that he was involved in the drug trade. After questioning Place, he was allowed to board a plane for New York. The police then continued their investigation which further raised their suspicion. They then called DEA agents in New York. When Place arrived in New York, DEA agents observed him. Place aroused their suspicions and was confronted by the agents who sought consent to search his suitcases. Place denied the officers consent and left when told he was not under arrest, but the officers seized the suitcases. Ninety minutes later, the suitcases were subjected to a drug sniffing dog which gave a positive indication of drugs. The suitcase was opened and cocaine was found inside. Place's attempt to have the drugs suppressed at trial failed, but the decision was reversed by the Court of Appeals of the Second Circuit. The Supreme Court then granted *certiorari*.

In its decision in *Place,* the Court's majority opinion by Justice O'Connor started by stating that the seizure of personal property was per se unreasonable without a warrant unless the circumstances fit into one of the exceptions to the warrant requirement and probable cause existed. *Terry v. Ohio* (1968), however, allowed limited investigatory seizures when police had reasonable suspicion to believe a crime had been committed. In such circumstances the Court balanced the competing interests to determine if the seizure is reasonable. The Court then declared that allowing law enforcement agencies to seize property, rather than persons as in *Terry,* when they had a reasonable suspicion, was a natural extension of the general interest in "effective crime prevention and detection" which had been recognized in *Terry.*[124] Even though there was no reason to suspect that the luggage presented a danger to officers, the Court believed that the interest in general law enforcement carried the greater weight when balanced against the intrusiveness of such seizures. Despite these expansions of the *Terry* doctrine, the Court affirmed the decision of the Second Circuit because the length of time which the police seized the suitcase was unreasonable considering the DEA agents knew in advance of Place's arrival in New York that they would need a drug sniffing dog. While finding that *Terry* stop limitations apply to possessions as well as persons, the Court believed that the ninety minute seizure of the luggage was unreasonable. Factored into the Court's decision was the failure of DEA agents to inform Place about where his luggage was and how it would be returned. The Court did not, however, place a specific time limit on *Terry* stops. In fact, the Court rejected the argument that *Terry* stops should be limited to twenty minutes. Instead, Justice O'Connor's opinion explained that such stops should be minimally intrusive, but Courts should be deferential to police when they diligently conducted their investigation.

The Rehnquist Court and *Terry*

The Rehnquist Court continued the law and order approach to the Fourth Amendment and *Terry* stops that had begun during the Burger Court years. *Minnesota v. Dickerson* (1993)[125] provides an example in which the Rehnquist Court upheld the principle that the purpose of stop and frisks is to protect the officer and public by determining if an individual has weapons. In *Dickerson* police observed Dickerson leaving a reputed crack house. When Dickerson saw the police he abruptly changed directions and tried to avoid any contact with the police, raising further police suspicions. When police confronted Dickerson they subjected him to a frisk. The officer who conducted the frisk felt no weapon, but did feel a small lump in Dickerson's pocket. The officer slid, squeezed and manipulated the lump until he was satisfied that it was a rock of crack cocaine whereupon he removed it from Dickerson's pocket only to have his suspicions confirmed. The trial court allowed use of the cocaine at trial and Dickerson was convicted. The conviction was overturned by the Minnesota Court of Appeals and its decision was upheld by the Minnesota State Supreme Court. When Minnesota sought *certiorari* it was granted by the Supreme Court.

The Court in *Minnesota v. Dickerson* found that the crack could not be admitted as evidence because the officer exceeded the allowable scope of a *Terry* search once he determined that the rock of crack could not have been a weapon and continued to manipulate the object in Dickerson's pocket. The Court went on, however, and clarified that when a justifiable search for weapons was made under *Terry* it did not disallow the seizure of nonthreatening contraband items when they were discovered through the plain feel of the officer. The Court argued that the "very premise of *Terry*, after all, is that officers will be able to detect the presence of weapons through the sense of touch and *Terry* upheld precisely such a seizure."[126]

While the Court may grant deference to the observations of police when conducting a *Terry* stop, its willingness to grant such deference when police conduct a stop based on an anonymous tip has been mixed. In *Alabama v. White* (1990)[127] the Court found that an anonymous tip which could be corroborated by the observation of officers did constitute reasonable suspicion. In that case, the suspect followed a particular series of specific activities which had been described in the tip as police had the suspect under observation. In *Florida v. J.L* (2000)[128] a unanimous Court, with an opinion written by Justice Ruth Bader Ginsberg, ruled that an anonymous tip which has no corroboration cannot serve as the basis for a *Terry* stop. The case came to the Court after police had received an anonymous tip that a young African-American male standing at a specific bus stop and wearing a plaid shirt would have a gun on his person. Police acted on the tip, frisked a youth who was wearing a plaid shirt and found a gun. After the trial court suppressed the gun in a decision eventually supported by the Florida Supreme Court, it came to the United States Supreme Court. Justice Ginsberg's opinion found that the tip lacked the necessary indications of reliability needed to create the reasonable suspicion to justify a stop. The real problem with the tip was that it contained no predictive information that would allow police to determine the reliability of the information. The mere fact that the stop wielded a gun as the tip predicted could not be taken into consideration because reasonable suspicion must exist prior to a stop. It is the knowledge of the police prior to a stop that determines whether the stop was justified, not the fruits of the stop.

Reasonableness in Non-*Terry* Stop Contexts

The language used in the opinions of *Camara* and *Terry* opened the door for possible wider uses of the reasonableness approach to the Fourth Amendment beyond administrative searches and investigatory stops. The ability to apply a reasonableness approach to non-*Terry* stop cases had previously been demonstrated by Justice Minton in *Rabinowitz*. Due to the efforts of the majority of the Warren Court, such an approach was rejected in favor of the cardinal principle that searches without a warrant were *per se* unreasonable unless the situation fit into one of the well delineated exceptions. Even though the Warren Court itself rejected broadening the reasonableness approach, its opinions had opened the door for other justices and courts to do so. By balancing the interest of the government to advance effective law enforcement against an individual's liberty interest the Warren Court in *Terry* created the opportunity for more conservative courts to reach a balance which put even more weight on the need to advance effective law enforcement. Such an approach would allow full blown searches and seizures in incidents when there was no probable cause and in some instances even when there was no individualized suspicion which pointed at a particular suspect. The Burger, Rehnquist, and Roberts Courts have accepted the reasonableness approach in their opinions. One of the first members of the Burger Court to advance this approach was Justice William Rehnquist. As early as 1979 in *Delaware v. Prouse,* Justice Rehnquist in a dissenting opinion argued that random suspicionless spot searches of individuals in automobiles for license and registration checks were not unreasonable. In 1981, in another dissent, Justice Rehnquist attacked the warrant requirement.[129] This was followed up with his dissent in the 1983 case of *Florida v. Royers* in which he advocated an ad hoc test of general reasonableness to be the standard in all search and seizure cases.

A majority of the Court endorsed the reasonableness approach in 1985 with *New Jersey v. T.L.O.* (1985).[130] This case came to the Court after a teacher witnessed T.L.O., who was fourteen, and another girl violating school rules by smoking in the restroom. The girls were taken to the office of the Assistant Vice-Principal, Theodore Choplick. When T.L.O. claimed that she didn't smoke, Choplick took her purse and opened it, finding a pack of cigarettes. While looking in the purse he also saw a package of rolling papers which he associated with marijuana use. He decided to continue his search of the purse and discovered a small amount of marijuana, a pipe, empty plastic bags, a large number of one-dollar bills, some notes seemingly listing students who owed her money, and two letters implicating her in selling marijuana. At her delinquency hearing, T.L.O. sought to have all the evidence discovered by Choplick suppressed claiming that its discovery came through a violation of the Fourth Amendment.

After granting *certiorari,* the Court rejected the view that the Fourth Amendment should not apply in schools because school officials were not law enforcement officials. Justice White, who wrote the majority opinion, refused to accept the State's argument that the doctrine of *in loco parentis* allowed school officials to act as parents and conduct warrentless searches. The opinion also found flawed the argument put forward by the State that students should maintain their privacy interest in personal private property by just leaving the property at home. The reason was students found it necessary to bring a wide variety of items to school and since not all of it was contraband they shouldn't be expected to give up all their privacy interests simply by being in a school environment. Despite this, the Court upheld the ability of a school official to conduct a warrantless search of a student's purse to try to find evidence of a school violation. The Court thought it appropriate to balance the pupil's legitimate expectation of privacy against "the substantial interest of teachers and administrators in maintaining discipline in the classroom and on school grounds."[131] In drawing a balance, the Court found that "It is evident that the school setting requires some easing of the restrictions to which searches by public authorities are ordinarily subject."[132]

Despite stressing the importance to maintain Fourth Amendment oversight of the actions of school officials, Justice White, relying on *Camara* and *Terry,* wrote that the foundation of the Fourth Amendment was that all searches must be reasonable, and that while "the concept of probable cause and the requirement of a warrant bear on the reasonableness of a search, . . . in certain limited circumstances neither is required."[133] Justice White ruled that schools were one place where the concepts were not required. School searches would be legal if they were deemed reasonable and the Court borrowed directly from *Terry* for a standard of understanding reasonableness:

> Determining the reasonableness of any search involves a twofold inquiry: first, one must consider "whether the . . . action was justified at its inception;" second, one must determine whether the search as actually conducted "was reasonably related in scope to the circumstances, which justified the interference in the first place." Under ordinary circumstances a search of a student by a teacher or other school official will be "justified at its inception" when there are reasonable grounds for suspecting that the search will turn up evidence that the student has violated or is violating either the law or the rules of the school. Such a search will be permissible in its scope when the measures adopted are reasonably related to the objectives of the search and not excessively intrusive in light of the age and sex of the student and the nature of the infraction.[134]

In applying this standard to the facts of *T.L.O.* the Court found that Choplick's search of T.L.O.'s purse was reasonable and did not constitute a Fourth Amendment violation. Central to a finding that Choplick's actions were justified was the individualized suspicion which centered on T.L.O. which triggered the entire process.

Justice Blackmun wrote a concurring opinion in *T.L.O.* that has proven to be influential in subsequent cases. In his opinion Justice Blackmun advanced the view that the reasonableness standard was appropriate in cases in which the government had "special needs" that went beyond the normal needs of law enforcement. Such circumstances existed in *T.L.O.* because "The special need for an immediate response to behavior that threatens either the safety of schoolchildren and teachers or the educational process itself justifies the Court in excepting school searches from the warrant and probable-cause requirement. . . ."[135] One of the reasons why Justice Blackmun's opinion has become influential is that it does not specify what constitutes other possible special need situations. Thus, it establishes a flexible concept which provides no unifying principle to explain exactly when exceptional circumstances and special needs will make the warrant provision and probable cause impracticable and allow the balancing of the interests. It also does not hint at what may constitute the special needs of government outside of the school environment.

Justices Brennan, Stevens, and Marshall dissented in *T.L.O.* because they believed the Court unnecessarily departed from the probable cause standard. Their position was that full blown searches, such as that of the purse in this case, have historically required probable cause to be legitimate under the Fourth Amendment. They saw no reason not to apply the standard in this case.

Both the dissenters in *New Jersey v. T.L.O.* and commentators at the time concentrated their comments on the inappropriateness of ignoring the probable cause standard in favor of the reasonableness standard in the school environment.[136] In doing so they missed the broader importance of the case by not discussing the possibility that the reasonableness standard which was enunciated by the majority could be applied to a broader variety of situations outside of school systems. The balancing approach of the Court in *T.L.O.* was not novel. As has been demonstrated by examining the *Terry* stop cases, balancing became commonplace after *Camara* and *Terry*. What is different about *T.L.O.* is that it allowed a full blown search without probable cause being present. It also moved beyond *Terry*, as had *United States v. Place*, by allowing the scope of the search to move beyond weapons to become a general search for related evidence.

The Special Needs Test

President Ronald Reagan's decision to elevate William Rehnquist to the position of Chief Justice after the retirement of Warren Burger in 1986 facilitated the Court's trend of allowing a wider variety of searches to be found reasonable under the Fourth Amendment. President Reagan followed Richard Nixon's pattern of placing law and order oriented justices on the Court. All of his appointments which included Justice Sandra Day O'Connor, Justice Antonin Scalia, and Justice Anthony Kennedy would come to accept a reasonableness approach to the Fourth Amendment. Justice Scalia endorsed the reasonableness approach in *California v. Acevedo* (1991)[137] where he stated: "The Fourth Amendment does not by its terms require a prior search warrant for searches and seizures; it merely prohibits searches and seizures that are 'unreasonable.'"[138] Justice Scalia continued, "the supposed 'general rule' that a warrant is always required does not appear to have any basis in common law . . . and confuses rather than facilitates any attempt to develop rules of reasonableness."[139] Justice Scalia has also complained that the Court took on too many Fourth Amendment cases noting, "I think we can tolerate a fair degree of diversity in what courts determine to be reasonable seizures."[140] Justice O'Connor voiced her support for a reasonableness approach to the Fourth Amendment in her majority opinion in *O'Connor v. Ortega* (1987).[141] Justice Kennedy came out in favor of a reasonableness approach in his majority opinion in *National Treasury Employees Union v. Von Raab* (1989).[142]

President George H. W. Bush's two appointments to the Supreme Court have both accepted a reasonableness approach to the Fourth Amendment. Justice David Souter wrote an opinion which indicated acceptance of the reasonableness approach in *Georgia v. Randolph* (2006),[143] although he found that the search in that case was not reasonable. Justice Clarence Thomas has been one the Court's most supportive votes for the reasonableness approach as demonstrated in his opinion in *Board of Education v. Earls* (2002).[144] Both of President William Jefferson Clinton's appointments, Justices Ruth Bader Ginsburg and Stephen Breyer, voiced support for the reasonableness approach to the Fourth Amendment in *Vernonia School District 47J v. Acton.*[145]

Since *New Jersey v. T.L.O.* the reasonableness approach has been applied to an increasing number of instances in which the Fourth Amendment is relevant to a factual situation, but where the Court believes the governmental interests outweigh individual interests. The inability of the Court to provide any specific methods by which to determine what weight privacy interest versus governmental interest would be given has meant that the reasonableness approach has been built on a slippery slope rather than bedrock. Since *New Jersey v. T.L.O.* the Court has expanded the settings in which governmental searches or seizures are reasonable due to the government's special needs. Under the special needs approach to the Fourth Amendment, the government is allowed to search and seize without a warrant or probable cause, but the purpose of the search cannot be to advance the normal needs of law enforcement. When the Court applies the special needs test it balances the importance of the governmental interest served by the search or seizure against the intrusion that it has on a person's expectation of privacy. In doing so it attempts to ensure that the government will not treat people in an arbitrary manner by limiting the government's use of discretion. The Court has broadened the special needs which allow the government to bypass warrants in a number of ways. These include broadening what the Court perceives to be vital governmental functions, expanding on the need for government efficiency in these areas, and dropping concerns that individualized suspicion be a component of reasonableness.

In *O'Connor v. Ortega* (1987)[146] the new governmental special need that justified searching a governmental employee's desk for a work related offense was ensuring that public agencies were operated in an effective and efficient manner. In a plurality opinion, Justice O'Connor, emphasized that the search was conducted by a supervisor, not law enforcement officials, at the place of employment. She stated that even though an employee might have an expectation of privacy in their office, society would not be willing to respect it. The opinion found that when there are claims of impropriety in the workplace, intrusions, such as searches, which do intrude on constitutionally protected privacy interests, should be judged by the "standard of reasonableness under all the circumstances."[147] When applying the standard of reasonableness the Court noted that the warrant requirement isn't appropriate when the warrant is likely to "frustrate the governmental purpose behind the search."[148] Justice Scalia who provided the fifth vote for the outcome did not accept the special needs analysis of the plurality. He found that searches of government offices for work-related materials are reasonable and do not violate the Fourth Amendment. While remanding this case to determine if the search of the employee's desk was reasonable since there were grounds to believe that it would turn up evidence of work related misconduct, the Court went on and found that the public expectation in efficient governmental operations created the special needs to justify both investigative searches when there were suspicions of employee misconduct and noninvestigative searches when a supervisor found it necessary to search an employee's work area for reasons related to the operation of the workplace.

The next use of special needs test which applied the reasonableness standard came in *Griffin v. Wisconsin* (1987).[149] In *Griffin* the Court upheld a state regulation that allowed the homes of probationers to be searched when there was a reasonable basis for believing that such a search would result in finding contraband or behavior involving misconduct. Despite ruling that "a probationer's home, like anyone else's, is protected by the Fourth Amendment's requirement that searches be 'reasonable'" the Court went on and ruled that the special need of maintaining a probation system justified the departure from the probable cause standard.[150] In explaining what justifies the use of the reasonableness standard when special needs exist, Justice Scalia said in *Griffin* that all of these cases involved searches in which there was "an ongoing supervisory relationship—and one that is not, or at least not entirely, adversarial—between the object of the search and the decision-maker."[151] *Griffin* was the first case in which the Court used the reasonableness standard to allow a search of an individual's home without probable cause. The majority rejected requiring a warrant in this situation because it believed that it would have interfered with the probation system, slowed down the probation officer's ability to respond quickly to reports of a probation violation, and reduced the deterrent effect that such expedited searches would have on probationers. The Court also found that there was a special governmental need to protect the community from the danger posed by probationers. Felons, given their probation status, the Court added, have a lesser expectation of privacy than other citizens. The Court in *United States v. Knights* (2001)[152] went still further and found that states could require people to give consent to suspicionless and warrantless searches as a condition for being released on probation.

The Court first used the special needs rationale to justify a search which lacked individualized suspicion in *New York v. Burger* (1987).[153] This case came to the Court's attention due to a New York law which allowed police to conduct suspicionless searches of automobile salvage yards and related businesses. After Burger's business was searched in pursuance of the statute, stolen property was uncovered and he was convicted. He challenged the constitutionality of the law. The Court found no Fourth Amendment violations. Justice Blackmun's opinion relied on the fact that the auto salvage business was a pervasively regulated industry. Therefore, those in the business had a lower expectation of privacy. This lower expectation of privacy made it reasonable to conduct routine property inspections. Furthermore, "as in other situations of 'special need,' . . . where the privacy interests in regulating particular businesses are concomitantly heightened, a warrantless inspection of commercial premises may well be reasonable within the meaning of the Fourth Amendment."[154] The Court explained that the warrantless searches of closely regulated businesses would be allowed if three factors existed. The first was that the government had to demonstrate a substantial governmental interest to justify the inspection. In this case, stopping traffic in stolen car parts. The second factor was that the government had to show that the inspections were necessary to further the regulatory scheme. Third, the government had to show its inspection program provided "a constitutionally adequate substitute for a warrant" by including provisions which adequately informed business owners that they were subject to inspections under the law.[155] *Burger* again broadened the special needs rationale. It did so by allowing, for the first time, a search to be conducted by law enforcement officials versus other types of governmental employees to be found reasonable. Furthermore, the special need of closely regulating the auto salvage industry is, unlike previous cases involving special needs, directly related to ferreting out criminal conduct.

In *National Treasury Employees Union v. Von Raab* (1989) and *Skinner v. Railway Labor Executives' Association* (1989),[156] decided on the same day, the Court found a special need for drug testing of employees without a warrant due to its reasonableness. In doing so, the Court, for the first time, found the suspicionless search of a person to be reasonable. Historically, individualized suspicion had been central to whether a search violated the Fourth Amendment. Individualized suspicion limits the discretion of the government to conduct searches by performing a gate keeping function. A policy based on no suspicion, no search, combated the ability of the government to engage in arbitrary searches where it had no evidence to believe a crime had been committed or that a particular individual had been involved. Individualized suspicion also limited the scope of searches by requiring that intrusions by the government be rationally related to the circumstances which justified the search.

One of the things that triggered the *Von Raab* and *Skinner* cases was President Reagan's decision to issue Executive Order No. 12,564. It explained that use of illegal drugs both on and off the job resulted in lost productivity and increased risk to public health, safety, and national security. It further noted that people who use illegal drugs are more likely to engage in crime and other forms of irresponsible behavior. It drew the conclusion that people who used illegal drugs were unfit for federal employment. It ordered all executive agencies to test all new job applicants for illegal drug use, to determine which jobs involved sensitive positions, and develop a program by which to test employees who held those positions. The result of the Executive Order was that by 1988 forty-two federal agencies had initiated testing procedures for their own employees as well as employees in regulated private industries such as railroads, airlines, the merchant marines, and pipeline construction.

In *Von Raab* the Commissioner of the United States Customs Service, a bureau within the Department of Treasury, established a policy to conduct a drug test of any employee promoted to a position where they would carry a firearm, be directly involved in drug interdiction, or have access to classified materials. Customs agents who failed the test and could not explain why to the satisfaction of the bureau were subject to dismissal, although the test results could not be shared with any other agency or law enforcement organization. The National Treasury Employees Union challenged the policy for violating the Fourth Amendment because the drug tests were not based on probable cause or individualized suspicion.

Although the Court in *Von Raab* recognized that the drug tests were searches under the Fourth Amendment, it rejected the claims of the union and found no constitutional violation. It did so by applying the special needs test and using a reasonableness approach based on balancing. The Court, through an opinion by Justice Kennedy, explained that normally individualized suspicion was required for a reasonable search to exist. However, when special governmental needs are present reasonableness is determined by balancing the individual's expectation of privacy against the need of the government to take measures beyond normal law enforcement techniques to ensure that its special needs are met. There were a number of special needs in this case which allowed the government to bypass the warrant and probable cause requirements. These included protecting public safety from custom agents who used drugs and carried weapons, protecting the integrity of the customs bureau, and insuring that customs agents had the physical fitness and judgment for the job.

The balance in this case tilted in favor of the governmental policy for a number of reasons. First, the Court believed that obtaining a warrant would divert important governmental resources from the bureau's primary mission. Furthermore, the drug tests were administrative in nature, not criminal, so the probable cause standard was not appropriate. Other administrative searches had shown that suspicionless searches were acceptable to prevent, not detect, hidden conditions that posed a threat to the general public. The drug testing of customs agents was acceptable given that those agents involved in drug interdiction were subject to contact with criminals which created the potential for corruption. Likewise, those agents who carried weapons presented a potential danger to other individuals. The Court ruled that the potential these dangers posed carried more weight than the privacy expectations of agents. This was because as the Court had ruled in previous cases, "the 'operational realities of the workplace' may render reasonable certain work-related intrusions by supervisors and co-workers that might be viewed as unreasonable in other contexts."[157] As a result, those individuals who applied for these jobs had lessened expectations of privacy. That was because they should expect the government to investigate their mental and physical fitness for the positions. Not only did the Court in *Von Raab* accept suspicionless searches, it found such searches justified even though the government had not demonstrated that drug use was a problem within the Customs Service. This was because the Court found that the drug testing procedures advanced the special needs of the government by both detecting drug use, if it existed, and by deterring possible future drug use. The Court remanded to the lower court to determine if the testing of agents who handled classified materials was reasonable.

Justice Scalia dissented in *Von Raab* because he was bothered by the fact that there was no factual record to indicate that there was widespread drug use by customs agents. He was also bothered by the breadth of the opinion and pointed out that if one extrapolated on the reasoning of the Court, it would allow for drug testing of many more groups of people within our society. Examples could include anyone whose job required carrying a firearm, or any person whose performance might endanger others such as construction workers, school crossing guards, and all people who drive vehicles.

Building on both *Burger* and *Von Raab* the Court decided *Skinner v. Railway Labor Executives' Association*. *Skinner* came to the Court when the Federal Railroad Administration issued a regulation which required drug testing of a railroad employee's blood, breath, and urine when he or she or the crew a person was on was involved in a train accident in which someone died, there was release of hazardous material which resulted in an evacuation, there was property damage of at least $500,000, or a reportable injury. It also gave railroad officials discretion to order a drug test after some rule violations or when a supervisor reasonably believed that someone was impaired by drug usage. The regulation was challenged by the Railway Labor Executive's Association who sued Samuel Skinner, the Secretary of Transportation.

The Court in an opinion by Justice Kennedy found that the drug tests triggered the protection of the Fourth Amendment because they intruded on the integrity of the bodies of railroad employees, violated their personal dignity, and revealed their private medical facts. Because the drug tests constituted searches the Court then suggested that the policy could not withstand traditional scrutiny. Despite announcing a preference for warrants, the Court went on and found that it was unnecessary to apply the traditional standard for the Fourth Amendment. This was because special governmental needs existed to ensure railroad safety and protect society from possible drug abuse within the railroad industry. The governmental needs were special because, as in schools and other regulated industries, they did not involve normal law enforcement needs. Furthermore, the government's desire to promote railroad safety would only be frustrated by the warrant requirement. Therefore, the proper standard of scrutiny to apply was reasonableness. The Court was so comfortable in *Skinner* with the reasonableness standard for the Fourth Amendment that it omitted the probable cause clause of the Fourth Amendment when it quoted the amendment. Once the Court rejected use of the warrant requirement it noted that the drug tests were also not bound by the probable cause standard. In fact, drug tests did not require a "Quantum of individualized suspicion."[158] Justice Kennedy justified this stating:

> In limited circumstances, where the privacy interests implicated by the search are minimal, and where an important governmental interest furthered by the intrusion would be placed in jeopardy by a requirement of individualized suspicion, a search may be reasonable despite the absence of such suspicion. We believe this is true of the intrusions in question here.[159]

Applying the reasonableness standard the Court had no problem, despite the lack of individualized suspicion required by the program, accepting the part of the regulation involving blood testing which it compared to the mandatory blood tests for people suspected of driving while intoxicated. It found it even easier to rule in favor of breath tests which involved less bodily invasion than the blood tests. The Court was bothered by the urine tests due to the greater privacy interests at stake. Despite these concerns, Justice Kennedy noted that providing a urine sample, unlike a blood test, involved no penetration of the body nor did it have to be directly observed by another person. Furthermore, the Court pointed out that the procedures adopted in the regulations tried to limit the intrusiveness of the urine tests as much as possible and therefore ruled in favor of the policy. Overall, the Court found the drug testing program was acceptable because personal expectations of privacy were diminished in such a widely regulated industry. Balancing the reduced privacy expectation of the railroad worker against what the Court called the compelling governmental interest of insuring railroad safety led the Court to favor the governmental interest. The Court added that using a tougher standard such as requiring a warrant or individualized suspicion would impede the government's ability to both detect and deter drug use among railroad employees.

Justice Marshall dissented in *Skinner*. He noted his disappointment that in its zeal to combat drug abuse the majority had discarded the heart of the Fourth Amendment, the warrant and probable cause requirements, as being impractical in favor of a flexible special needs approach that relied on a balancing of interests to determine if a search was reasonable. Justice Marshall pointed out that this case was different from previous cases which had used a balancing approach because it involved the direct search of a person, not their possessions. It also allowed use of the special needs rationale to justify a search when there was no individualized suspicion. Tying together his reasoning Justice Marshall chided the majority stating: "Constitutional requirements like probable cause are not fair-weather friends, present when advantageous, conveniently absent when 'special needs' make them seem not."[160]

The impact of *Von Raab* and *Skinner* was that it once again enlarged the Court's view of what constitutes a special need of government to include maintaining the integrity of customs agents and expanding safety of the rail system. The rationale of Justice Kennedy's opinion, like that of Chief Justice Warren's in *Terry*, used a flexibility that invited further expansion. It invites an unlimited use of future governmental claims to special needs and the Court applying the balancing approach of reasonableness. The lower courts have followed the lead and ruled that other heavily regulated industries are subject to employee drug testing including the trucking and shipping industries. Other jobs with special needs related to safety have included "nuclear power plant employees, firefighters, hazardous material inspectors, aircraft mechanics, pilots, air traffic controllers, . . . school bus attendants, airline attendants, and government motor vehicle operators."[161] What further sets *Van Rabb* and *Skinner* apart from earlier cases in which the Court had applied the reasonableness standard was that the Court dropped individualized suspicion as a necessary component of the reasonableness decision for a search of an individual, rather than a business. Although the Court had in the previous year in *Michigan Department of State Police v. Sitz* allowed the brief seizure of an individual without suspicion in drug checkpoints, *Van Rabb* and *Skinner* were the first time that the Court allowed the search of a person without individualized suspicion.

In the case of *Vernonia School District 47J v. Acton* (1995)[162] the application of the reasonableness approach of the Fourth Amendment returned to the school environment where the special needs rationale was first mentioned in Justice Blackmun's concurring opinion in *T.L.O.* This time the Court concentrated on a suspicionless drug testing program. *Acton* came to the Court as a result of the Vernonia School District initiating a policy which included mandatory and random drug testing of student athletes. The school district announced the policy after it had noticed an increase in student drug use and concurring disciplinary problems. The school believed that its athletes were the primary drug abusers and thought that their drug use could lead to injuries and possibly increased drug use among other students who looked up to the athletes. The policy required every student who wanted to participate in athletics to sign a form authorizing the district to perform a drug test on their urine at the beginning of each sport season in which they participated. During the season, athletes would randomly be tested on a weekly basis. According to the policy, the student would complete the urine test while a faculty member of the same sex monitored the process to ensure that there was no tampering. The results of the test would be released to the superintendent, principals, vice-principals, and athletic directors. When a student tested positive a second test would be administered and if it was positive, the student could exercise the following options. First, they could participate in a drug counseling program for six weeks and continue to undergo weekly drug testing. Second, the student could accept a suspension from athletics for that season and the entire following season. James Acton, a seventh grader in the district, refused to sign the consent form before joining the football team. James and his parents then challenged the policy arguing that the policy violated the Fourth Amendment since there was no evidence that James used drugs. The district court found the policy to be reasonable. The court of appeals reversed and the school district was granted *certiorari*.

In a 6-3 decision the majority of the Court, through an opinion by Justice Scalia found in favor of the school district. The Court ruled that because there were special needs to protect kids from the harm caused by drugs that went beyond normal law enforcement the warrant and probable cause requirements were impractical. As in other special needs cases, the constitutionality of the search was dependant on assessing the reasonableness of the search by balancing the privacy interest of the individual against the governmental interest. The Court found two factors which limited the privacy interest in this case. First, in reasoning that seemed to move away from the decision in *T.L.O.* when the Court found that schools do not act *in loco parentis* to students, the Court found that the individuals involved were children and were under the temporary custody of the state while they were in school. As a result, they only held an expectation of privacy which was appropriate for children in a school which acted as guardian and tutor. Second, student athletes had a lesser expectation of privacy due to the fact that they shared locker rooms and were required to have pre-season physicals. In examining the intrusiveness of providing a urine sample Justice Scalia backed off his view in *Von Rabb* that the procedure was "particularly destructive of privacy and offensive to personal dignity" and instead noted that it was a relatively unobtrusive procedure.[163] Justice Scalia also noted that students voluntarily participated in athletics in a way that made it comparable to a closely regulated industry. Finally, the Court noted that because so few school officials had access to the results of the test the invasion of privacy was lessened.

After examining the privacy interest, the Court examined the governmental interest. The Court found that it was unnecessary for the school to have a compelling interest to justify the program. Despite this, it found that preventing the harmful psychological and physical effects of drugs created an important governmental interest that was nearly compelling. The opinion concentrated on how the program only tested student athletes and noted that the risks of harm to them through sports related injury was particularly high. It also noted that the scope of the program was appropriately aimed at athletes because school officials had found them to be a larger part of the problem and because they were role models for other students. Comparing the two interests which had to be balanced the Court ruled that the drug testing program was reasonable and did not violate the Fourth Amendment. The Court also noted that suspicionless searches would be less intrusive on the rights of individuals and better advance the goals of the government than would suspicion based searches.

The line of cases from *T.L.O.* through *Acton* resulted in an unbroken series

Justice O'Connor dissented and pointed out that in the past suspicionless searches had only been approved when it was "clear that a suspicion-based regime would be ineffectual."[164] This decision, the dissent pointed out, would give approval to conducting an intrusive bodily search on millions of student athletes who were not suspected of using drugs. The dissent reminded the majority that this was reminiscent of the general blanket searches that the framers of the Fourth Amendment had meant to stop. Justice O'Connor unsuccessfully urged the Court to require suspicion to be a necessary precondition for lawful searches.

The line of cases from *T.L.O.* through *Acton* resulted in an unbroken series of cases in which the Court accepted the special needs analysis of the Fourth Amendment. In these cases the Court ruled that when a special need was present, reasonableness would be determined by balancing an individual's privacy interest against the competing governmental interests. The Court's seeming willingness to accept a growing variety of searches as being outside the warrant and probable cause requirements in this series of cases made the special needs analysis of the Fourth Amendment a subject of scholarly attention.[165]

It wasn't until 1997 when the Court decided *Chandler v. Miller*[166] that the Court failed to uphold a search when a governmental special need was claimed. *Chandler v. Miller* came to the Court as a result of a 1990 Georgia state law which required drug testing of candidates for state offices. The law stated that in order for candidates to qualify for the ballot they had to be able to certify that they had been proven to be drug free 30 days prior to be being placed on either a primary or general election ballot. Candidates were given their choice of providing a urine specimen at a state approved laboratory or going to their personal physician and providing a sample which would then be sent to an approved lab. The specimen was then tested for five drugs. If the sample tested positive and the individual chose not to file and run for office, the results would not be given to law enforcement agencies. In 1994 the law was challenged by Walker Chandler, the Libertarian Party candidate for lieutenant governor. The U.S. district court and the court of appeals both ruled that law did not violate the Constitution. Chandler was then granted *certiorari*.

In an 8-1 decision, with an opinion written by Justice Ginsburg, the Court overruled the lower courts and found that the Georgia law violated the Fourth

Amendment. The opinion reviewed the special needs balancing test coming out of the Court's prior cases involving drug testing, but never used it to reach its decision. This was because the Court changed its definition of what constituted a special need. Prior to *Chandler*, the Court had found that a special need existed anytime that a governmental function or goal was outside of normal law enforcement concerns. In *Chandler* the Court established a new judicial standard for special needs. According to this standard, unless the governmental interests that a drug testing policy was created to protect are important or substantial enough, the procedure is unreasonable and unconstitutional. As defined by Justice Ginsburg the interest had to be substantial enough "to override the individual's acknowledged privacy interest, sufficiently vital to suppress the Fourth Amendment's normal requirement of individualized suspicion."[167] When the Court applied this standard it found that the Georgia law failed due to four principle weaknesses. The first was that the record failed to show that there was a history of drug abuse among state officials. Second, the Court also noted that the law was not an efficient method of either combating drug use by elected officials or deterring candidates who used drugs since they controlled when they would be tested. Another weakness in the law was that the elected offices covered by the law were not safety-sensitive positions. The final weakness was that drug testing was not necessary for public officials since they are "subject to relentless scrutiny—by their peers, the public, and the press."[168] The Court believed that the only interest advanced by the state law was for candidates to serve as good examples for others in the community.

Chief Justice Rehnquist used his dissent in *Chandler* to point out that in previous special needs cases the term did not refer to especially important governmental goals, only ones that were outside of normal law enforcement concerns. If his understanding of special needs was used in this case, as he urged, the Georgia law would stand up to scrutiny because insuring that elected office seekers are drug free is a special need of the government.

The decision in *Chandler* changed the jurisprudence of special needs. Prior to *Chandler*, special needs were used when the Court believed that the search fell outside the normal needs of law enforcement. Special needs provided a rationale for not applying the warrant or probable cause requirements of the Fourth Amendment. As a result, the only other consideration the Court had to make was whether the search was reasonable when the Court balanced the privacy interests against the interests of the state. In reaching a balance, the governmental interest did not have to be compelling, only of sufficient importance to outweigh the privacy interest. After *Chandler*, the governmental goals that triggered special needs analysis had to be important or substantial. Another change in special needs jurisprudence noticeable in *Chandler* concerns the need for governmental drug testing policies to be efficient. In *Chandler* the Court ruled that one of the flaws with the Georgia law was that it would be inefficient at accomplishing its goal because it was "not well designed to identify candidates who violate antidrug laws. Nor is the scheme a credible means to deter illicit drug users from seeking election to state office."[169]

The Court's unwillingness to accept every claim of governmental special needs continued in *Ferguson v. Charleston* (2001).[170] In this case, the Medical University of South Carolina (MUSC) reacted to a perceived increase in babies which were born to mothers who used crack cocaine by creating a policy to screen the urine of pregnant mothers. The policy had provisions which encouraged women who tested positive to receive treatment. It gave added incentive to get treatment by providing the threat that if patients did not, law enforcement officials would be notified. The last part of the policy then explained the procedures that law enforcement officials should take when they were notified of individual drug abusers. The policy was challenged by ten women who had received medical care at MUSC and who were arrested after testing positive for cocaine. The women claimed that the policy violated the Fourth Amendment. MUSC responded that the petitioners had consented to the drug tests and if that was not the case, the searches were reasonable because they were justified by special non-law enforcement needs. At trial the jury found that consent for the searches had been given. The case was eventually granted review by the U.S. Supreme Court.

In *Ferguson* the majority of the Court found that the drug testing did violate the Fourth Amendment. Justice Stevens wrote the majority opinion. In it the Court assumed that the women who brought suit had not consented to the urine test which the Court considered to be a search under the Fourth Amendment. The issue before the Court was then narrowed to whether there were special needs existing which allowed the government, acting through a state medical facility, to bypass probable cause requirements. In his discussion of whether a special need existed, Justice Stevens distinguished *Ferguson* from previous special needs cases involving drug testing in several ways. The first was that the Court pointed out that in *Ferguson* different use was made of these drug tests than in prior cases. In this case, the patients assumed they were getting routine medical care for pregnancy not knowing that the results would possibly be turned over to law enforcement officials. Related to this, in the prior cases there had been precautions not to disseminate the results to third parties. In *Ferguson*, however, the results were immediately handed over to third parties. Another thing that distinguished *Ferguson* from previous cases was that in *Ferguson* the women receiving treatment had a reasonable expectation of privacy that the results of their test would not be shared with others. The critical difference between *Ferguson* and previous "special needs" cases was, however, that in all the previous cases the special need fell outside of normal law enforcement needs. In *Ferguson* law enforcement played a central role in the overall program since the threat of law enforcement provided the incentive for expectant mothers to enter rehabilitation programs. The Court therefore believed that even though the main goal of the program may have been to improve the health of the women involved in the program, the immediate goal was gathering information for law enforcement purposes. The Court found that this immediate goal had to be its first consideration in determining the constitutionality of the program since the ultimate goal of almost all police actions is to advance some societal good.

Justice Scalia, joined by Chief Justice Rehnquist and Justice Thomas, dissented because they believed that the defendants, who had been given medical care, consented to the urinalysis which was the foundation of the search. Even if consent had not been given they would have allowed the use of the urinalysis because they thought that a special need was present. They did this by distinguishing the ultimate purpose of the urinalysis, to protect infant and maternal health, and the immediate purpose, to obtain evidence that incriminated patients at the medical center. The dissent went on and argued that the ultimate purpose of the urinalysis trumped the immediate purpose and created a special need under the Fourth Amendment.

One year after *Ferguson* it became clear that the Court was not ready to abandon the special needs approach to the Fourth Amendment. The case, *Board of Education v. Earls* (2002),[171] once again involved the role of the Fourth Amendment in America's schools. As in *Acton* the Court was examining a drug testing program. This time it was one that applied to all students who wanted to participate in any extracurricular activity. The policy adopted by the School District of Tecumseh, Oklahoma required students to submit to a drug test prior to participating in any extracurricular activity. It used continued random testing, and testing any time there was reasonable suspicion. Earls, a student in the district, challenged the policy which was upheld by the district court, but overturned by the court of appeals. The Supreme Court then granted *certiorari*.

The Supreme Court, splitting 5-4 in an opinion by Justice Thomas, reversed and found the testing program to be within the Fourth Amendment. The Court found that schools need not meet the probable cause standard of the Fourth Amendment because such a standard would "unduly interfere with the maintenance of the swift and informal disciplinary procedures needed" in schools.[172] Due to the important safety concerns of school officials they could bypass probable cause standards when there are special needs. In a move which reinforced *Acton*, but again seems at odds with *T.L.O.*, the Court found that the public school environment created a special need because school officials have "custodial and tutelary responsibility for children."[173]

After finding a special need, Justice Thomas went on and applied the balancing test which had been used in *Acton*. The opinion found that a student's privacy interest is limited within the public school environment because the state is responsible for maintaining discipline, health, and safety within the school. The Court then examined the intrusion created by the policy and found the method by which urine samples were collected to be minimally intrusive and even less intrusive than the procedures used in *Acton*. Furthermore, the Court noted that results were never made known to law enforcement officials and it wasn't until the third failed test that a student was suspended from extracurricular activities. After examining the privacy expectations of students and the invasion on that privacy, the Court turned to a determination of the importance of the governmental interests. The Court found that the nationwide drug epidemic combined with specific evidence that there was drug usage within the school district were of sufficient weight to override the privacy interests of students. In a message to other school districts the Court emphasized the existence of the governmental interest by noting that it would be wrong to read *Acton* to require a pervasive drug problem in a school before drug testing policies could pass scrutiny. The Court also noted that the policy the school board had put together was a reasonably effective means of attacking the drug problem.

Justice Ginsburg wrote a dissent which sought to distinguish *Earls* from *Acton* due to the presence of the lesser privacy expectations for student athletes, the connection between safety when drug use and physical activity were combined, and the lack of a major drug problem being present in the Tecumseh schools.

With *Acton* and *Earls* the reasonableness approach that was announced in *T.L.O.* was again applied in schools. By the time that those cases were decided it was a much different standard than had been applied in *T.L.O.* The reasonableness standard as applied in *T.L.O.* was a direct descendent of *Terry v. Ohio* in which the reasonableness of a search was dependent on two things. First, the action had to be justified at its inception by school officials having reasonable grounds to suspect the student had violated either school rules or the law. Second, whether the search was reasonably related in scope to the justification for the search. By the time of *Acton* and *Earl* the reasonableness approach is closer to *Camara* than *Terry*. This is because it no longer included the necessity of individualized suspicion which had previously been the trigger for the application of reasonableness. Instead, the trigger which is necessary to apply the reasonableness approach is the Court's finding that the government has substantial special needs that go beyond law enforcement and a policy in place which advances the governmental interest. As developed the special needs rationale is used by the Court to eliminate the need for individualized suspicion whenever the Court determines that a governmental policy is necessary to advance a public interest, there is a minimal intrusion in a person's privacy, and the search is reasonably related to remedying the problem identified in the policy. The more compelling the governmental interest, the more likely the Court has been to reach the balance in favor of the government. An overview of the Court's special needs cases points out that a number of things must be present for the Court to apply the special needs rule. These include: (1) the situation in which special needs exist must be one in which a warrant would be impracticable; (2) there must be substantial special need; and (3) a search based on special needs cannot involve law enforcement officers in an intricate way.

Conclusion

Under the reasonableness approach to the Fourth Amendment the two clauses of the Fourth Amendment are not seen as being interconnected. Thus, the only real limitation on the power of the government to search and seize is that its behavior must be reasonable. While the existence of a warrant or probable cause can be an indication of reasonableness, they are not seen as required in all circumstances. Even though the Warren Court was a strong believer in the traditional approach and turned its back on a general reasonableness approach to the Fourth Amendment, the language it used in *Camara v. Municipal Court* and *Terry v. Ohio* clearly opened the door for such an approach to be used by later courts. Starting with *Camara v. Municipal Court*, the Warren Court sought to enlarge the protections of the Fourth Amendment to a situation that had not previously implicated the amendment. The Warren Court believed that achieving this was so important that it was willing to overrule the precedent of *Frank v. Maryland* to bring Fourth Amendment protection to administrative searches. The Warren Court may not have realized it, but in its rush to extend the coverage of the Fourth Amendment it used language that would create opportunities for later courts to limit the protections of the Fourth Amendment. By emphasizing the reasonableness of governmental actions in administrative searches and then doing the same in *Terry v. Ohio* for investigative stops, the Warren Court clearly found that not all situations in which the Fourth Amendment is implicated require warrants based upon probable cause. The Warren Court's decision that when the warrant provision was not practical it was reasonable to balance governmental interests against an individual's privacy expectations had broad implications that it failed to realize. The Warren Court's broadly written opinions, therefore, set the stage so later courts could rule that there were other scenarios in which the warrant provision would also not be applicable.

The Warren Court's reasoning which balanced the interests of the government against the liberty interests of citizens had the potential to open the Fourth Amendment up to very different readings than had existed under the traditional approach. The Burger Court showed little hesitation in taking advantage of the opening and expanding the reasonableness approach to the Fourth Amendment. After examining the Supreme Court's Fourth Amendment cases in 1983, Wayne LaFave commented about the Burger Court that "it is almost as if a majority of the Court was hell-bent to seize any available opportunity to define more expansively the constitutional authority of law enforcement officials."[174] Carolyn Long added that "The Rehnquist Court's most significant contribution to Fourth Amendment jurisprudence has been its expansion of permissible searches based on the lesser standard of 'reasonableness' rather than probable cause."[175] The Court is now so favorably disposed towards the reasonableness approach that Chief Justice John Roberts has written that "the ultimate touchstone of the Furth Amendment is 'reasonableness.'"[176]

Starting with the Warren Court the balancing test used by the Court in its application of the reasonableness approach weighed the importance of the governmental interest served by the search or seizure against the government's intrusion into the privacy expectations of the individual. The Courts that have followed the Warren Court have used the reasonableness approach to enlarge the powers of the government to search and seize in two ways. The first was by opening the door to an increasing number of *Terry* stop scenarios in which investigative stops and seizures are declared to be reasonable. However, unlike *Terry,* which had required individualized and articulable suspicion that a person was doing something wrong and was armed and dangerous, some of these new situations did not require individualized suspicion that a person was either engaged in criminal activity or dangerous. Both the Burger and the Rehnquist Courts expanded the precedent from *Terry* to allow investigative stops when the reasonable suspicion for the stop is based on innocent conduct. For example, in *United States v. Sokolow*, the Court said that it was reasonable to stop a person for investigative reasons, even if there is no individualized suspicion, when the person matched a number of characteristics law enforcement agents believe describe the actions of drug couriers. Likewise, in *Michigan Department of State Police v. Sitz* the Court found that drunk driving checkpoints which systematically stopped vehicles were acceptable despite the lack of individualized suspicion against any of the drivers. In both of these cases the importance of the governmental interests, winning the war on drugs and stopping drunk driving, trumped what was perceived to be as a slight intrusion on a person's expectation of privacy within our society. The Court has also instructed lower courts to be deferential to the decisions of law enforcement officers in judgments as to whether reasonable suspicion for an investigative stop existed. The length of investigative stops has grown in some instances beyond the brief duration allowed in *Terry*. The basis of searches in investigative stops has grown from a pat down search of persons when there are articulable suspicions that they are involved in criminal activity and armed and dangerous, to blanket frisks of all persons suspected of certain categories of crime. The scope of these searches has grown beyond a pat down for weapons to include vehicle interiors even when the person is no longer in the vehicle. The purpose of investigative searches has also been enlarged beyond the need to protect officers to include searches of containers to determine if they contain contraband.

A second method by which the protections of the Fourth Amendment were lessened through a reasonableness approach was to open its use to cases that fall outside of *Terry* investigative stops. The majority of the Court accepted this expansion of the reasonableness approach to the Fourth Amendment in *New Jersey v. T.L.O.* In that case Justice Byron White quoted from *Terry* and went on to explain that because the original stop of T.L.O., for smoking in school, was justified, the search of T.L.O's purse was reasonably related to the purpose of the stop. Justice Harry Blackmun's concurring opinion in *T.L.O.* further explained that when the government had "special needs" that went beyond law enforcement the Court should apply the reasonableness approach to the Fourth Amendment rather than strictly adhering to the warrant requirement. The majority of the Court went on to give its support to the "special needs" test in *O'Connor v. Ortega*. As it has evolved the special needs doctrine has dropped the probable cause requirement and allows searches and seizures to be justifiable if the search is reasonable in light of the perceived public policy objective. The Court has also allowed special needs searches to be broadened in scope beyond the original search to protect the safety of the officer established in *Terry*.[177] Presently, under the special needs test when a case doesn't involve traditional law enforcement and there is not a warrant the Court examines the policy goals of the government and balances the policy against the intrusions on a person's expectation of privacy. In *Chandler v. Miller* the Court expressed its belief that the government interest needed to be sufficiently vital, without clarifying the term, to allow it to override the Fourth Amendment's normal requirement of individualized suspicion.

The willingness of the Court to accept the reasonableness approach to the Fourth Amendment has changed its focus from the facts of the case which explained how an individual came under governmental scrutiny, to an examination of the importance of the governmental policy. The Court has shown a willingness to dispense with probable cause or even individualized suspicion when there is a special need. In such cases it has argued that suspicionless searches are less intrusive on the rights of citizens than would searches based on individualized suspicion. Suspicionless searches, the Court has also noted, have the added benefit of better advancing the goals of the government than would searches which required individualized suspicion. Despite the Court's claim that special needs only applies to non-law enforcement situations, in *New York v. Burger* it was used to regulate the auto salvage industry which clearly is meant to facilitate law enforcement's need to halt auto thefts and the stolen parts industry.

All the changes brought about through the reasonableness approach to the Fourth Amendment were done so without overruling a single precedent of the Warren Court. Given their predispositions to emphasize law and order, it is difficult to say that the later Courts would not have moved as fast and as far in limiting the protections of the Fourth Amendment if it weren't for the opinions of the Warren Court. It is true, however, that these Courts did not have to develop new approaches to the Fourth Amendment to move the law in the direction they desired. The foundations of the reasonableness approach and balancing of interests had already been developed by the Warren Court. Change was made possible because the reasoning that the Warren Court used in its pragmatic protection of the Fourth Amendment and government interest created a flexible framework for interpreting the Fourth Amendment. Later Courts have used that reasoning and emphasized the reasonableness of the government's actions, given the importance of its goals when compared to the privacy interests of the citizen. This approach to determining the constitutionality of searches and seizures is highly subjective and dependent on the judges who hear a case and the weight they put on the competing interest of personal liberty versus the goals of the governmental policy. For that reason it has not been without controversy.[178] Despite the controversy, anytime that the public policy objective seems to be weighty enough, procedural requirements of the Fourth Amendment, other than the command that governmental actions be reasonable, may be bypassed and what would otherwise be an unconstitutional search will pass scrutiny. This change in the application of the Fourth Amendment has caused individual citizens to lose some control over when they will be subjected to Fourth Amendment intrusions. Under the traditional approach of the warrant rule, a citizen would only be subjected to governmental interference if their personal behavior gave police probable cause to believe they had committed a crime. That is no longer true. Today activities which are perfectly innocent like driving down the street, applying for a job with the government or in a highly regulated industry, or wanting to participate in extra-curricular activities as a student, may subject a person to a governmental search and seizure because the government has generic policy goals which may be advanced if everyone is subject to search and seizure.

Illustrative Case Reprise

In the case of *Los Angeles County, California v. Rettele* (2007), which began the chapter, Rettele and the Sadler lost their case. The district court, noting that there had been a legal warrant issued, granted summary judgment to the Sheriff's Department. The Court of Appeals for the Ninth Circuit reversed because it believed that a reasonable deputy would have stopped the search upon finding that no one in the house matched the race of the suspects. It also believed that it was unreasonable for the deputies to require Rettele and Sadler to get out of their bed while naked. The Supreme Court in a *per curiam* opinion reversed the decision of the Court of Appeals and let stand the summary judgment of the district court.

The Court's opinion held that the warrant which was used to search Rettele's house was a valid warrant. Under the Fourth Amendment warrants are issued on probable cause which often falls short of absolute certainty that a location will reveal evidence of criminal behavior. A warrant may be valid and fail to lead to the suspected criminal behavior. When it does, as in this case, the innocent bear the costs. These costs may include being caught engaged in a private activity which is embarrassing and humiliating. Despite these costs, if an officer serves a warrant in reasonable manner, the Fourth Amendment is not violated. The Court also held that when officers are executing a warrant they may detain those persons found on the premises. When there is a valid warrant detention of suspects presents little additional intrusion on a person's liberty. This intrusion must be balanced against the possible dangers to the officers who serve the warrant, possible interruption of the officer's completion of the search and risk of flight of suspects if they are not detained. There is no doubt that when executing a warrant, the risk of harm to law enforcement and whoever might be in the premises is minimized when officers take clear command of the premises. The test that is used to determine if an officer's detention of a person while serving a warrant violated the Fourth Amendment is one of reasonableness. Reasonableness is an objective test. Examples of when the detainment of an individual would be unreasonable are when officers cause unnecessary pain or individuals are detained for a prolonged period past the time necessary for the officers to complete their duties. In this case, the detainment was not unreasonable so there was no Fourth Amendment violation. The Court concluded by ruling that when there are no constitutional violations, law enforcement officers are given qualified immunity for their actions from title 42 U.SC., section 1983 suits.

In the *Rettele* case the Court believed that there was no constitutional violation because the police had acted reasonably given the circumstances. As a result neither the officers nor the government were subject to any penalty. The next chapter examines what happens when the police do not act so reasonably and there is a violation of the Fourth Amendment by concentrating on the exclusionary rule which places a penalty on the government for violating the Constitution.

Notes

1. Jacob W. Landynski, "Reasonability and the Fourth Amendment: Comments," *Criminal Law Bulletin* 25 (1989): 54. Landynski is commenting on H. Richard Uviller's article "Reasonability and the Fourth Amendment: A (Belated) Farewell to Justice Potter Stewart," *Criminal Law Bulletin* 25 (1989).
2. George M. Derry, III, "Are Politicians More Deserving than School Children? How *Chandler v. Miller* Exposed the Absurdities of the Fourth Amendment 'Special Needs' Balancing," *Arizona Law Review* 40 (1998): 102.
3. *Los Angeles County, California v. Rettele,* 127 S.Ct. 1989 (2007).
4. Omar Saleem, "The Age of Unreason: The Impact of Reasonableness, Increased Police Force, and Colorblindness on Terry 'Stop and Frisk,'" *Oklahoma Law Review* 50 (1997): 452; and Bernard Schwartz, *A History of the Supreme Court* (New York: Oxford University Press, 1993), 279.
5. Telford Taylor, *Two Studies in Constitutional Interpretation: Search, Seizure and Surveillance and Fair Trial and Free Press* (Columbus: Ohio State University Press, 1969).
6. Akhil Reed Amar, "Fourth Amendment and First Principles," *Harvard Law Review* 107 (1994): 757-819.
7. Telford Taylor, *Two Studies in Constitutional Interpretation,* 41.
8. For another supporter of the reasonableness approach, see, H. Richard Uviller, "Reasonability and the Fourth Amendment: A (Belated) Farewell to Justice Potter Stewart," *Criminal Law Bulletin* 25 (1989): 29-50.
9. Amar, "Fourth Amendment and First Principles," 759.
10. Debra Livingston, "Police, Community Caretaking, and the Fourth Amendment," *University of Chicago Law Forum* (1998): 263.
11. William W. Greenhalgh and Mark J. Yost, "In Defense of the "Per Se" Rule: Justice Stewart's Struggle to Preserve the Fourth Amendment's Warrant Clause," *American Criminal Law Review* 31 (1994): 1019-1036; Thomas Y. Davies, "Recovering the Original Fourth Amendment," *Michigan Law Review* 98 (1999): 547-667; Jacob W. Landynski, "The Supreme Court's Search for Fourth Amendment Standards," *Connecticut Bar Journal* 45 (1971): 2-39; Tracey Maclin, "The Complexity of the Fourth Amendment: A Historical Review," *Boston University Law Review* 77 (1997): 925-974; and Donald Dripps, "Akhil Amar on Criminal Procedure and Constitutional Law: "Here I Go Down the Wrong Road Again," *North Carolina Law Review* 74 (1996): 1559-1639.
12. Landynski, "Reasonability and the Fourth Amendment: Comments," 54.

13. Davies, "Recovering the Original Fourth Amendment," 552.

14. Martin Grayson, "The Warrant Clause in Historical Context," *American Journal of Criminal Law* 14 (1987): 114.

15. Craig S. Lerner, "The Reasonableness of Probable Cause," *Texas Law Review* 81 (2003): 973.

16. Carol S. Steiker, "Second Thoughts About First Principles," *Harvard Law Review* 107 (1994): 824-825.

17. *United States v. Rabinowitz*, 339 U.S. 56 (1950).

18. *United States v. Rabinowitz*, 339 U.S. at 60.

19. *United States v. Rabinowitz*, 339 U.S. at 65-66.

20. *United States v. Rabinowitz*, 339 U.S. at 70 (Frankfurter, J., dissenting).

21. *Chimel v. California*, 395 U.S. 752 (1969).

22. *Henry v. United States*, 361 U.S. 98 (1959).

23. *Henry,* 361 U.S. at 102.

24. *Henry,* 361 U.S. at 104.

25. *Mapp v. Ohio*, 367 U.S. 641 (1961).

26. Silas J. Wasserstrom, "The Court's Turn Toward a General Reasonableness Interpretation of the Fourth Amendment," *American Criminal Law Review* 27 (1989): 119-148; Brian J. Serr, "Great Expectations of Privacy: A New Model for Fourth Amendment Protection," *Minnesota Law Review* 73 (1989): 583-642; James Sokolowoski, "Special Project: Government Drug Testing: A Question of Reasonableness," *Vanderbilt Law Review* 43 (1990): 1343-1376; and Thomas K. Clancy, "The Role of Individualized Suspicion in Assessing the Reasonableness of Searches and Seizures," *University of Memphis Law Review* 25 (1994): 483-635.

27. *Camara v. Municipal Court*, 387 U.S. 523 (1967).

28. *See v. City of Seattle*, 387 U.S. 541 (1967).

29. *Terry v. Ohio*, 392 U.S. 1 (1968).

30. *Frank v. Maryland*, 359 U.S. 360 (1959).

31. *Camara v. Municipal Court*, 387 U.S. 523, 534 (1967).

32. *Camara,* 387 U.S. at 539.

33. *Camara,* 387 U.S. at 539.

34. *Camara,* 387 U.S. at 537.

35. *Camara,* 387 U.S. at 539.

36. Scott E. Sundby, "A Return to Fourth Amendment Basics: Undoing the Mischief of *Camara* and *Terry*," *Minnesota Law Review* 72 (1988): 401

37. Peter S. Greenberg, "The Balance of Interests Theory and the Fourth Amendment: A Selective Analysis of Supreme Court Action since *Camara* and *See*," *California Law Review* 61 (1973): 1011-1064; and Barry Jeffrey Stern, "Warrants Without Probable Cause," *Brooklyn Law Review* 59 (1994): 1390-1405.

38. For examples of scholars who believe that *Terry v. Ohio* has been positive for the legal system see: Stephen A. Saltzburg, "*Terry v. Ohio*: A Practically Perfect Doctrine," *St. John's Law Review* 72 (1998): 911; Akhail Reed Amar, "*Terry* and Fourth Amendment First Principles," *St. John's Law Review* 72 (1998): 1097-1131; Christopher Slobogin, "Let's Not Bury *Terry*: A Call for Rejuvenation of the Proportionality Principle," *St. John's Law Review* 72 (1998): 1053-1095. For examples of people who have criticized *Terry* or its application by lower courts see, Thomas K. Clancy, "Protective Searches, Pat-Downs, or Frisks?: The Scope of the Permissible Intrusion to Ascertain if a Detained Person is Armed," *Marquette Law Review* 82 (1991): 491-533; David A. Harris, "Frisking Every Suspect: The Withering of *Terry*" *University of California-Davis Law Review* 28 (1994): 1-52; Omar Saleem, "The Age of Unreason: The impact of Reasona-

bleness, Increased Police Force, and Colorblindedness on *Terry* 'Stop and Frisk,'" *Oklahoma Law Review* 50 (1997): 451-493; and Tracey Maclin, "*Terry v. Ohio's* Fourth Amendment Legacy: Black Men and Police Discretion," *St. John's Law Review* 72 (1998): 1271-1321.

39. *Terry v. Ohio*, 392 U.S. 1, 16 (1968).

40. *Terry*, 392 U.S. at 20.

41. *Terry*, 392 U.S. at 19.

42. Saltzburg, "*Terry v. Ohio*: A Practically Perfect Doctrine," 952.

43. *Terry*, 392 U.S. at 33 (1968) (Harlan, J., concurring).

44. *Terry*, 392 U.S. at 34 (White, J., concurring).

45. *Terry*, 392 U.S. at 37 (Douglas, J., dissenting).

46. Kenneth H. Pollack, "Stretching the Terry Doctrine to the Search for Evidence of Crime: Canine Sniffs, State Constitutions, and the Reasonable Suspicion Standard," *Vanderbilt Law Review* 47 (1994): 809-26.

47. Sundby, "A Return to Fourth Amendment Basics: Undoing the Mischief of *Camara* and *Terry*," p. 399.

48. Yale Kamisar, "The Warren Court and Criminal Justice," in *The Warren Court: A Retrospective*, ed. Bernard Schwartz, (New York: Oxford, 1996), 117.

49. *Mincey v. Arizona*, 437 U.S. 385 (1978).

50. *Katz v. United States*, 389 U.S. 347 (1967).

51. *Mincey v. Arizona*, 437 U.S. 385, 390 (1978).

52. *New York v. Belton*, 453 U.S. 454 (1981).

53. *New York v. Belton*, 453 U.S. at 457. For other examples see *Arkansas v. Sanders*, 442 U.S. 753, 758 (1979); *Robbins v. California*, 453 U.S. 420, 423 (1981); and *California v. Carney*, 471 U.S. 386, 390-391 (1985).

54. Thomas N. McInnis, *The Christian Burial Case* (Westport, CT: Preager, 2001), 172-177; Silas J. Wasserstrom, "The Incredible Shrinking Fourth Amendment," *American Criminal Law Review* 21 (984): 259; Robert M. Bloom, "The Supreme Court and its Purported Preference for Search Warrants," *Tennessee Law Review* 50 (1983): 50; Craig Bradley, "Criminal Procedure in the Rehnquist Court: Has the Rehnquisition Begun?," *Indiana Law Journal* 62 (1989): 285; Warren E. Burger, "Who Will Watch the Watchman," *American University Law Review* 14 (1964): 1-23; and Timothy E. Gammon, "The Exclusionary Rule and the 1983-1984 Term," *Marquette Law Review* 68 (1984): 1-25.

55. Chief Justice Burger and Justice Rehnquist indicated their acceptance of a reasonableness approach by signing onto Justice White's majority opinion in *New Jersey v. T.L.O.*, 469 U.S. 325 (1985). Justice Powell in *New Jersey v. T.L.O.* concurred that when there are "reasonable grounds for suspecting that [a] search will turn up evidence that the student has violated or is violating" a law or school rule a search of the student's person or belongings is justified, although he emphasized that this was due to the lesser expectation of privacy that students have in schools, *New Jersey v. T.L.O.*, 469 U.S. 325, 350 n. 3 (1985) (Powell, J., concurring). Justice Blackmun also indicated an acceptance of the reasonableness approach whenever the government had special needs that were not related to law enforcement in his concurring opinion in *New Jersey v. T.L.O.*

56. Anthony Amsterdam, "Perspectives on the Fourth Amendment," *Minnesota Law Review* 58 (1974): 394.

57. Silas J. Wasserstrom, "The Incredible Shrinking Fourth Amendment," 260-261, points out, for example, that in the 1983 Term the Court found that challenged police conduct in the area of search and seizure was acceptable in 7 of 9 cases and that in the two cases in which law enforcement behavior went beyond the power of the government,

the Court expanded the powers of the government to conduct searches and seizures beyond what it had been prior to the case.

58. The companion cases to *Terry* were *Sibron v. New York* and *Peters v. New York*, 392 U.S. 40 (1968).

59. *Adams v. Williams*, 407 U.S. 143 (1972).

60. *Adams*, 407 U.S. at 145.

61. *Ybarra v. Illinois*, 444 U.S. 85 (1979).

62. *Ybarra*, 444 U.S. at 93-94.

63. *Ybarra*, 444 U.S. at 94.

64. *Ybarra*, 444 U.S. at 106-107 (Rehnquist, J., dissenting).

65. *Almeida-Sanchez v. United States*, 413 U.S. 266 (1973).

66. *Almeida-Sanchez*, 413 U.S. at 270.

67. *United States v. Brignoni-Ponce* 422 U.S. 873 (1975).

68. *United States v. Brignoni-Ponce* 422 U.S. at 881-882.

69. *United States v. Ortiz*, 422 U.S. 891 (1975).

70. *United States v. Martinez-Fuerte*, 428 U.S. 543 (1976).

71. *Delaware v. Prouse*, 440 U.S. 648 (1979).

72. *Delaware v. Prouse*, 440 U.S. at 653-654.

73. *Delaware v. Prouse*, 440 U.S. at 661.

74. *Delaware v. Prouse*, 440 U.S. at 663.

75. *Brown v. Texas*, 443 U.S. 47 (1979).

76. *Brown*, 443 U.S. at 51.

77. *Michigan Department of State Police v. Sitz*, 496 U.S. 444 (1990).

78. *Michigan Department of State Police*, 496 U.S. at 450.

79. *Michigan Department of State Police*, 496 U.S. at 453.

80. *City of Indianapolis v. Edmond*, 531 U.S. 32 (2000).

81. *Illinois v. Lidster*, 540 U.S. 419 (2004).

82. *United States v. Mendenhall*, 446 U.S. 544 (1980).

83. *United States v. Mendenhall*, 446 U.S. at 554.

84. *United States v. Mendenhall*, 446 U.S. at 554.

85. *Florida v. Royer*, 460 U.S. 491 (1983).

86. *Florida v. Royer*, 460 U.S. at 507.

87. *United States v. Sokolow*, 490 U.S. 1 (1989).

88. *United States v. Sokolow*, 490 U.S. at 10.

89. The Court has also accepted use of a drug courier profile in *Florida v. Rodriquez*, 469 U.S. 1 (1984), but ruled against one in *Reid v. Georgia*, 448 U.S. 438 (1980).

90. Roger S. Hanson, "The Common Carrier Drug Courier Profile: The Drug Interdiction Program and its Development in the Federal Courts," *Western State University Law Review* 18 (1991): 654-664.

91. *Illinois v. Wardlow*, 528 U.S. 119 (2000).

92. *Illinois v. Wardlow*, 528 U.S. at 124.

93. *Illinois v. Wardlow*, 528 U.S. at 124.

94. *Illinois v. Wardlow*, 528 U.S. at 125.

95. *Illinois v. Wardlow*, 528 U.S. at 128-129 (Stevens, J., concurring in part, dissenting in part).

96. *Michigan v. Chesternut*, 486 U.S. 567 (1988).

97. *California v. Hodari D.*, 499 U.S. 621 (1991).

98. *Michigan v. Chesternut*, 486 U.S. 567, 576 (1988).

99. Robert J. Burnett, "Comment: Random Police-Encounters: When is a Seizure a Seizure?" *Duquesne Law Review* 33 (1995): 287.

100. Burnett, "Comment: Random Police-Encounters: When is a Seizure a Seizure?" 288.

101. *United States v. Cortez*, 449 U.S. 411 (1981).

102. *United States v. Cortez*, 449 U.S. at 417-418.

103. *United States v. Cortez*, 449 U.S. at 418.

104. Margaret Anne Hoehl, "Casenote: Usual Suspects Beware: 'Walk Don't Run' Through Dangerous Neighborhoods," *University of Richmond Law Review* 35 (2001): 140-41.

105. Hoehl, "Casenote: Usual Suspects Beware," 143-44.

106. *United States v. Arvizu*, 534 U.S. 266, 277 (2002).

107. Sheri Lynn Johnson, "Race and the Decision to Detain a Suspect," *Yale Law Journal* 93 (1983): 219-220.

108. David T. McTaggert, "Note: Reciprocity on the Streets: Reflections on the Fourth Amendment and the Duty to Cooperate with the Police," *New York University Law Review* 76 (2001): 1249-1250.

109. *Hiibel v. Sixth Judicial District Court*, 542 U.S. 177 (2004).

110. *United States v. Sharpe*, 470 U.S. 675 (1985).

111. *United States v. Sharpe*, 470 U.S. at 685.

112. *United States v. Montoya de Hernandez*, 473 U.S. 531 (1985).

113. *Pennsylvania v. Mimms*, 434 U.S. 106 (1977).

114. *Pennsylvania v. Mimms*, 434 U.S. at 107.

115. *Maryland v. Wilson*, 519 U.S. 408 (1997).

116. *Michigan v. Long*, 463 U.S. 1032 (1983).

117. *New York v. Belton*, 453 U.S. 454 (1981).

118. *New York v. Belton*, 453 U.S. at 561.

119. *Michigan v. Long*, 463 U.S. at 1052 n.16 (1983).

120. Harris, "Frisking Every Suspect: The Withering of Terry," 22-31.

121. David A. Harris, "*Terry* and the Fourth Amendment: Particularized Suspicion, Categorical Judgments: Supreme Court Rhetoric versus Lower Court Reality under *Terry v. Ohio*," *St. John's Law Review* 72 (1998): 991-996.

122. Amsterdam, "Perspectives on the Fourth Amendment," 394.

123. *United States v. Place*, 462 U.S. 696 (1983).

124. *United States v. Place*, 462 U.S. at 704.

125. *Minnesota v. Dickerson*, 508 U.S. 366 (1993).

126. *Minnesota v. Dickerson*, 508 U.S. at 376.

127. *Alabama v. White*, 496 U.S. 325 (1990).

128. *Florida v. J.L.*, 529 U.S. 266 (2000).

129. *Robbins v. California*, 453 U.S. 420, 437 (1981) (Rehnquist, J., dissenting).

130. *New Jersey v. T.L.O.*, 469 U.S. 325 (1985).

131. *New Jersey v. T.L.O.*, 469 U.S. at 339.

132. *New Jersey v. T.L.O.*, 469 U.S. at 340.

133. *New Jersey v. T.L.O.*, 469 U.S. at 340.

134. *New Jersey v. T.L.O.*, 469 U.S. at 341-342.

135. *New Jersey v. T.L.O.*, 469 U.S. at 353 (Blackmun, J., concurring).

136. For Justice Brennan's focus on school systems see, *New Jersey v. T.L.O.*, 468 U.S. 325, 353 (1985) (Brennan, J., dissenting). For the narrowness of other commentary see, Neal I. Aizenstein, "Fourth Amendment—Searches by Public School Officials Valid on 'Reasonable Grounds': *New Jersey v. T.L.O.*, 105 S. Ct.733 (1985)," *Journal of Criminal Law and Criminology* 76 (1985): 898-932; Sunil H. Mansukhami, "School Searches After *New Jersey v. T.L.O.*: Are There Any Limits?" *University of Louisville Journal of*

Family Law 34 (Spring 1995/1996): 345-378; and Charles W. Hardin, Jr., "Searching Public Schools: *T.L.O.* and the Exclusionary Rule," *Ohio State Law Journal* 47 (1986): 1099-1114.

137. *California v. Acevedo*, 500 U.S. 565 (1991).

138. *California v. Acevedo*, 500 U.S. at 583 (Scalia, J. concurring).

139. *California v. Acevedo*, 500 U.S. at 583-584 (Scalia, J. concurring).

140. Antonin Scalia, "The Rule of Law as a Law of Rules," *University of Chicago Law Review* 56 (1989): 1186.

141. *O'Connor v. Ortega*, 480 U.S. 709 (1987).

142. *National Treasury Employees Union v. Von Raab*, 489 U.S. 656 (1989).

143. *Georgia v. Randolph*, 547 U.S. 103 (2006).

144. *Board of Education v. Earls*, 536 U.S. 822 (2002).

145. *Vernonia School District 47J v. Acton*, 515 U.S. 646 (1995).

146. *O'Connor v. Ortega*, 480 U.S. 709 (1987).

147. *O'Connor*, 480 U.S. at 725-726.

148. *O'Connor*, 480 U.S. at 720.

149. *Griffin v. Wisconsin*, 483 U.S. 868 (1987).

150. *Griffin*, 483 U.S. at 873.

151. *Griffin*, 483 U.S. at 879.

152. *United States v. Knights*, 534 U.S. 112 (2001).

153. *New York v. Burger*, 482 U.S. 691 (1987).

154. *New York v. Burger*, 482 U.S. at 702.

155. *New York v. Burger*, 482 U.S. at 703.

156. *Skinner v Railway Labor Executives' Association*, 489 U.S. 602 (1989).

157. *National Treasury Employees Union v. Von Raab*, 489 U.S. 656, 671 (1989).

158. *Skinner*, 489 U.S. at 624.

159. *Skinner*, 489 U.S. at 624.

160. *Skinner*, 489 U.S. at 637(Marshall, J., dissenting).

161. James Sokolowski, "Government Drug Testing: A Question of Reasonableness," *Vanderbilt Law Review*, 43 (1990): 1369-1370.

162. *Vernonia School District 47J v. Acton*, 515 U.S. 646 (1995).

163. *National Treasury Employees Union*, 489 U.S. at 680 (Scalia, J., dissenting).

164. *Vernonia School District 47J*, 515 U.S. at 668 (O'Connor, J., dissenting).

165. Kenneth Nuger "The Special Needs Rationale: Creating a Chasm in Fourth Amendment Analysis," *Santa Clara Law Review* 32 (1992): 89-136; Jennifer Y. Buffaloe, "Note: 'Special Need' and the Fourth Amendment: An Exception Poised to Swallow the Warrant Preference Rule," *Harvard Civil Rights-Civil Liberties Law Review* 32 (1997): 529-564; and David J. Gottlieb, "Drug Testing, Collective Suspicion, and a Fourth Amendment Out of Balance: A Reply to Professor Howard," *Kansas Journal of Law and Public Policy* 6 (1997): 27-36.

166. *Chandler v. Miller*, 520 U.S. 305 (1997).

167. *Chandler*, 520 U.S. at 315.

168. *Chandler*, 520 U.S. at 321.

169. *Chandler*, 520 U.S. at 319.

170. *Ferguson v. Charleston*, 532 U.S. 67 (2001).

171. *Board of Education v. Earls*, 536 U.S. 822 (2002).

172. *Board of Education v. Earls*, 536 U.S. at 828-29.

173. *Board of Education v. Earls*, 536 U.S. at 830.

174. Wayne LaFave, "Fourth Amendment Vagaries (Of Improbable Cause, Imperceptible Plain View, Notorious Privacy, and Balancing Askew)," *Journal of Crime and Criminology*, 74 (1983): 1222.

175. Carolyn Long, *Mapp v. Ohio: Guarding Against Unreasonable Search and Seizure* (Lawrence, KS: University Press of Kansas, 2006), p. 190.

176. *Brigham City, Utah v. Stuart*, 547 U.S. 398, 403 (2006).

177. Searches that are broader in scope than those allowed under the limited searches to protect public safety in *Terry* now include: (1) the desks and offices of governmental workers, *O'Connor v. Ortega*, 480 U.S. 709 (1987); (2) the homes of probationers, *Griffin v. Wisconsin*, 483 U.S. 868 (1987); (3) the inventory of auto salvage yards, *New York v. Burger*, 482 U.S. 691 (1987); (4) drug testing of railroad employees, *Skinner v. Railway Labor Executives' Association*, 489 U.S. 602 (1989), customs officers, *National Treasury Employees Union v. Von Rabb*, 489 U.S. 656 (1989), and students who participate in extracurricular activities, *Board of Education v. Earls*, 536 U.S. 822 (2002).

178. As would be expected, commentators have criticized the Court for placing too much weight on the governmental interest in these cases or being unprincipled. See Nuger, "The Special Needs Rationale: Creating a Chasm in Fourth Amendment Analysis," 97 and George M. Derry, III, "Are Politicians More deserving than School Children? How *Chandler v. Miller* Exposed the Absurdities of the Fourth Amendment 'Special Needs' Balancing," *Arizona Law Review* 40 (1998): 73.

Chapter 6
The Exclusionary Rule of Justice

Too often, what might seem at worst a minor sidestep at the time turns out, when viewed from the clearest perspective provided by the passage of time, to have been a step over the cliff. Minor constrictions on the Fourth Amendment often take on broader dimensions when revisited by the Supreme Court.[1]

Illegitimate and unconstitutional practices get their first footing . . . by silent approaches and slight deviations from legal modes of procedure. This can only be obviated by adhering to the rule that constitutional provisions for the security of person and property should be liberally construed. A close and literal construction deprives them of half their efficacy, and leads to gradual depreciation of the right, as if it consisted more in sound than in substance. It is the duty of courts to be watchful for the constitutional rights of the citizen, and against any stealthy encroachments thereon.[2]

Illustrative Case

On September 26, 1989 Luis Arciniega was driving a 1976 Cadillac down an Arizona interstate. He was driving slightly over the 65 m.p.h. speed limit when he came upon the vehicle of an Arizona State Trooper. The officer driving the trooper vehicle, Russell Fifer, testified that Arciniega was not going so fast over the speed limit to warrant being stopped and given a ticket. The officer said, however, that his interest was aroused because when Arciniega passed the officer he acted suspiciously by jerking his head and stiffened. According to Officer Fifer, he also found it suspicious because Arciniega continued to watch the trooper vehicle through his side mirror. Officer Fifer followed Arciniega's vehicle for eleven miles during which time Arciniega's vehicle traveled between 50 to

60 miles per hour. During this time Officer Fifer radioed State Patrol Headquarters the plate number of the vehicle Arciniega was driving. He was told that those plates belonged to a Pontiac, not a Cadillac.

Despite the fact that there was no posted minimum speed for the interstate, Officer Fifer pulled over Arciniega for driving too slow. He believed the speed was not reasonable and prudent given the road conditions. Arciniega showed Officer Fifer a valid drivers's license, registration, and proof of insurance which showed the vehicle was owned by Donald Simpson, who worked for the U.S. Customs Service. While questioning Arciniega, Officer Fifer learned at 11:46 a.m. that the plates were correct and did not belong to a Pontiac. During the stop another officer, Robert Williamson, arrived at the scene. The two officers consulted with each other and decided that Arciniega's characteristics fit those of a drug courier profile. At that time they asked for consent to search the trunk of his vehicle. Arciniega gave them permission and the officers found 560 pounds of cocaine. He was immediately placed under arrest at 11:50 a.m. A third officer, Vanderpoole, arrived at the scene and told Arciniega that "he was looking at at least twenty five years in prison; and since he was 50, he might not make it out of prison."[3] Arciniega was then told that if he cooperated with them, he would not be charged.

After Arciniega agreed to cooperate, he was interrogated. His statements caused the officers to believe that he was merely transporting the cocaine for others. He and the vehicle were taken to a motel in Tempe, Arizona where he was told to call his contact. He spoke to a person who promised to send someone by to pick up the drugs. Later, Jorge Padilla and Suzy Padilla arrived to pick up the Cadillac and were arrested as they tried to leave. Police searched the vehicle they came in and found documentation to show that it had been rented by Xavier Padilla, who was Jorge's brother and Suzy's husband. After questioning Suzy, she gave them a lead that Alicia Padilla Romero may have also been involved in the crime. Officers went to her house and were questioning her when Xavier Padilla arrived. They also questioned him, but he did not implicate himself in the crime.

The next day, the state troopers informed the U.S. Customs Service that Donald Simpson's vehicle had been used to transport a large amount of drugs. The two agencies then interrogated Luis Arciniega who implicated Mr. Simpson in the crime. Based on this information a search warrant was issued for Simpson's home and evidence implicating him and his wife was found and seized.

Police later interrogated an informant who had been arrested with cocaine and decided to cooperate with police. He gave them insight into the drug operation of Luis Arciniega and Xavier Padilla. Members of various law enforcement agencies met on October 6, 1989, to try to determine the structure of the organization. This meeting produced a clearer picture of what had happened leading up to the seizure of the cocaine from Arciniega. The picture showed that while Xavier Padilla and the Simpsons never owned the cocaine. They had conspired to provide the service of transporting the contraband over the border for the "El Tejano" drug cartel. This was the fourth time they had moved drugs for the cartel. It was not clear if Jorge and Suzy Padilla were just employees or played a larger role in the conspiracy to bring drugs across the border. Based on this information all of the people involved in the transportation and the conspiracy to transport the drugs into the United States were arrested and charged with conspiracy to distribute and possession with intent to distribute cocaine. Before the trial began all of the defendants challenged the admission of the cocaine that was seized arguing that the initial stop of Luis Arciniega had violated the Fourth Amendment since there was no suspicion for the continuation of the stop beyond the point in which the license plate mix up had been resolved and that therefore the evidence could not be used. They further argued that because all of the other evidence against them was gained as a result of the initial vehicle search it should also be suppressed. The case of *United States v. Padilla* (1993)[4] presents a number of interesting issues. For example, if the initial search was a violation of the Fourth Amendment, must the evidence be suppressed? Under what conditions can illegally seized evidence be used? Who can challenge the admission of illegally seized evidence to be used against them? These and other questions involving the exclusionary rule are examined in this chapter.

Foundations of the Exclusionary Rule

In the chapters leading up to this point we have examined what constitutes a violation of the Fourth Amendment. As we have seen, the Fourth Amendment has changed over time and the power of the government to engage in search and seizures has been broadened. The parameters of the Fourth Amendment are important due to the exclusionary rule. The primary purpose of the exclusionary rule, according to Jacob Landynski, has been "to protect the vitality of the Fourth Amendment" by making unprofitable any benefit of evidence that might be gained through a violation of the Fourth Amendment.[5] Justice Tom Clark in his majority opinion in *Mapp v. Ohio* (1961)[6] clearly understood that the Fourth Amendment was meaningless unless there was some way to enforce it. The Constitution, however, fails to mention the exclusionary rule. Despite this, the values inherent in the rule are important for helping to protect rights which are specifically found in the Bill of Rights. Bradley Canon summarizes these values by stating: "Inherent in the rule are respect for privacy and individual autonomy, for the rule of the law, that is the law serving as a constraint on the governors as well as those being governed, and fair treatment in the relationship between government and citizen."[7] Much of the exclusionary rule debate has been framed around the Fourth Amendment. Other provisions of the Constitution which have also been involved in the exclusionary rule debate include the Fifth Amendment's right against self-incrimination, the Sixth Amendment's right to counsel, and the Fourteenth Amendment's Due Process Clause.

The debate over the exclusionary rule is created from the Constitution's inability to define what consequences the government would be subject to should it violate the provisions of the Bill of Rights. The Constitution at no point states that evidence which is seized in violation of its provisions shall be excluded from submission in courts of law. Critics of the exclusionary rule have been quick to point out that exclusion should not therefore be considered a constitutional requirement. Judge Malcom Wilkey, for example, has complained "This rule of evidence did not come from on high. It's man-made. . . . It's not even in the Constitution."[8] Supporters of the exclusionary rule, on the other hand, have argued that the Constitution does not have an addendum which states that the government is free to benefit from constitutional violations. Yale Kamisar has written "Because the fourth amendment has *nothing to say* about *any* consequences that might flow from its violation, reading it as *permitting* the use of evidence obtained by means of an unreasonable search and seizure . . . strikes me as no less 'creative' or 'judge-made' than" applying the exclusionary rule.[9]

The Supreme Court had already created confusion regarding the source of the exclusionary rule and when it should be applied prior to *Mapp v. Ohio* (1961). Most of the confusion can be traced back to two earlier decisions. The first is *Weeks v. United States* (1914)[10] and the second is *Wolf v. Colorado* (1949).[11] In *Weeks v. United States*, the Court ruled that the exclusionary rule was a constitutional necessity as a part of the Fourth Amendment. Justice William Day, who wrote the *Weeks* opinion, reasoned that the exclusionary rule was necessary because, "If letters and private documents can thus be seized and held and used in evidence against a citizen accused of an offense, the protection of the Fourth Amendment declaring his right to be secure against such searches and seizures is of no value, and, so far as those thus placed are concerned, might as well be stricken from the Constitution."[12] He went on to explain that another reason for the exclusionary rule was the need to maintain judicial integrity. His argument that exclusion was necessary to promote judicial integrity demonstrates his acceptance of a unitary model of government that holds that a constitutional violation by one part of the government disbars the entire government from making use of the violation. This theory sees the government as a monolith in which each part must live with the mistakes of any part of the whole.

In *Wolf v. Colorado*, Justice Felix Frankfurter introduced a very different understanding of the rule when he wrote that the exclusionary rule was not a constitutional requirement. It was, instead, a judicial remedy which the Court had created to act as a deterrent to future police violations. As a judicially created remedy, the rule did not require exclusion of evidence in all cases in which there was a violation of the Fourth Amendment. Justice Frankfurter's approach to the exclusionary rule shows his acceptance of a fragmented model of government in which a constitutional violation of a person's right by one arm of the government is seen as a separate incident than the use of the tainted evidence by a separate part of the government. As a result, he believed the courts can make an independent choice about whether evidence which has been illegally gathered needs to be suppressed at trial.

As discussed in Chapter 2, the *Mapp v. Ohio* (1961)[13] decision is monumental for incorporating the exclusionary rule and holding that it is constitutionally required in all courts, state and federal. It did not, however, build this monument on the firmest foundation possible since the decision still did not clarify the exact source of the exclusionary rule. Rather than following the reasoning and approach of either *Weeks* or *Wolf*, the decision referred to both. Justice Tom Clark, writing for the majority, relied on the primacy of the *Weeks* tradition and reasoned that the exclusionary rule was an essential part of the Fourth Amendment. In Justice Clark's words "the plain and unequivocal language of *Weeks*" despite anything said in *Wolf* was that "the *Weeks* rule is of constitutional origin" and "remains entirely undisturbed" by *Wolf*.[14]

Justice Clark stated that the rule was also necessary in order to promote judicial integrity. This desire to promote judicial integrity demonstrates a unitary view of government in that the Court believed that if there was a constitutional violation by any branch of the government, no part could gain from the violation. As Justice Clark explained when there is a constitutional violation and evidence is excluded, "The criminal goes free, if he must, but it is the law that sets him free. Nothing can destroy a government more quickly than its failure to observe its own laws, or worse, its disregard of the charter of its own existence."[15]

Finally, Justice Clark also included a secondary argument that the rule's purpose was to act as a deterrent to future constitutional violations. This argument was included to justify the break the Court was making with the precedent of *Wolf*. Justice Clark made it clear that a deterrent rationale was "not basically relevant to a decision that the exclusionary rule is an essential ingredient of the Fourth Amendment," but included the argument to demonstrate that the facts had changed enough since the decision in *Wolf* to allow its result to be overturned because "more than half those [states] since passing upon it [the exclusionary rule], by their own legislative or judicial decision have wholly or partly adopted or adhered to the *Weeks* rule."[16] The Court believed that movement in the states toward adopting the exclusionary rule demonstrated that "other remedies have been worthless and futile."[17] Consequently, reason and truth required the exclusionary rule to apply to the states as well as the federal government.

Justice Black wrote a concurring opinion that helped to confuse the issue as to what was the foundation of the exclusionary rule. Despite Justice Clark's statement that "the *Weeks* rule is of constitutional origin,"[18] Justice Black's opinion stated, "I agree with what appears to be a plain implication of the Court's opinion that the federal exclusionary rule is not a command of the Fourth Amendment but is a judicially created rule of evidence which Congress might negate."[19] For Black, the exclusionary rule did not have a constitutional basis unless there was a Fourth Amendment violation considered together with a Fifth Amendment violation against compelled self-incrimination. Justice Douglas also wrote a concurring opinion which may have caused confusion by explaining that when *Wolf* was decided the Court had left open to states the ability to develop alternative methods of deterring state officials from violating the Fourth Amendment. Failure of the states to do so made *Mapp* an appropriate case to incorporate the exclusionary rule because it presented "the casual arrogance of those who have the untrammeled power to invade one's home and to seize one's property."[20]

Working off of the primacy of the *Weeks* tradition the Court did put forth a strong precedent in *Mapp* when it stated: "We hold that all evidence obtained by searches and seizures in violation of the Constitution is, by that same authority, inadmissible in a state court."[21] However, as a result of Justice Clark's opinion, especially his desire to cover all bases to demonstrate the wisdom behind incorporating the exclusionary rule, and the concurring opinions of Justice Black and Douglas, debate has continued both on and off the Court as to where the justification for excluding evidence comes from in the Constitution and when it is appropriate to do so.

In 1961 when the exclusionary rule was incorporated there were two exceptions to the rule. They were the independent source[22] and attenuation exceptions.[23] Despite the lack of clarity over the source of the exclusionary rule in *Mapp v. Ohio*, the Warren Court continued to be firmly committed to the application of the rule at both the federal and state levels when governmental officials violated the Fourth Amendment. Researchers have called the mid-1960's the high-water mark for the exclusionary rule.[24] This was because of the consistent manner in which the Court applied the exclusionary rule when there were Fourth Amendment violations.

Despite the mid-1960s being a high water mark for the exclusionary rule, the Warren Court did make a ruling in 1965 that further questioned the foundations of the rule. In *Linkletter v. Walker*[25] the Court had to decide if *Mapp* would be applied retrospectively, Justice Clark, who had written the majority opinion in *Mapp* and now wrote for the majority again, seemed to narrow the foundation for the exclusionary rule in the *Linkletter* decision. He did so by concentrating on a deterrence rationale for the rule which implied that the purpose for excluding illegally gathered evidence was to discourage future illegal behavior. As Justice Clark stated, "*Mapp* had as its prime purpose the enforcement of the Fourth Amendment through the inclusion of the exclusionary rule within its rights. This, it was found, was the only effective deterrent to lawless police action."[26] Justice Clark stated that in every case since *Wolf* where the Court had ruled in favor of exclusion it had done so "based on the necessity for an effective deterrent to illegal police action."[27] If the purpose of the exclusionary rule was to deter constitutional violations, the Court found that it made little sense to apply the rule retrospectively. This was because, "The misconduct of the police prior to *Mapp* has already occurred and will not be corrected by releasing the prisoners involved."[28] Justice Clark also undercut the argument promoting judicial integrity that he had put forward in *Mapp*. He did this by finding that applying *Mapp* retrospectively would place new pressures on the judicial system as it was forced to have hearings on the excludability of evidence that may no longer exist, and rely on witnesses who, if they were available, would have difficulty remembering how evidence was gathered. After finding that the image of justice would not be promoted by applying the rule retrospectively, Justice Clark broke further with the Court's reasoning in *Mapp* and hinted that the possibility of guilt should be taken into consideration when it came to the application of the exclusionary rule. He concluded that "To thus legitimate such an extraordinary procedural weapon that has no bearing on guilt would seriously disrupt the administration of justice."[29]

Narrowing the Ability to Challenge an Illegal Search

In 1967 the Court decided *Katz v. United States*[30] and ruled that electronic surveillance of a phone conversation without a warrant violated the Fourth Amendment because it protected people, not places. Despite the decision in *Katz* by the Warren Court to broaden the protections of the Fourth Amendment, the Burger Court used *Katz* to narrow its view of who has been injured by a violation of the Fourth Amendment and thus would have standing to ask a trial court to suppress the evidence through application of the exclusionary rule. This is because if a criminal defendant moves to have evidence suppressed at trial because it was gathered through a violation of the Fourth Amendment, he must have a legal right to do so. The Court has long had established threshold requirements that must be met before an individual can have standing to raise constitutional claims. These include the need for a real case or controversy to exist, the issues involved to be ripe, and the need for the party bringing the case to have a direct injury which the courts can remedy.

For a period starting in 1960 any person charged with possession of contraband who claimed that a search had violated their rights had the ability to challenge the legality of the search and subsequent admission of evidence. The automatic standing rule was adopted in *Jones v. United States* (1960).[31] In *Jones* the Court had to determine if an individual, Jones, who was a guest in a friend's apartment, had standing to contest a search of the apartment. The Court ruled that Jones did have standing to challenge the legality of the search under two different theories. The first was that a person had automatic standing to contest a search which resulted in seizure of contraband when they were charged with possessing the contraband. The second theory was that "anyone legitimately on premises where a search occurs may challenge its legality by way of a motion to suppress, when its fruits are proposed to be used against him."[32]

In *Alderman v. United States* (1969)[33] the Court used language which created an opening for future courts to weaken the protections of the exclusionary rule. The case concerned whether a defendant had standing to challenge the use of evidence which was gathered through illegal electronic surveillance. The Court had ruled in *Katz v. United States* that the Fourth Amendment could protect people in phone conversations and that warrants were required by law enforcement to listen in on phone conversations. What differs in *Alderman* was the question as to whether conversations gathered through illegal electronic surveillance could be used against third parties whose phones were not tapped and whose conversations were not heard. The government in *Alderman* had used illegal electronic surveillance against several suspects in a number of criminal conspiracy cases. The information gathered through the surveillance implicated a number of other individuals as co-conspirators and was used to help gain convictions against them. When the co-conspirators found out that part of the evidence used to convict them was gained through the use of illegal electronic surveillance they challenged their convictions. Justice Byron White's majority opinion examined the precedents regarding who could object to the use of illegally seized evidence and clarified that "Fourth Amendment rights are personal rights which, like some other constitutional rights, may not be vicariously asserted."[34] For that reason the owner of a location which was subject to electronic eavesdropping had standing to challenge admission of any evidence gained, as would any person whose conversations were illegally overheard, but not those who were merely mentioned in overheard conversations. The Court acknowledged that its exclusionary rule precedents such as *Linkletter v. Walker* recognized that the rule acted as a deterrent against future constitutional violations. The Court went further and stated "Neither those cases nor any others hold that anything which deters illegal searches is thereby commanded by the Fourth Amendment."[35] For the Court the necessity of being able to demonstrate a personal violation of the Fourth Amendment was so important that it took priority over any deterrent effect that had been recognized by the Court in earlier exclusionary rule cases. The Court then limited the application of the exclusionary rule by balancing its substantial costs of setting free criminals against its benefits of serving as a future police deterrent to constitutional violations and found the costs too high. Justice White reasoned:

> The deterrent values of preventing the incrimination of those whose rights the police have violated have been considered sufficient to justify the suppression of probative evidence even though the case against the defendant is weakened or destroyed. . . . But we are not convinced that the additional benefits of extending the exclusionary rule to other defendants [whose personal rights were not infringed] would justify further encroachment upon the public interest in prosecuting those accused of crime and having them acquitted or convicted on the basis of all the evidence which exposes the truth.[36]

The Court in *Alderman* tried to make it clear that it was not belittling or showing disrespect for the Fourth Amendment and that its protections were still fundamental to our system of government. In an odd comment from a Court that had as recently as *Mapp v. Ohio* (1961) stated that remedies other than exclusion to Fourth Amendment violations were futile, Justice White noted that those who flout the amendment could be prosecuted for violating a law which made unauthorized electronic surveillance a serious crime. Furthermore, Congress or state legislatures could legislatively make illegally seized evidence inadmissible against anyone for any purpose. The Court was unwilling to do so, however, and ruled that in cases of Fourth Amendment violations only individuals whose personal rights were infringed would be allowed to assert their Fourth Amendment rights to challenge the legality of the surveillance. The broad ruling of *Mapp* that "all evidence obtained by searches and seizures in violation of the Constitution, is, by that same authority"[37] to be excluded in courts was narrowed considerably in *Alderman*. The Court also dropped support for a unitary model of government whereby any use of constitutional violations was thought to create complicity by the entire government in the violation. *Alderman* supported the fragmented model of government and allowed the government to be rewarded for its constitutional violation. After *Alderman*, the Court continued to show a willingness to turn its back on the use of evidence gained through constitutional violations as long as it was not used against the individuals whose actual rights had been violated. By deciding that it was not necessary to exclude evidence anytime that it may create a possible deterrent effect on future constitutional violations *Alderman* established a precedent and a line of reasoning that would continue to be used by Courts after the Warren years to weaken enforcement of the Fourth Amendment. It also added a new tool that could be used to weaken the exclusionary rule, the ability to balance societal interests against the deterrent effect that exclusion may have.

The first of the decisions building on *Alderman* and further changing the rules of standing was *Rakas v. Illinois* (1978).[38] *Rakas* came to the Court when passengers within a vehicle which was illegally searched sought to have the evidence discovered from being introduced in their trial for armed robbery. In *Rakas* the Court eliminated the "legitimately on the premises" foundation of the automatic standing rule due to its "superficial clarity."[39] The Court believed that a demonstration that they had suffered an injury and that a person's rights were violated "is more properly placed within the purview of the substantive Fourth Amendment law than within that of standing."[40] Thus, individuals had to demonstrate that their personal Fourth Amendment rights were violated in order to challenge the submission of evidence at trial. In making its decision the Court rejected the target theory that anyone against whom a search was directed should have standing to challenge the admissibility of the evidence. The Court found that *Katz*'s requirement that an individual needs to have a legitimate expectation of privacy in the invaded space before there could be a Fourth Amendment violation provided better guidance. The Court's decision directed lower courts to examine sources outside the Fourth Amendment to help determine if an individual had a legitimate expectation of privacy. In the Court's view the key sources that needed to be examined included (1) the concepts of real and personal property, (2) the use of a location, (3) societal understandings, and (4) steps undertaken by a person to exclude others. The Court's decision in *Rakas* focused on the first of these sources, property interests, and denied the passengers of a car standing to challenge the search of the car because they asserted no possessory or property interest in the vehicle, especially under the seats and the glovebox where evidence was found. They also had no possessory interest in the items seized. As a result, the defendants failed to demonstrate a legitimate expectation of privacy in the areas searched. This was true despite the fact that the passengers had legitimately been in the car with the permission of the owner. The Court drew a distinction between being legitimately on the premises and having a legitimate expectation of privacy in the particular areas searched within the car.

The second decision weakening the rules of standing was *United States v. Salvucci* (1980).[41] The case came about after stolen checks which were found at a co-defendant's mother's house through a faulty warrant were used to gain a conviction against Salvucci. In *Salvucci* the Court ended that part of the automatic standing rule in Fourth Amendment cases that had stood since *Jones v. United States* that allowed challenges to any illegally seized contraband you were charged with possessing from being introduced at trial. Justice William Rehnquist examined the reasons behind the automatic standing rule in *Jones* and found two explanations. The first had been to prevent the danger of self-incrimination from having the defendant's testimony from the suppression hearing used at trial. The Court found this purpose behind the automatic standing rule was no longer valid due to the Court's decision in *Simmons v. United States* (1968)[42] which ruled that a defendant's testimony in a suppression hearing couldn't be used as evidence of their guilt. The second reason for the automatic standing rule had been to stop prosecutors from contradicting themselves by first arguing for standing purposes that the defendant's Fourth Amendment rights were not violated, but later, in order to gain a conviction arguing that the defendant did indeed possess the materials. Justice Rehnquist pointed out that the Court in *Rakas* had decided that this contradiction in prosecutorial tactics was acceptable. Therefore, Justice Rehnquist explained that "defendants charged with crimes of possession may only claim the benefits of the exclusionary rule if their own Fourth Amendment rights have been violated."[43] Justice Rehnquist further reasoned that "an illegal search only violates the rights of those who have a 'legitimate expectation of privacy in the invaded place.'"[44] Furthermore, the Court was unwilling to use "possession of a seized good as a substitute for a factual finding that the owner of the good had a legitimate expectation of privacy in the area searched."[45] Since Salvucci had not made the claim in his suppression hearing that he had a legitimate expectation of privacy in the place where the evidence against him was found, it was admissible.

The same day that *Salvucci* was decided the Court ruled on *Rawlings v. Kentucky* (1980).[46] In *Rawlings* police had an arrest warrant for a person named Marquees and went to Marquees' house to serve the warrant. When the police arrived, Marquees was not there, but they did smell marijuana, see pipes, and found four guests in the house. They required all the guests to wait in the house unless they were willing to allow a full body search until a search warrant for marijuana arrived for the house. While the guests were being held, David Rawlings stashed some of his property, 1800 tabs of LSD, into the purse of another guest, Vanessa Cox. When the warrant arrived forty-five minutes later the police ordered Cox to empty her purse. When the 1800 tabs of LSD were discovered David Rawlings immediately claimed the LSD as his property. Under *Jones*,

Rawlings would have had standing to challenge the evidence since he claimed possession of the drugs which were the basis of the charges brought against him. When the case came to the Supreme Court it held that Rawlings lacked standing to challenge the constitutionality of the search of the purse. The Court found that even though Rawling's ownership of the drugs in Cox's purse had to be taken into consideration, the decision in *Rakas* had rejected the principle that Fourth Amendment claims could be asserted based on outdated concepts of property law. The Court pointed out that while Cox certainly had a legitimate expectation of privacy in her purse that expectation did not extend to everyone who happened to be in the house. The Court reasoned that Rawlings did not have a legitimate expectation of privacy in the purse for a number of reasons. These included: (1) he had no right to exclude others from the purse, (2) he had taken no precautions to maintain privacy in the purse, (3) he did not have access to the purse prior to the police search, (4) he hadn't known Cox very long, (5) others had looked in the purse while they were in the house together, and (6) he had never before used the purse. All of these factors indicated to the Court that Rawlings had not taken "normal precautions to maintain his privacy."[47] The Court also noted that Rawlings lacked a subjective expectation of privacy in Cox's purse due to his admission that he did not believe the purse would be free from governmental intrusion. Even though he had hidden his illicit drugs there, Rawlings lacked a legitimate expectation of privacy in the purse since it was the property of another person. Therefore, his Fourth Amendment rights had not been violated by the purse's search and seizure and he had no standing to challenge the evidence found within the purse.

After rejecting the automatic standing rule, the Court next created a bright line rule which applied to individuals who are invited to be guests in someone else's home. The Court reasoned that when a person is invited as an overnight guest society is willing to respect as reasonable the legitimate expectation of privacy they have to stay without having their privacy interfered with by those who do not reside at the home. However, when a person is a guest in someone's home, but not invited to spend the night, they have no such expectation of privacy. In making that decision, the Court examined three of the sources for determining if an individual had a legitimate expectation of privacy that had been brought out in *Rakas*. The first was property interests. The Court reasoned that because the Fourth Amendment protects persons, not property, something other than merely being in another person's home had to exist to create an expectation of privacy. Therefore, the Court went on and examined the societal understandings source. The Court had no trouble ruling in *Minnesota v. Olson* (1990)[48] that society would be willing to protect the privacy expectations of overnight guests. Whether society would find the privacy claims of guests who were not staying the night to be reasonable was the issue in *Minnesota v. Carter* (1998).[49] The answer was dependant on the use those guests made of the property. The Court explained that there were three factors which had to be evaluated to determine if what a short term guest did at the property gave them a legitimate expectation of privacy in a searched premise. The first was an examination of the use of the property made by the guest. The Court noted that business use would be considered to create a lesser expectation of privacy compared to personal use. The second factor was how long the guest had spent on the premises, the longer a person was on the premises the greater was their expectation of privacy. Third, the relationship between the host and the guest needed to be examined and in order for the guest to have an expectation of privacy some previous connection must exist between the host and guest. In *Carter* the Court rejected the claim that Carter had a legitimate expectation of privacy to challenge evidence found in another person's apartment because he was invited into the apartment solely to complete a business transaction, weighing out cocaine. It was for a short period of time, two and a half hours. Finally, there was no other relationship between Carter and the apartment tenant other than the transaction.

The Court's determination to reinforce its ruling that defendants lacked standing unless their Fourth Amendment rights have been violated was demonstrated by its decision in *United States v. Payner* (1980).[50] *Payner* came to the Court as a result of Jack Payner's efforts to suppress evidence at his trial for falsifying his 1972 income tax return. The trial court found that most of the evidence used against Payner resulted from government agents knowingly and willfully unlawfully seizing the briefcase of a third party. The trial court also found that "the government affirmatively counsels its agents that the Fourth Amendment standing limitation permits them to obtain evidence against third parties."[51] The trial court ruled that while Payner did not have standing to object to the evidence, it would still be suppressed based on the power of federal courts to supervise the administration of justice. The government was then granted *certiorari*. In an opinion by Justice Powell, the Court quickly reaffirmed the holding of *Rakas* that defendants could only object to the use of evidence which was gathered through a violation of their own Fourth Amendment rights and this required the government to invade their legitimate expectation of privacy, not those of the third party. While stating: "No court should condone the unconstitutional and possibly criminal behavior of those who planned and executed this 'briefcase caper,'"[52] the Court nevertheless rejected suppression of the evidence based on the supervisory powers of courts. The Court thought this it was necessary to do this because the social costs of impeding the truth-finding function of a trial were too high and "the interest in deterring illegal searches does not justify the exclusion of tainted evidence at the instance of a party who was not the victim of the challenged practices."[53]

Susan Bandes points out the problem with the new standing rules stating, "Standing doctrine permits law enforcement to engage in conduct that would be illegal if certain litigants complained about it, so long as it directs it at those without the right to complain."[54] The bright line rule of *Minnesota v. Carter*, according to Stephen Jones, also results in the questionable outcome in which "the police can intentionally knock down someone's front door at night without a warrant, search the entire house, and charge all the non-overnight guests with constructive possession of any contraband found in the house and their flagrant violation of the Fourth Amendment can never be challenged if the owner is not charged."[55] In the same scenario, even though all houseguest should reasonably have the same expectation of privacy when they enter a person's home, overnight guests and the owner of a home would be protected by the Fourth Amendment from having any evidence seized from being introduced at trial. A Court that was serious about *Katz* would remember its words that "the Fourth Amendment protects, people, not places"[56] and honor a person's expectation of privacy regardless of whose car or home they are in just as it did the public phone booth in *Katz*.

The Burger Court and the Exclusionary Rule

As stated in *Mapp* the Warren Court had considered the exclusionary rule as a constitutional requirement of the Fourth Amendment. In *Linkletter*, however, the rule was promoted as tool that could be used to deter future violations of the Fourth Amendment. The two opinions penned by Justice Clark left the foundation and purpose of the exclusionary rule in disarray. It also created opportunities for later courts to take the exclusionary rule in a number of different directions depending on their predilections. The decisions of the Warren Court, like *Mapp*, which extended the rights of the criminally accused were immensely unpopular with both members of law enforcement and legal commentators.[57] The decisions were so unpopular that they became an issue in the presidential election of 1968 when candidate Richard Nixon promised that if he were elected he would only appoint judges and justices who would advance the cause of "law and order" and narrow the scope of the decisions of the Warren Court. After winning the election, President Nixon quickly got his chance to start rebuilding the Supreme Court. President Nixon appointed four justices, Chief Justice Warren Burger and associate justices, Harry Blackmun, Lewis Powell, and William Rehnquist. Compared to the Warren Court the Burger Court developed a fundamentally different approach to constitutional adjudication in the area of the rights of the criminally accused, especially concerning the exclusionary rule. The approach was summarized by John Burkhoff as follows:

> The Burger Court consider[ed] the exclusionary rule as a strictly prophylatic, judicially created device legitimate only to the extent that it deters unlawful police conduct. It is not, in this view, an inherent or necessary part of the fourth amendment; rather, it is one of many possible remedial devices theoretically available to protect and preserve fourth amendment interests.[58]

The changes that were made by the Burger Court in cases involving the application of the exclusionary rule were pushed with the leadership of Chief Justice Warren Burger who had a long history of skepticism of the rule.[59] Once on the Court, Chief Justice Burger continued to make his unhappiness with the exclusionary rule known. He expressed his view of the rule by using the case of *Bivens v. Six Unknown Named Agents* (1973)[60] as his vehicle. In his dissenting opinion, Chief Justice Burger disclaimed the theories which had served to justify the exclusionary rule in past cases and declared that the exclusionary rule rested solely on the deterrence rationale. He also discussed the possibility of applying other alternative remedies which could serve a deterrent function without the cost of letting criminals go free. More specifically, Chief Justice Burger indicated a desire for Congress to pass legislation which would: (1) waive sovereign immunity for law enforcement officers who commit illegal acts in the performance of their duties; (2) create a cause of action for damages resulting from such illegal actions; (3) create a quasi-judicial tribunal to adjudicate damages for such claims; (4) clarify that this process would be in lieu of exclusion of evidence; and (5) provide that no evidence be excluded from criminal trials due to violations of the Fourth Amendment.

In 1974 Chief Justice Burger's approach to the exclusionary rule became the standard for future applications in *United States v. Calandra*.[61] *Calandra* came to the Court after a witness, John Calandra, who had been summoned to appear before a grand jury investigating loan sharking, refused to answer some questions on the grounds that the source of the questions was based on the fruits of an unlawful search of his business. In determining if such questions had to be excluded from grand jury inquiries, the Supreme Court in a 6-3 decision with the opinion written by Justice Lewis Powell ruled that the exclusionary rule was inapplicable. The first thing that was made clear by the opinion was that the exclusionary rule was no longer considered by the Supreme Court to be required directly by the Constitution or to protect judicial integrity. Instead, Justice Powell wrote that the exclusionary rule was "a judicially created remedy designed to safeguard Fourth Amendment rights generally through a deterrent effect, rather than a personal constitutional right of the party aggrieved."[62] As a remedy, the sole purpose of the exclusionary rule was "to deter future unlawful police conduct and thereby effectuate the guarantee of the Fourth Amendment against unreasonable search and seizures."[63] As a deterrent the rule would not be automatically applied in all future cases. Instead, the Court held that "despite its broad deterrent purpose, the rule has never been interpreted to proscribe the use of illegally seized evidence in all proceedings against all persons" and its application should be "restricted to those areas where its remedial objectives are thought most efficiously served."[64]

The Court reached out in *Calandra* and made a broad ruling which would have even more serious implications for the exclusionary rule than had *Alderman v. United States*. Not only did *Calandra* make it clear that the cost-benefit balancing approach was the preferred method of determining whether the exclusionary rule should be applied, it also clarified that the Court was willing to consider societal costs other than the possibility of criminals going free. In reaching a balance in *Calandra* the Court weakened the interest of the person whose Fourth Amendment rights had been violated. This was done because the Court noted that the primary deterrent effect from the exclusionary rule came through the application of the rule to the prosecution's case-in-chief. Such a view of deterrence had the potential to allow use of illegally gathered evidence in a variety of settings that did not include the prosecution's case-in-chief. The Court ruled

> Whatever deterrence of police misconduct may result from the exclusion of illegally seized evidence from criminal trials, it is unrealistic to assume that application of the rule to grand jury proceedings would significantly further that goal. . . . We therefore decline to embrace a view that would achieve a speculative and undoubtedly minimal advance in the deterrence of police misconduct at the expense of substantially impeding the role of the grand jury.[65]

The Court also explained that exclusion would not only impact the ability of the grand jury to function, but use of illegally gathered evidence did not create a new violation of the individual's Fourth Amendment rights. The Court's willingness to explicitly state that the exclusionary rule was a judicially created remedy which did not disallow the government from benefitting as a result of all constitutional violations demonstrates that the Court's majority had firmly adopted the fragmented model of government in regard to the exclusionary rule.

Justice William Brennan, who promoted the unitary model of government, wrote a dissent in *Calandra,* joined by Justices William Douglas and John Marshall, which recognized the potential that adoption of a fragmented model of government could have on the future of the exclusionary rule. Speaking for the last remaining justices who had been in the *Mapp* majority, he complained that the Court misunderstood the historic purpose of the exclusionary rule which "accomplished twin goals of enabling the judiciary to avoid the taint of partnership in official lawlessness and of assuring the people—all potential victims of unlawful government conduct—that the government would not profit from its lawless behavior."[66]

The Burger Court consistently insisted that the sole purpose of the exclusionary rule was to serve as a deterrent remedy for future constitutional violations. In doing so, it applied the cost-benefit balancing approach to determine if the exclusionary rule would serve as a future deterrent. In all of the cases which follow the Court found that under the circumstances involved the use of the exclusionary rule was inappropriate. In *United States v. Janis* (1976)[67] the Court held that evidence which was illegally obtained by state police was admissible in a federal civil tax proceeding. The Court believed that the societal costs of excluding evidence which was gathered by police officers representing one government from use in civil courts by another government was too high to allow exclusion. Furthermore, there was an insufficient likelihood that exclusion in a federal civil court would have a deterrent effect on the actions of state officers. In 1976 the Court ruled in *Stone v. Powell*[68] that in federal *habeas corpus* proceedings Fourth Amendment claims, including claims that the exclusionary rule was not properly applied could no longer be reviewed. The Court reasoned that where state courts had given a defendant a full and fair hearing on their Fourth Amendment claims it would be inappropriate to then review and exclude evidence in the *habeas* process because "the contribution of the exclusionary rule to the effectuation of the Fourth Amendment is minimal, and the substantial costs of application of the rule persist with special force."[69] In 1980 the Court ruled in *United States v. Haven*[70] that evidence gathered through a violation of the Fourth Amendment which is inadmissible in the prosecution's case-in-chief can be used by the prosecutor to impeach a defendant who testifies at a criminal trial. In 1984 the Court ruled in *United States v. Lopez-Mendoza*[71] that the exclusionary rule did not apply to deportation proceedings. As a result of not applying the exclusionary rule to the preceding judicial hearings, the only type of judicial proceeding other than criminal trials in which the rule is applied to is civil forfeiture proceedings wherein the government seeks the forfeiture of non-contraband personal property because it was used in the commission of a crime.[72]

Since settling on a cost-benefit approach to the exclusionary rule, the Burger Court's interest balancing between the costs associated with the exclusionary rule versus its benefits has been an easy calculation for it. Time and time again the Burger Court noted the high cost of freeing those criminals who are plainly guilty because they were caught with the evidence. Other social costs of the exclusionary rule to which the Court has referred include impeding the search for the truth and creating disrespect for the law. The benefits of the exclusionary rule are more difficult to conceptualize. It is difficult to determine how often the police would violate the Fourth Amendment were it not for the exclusionary rule. How does one know what value we should put on the privacy of the lives of citizens due to the role of the exclusionary rule? For the Burger and then the Rehnquist Courts the benefits of the exclusionary rule were so difficult to determine, they became speculative.

The Court's balancing of interests has not been accepted by all legal scholars without criticism. Yale Kamisar, observing the vagueness of the basis of competition between the values at stake, asked the following questions of this approach to the exclusionary rule:

> Does interest-balancing, at least when applying the exclusionary rule, turn largely, if not entirely, on *how* one identifies the competing interests and *how* one "weighs" them? How does one go about doing this: How for example, does one "quantify" the "privacy" or "individual liberty" the fourth amendment is supposed to protect and the exclusionary rule is supposed to effectuate? Is interest-balancing the "real" basis for judgment in the way to write an opinion once a judgment has already been reached on the basis of individual, subjective values?[73]

Criticisms of the Burger Court's interest balancing did not, however, sway its approach to the exclusionary rule. The knowledge by prosecutors and trial judges that the Burger Court was rewriting the dimensions of the exclusionary rule may have emboldened some to keep testing the limits of what types of illegally gathered evidence would be admissible at trial and whether it could be included in the prosecution's case-in-chief.

Continuing unhappiness with the societal costs of the exclusionary rule resulted in clear signals by some of the justices that they might also be willing to relax the application of the exclusionary rule to allow illegally gathered evidence to be used in the prosecution's case-in-chief. One clear signal was sent by Justice Lewis Powell who hinted in his majority opinion in *Brewer v. Williams* (1977)[74] that the Court might look favorably on arguments for an "inevitable discovery" exception that would allow evidence which is gathered illegally to be admissible if it could be demonstrated that it would have also been discovered through legal means. Beyond that, by 1984 five of the sitting justices, Chief Justice Warren Burger and Justices William Rehnquist, Byron White, Lewis Powell, and Sandra Day O'Connor, had indicated a willingness to adopt a "good faith" exception to the exclusionary rule. Both an "inevitable discovery" and a "good faith" exception to the exclusionary rule, would allow illegally seized evidence to be used in the prosecution's case-in-chief. In 1984 the Court granted *certiorari* in a series of cases involving these possible exceptions to the exclusionary rule which had the potential of removing limitations on when illegally gathered evidence could be admitted in all phases of a trial.

The Court's opportunity to add an inevitable discovery exception to the exclusionary rule came in *Nix v. Williams* (1984).[75] *Nix* came to the Court as a result of the Supreme Court overturning a prior first degree murder conviction of Robert Anthony Williams in 1977 due to a violation of his Sixth Amendment right to counsel.[76] When Williams was tried again tainted evidence, in the form of a body and forensic tests conducted on it, was admitted on the theory that it would have been inevitably discovered if there had not first been constitutional violations which led to its discovery. The judge allowed the evidence because of testimony which showed that police had organized a search party of around 200 volunteers. These searchers had divided the area of the search in grid fashion and then split into teams responsible for specific areas where they were instructed to "check all the roads, the ditches, any culverts . . . or any other places where a small child could be secreted."[77] There was additional testimony that, had Williams not led the police to the body, the search would have been resumed and discovered the body in an additional three to five hours. The trial judge believed that based on this testimony the body would have been found in similar condition had there not been a violation of William's rights and admitted the challenged evidence in question. After his second conviction for first degree murder was upheld by the Iowa Supreme Court, Williams filed a petition for writ of *habeas corpus* in federal court. The petition was denied by the district court. After that decision was overturned by the court of appeal, the Supreme Court granted *certiorari*.

The Court in a 7-2 decision reversed the grant of *habeas corpus*. The majority opinion, written by Chief Justice Burger, started with a review of the facts to the case and its history. Chief Justice Burger then discussed the heart of the case, the role of the exclusionary rule in the American legal system. The opinion pointed out that Williams' arguments in favor of upholding the grant of *habeas corpus* because the body and the related physical evidence should not have been admitted at trial was based upon two things. The first was that the body and all resulting evidence should have been considered "fruit of the poisonous tree" since it was directly found through the violation of Williams' right to counsel. The second was that if the inevitable discovery exception to the exclusionary rule was constitutionally permissible, it had to include the element of police good faith which Williams claimed had not existed when his rights were violated.

Chief Justice Burger's opinion selectively read the history of the exclusionary rule by emphasizing the Court's acceptance of a fragmented model of government. The central point in the majority opinion's reading of the history of the exclusionary rule was that our judicial system has accepted the exclusionary rule due to its deterrent effect despite its high social cost of, at times, letting the guilty go free. This has been acceptable since the "prosecution is not to be put in a better position than it would have been in if no illegality had transpired."[78] The Court believed that in cases where there was police misconduct a balance had to be reached between the competing interests of deterring police abuses and allowing juries all probative evidence. The Court then pointed out that in past cases involving the independent source doctrine it had been understood "that the interest of society in deterring unlawful police conduct and the public interest in having juries receive all probative evidence of a crime are properly balanced by putting the police in the same, not a *worse*, position that they would have been in if no police error or misconduct had occurred."[79] As a result of this past history, even though there was a difference between the independent source and inevitable discovery exceptions, the Court believed there was "a functional similarity between these two doctrines in that exclusion of evidence that would inevitably have been discovered would also put the government in a worse position, because the police would have obtained that evidence if no misconduct had taken place."[80]

Having accepted the inevitable discovery exception to the exclusionary rule into our body of law, the Court then established some standards for its application. The Court stated that tainted evidence would be admissible if the prosecution could prove by a preponderance of the evidence that the information would inevitably have been found by lawful means. When such a situation exists Chief Justice Burger explained, "then the deterrence rationale has so little basis that the evidence should be received."[81] The Court also held that in meeting its burden the prosecution did not have to show that the police acted in good faith. This was because such a showing would place courts in the position of withholding truthful evidence from juries which would place the "police in a *worse* position than they would have been if no unlawful conduct had transpired."[82] This, the Court believed, would have placed too high of a societal cost on our system of justice and its search for truth. Furthermore, the Court believed that a showing of good faith on the part of police wouldn't affect future deterrence because "when an officer is aware that the evidence will inevitably be discovered, he will try to avoid engaging in any questionable practice" to ensure the evidence's admissibility.[83] The Court accepted the ruling of the trial court judge and believed that it was clear that the body and additional evidence would have inevitably been discovered by lawful means and overruled the judgment of the court of appeals.

Justice Brennan filed a dissenting opinion which was joined by Justice Marshall. The opinion agreed that the inevitable discovery exception was constitutionally permissible due to the similarities between it and the independent source exception to the exclusionary rule. Despite this similarity, Justice Brennan believed that the majority's opinion showed disrespect for the exclusionary rule causing the majority to be overly zealous in its desire to undermine the rule. Justice Brennan stated, "to ensure that this hypothetical finding is narrowly confined to circumstances that are functionally equivalent to an independent source, and to protect fully the fundamental rights served by the exclusionary rule, I would require clear and convincing evidence before concluding that the government had met its burden of proof on this issue."[84]

The second exception to the exclusionary rule that the Court considered in 1984 was the "good faith" exception. The Court examined this exception in *United States v. Leon*[85] and its companion case *Massachusetts v. Sheppard*.[86] The facts to *Leon* were that police received a tip from an anonymous informant, who had no track record for reliability, that two people were selling drugs from their home. The police then undertook an investigation to collaborate the tip. Six months later a warrant application was made based on the original tip. Police also included in the affidavit corroborative evidence gathered through one month of surveillance that placed Leon and his codefendants in a pattern of contacts with people who had narcotics records. Police secured search warrants for three homes and several vehicles. In the searches conducted pursuant to the warrants, drugs were found. The lower courts ruled, and the Supreme Court accepted as fact, that the warrants were invalid and should not have been issued. This was because the informant's tip that was used in the affidavit had become stale and the evidence gained from the surveillance was as consistent with innocent behavior as guilty behavior. The lower court also concluded that the officers in this case had acted with good faith when the warrant was served.

In *Sheppard*, police had the probable cause necessary to get a search warrant to search Sheppard's home in a murder case. The police did not have the right warrant form available and the application was drawn up on a warrant form that was standardized for the search of drugs. When police applied for the warrant, they informed the judge about the problems with the warrant application and the judge said that he would make the necessary changes. Unfortunately, the judge did not make all the necessary changes and the warrant which was issued only allowed a search for drugs, not for evidence of a murder, and did not have attached to it the affidavit which set out the items for which the police had planned to search. When police conducted the search they found items related to the murder which had been in the original affidavit, but were not mentioned in the warrant. The trial court found that although the police had acted in good faith the warrant was constitutionally defective.

The Supreme Court granted *certiorari* in these two cases to determine if there was a good faith exception. The Court in a 6-3 decision ruled that there was indeed a good faith exception to the exclusionary rule. As a result, evidence which is discovered when police have acted in reasonably good faith on a warrant issued by a neutral and detached magistrate will not be suppressed. Justice White wrote the Court's opinion. In a complete turnaround from the judicial integrity argument put forth in *Weeks* and *Mapp* the Court stated that excluding evidence in cases when the police have acted properly had the potential to generate disrespect for the law and the administration of justice. Justice White also made it clear that "the use of fruits of a past unlawful search or seizure 'work no new Fourth Amendment wrong'" so courts would not be violating the Fourth Amendment by allowing tainted evidence to be admitted.[87] Justice White found no deterrent benefits in suppressing evidence under these circumstances that would produce better performance by the issuing magistrate. Justice White reasoned:

> First, the exclusionary rule is designed to deter police misconduct rather than to punish the errors of judges and magistrates. Second, there exists no evidence suggesting that judges and magistrates are inclined to ignore or subvert the Fourth Amendment. . . . Third [we don't think] that exclusion of evidence seized pursuant to a warrant will have a significant deterrent effect on the issuing judge or magistrate.[88]

Justice White next examined the exclusionary rule itself. His reasoning was based on the Burger Court's well established preference for a balancing test to determine if exclusion of illegally gathered evidence was necessary. Justice White explained

> Whether the exclusionary sanction is appropriately imposed in a particular case, our decisions make clear is "an issue separate from the question whether the Fourth Amendment rights of the party seeking to invoke the rule were violated by police conduct." Only the former question is currently before us, and it must be resolved by weighing the costs and benefits of preventing the use in the prosecution's case-in-chief of inherently trustworthy tangible evidence obtained in reliance on a search warrant issued by a detached and neutral magistrate that ultimately is found to be defective.[89]

The Court found that the social cost of the exclusionary rule was too high in cases such as these. Justice White pointed to empirical evidence which confirmed that a number of convictions were lost due to the exclusionary rule. Justice White went on and stated that the cases which went to court and resulted in no conviction due to the suppression of evidence "mask a large absolute number of felons who are released because the cases against them were based in part on illegal searches or seizures."[90] Weighed against these substantial costs was the Court's view that there were no benefits in the form of a deterrent effect on future constitutional violations if it excluded evidence in cases such as this. That was because in these cases the police followed the procedures laid out in the Fourth Amendment by seeking warrants prior to the searches. Therefore, applying the exclusionary rule would not change the behavior of the police and serve as a future deterrent.

Justice Harry Blackmun, who concurred in the opinion, made it clear that his support for the good faith exception was tentative and dependent on the future behavior of law enforcement. He reasoned:

> If it should emerge from experience that, contrary to our expectation, the good faith exception to the exclusionary rule results in a material change in police compliance with the Fourth Amendment, we shall have to reconsider what we have undertaken here. The logic of a decision that rests on untested predictions about police conduct demands no less.[91]

In *Leon* the Court made it clear that evidence which came about through the issuance of a warrant did not give the police a blank check to commit constitutional violations. This was because their actions would not fall under the good faith exception if a reasonably well-trained officer would have realized the warrant was improperly issued. Justice White gave four examples in which it would be unreasonable for an officer to claim that he or she had acted in good faith. These were: (1) when the affidavit knowingly included false information; (2) when the magistrate abandoned his or her neutral and detached role; (3) when the affidavit so lacked an indication of probable cause that belief that it did would be unreasonable; and (4) when the warrant itself was facially deficient. What Justice White seemed to have forgotten was that in *Franks v. Delaware* (1978)[92] the Court had created rules that made it difficult to show that a warrant was based on false information. The Court in *Franks* ruled that in order to invalidate a warrant based on false information being included in the affidavit an individual would have to first provide a specific proof to demonstrate that the officer who applied for the warrant made the false statement knowingly and intentionally or with reckless disregard for the truth. Next, the individual hoping to get a warrant thrown out and evidence excluded would have to demonstrate through a preponderance of the evidence that the false statements were a necessary part of the determination that probable cause existed.

As was traditional during the Burger Court, Justices Brennan and Marshall opposed weakening the exclusionary rule or the Fourth Amendment and argued in favor of a unitary model of government. In his dissent in *Leon* Justice Brennan reminded the Court that according to *Weeks v. United States* the exclusionary rule was integral to protecting the Fourth Amendment and the amendment would mean little if the government could make use of illegally seized evidence. Furthermore, the original purpose of the exclusionary rule was not only to act as a deterrent to future Fourth Amendment violations, it was to ensure that the government did not benefit from the use of illegally obtained evidence. As a result, once it was determined that evidence was illegally gathered the Court's duty was to find the evidence inadmissible, not determine the good or bad faith of those officers involved in the seizure. He further argued that the judicial branch needed to continue to play an important role in preserving constitutional principles so it was necessary for courts to suppress evidence which was gathered through a violation of the Fourth Amendment. Justice Brennan's dissent argued that the Court was not being fair in the manner it determined the cost/benefit analysis of the exclusionary rule. This was because the empirical evidence demonstrated that only 0.2% of all felony arrests were declined for prosecution due to the exclusionary rule and even less of those would fall into the category of cases in which police had relied on good faith.[93] While the costs were exaggerated, Brennan complained that "the benefits of such exclusion are made to disappear with the mere wave of a hand."[94] Finally, Justice Brennan believed that the exception carved out by the Court took away the institutional incentive for police departments to educate themselves about the Fourth Amendment and provided incentive to promote police ignorance rather than education of Fourth Amendment principles.

In *Sheppard v. Massachusetts* the Court reasoned that since the officer who sought the warrant told the judge who issued it about the problems with the application and what would be necessary to correct them, the judge indicated that he would make the corrections, the officer watched the judge do so, and the judge then said the warrant was okay, it was reasonable for the officer to rely on the warrant. The Court ruled that the evidence should be admissible and the conviction stand because "there is little reason why [the officer] should be expected to disregard assurances that everything is all right, especially when he has alerted the judge to the potential problems."[95]

Leon and *Sheppard* help to clarify the Court's understanding of the deterrent role that the exclusionary rule should play. As the Court explained, "If exclusion of evidence obtained pursuant to a subsequently invalidated warrant is to have any deterrent effect, . . . it must alter the behavior of individual law enforcement officers or the policies of their departments.[96] Furthermore, even if application of the exclusionary rule would deter some police misconduct, "it cannot be expected, and should not be applied, to deter objectively reasonable law enforcement activity."[97]

The knowledge that officers have that if they obtain a warrant, the fruits of their search will be admitted as evidence gives officers good incentive to follow the warrant process in securing evidence. In this way the good faith exception helps to strengthen the Fourth Amendment. Unfortunately, due to the Court's acceptance of the fragmented model of government allowing use of evidence gathered through warrants that do not pass constitutional scrutiny is acceptable, at the same time the Court is giving police incentive to use warrants, it is also in part negating the Fourth Amendment. Due to the reasoning in *Leon* and *Sheppard* there are a variety of factual situations that will fall under the good faith exception to the exclusionary rule. These include cases in which a magistrate issued a warrant when there was a lack of probable cause, failures to incorporate the affidavit into the warrant, and warrants which are overly broad.

One problem some commentators have pointed out concerning the good faith exception is that it places considerable power in the hands of magistrates who may not be formally trained as attorneys but have the power to decide whether a warrant will be issued. This is because appellate review of whether a warrant should have been issued makes little sense if the evidence will be admitted any way.[98] David Esseks has characterized the changes resulting from the good faith and inevitable discovery exceptions for the exclusionary in the following way:

> The "old" Exclusionary rule read, essentially, "if the evidence is tainted, then suppress it from use in the prosecution's case-in-chief." With the [exceptions], the rule became, "if the evidence is tainted, then suppress it from the use in the prosecution's case-in-chief only if doing so will deter police misconduct."[99]

In yet another 1984 case, *Segura v. United States*,[100] the Court had to determine whether an initial illegal search into a person's apartment requires the exclusion of evidence which was subsequently seized pursuant to a valid warrant. This case came to the Court after the New York Drug Task Force got word that Segura and Colon were selling drugs out of their apartment. Agents then placed the suspects and their apartment under surveillance. The agents observed the suspects selling drugs to several people and then trailed those people to their homes and arrested them. One of those arrested, Rivudalla-Vidal, admitted that he had bought drugs from Segura and Colon. He also informed agents that Segura was going to call him later that evening to see if he needed more of the product. The agents then sought and received authorization from superiors to arrest Segura and Colon. Agents were told that a search warrant for the residence would be obtained the next day, but that the agents should secure the premises after the arrests to prevent the destruction of evidence. Segura was arrested outside the apartment. The agents then went to the apartment to arrest Colon. Prior to her arrest, the police did a security check of the apartment to ensure that their safety was not at risk and stop possible destruction of evidence. Along with Colon there were three other persons in the apartment and the agents saw drug paraphernalia in plain view. Colon and the others were then arrested and agents informed everyone that a search warrant was going to be issued. Two agents were left at the apartment to secure the evidence, but the warrant was not issued for another nineteen hours. When the warrant did arrive and a search was made, agents discovered close to three pounds of cocaine.

The defendants moved to suppress all the evidence against them. The district court held that there were no exigent circumstances which justified entry into the apartment so it found that the initial entry of the apartment, arrest of Colon, and seizure of the drug paraphernalia was illegal. The court went on and ruled that the evidence seized pursuant to the warrant would not have necessarily been discovered but for the illegal entry and impoundment of the apartment because it may have been moved or destroyed. As a result, this evidence had to be suppressed as fruit of the poisonous tree. The court of appeals affirmed in part and reversed in part. It affirmed that the evidence gathered in the security check of the apartment should have been suppressed since the security check was not justified. It reversed on all the other evidence and allowed it to be admitted under the belated warrant not accepting the "but for" reasoning of the lower court. The Supreme Court granted *certiorari*.

The Supreme Court in a 5-4 decision allowed the evidence that was gathered through a legal warrant executed the day after the agents had unlawfully entered and secured the apartment to be used. Chief Justice Burger wrote for the majority. The Court accepted the lower court's ruling that the security check of the apartment was an illegal action. The search of the apartment after arrival of the warrant was legal, however, due to the fact that none of the information contained in the affidavit came from the illegal security check. The opinion relied on the independent source exception to the exclusionary rule. The Court reasoned it was appropriate to make use of the evidence found through the warrant because the challenged evidence was the product of a search which was unrelated to the prior illegal entry in the form of the security check. Therefore, exclusion was not necessary in light of the fact that nothing contained in the affidavit for the warrant relied in any part on information gained during the illegal entry. This made the illegal entry of the apartment irrelevant to the question as to whether the evidence gained through the search warrant was admissible. Chief Justice Burger clarified that evidence would not be excluded as "'fruit [of the poisonous tree]' unless the illegality is at least the 'but for' cause of the discovery of the evidence. Suppression is not justified unless 'the challenged evidence is in some sense the product of illegal governmental activity.'"[101] Chief Justice Burger noted that this ruling was one which adhered to both logic and common sense. Furthermore, because the exclusionary rule "already exacts an enormous price from society and our system of justice" further expanding it to this case would "further 'protect' criminal activity."[102]

Justice John Paul Stevens wrote a dissent which did not distinguish between the initial illegal entry and the occupation of the apartment while agents waited for the warrant to arrive. Justice Stevens argued that the agents had occupied the apartment to ensure that evidence would not be lost. The desire to acquire the evidence before a warrant was issued was the motivating force for the agents to violate the Constitution. Therefore, in his mind there was a direct connection between the illegal actions of the government and the evidence which was gained. He also criticized the reasoning of the majority stating "a rule of law that is predicated on the absurd notion that a police officer does not have the skill required to obtain a valid search warrant in less than 19 or 20 hours or that fails to deter authorities from delaying unreasonably their attempt to obtain a warrant after they have entered a home, is demeaning to law enforcement and can only encourage sloppy, undisciplined procedures."[103] It should be noted that in a later case, *Maryland v. Buie* (1990),[104] the Court gave law enforcement officers authority to conduct a security sweep when serving an arrest warrant in a person's home.

The Rehnquist Court and the Exclusionary Rule

When Ronald Reagan was elected president he too sought to influence the Supreme Court on issues regarding the criminal justice process. Tinsley Yarbrough has written "to a greater degree arguably than all his predecessors, President Reagan closely reviewed the ideological leanings of prospective judicial nominees and maximized White house control over judicial selection."[105] At the beginning of his second term, two years before the promotion of William Rehnquist, President Reagan asked Attorney General Edwin Meese if there was any way they could limit the excesses of the Warren Court's decisions. In response the Attorney General's office produced eight reports collectively titled the "Truth in Criminal Justice Series." The report on the Fourth Amendment referred to *Mapp v. Ohio* as a case in which the Warren Court had improperly used its power to incorporate the exclusionary rule even though the rule could not be found in the original intent or meaning of the Constitution. It went on to condemn the rule for its high costs to society, especially releasing people who were factually guilty of criminal behavior. The conclusion of the report was that due to these high costs the administration should work to convince the Supreme Court to end its support for the exclusionary rule. President Reagan's first appointment to the Supreme Court was Sandra Day O'Connor, the first woman appointed to the Supreme Court, who was a pragmatic conservative. O'Connor proved to be a fairly reliable vote which sided with the government and against expanding the rights of criminal defendants. The promotion of William Rehnquist to the position of the Chief Justice was President Ronald Reagan's second appointment to the Supreme Court. The promotion of William Rehnquist, who at the time was the most conservative justice on the Court, was seen as another signal as to what type of Court President Reagan desired. The nomination of Antonin Scalia to fill Rehnquist's position sent another strong message that Reagan was hoping to build a Court of law and order conservatives. President Reagan tried to place another strong conservative on the Court in the person of Robert Bork, but the Senate failed to confirm the nomination. Anthony Kennedy was eventually placed on the Court. Justice Kennedy, like Justice O'Connor, is a moderate conservative.

President George Herbert Walker Bush strengthened the conservative base of the Rehnquist Court. Due to the retirements of Justices William Brennan and Thurgood Marshall, the two holdovers from the Warren Court who had continually argued in favor of a traditional approach to the Fourth Amendment and believed that the exclusionary rule was a constitutional requirement, President Bush got to nominate two justices. They were Justice David Souter, a moderate, and Justice Clarence Thomas, an ideological conservative. Both of these justices accept the view that the exclusionary rule is a judicially created remedy for constitutional violations. President Bill Clinton's appointees, Justices Ruth Bader Ginsburg in 1993 and Stephen Breyer in 1994, have also shown a willingness to accept the current orthodoxy that the exclusionary rule is a judicially created remedy which is applied only when it will have a deterrent effect.

As leadership on the Supreme Court passed from Chief Justice Warren Burger to Chief Justice William Rehnquist there was no change in the Court's view of the exclusionary rule. The Rehnquist Court continued to believe that the rule was a judicially created remedy which was only properly applied when it would serve as a deterrent to future constitutional violations by police. For the Rehnquist Court, exclusion was only necessary when the benefits outweighed the costs. The Court also continued to accept a fragmented model of government whereby evidence discovered through a constitutional violation by one branch of the government was seen as an isolated event and could be used at trial in another branch of the government.

During the Rehnquist years, the Supreme Court expanded the application of the good faith exception. One example may be found in *Illinois v. Krull* (1987).[106] *Krull* came to the Court after the trial court excluded evidence which was crucial in the prosecution of Albert Krull. His arrest was the result of investigative work undertaken by the Chicago Police Department who visited Krull's automobile wrecking yard. The police went to the yard based on the authority given to them by a state law which permitted officers the ability to search such facilities without a warrant. When police searched the yard they traced several VIN numbers and determined that three vehicles at the site were stolen. Krull was then arrested and prosecuted for various violations of the Illinois motor vehicle statutes. Krull objected to use of the evidence since he argued that the state law which gave police authority to conduct the search was unconstitutional. The trial court ruled that the state law did indeed violate the Fourth Amendment and thus required suppression of the evidence. The Illinois Supreme Court affirmed the lower court decision, so Illinois sought and was granted *certiorari*.

In a 5-4 decision the Supreme Court affirmed that the statute in question was unconstitutional, but nevertheless allowed the evidence which was the fruit of the search conducted under authority of the statute to be used under the good faith exception to the exclusionary rule. The majority opinion, written by Justice Blackmun, reaffirmed the basic premise of the exclusionary rule, that it stops illegally gathered evidence from being admitted in a criminal prosecution. He went on to explain that the rule's primary purpose is to deter police from committing future violations of the Fourth Amendment. The Court again noted that the rule was a judicially created remedy for constitutional violations and that the victim of an illegal search had no personal constitutional right to exclusion of the evidence. After laying out these basic principles the Court explained that the ruling precedent in this case was *Leon* which allowed evidence to be used when an officer acted in an objectively reasonable reliance on a search warrant that was later found to have been unconstitutionally issued. Excluding evidence in situations where police had in good faith tried to adhere to the letter of the law would not act as proper deterrent for future violations. The Court reasoned that the similarity between relying on a warrant that an officer thought was valid and a statute was similar enough so that *Leon* should control the decision in *Krull*.

The Court's opinion again asserted a fragmented model of government by reasoning that a central question of inquiry was whether legislators were "inclined to ignore or subvert the Fourth Amendment."[107] The Court decided that even though legislators were not neutral judicial officers, they should not be seen as part of the law enforcement team. The Court found there was no evidence to indicate that legislators purposely tried to pass unconstitutional laws so excluding evidence in such cases would serve no deterrent against future actions of state legislatures. The truth was that legislators took an oath of office to uphold the Constitution. In both *Krull* and *Leon* police had in good faith followed the law and acted in an objectively reasonable manner so exclusion would not act as an effective deterrent for future violations.

Justice O'Connor wrote the dissent in *Krull*. It reasoned that even though *Leon* had been properly settled, the role of the magistrate who mistakenly issues a warrant and a legislature which creates an unconstitutional law are too different to be treated the same. The opinion pointed out that a main reason behind the Fourth Amendment was that laws during the colonial period allowed searches which were so broad that they were considered to be unreasonable. Furthermore, the Court's past efforts to ensure that evidence which was seized as a result of overly broad laws would be suppressed demonstrated that the Court believed that legislatures, unlike magistrates, did indeed present a significant threat to civil liberties. Justice O'Connor argued against giving police a window of opportunity in which unconstitutional laws could be passed and the evidence gathered under these laws would be admitted at trial until such time that the laws were declared unconstitutional by the courts. This, she believed, would give legislatures incentive to pass bad laws. Not expanding the good faith exception to instances where the police relied on an unconstitutional law would therefore, she argued, have a deterrent effect on the willingness of legislatures to pass unconstitutional laws.

Another example of the Rehnquist Court expanding the good faith exception is *Maryland v. Garrison* (1987).[108] In this case police received a tip from a reliable informant that marijuana was being sold out of the top floor apartment of a three story apartment building at 2036 Park Avenue. Police checked out the building to see if it matched the description given by the informant. When the description of the building matched, police went to the electric company and found out that the name of the person who had the third floor apartment was Lawrence McWebb. The police then took a picture of McWebb from an old arrest record to the informant who identified him as the person selling marijuana. The police then secured a search warrant for McWebb's third floor apartment. When police arrived to serve the warrant they noticed seven mailboxes and doorbells at the entrance to the building. Before they entered the building, McWebb drove up. Police detained him and told him about the search warrant. Police then went up to the third floor where they found a foyer with rooms to the left and to the right. Doors to both these rooms were open and one had a man, Harold Garrison, standing in the doorway. Police believed Garrison to be a guest of McWebb. The officers then searched the entire third floor of the building without noticing that the doors in the foyer room had numbers on them indicating that there were two separate apartments. The police found marijuana, heroin, and drug paraphernalia before they noticed that there were two kitchens indicating that there were two separate apartments. Realizing their mistake, the search was ended. Regardless of the fact that there had been no warrant to search Garrison's apartment he was prosecuted for possession of the drugs found in his apartment. At trial Garrison unsuccessfully moved to have the evidence gathered in the search suppressed. Eventually, the Court of Appeal of Maryland ruled that the evidence should be suppressed and Maryland then sought and was granted *certiorari*.

In an opinion by Justice Stevens the Court divided the case into two issues. In the first issue the Court determined that the search warrant which was used to gather evidence was facially valid. The Court believed that the validity of the warrant had to be determined by examining the information that was actually disclosed by the officer in the affidavit and any information the officer should have discovered and disclosed. The Court then noted that if the officers either knew or should have known that the third floor had two apartments the warrant could not be considered valid. After examining the facts, the Court determined that the police did not have sufficient information to be able to know that there were two apartments on the third floor. Therefore, the warrant was valid.

The second question that the Court had to answer was whether the police had acted reasonably when they served the warrant. The Court explained that a search that would normally be invalid due to the over breadth of the warrant, is not necessarily so when police have objectively believed with good reason that the warrant was valid. That was the foundation behind the Court creating a good faith exception to the exclusionary rule. Therefore, in this case it was crucial to determine if the failure of the police to understand the over breadth of the warrant was objectively reasonable and understandable. Given the facts of the case, the Court concluded that even though there was evidence that the police could have discovered that the warrant did not cover the entire third floor of the apartment building, the officers were reasonable when they served the warrant and read the warrant to authorize the search of the entire third floor.

Justice Blackmun wrote a dissent which was joined by Justices Brennan and Marshall. Justice Blackmun pointed out that multi-unit apartments deserved the same protections under the Fourth Amendment as single homes. Thus, unless there was a valid warrant or an exigent circumstance which could justify entry into Garrison's apartment, there was a constitutional violation. In this case there were neither. The warrant was not valid because it did not with particularity describe the place to be searched and could only have been justifiably served on McWebb's apartment, not Garrison's. There was no exigent circumstance in this case. Justice Blackmun further believed that police could not rely on the good faith exception to excuse their error. This was because he thought that with diligent effort, police could have discovered prior to the issuance of the warrant that there were two apartments on the third floor. Furthermore, he believed that even though they had not discovered the existence of two apartments prior to gaining the warrant a number of things should have given officers a red flag when the warrant was served. These items included the number of mailboxes at the address which should have indicated the presence of two apartments on the third floor, the presence of two doors off the foyer on the third floor, and the decision of police not to go to the trouble of asking Garrison where he lived while they conducted the search of his apartment. All of these factors meant that police had not acted reasonably so the evidence should have been excluded from trial.

Another case in which the Court reexamined the good faith exception and expanded its application was *Arizona v. Evans* (1995).[109] *Evans* came to the Court after Isaac Evans was stopped for a traffic violation, going the wrong way on a one way street. Police then ran a computer check on him which indicated that there was an outstanding arrest warrant on Evans. Evans was placed under arrest and the search incident to that arrest resulted in some marijuana being discovered hidden in his hands and inside Evan's car under the passenger seat. It was established at the suppression hearing that the arrest warrant was issued by a justice of the peace on December 13, 1990 when Evans failed to make a court appearance, but that the warrant was ordered quashed on December 19, 1990 by the same justice of the peace when Evans appeared in court. The arresting officer testified that if it were not for the arrest warrant, he would not have arrested Evans. Standard operating procedure in the jurisdiction, which was not followed in this case, was for the justice of the peace's court clerk to inform the sheriff about the quashed warrant and for the sheriff then to remove the warrant from the computer records. Which office, the clerk of the court or the sheriff's, was at fault was not determined. The trial court suppressed the evidence because the State had been at fault in not purging Evan's record of the arrest warrant. The state court of appeals reversed stating that exclusion was not appropriate when mistakes were made by public employees not directly associated with the arresting officers or a law enforcement agency. The Arizona Supreme Court reversed this decision believing that no distinction could be made between the clerical errors made by court employees and mistakes made by law enforcement personnel. The U.S. Supreme Court then granted *certiorari*.

The Court overruled the decision of the Arizona Supreme Court in a 7-2 decision. Chief Justice Rehnquist set out the Court's narrow view of the exclusionary rule "We have recognized . . . that the Fourth Amendment contains no provision expressly precluding the use of evidence obtained in violation of its commands."[110] He then explained that a proper reading of both *Leon* and *Krull* demonstrated:

> If court employees were responsible for the erroneous computer record, the exclusion of evidence at trial would not sufficiently deter future errors so as to warrant such a severe sanction. First, as we noted in *Leon*, the exclusionary rule was historically designed as a means of deterring police misconduct, not mistakes by court employees. Second, respondent offers no evidence that court employees are inclined to ignore or subvert the Fourth Amendment or that law-

lessness among these actors requires application of the extreme sanction of exclusion.[111]

Chief Justice Rehnquist then emphasized that suppressing evidence under
these circumstances would not act as a future deterrent and result in fewer violations of the Fourth Amendment. That was because court clerks, unlike police,
have no stake in the outcomes of cases and are not actively engaged in trying to
ferret out criminals. The critical question that had to be answered in this case
was whether the good faith exception should be expanded to cover an arrest
made by an officer reasonably relying on inaccurate computer records showing
an arrest warrant on Evans. The Court concluded that suppression of evidence in
this circumstance would have no deterrent effect on police, because police officers would continue to make arrests anytime there was a warrant issued for arrest
and police came across the individual. Therefore, the Court found it was perfectly reasonable not to suppress evidence in this circumstance.

Justices O'Connor, Souter, and Breyer concurred but held out the possibility that in future cases even if the error was made by a court clerk, it could still
be questioned whether police "acted reasonably in their reliance *on the record
keeping system itself*."[112] This was especially true if police relied on a record
keeping system that contained no mechanism to ensure accuracy.

Justice Souter wrote a separate concurrence which was supported by Justice
Breyer that expressed some uneasiness with the existence of constitutional violations in a fragmented model of government. Despite agreeing with the majority,
he pointed out that he reserved the right to decide at a later date whether the
"concept of deterrence by exclusion of evidence should extend to the government as a whole, not merely the police, on the ground that there would otherwise
be no reasonable expectation of keeping the number of resulting false arrests
within an acceptable minimum limit."[113]

Justice Stevens dissented and criticized the deterrence rationale of the exclusionary rule found in the majority opinion. Justice Stevens firmly argued in
favor of a unitary model of government. He stated:

> Both the constitutional text and the history of its adoption and interpretation
> identify a more majestic conception. The Amendment protects the fundamental
> "right of the people to be secure in their persons, houses, papers, and effects,"
> against all official searches and seizures that are unreasonable. The Amend-
> ment is a constraint on the power of the sovereign, not merely on some of its
> agents. The remedy for its violation imposes costs on the sovereign, motivating
> it to train all its personnel to avoid future violations.[114]

The Rehnquist Court also extended the types of proceedings in which illegally gathered evidence could be used by the government. In 1998 in *Pennsylvania Board of Probation and Parole v. Scott*[115] the Rehnquist Court ruled that
the exclusionary rule did not disbar illegally gathered evidence from parole re-
vocation proceedings.

The Roberts Court and the Exclusionary Rule

The Court has not made any great changes in its approach to the exclusionary rule since *United States v. Calandra*. Instead, what it has done is extended the logic of *Calandra* so as to find more and more situations in which the costs of exclusion are too high for the government not to make use of evidence which was gathered through a constitutional violation. It also created exceptions which allowed the use of tainted evidence to be used in the prosecution's case-in-chief. Given the support that the deterrence rationale currently has on the Court, there seems little likelihood that the Court will change its approach. The area to watch in future exclusionary rule cases will be how far the Court will expand the exceptions which already exist in application of the exclusionary rule. For example, one danger not discussed by the Court in its good faith cases is that if we need not pay attention to the errors of individuals other than police officers which may result in constitutional violations such as legislators who pass laws, judges who issue warrants, and clerks who don't do paperwork because excluding the evidence which results will not change police behavior, what about others who violate the Fourth Amendment. Will the products of illegal searches conducted by school officials, building inspectors, firefighters, EPA inspectors, etc. be admissible because suppression of such evidence cannot act as a deterrent to future constitutional violations by the police? So far, the Court has believed exclusion to be necessary when it will advance the deterrent benefits of the exclusionary rule to those governmental actors who are actively engaged in the gathering of evidence, but not to other types of governmental actors.

The fragmented model of government that the Court has adopted allows it to turn a blind eye to many constitutional violations and allows use of the evidence if excluding it would not act as a proper police deterrent. This is no longer surprising. What is surprising about the Court's attitude in these cases is that the Court seems to no longer care that the government is violating the Constitution. The Court rarely discusses the available remedies a person should have when the government has violated Fourth Amendment rights and the Court believes exclusion to be an inappropriate remedy. This inability to have clear remedies that would act to compensate citizens who were subject to Fourth Amendment violations was a central reason why the Court acted in *Mapp v. Ohio* (1961) to incorporate the exclusionary rule.

Currently, the Court does provide for civil remedies when officers violate a person's Fourth Amendment rights. *Bivens v. Six Unknown Agents of Federal Bureau of Narcotics* set the precedent that federal agents could be sued in a civil court for injuries caused when an agent acting under the color of his authority violated a person's Fourth Amendment rights. In a similar manner, civil suits can be brought against state officials who violate a person's Fourth Amendment rights under Title 42 U.S.C. section 1983. State and federal officers who are sued for violations of the Fourth Amendment have a "good faith" qualified immunity defense. Under this defense if an officer can demonstrate that when the violation occurred the officer could have believed, based on clearly established legal rules, that the search or seizure was legal, the officer is entitled to a summary judgment. In the determination as to whether an officer should be granted summary judgment the presiding judge needs to go through the following two step process:

> (1) taken in the light most favorable to the party asserting the Fourth Amendment injury, do the facts alleged show the . . . officer's conduct clearly violated a Fourth Amendment right of the party complaining? (2) If so, was this right clearly established in the specific factual context of the case, so that it would be clear to a reasonable officer that his conduct was unlawful in the factual situation that he confronted?[116]

If the answer to either question is no, a summary judgment should be granted. If not, the case should proceed.

It seems clear that unless the Supreme Court provides leadership to ensure that the Fourth Amendment is not violated, violations will continue and under current practice will only be remedied by exclusion of evidence when the Court believes that it will teach law enforcement agents a lesson. It looks doubtful that leadership for a different direction will come from either Chief Justice John Roberts who was appointed to the Supreme Court by President George W. Bush in 2005 or Justice Samuel Alito who was also appointed by President Bush in 2006. In *Hudson v. Michigan* (2006),[117] a case dealing with whether the fruits of a search that violated the knock and announce rule should be excluded, both new members of the Court signed onto Justice Scalia's majority opinion. It ruled that despite the constitutional soundness of the knock and announce rule, violations did not require exclusion. Justice Scalia recognized the broadness of the exclusionary rule coming from *Mapp*, but noted that the Court had long rejected such an approach. Instead, he declared "Suppression of evidence . . . has always been our last resort, not our first impulse."[118] Justice Scalia went on to point out that the knock and announce rule did protect some important interests. These interests include protection of life and limb from unannounced entry, protection of property from being broken into when a warrant is served, and elements of privacy that can be destroyed by sudden entrance. Nevertheless, none of these interests are related to stopping the government from gathering evidence named in a warrant. Therefore, a determination of whether evidence gathered after police have violated the rule is dependent on whether the deterrent effect of doing so outweighed the substantial social costs. Justice Scalia pointed out that few incentives existed for police to bypass the knock and announce rule. Justice Scalia then balanced the deterrent benefits that would exist if evidence were excluded against the social costs stating, "ignoring knock-and-announce can realistically be expected to achieve absolutely nothing except the prevention or destruction of evidence and the avoidance of life-threatening resistance by occupants of the premises—dangers which, if there is even 'reasonable suspicion' of their existence, suspend the knock-and-announce requirement anyway."[119] Justice Scalia continued to state that the Fourth Amendment no longer required exclusion of all evidence which could have a deterrent benefit. The opinion explained that times had changed since *Mapp* was decided and exclusion was less necessary today because of a variety of other remedies which would have a deterrent effect on police violating the Fourth Amendment. These remedies included bringing civil suits under Title 42 U.S.C., section 1983 and the increasing professionalism of police forces with their emphasis on internal police discipline.

Justice Breyer in a dissenting opinion joined by Justices Stevens, Souter, and Ginsberg complained that the Court's decision undercut any desire that police might have to follow the constitutional requirement of the knock and announce rule. While agreeing that "the driving legal purpose underlying the exclusionary" is "the deterrence of unlawful government behavior," he also pointed out that *Mapp* was law, not *Wolf*.[120] Due to this fact, he argued the Court should apply the exclusionary rule rather than examining whether other possible remedies might exist which would deter police from violating the Fourth Amendment.

Conclusion

There is no doubt that the Warren Court was serious about using the exclusionary rule as a tool to enforce the Fourth Amendment. This can be demonstrated by the Court's decision in *Mapp v. Ohio*. Despite this, the Warren Court's inability to clearly explain the rationale for the exclusionary rule provided later courts with options as to when exclusion was necessary. The problem is that while Justice Tom Clark's majority opinion in *Mapp* made it clear that the Fourth Amendment would be meaningless and ignored by law enforcement officers unless it mandated exclusion of evidence that was illegally gathered, he also provided a couple of other explanations for the exclusionary rule. One was that the exclusionary rule protected the integrity of the judicial system. To explain why *Wolf* should be overruled, the opinion also noted that exclusion acted as a deterrent against future constitutional violations. When *Mapp* was decided there were only two exceptions to the exclusionary rule that had been recognized. Those were the independent source and attenuation exceptions. In its oversight of the Fourth Amendment, the Warren Court would create no further exceptions to the exclusionary rule.

Interfering with a clear application of the exclusionary rule was the fact that in both *Linkletter v. Walker* and *Alderman v. U.S.* the Warren Court changed its reasoning for the foundation of the exclusionary rule. In *Linkletter* the Court presented the deterrence argument front and center as the foundation for the exclusionary rule and in *Alderman* the Court went a step further and found that even if exclusion would act as a deterrent it was not always necessary to exclude evidence. This confusion in precedents left later courts with a lot of opportunities to bend the precedents of the Warren Court in whatever direction they desired.

If it were not for the Court's dislike of the exclusion of evidence gathered through violations of the Fourth Amendment, many of the changes in the Fourth Amendment which have taken place since *Mapp v. Ohio* was decided may not have taken place. The dislike of the exclusionary rule also explains why the rule is quite different today than when the Court decided *Mapp v. Ohio*. The Burger Court believed that the societal costs of the exclusionary rule were too high, so it sought to limit its application. One way this was accomplished was by limiting the ability of individuals to challenge the admissibility of illegally gathered evidence unless their personal Fourth Amendment rights were violated. The primary method, however, by which the Burger Court limited the exclusionary rule was to follow the *Linkletter* precedent and declare that the sole purpose for the exclusionary rule was to deter future unlawful police behavior and thereby protect the constitutional guarantees of the Fourth Amendment. In 1974 when the Court decided *United States v. Calandra* the Court made it clear that the exclusionary rule was a judicially created remedy, not a personal constitutional right. This allowed the Court to examine violations of the Fourth Amendment through a fragmented model of government and allowed evidence which had been illegally gathered by one branch of the government to be introduced as evidence at hearings and trials conducted by another branch of the government. The Burger Court developed a cost-benefit balancing test to determine when it was appropriate to allow use of illegally gathered evidence and found that in an increasing number of circumstances the societal costs of suppressing evidence, releasing the guilty, interfering in the truth seeking process of trials, and creating disrespect for the law, carried more weight than the benefit, the deterrent effect on future police violations of the Fourth Amendment.

In 1984 the Burger Court also created two new exceptions to the exclusionary rule. The inevitable discovery exception allowed use of illegally gathered evidence in the prosecution's case-in-chief if a trial court judge could be convinced that law enforcement officials would have hypothetically found the evidence through legal means, had there not first been a constitutional violation. The good faith exception allowed use of evidence when police had in good faith tried to follow the requirements of the Fourth Amendment by obtaining a warrant which subsequently was found to be unlawfully granted. In both cases, it was believed that the deterrent effect on future constitutional violations would be minimal when compared to societal harms. Due to the openings left by the Warren Court's opinions, all of these changes were made without overruling *Mapp* or any other major decision of the Warren Court. The Rehnquist Court did not add any new exceptions to the exclusionary rule, but it expanded the application of the good faith exception. The Roberts Court has already created one exception to the exclusionary rule. It is when the government fails to follow the knock and announce rule for serving warrants.

The changes in the exclusionary rule are best demonstrated by comparing the rule as it existed at the time of its incorporation with the current rule. When

Mapp was decided tainted evidence could not be used at trial for any purpose. Under the current rule, tainted evidence will be suppressed only from the prosecution's case-in-chief, only if it will deter future *police* misconduct. As with other aspects of the Fourth Amendment the exclusionary rule now seems to be driven by a question of reasonableness. The Court in balancing the competing interests of the costs of exclusion versus the benefits of exclusion asks what is reasonable in our society today. In accordance, the good faith exception is a polite way of referring to what the Court clearly sees as a reasonable mistake on the part of law enforcement agencies to gather evidence.

The new rule has flexibility, but has added uncertainty about when governmental misconduct will actually lead to suppression of evidence. The Roberts Court has gone as far as forgetting that the Warren Court had actively used suppression as a tool to require the government to honor the Fourth Amendment and stated "Suppression of evidence . . . has always been our last resort, not our first impulse."[121] In creating uncertainty about when evidence will be suppressed, the Court has given an open invitation to the government to test the willingness of the Court to allow evidence into trial.

Illustrative Case Reprise

When the *Padilla* case discussed at the start of this chapter came before the courts each looked at the issues differently. The district court ruled that because the traffic stop lasted beyond the point that Officer Fifer learned that there was no falsification of the license plates he had unconstitutionally seized Luis Arciniega. As a result of this, the district court had found that the permission that Arciniega gave for the search of the vehicle's trunk was not voluntarily given. The district court also ruled that all the individuals involved in the cocaine ring had standing to challenge not only the cocaine in the car, but all the subsequent evidence found as a result of that stop. This was because the illegal stop "clearly led to the subsequent activities of the day when the car was delivered to Tempe; that without that stop, there would not have been any involvement by the DPS [Department of Public Safety], nor would they have informed Customs and DEA about that."[122] The Court of Appeals of the Ninth Circuit agreed that the search was unconstitutional because Arciniega had been improperly seized. It also allowed all the members of the cocaine transporting conspiracy to challenge the admission of the evidence. The Court of Appeals of the Ninth Circuit stated that "a coconspirator's participation in an operation or arrangement that indicates joint control and supervision of the place searched establishes standing" to challenge the admission of the evidence.[123] It then found that the vehicle was part of a joint enterprise so everyone involved in the conspiracy had standing to claim a legitimate expectation of privacy in the vehicle and seized cocaine. In the view of the court of appeals each member of the conspiracy who played an essential role in the criminal activity could challenge the evidence. Those members were Mr. and Mrs. Donald Simpson and Xavier Padilla. The court remanded the case for Jorge and Suzy Padilla since it couldn't be known whether they were central players in the conspiracy or just employees.

The Supreme Court overruled the coconspirators rule that had been developed by the Ninth Circuit. In doing so, the *per curiam* opinion relied on *Alderman v. United States* (1969) and the precedent that only those whose personal Fourth Amendment rights have been violated have standing to challenge the admission of illegally seized evidence. Under this rule, coconspirators and codefendants have no power to challenge the admission of evidence which was seized in violation of someone else's constitutional rights. As a result, in this case the only one that could challenge the admission of the evidence seized in the illegal car search was Luis Arciniega.

In the series of Fourth Amendment standing cases beginning with *Alderman* and going through *Rawlings v. Kentucky* the Court found that third parties had no right to challenge the admissibility of evidence which was gained through a violation of another person's constitutional rights. In these cases the Court's reasoning was an extension of the Court's opinion in *Katz v. United States*. In the standing cases the Court limited the impact of *Katz* by ruling that the Fourth Amendment only protected *legitimate* expectations of privacy and emphasized an individual had no legitimate expectation in the privacy of others. In the next chapter we examine the case of *Katz v. United States* and see that while the Court originally used the case to expand the protections of the Fourth Amendment, more recently, the Court has used *Katz* to narrow what constitutes a search under the amendment. This is a critical issue because if an investigative technique is not considered a search under the Fourth Amendment, all evidence found through the technique will be admissible because the exclusionary rule will not apply to it.

Notes

1. Wayne R. LaFave, "Computers, Urinals and the Fourth Amendment: Confessions of a Patron Saint," *Michigan Law Review* 94 (1996): 2581.
2. *Boyd v. United States*, 116 U.S. 616, 635 (1886).
3. *United States v. Padilla*, 960 F.2d 854, 856 (1992).
4. *United States v. Padilla*, 508 U.S. 77 (1993).
5. Jacob W. Landynski, *Search and Seizure and the Supreme Court: A Study in Constitutional Interpretation* (Baltimore: John Hopkins Press, 1966), 76.
6. *Mapp v. Ohio*, 367 U.S. 643 (1961).
7. Bradley C. Canon, "Ideology and Reality in the Debate Over the Exclusionary Rule: A Conservative Argument for its Retention," *South Texas Law Review* 23 (1982): 579-580.
8. Cited in Charles McC. Mathias, Jr., "The Exclusionary Rule Revisited," *Loyola Law Review* 28 (1982): 7. For other criticisms see also Bradford Wilson, "The Origins

and Development of the Federal Rule of Exclusion," *Wake Forest Law Review* 18 (1982): 1073-1109.

9. Yale Kamisar, "Does (Did) (Should) the Exclusionary Rule Rest on a 'Principled Basis' Rather than an 'Empirical Proposition'?," *Creighton Law Review* 16 (1983): 585.

10. *Weeks v. United States*, 232 U.S. 383 (1914).

11. *Wolf v. Colorado*, 338 U.S. 25 (1949).

12. *Weeks*, 232 U.S. at 393.

13. *Mapp v. Ohio*, 367 U.S. 643 (1961).

14. *Mapp*, 367 U.S. at 649.

15. *Mapp*, 367 U.S. at 659.

16. *Mapp*, 367 U.S. at 651.

17. *Mapp*, 367 U.S. at 652.

18. *Mapp*, 367 U.S. at 649.

19. *Mapp*, 367 U.S. at 661 (Black, J., concurring).

20. *Mapp*, 367 U.S. at 671 (Douglas, J., concurring).

21. *Mapp*, 367 U.S. at 655.

22. *Silverthorne Lumber Co. v. United States*, 251 U.S. 385 (1920).

23. *Nardone v. United States*, 308 U.S. 338 (1939).

24. James Duke Cameron and Richard Lustiger, "The Exclusionary Rule: A Cost-Benefit Analysis," *Federal Rules Decisions* 101 (1984): 118.

25. *Linkletter v. Walker*, 381 U.S. 618 (1965).

26. *Linkletter*, 381 U.S. at 636.

27. *Linkletter*, 381 U.S. at 637.

28. *Linkletter*, 381 U.S. at 637.

29. *Linkletter*, 381 U.S. at 637-638.

30. *Katz v. United States*, 389 U.S. 347 (1967).

31. *Jones v. United States*, 362 U.S. 257 (1960).

32. *Jones*, 362 U.S. at 267.

33. *Alderman v. United States*, 394 U.S. 165 (1969).

34. *Alderman*, 394 U.S. at 174.

35. *Alderman*, 394 U.S. at 174.

36. *Alderman*, 394 U.S. at 174-175.

37. *Mapp*, 367 U.S. at 655.

38. *Rakas v. Illinois*, 439 U.S. 128 (1978).

39. *Rakas*, 439 U.S. at 147.

40. *Rakas*, 439 U.S. at 140.

41. *United States v. Salvucci*, 448 U.S. 83 (1980).

42. *Simmons v. United States*, 390 U.S. 377 (1968).

43. *United States v. Salvucci*, 448 U.S. 83, 85 (1980).

44. *United States v. Salvucci*, 448 U.S. at 91-92 (quoting *Rakas v. Illinois*, 439 U.S. 128, 140 (1978).

45. *United States v. Salvucci*, 448 U.S. at 92.

46. *Rawlings v. Kentucky*, 448 U.S. 98 (1980).

47. *Rawlings*, 448 U.S. at 105.

48. *Minnesota v. Olson*, 495 U.S. 91 (1990).

49. *Minnesota v. Carter*, 525 U.S. 83 (1998).

50. *United States v. Payner*, 447 U.S. 727 (1980).

51. *United States v. Payner*, 447 U.S. at 730.

52. *United States v. Payner*, 447 U.S. at 733.

53. *United States v. Payner*, 447 U.S. at 735.

54. Susan Bandes, "Power, Privacy and Thermal Imaging," *Minnesota Law Review* 86 (2002): 1381.

55. Stephen P. Jones, "Reasonable Expectations of Privacy: Searches, Seizures, and the Concept of Fourth Amendment Standing," *University of Memphis Law Review* 27 (1997): 975.

56. *Katz*, 389 U.S. at 351.

57. Steven Cann and Bob Egbert, point out that prior to 1980 most of the law review articles written about the exclusionary rule have been critical of the rule, "The Exclusionary Rule: Its Necessity in Constitutional Democracy," *Howard Law Journal* 23 (1980): 300.

58. John M. Burkhoff, "The Court that Devoured the Fourth Amendment: The Triumph of an Inconsistent Doctrine," *Oregon Law Review* 58 (1979): 152.

59. For an extended example see Warren E. Burger, "Who Will Watch the Watchman," *American University Law Review* 14 (1964): 1-23.

60. *Bivens v. Six Unknown Named Agents*, 403 U.S. 388 (1971).

61. *United States v. Calandra*, 414 U.S. 338 (1974).

62. *United States v. Calandra*, 414 U.S. at 348.

63. *United States v. Calandra*, 414 U.S. at 347.

64. *United States v. Calandra*, 414 U.S. at 348.

65. *United States v. Calandra*, 414 U.S. at 351-352.

66. *United States v. Calandra*, 414 U.S. at 357 (Brennan, J., dissenting).

67. *United States v. Janis*, 428 U.S. 433 (1976).

68. *Stone v. Powell*, 428 U.S. 465 (1976).

69. *Stone*, 428 U.S. at 495.

70. *United States v. Haven*, 446 U.S. 620 (1980).

71. *United States v. Lopez-Mendoza*, 468 U.S. 1032 (1984).

72. *One 1958 Pymouth Sedan v. Pennsylvania*, 380 U.S. 693 (1965).

73. Kamisar, "Does (Did) (Should) the Exclusionary Rule Rest on a 'Principled Basis' Rather than an 'Empirical Proposition'?," 642.

74. *Brewer v. Williams*, 430 U.S. 387 (1977).

75. *Nix v. Williams*, 467 U.S. 431 (1984).

76. For an extended account of *Brewer v. Williams* and *Nix v. Williams* see Thomas N. McInnis, *The Christian Burial Case* (Westport, CT: Praeger, 2001).

77. *Nix*, 467 U.S. at 448-449.

78. *Nix*, 467 U.S. at 443.

79. *Nix*, 467 U.S. at 443.

80. *Nix*, 467 U.S. at 444.

81. *Nix*, 467 U.S. at 444.

82. *Nix*, 467 U.S. at 445.

83. *Nix*, 467 U.S. at 445-446.

84. *Nix*, 467 U.S. at 459.

85. *United States v. Leon*, 468 U.S. 897 (1984).

86. *Massachusetts v. Sheppard*, 468 U.S. 981 (1984).

87. *United States v. Leon*, 468 U.S. at 906.

88. *United States v. Leon*, 468 U.S. at 916.

89. *United States v. Leon*, 468 U.S. at 906-907.

90. *United States v. Leon*, 468 U.S. at 907 n. 6.

91. *United States v. Leon*, 468 U.S. at 928 (Blackmun, J., concurring).

92. *Franks v. Delaware*, 438 U.S. 154 (1978).

93. *United States v. Leon*, 468 U.S. at 950 (Brennan, J., dissenting).

94. *United States v. Leon*, 468 U.S. at 950 (Brennan, J., dissenting).

95. *Massachusetts v. Sheppard*, 468 U.S. 981, 990.

96. *United States v. Leon*, 468 U.S. at 918.

97. *United States v. Leon*, 468 U.S. at 919.

98. Craig M. Bradley, "The 'Good Faith Exception' Cases: Reasonable Exercises in Futility," *Indiana Law Journal* 60 (1984): 293.

99. David Clark Esseks, "Error in Good Faith: The *Leon* Exception Six Years Later," *Michigan Law Review* 89 (1990): 654.

100. *Segura v. United States*, 468 U.S. 796 (1984).

101. *Segura*, 468 U.S. at 815.

102. *Segura*, 468 U.S. at 816.

103. *Segura*, 468 U.S. at 839.

104. *Maryland v. Buie*, 494 U.S. 325 (1990).

105. Tinsley Yarbrough, *The Rehnquist Court and the Constitution*, (New York: Oxford University Press, 2000), p. x.

106. *Illinois v. Krull*, 480 U.S. 340 (1987).

107. *Illinois v. Krull*, 480 U.S. at 350.

108. *Maryland v. Garrison*, 480 U.S. 79 (1987).

109. *Arizona v. Evans*, 514 U.S. 1 (1995).

110. *Arizona v. Evans*, 514 U.S. at 10.

111. *Arizona v. Evans*, 514 U.S. at 14-15.

112. *Arizona v. Evans*, 514 U.S. at 17.

113. *Arizona v. Evans*, 514 U.S. at 18 (Souter, J., concurring).

114. *Arizona v. Evans*, 514 U.S. at 18-19 (Stevens, J., dissenting).

115. *Pennsylvania Board of Probation and Parole v. Scott*, 524 U.S. 357 (1998).

116. Phillip A. Hubbart, *Making Sense of Search and Seizure Law: A Fourth Amendment Handbook* (Durham: Carolina Academic Press, 2005), 362.

117. *Hudson v. Michigan*, 126 S.Ct. 2159 (2006).

118. *Hudson*, 126 S.Ct. at 2163.

119. *Hudson*, 126 S.Ct. at 2166.

120. *Hudson*, 126 S.Ct. at 2173 (Bryer, J., dissenting).

121. *Hudson*, 126 S.Ct. at 2163.

122. *United States v. Padilla*, 1992 U.S. App. LEXIS 5562, 10 (1992).

123. *United States v. Padilla*, 508 U.S. 77, 80 (1993).

Chapter 7
Limiting the Definition of a Search

The decision to characterize an action as a search is in essence a conclusion about whether the fourth amendment applies at all. If an activity is not a search or seizure (assuming the activity does not violate some other constitutional or statutory provision), then the government enjoys a virtual carte blanche to do as it pleases.[1]

Science has perfected amplifying and recording devices to become frightening instruments of surveillance and invasion of privacy, whether by the policeman, the blackmailer, or the busybody.[2]

Illustrative Case

The Highland Town School District in Highland, Indiana had in the seven months prior to March 23, 1979 experienced some incidents of alcohol and drug use by students. To the best knowledge of officials at the school twenty-one students had been involved in these incidents. Due to their involvement in such activities thirteen out of the twenty-one students had been removed from school by March. Despite this, school Superintendant Omer Renfrow and Principal George Kurteff in conjunction with Highland Police Chief Al Prendergast decided to use trained drug dogs to determine if there was a wider drug problem in the school. On the morning of March 23, 1979 right before classes were scheduled to be adjourned for the next class all teachers throughout the school ordered students to remain seated until they were dismissed. At this time six teams consisting of a school official, a police officer, a trained drug detecting dog and its trainer swept through the school for the next two and a half hours. During this time, every classroom and every student were subjected to contact with a dog. During the search, students were required to sit quietly with their hands on their desks and all personal belongings in front of them in view of their teacher. Students were not allowed to use the restrooms unless accompanied by school staff. To insure that students did not try to hide any contraband items the halls were manned by police officers and school administrators. While students could not leave the school, the school did invite members of the media in to observe the search. The search was a systematic one in which the dogs were instructed to go down each aisle in the classrooms and move from student to student. Each student was inspected between one and fourteen different times by the dogs. If a student was found with drugs or alcohol, the plan was to deal with it administratively within the schools rather than through the criminal justice process.

When one of the teams came upon Denise Doe (the name is a pseudonym to protect her since she was a minor), a thirteen year-old student, the dog sniffed her body and then repeatedly pushed its nose into her legs. The officer believed that the dog had given a positive alert that Denise had drugs on her person. The officer then required Denise to stand and empty her pockets, but no drugs were found. The officer then subjected Denise to another sniff by the dog which again positively alerted that drugs could be smelled. Denise was then taken to the nurse's office for a more thorough inspection. In the nurse's office Denise was subjected to a search by two women, one of which was a police officer. Denise was ordered to strip naked. The two women then subjected her body to a visual inspection. They also inspected her clothes and subjected her hair to a physical examination. When no drugs were found, Denise was allowed to put her clothes back on and was taken back to the classroom.

The raids on Highland Junior High School where Denise went to school were not the only ones which took place in the school district that week. By the end of the week every junior and senior high school was subject to similar actions. By the end of the week each of the 2,780 junior and senior high school students had been subjected to such treatment. This was despite the fact that the school and police had no individualized suspicion that any particular student had possession of alcohol or drugs. Denise Doe was not the only student subject to special treatment because of a false alert by a dog. At least nine other students were subjected to special interrogations and searches, not including nudity, after dogs indicated they had drugs, but no drugs were found. Four other junior high girls were subjected to further interrogation and a strip search. None of these students were found with drugs either. On the other hand, out of the 2,780 students who went through the process, 17 students in the senior high, but none in the junior high were found to possess marijuana, drug paraphernalia, or cans of beer.

The case of *Doe v. Renfrow* (1979)[3] presents a number of interesting questions for the Fourth Amendment. These questions include whether school officials must have a warrant or some form of probable cause before they subject students to searches? Do dog sniffs constitute a search under the Fourth Amendment and therefore require a warrant or the existence of probable cause and an exigent circumstance? Would use of another surveillance technology which allowed government officials to pry into private behavior violate the amendment? Does a positive indication by a trained drug dog present probable cause to allow a search without a warrant? Should this include strip searches where the suspect is required to succumb to a visual inspection of the naked body? Some of these questions concerning the power of school officials to conduct searches without a warrant were answered in the last chapter and others will be examined in this chapter.

Protection of Privacy Interests over Property Interests: The Victory of *Katz*

Justice Potter Stewart once observed that there are two principle methods that can be used to lessen the impact of the Fourth Amendment. The first was to shrink the scope of the amendment so that it limits fewer governmental attempts to gather evidence by declaring those efforts outside the protections of the Fourth Amendment. The second was to limit the application of the exclusionary rule so that even if there was a constitutional violation, the evidence may be used.[4] In the last chapter we examined Justice Stewart's second method of curbing the impact of the Fourth Amendment, limiting the role of the exclusionary rule. The focus of this chapter will be on the first method Justice Stewart mentioned, limiting the impact of the Fourth Amendment.

The question as to what qualifies as a search or seizure is a critical issue in Fourth Amendment analysis. One thing that has long been clear regarding the Fourth Amendment is that it is only triggered when a government official executes a search or seizure.[5] In its decisions the Warren Court broadened the definition of what constituted a violation of the Fourth Amendment bringing more governmental actions into regulation by the amendment. Movement in this direction resulted from the Warren Court's attempt to better protect the rights of American citizens charged with crimes. Despite the efforts of the Warren Court to broaden the protections of the Fourth Amendment, later courts used the reasoning and language of the opinions of the Warren Court to narrow its protections. Due to their desire to prevent crime through more aggressive police tactics and their dislike of the exclusionary rule, the Burger and Rehnquist Courts relied on the language of the Warren Court to actively narrow the scope of the Fourth Amendment.[6]

One area in which the Warren Court broadened the protections of the Fourth Amendment was in the area of electronic surveillance. Once the Warren Court incorporated the exclusionary rule in *Mapp v. Ohio* another issue that it reconsidered was whether the use of technology, in the form of wire taps, in the collection of evidence constituted a search and seizure. The ruling precedent in this area had been made in *Olmstead v. United States* (1928).[7] The decision in *Olmstead* limited Fourth Amendment protection to those things specifically mentioned in the language of the amendment, houses, persons, papers, and effects, by basing its protections on the law of trespass. After *Olmstead*, Fourth Amendment protection involved a two part inquiry to determine if there had indeed been a trespass. The first issue was, had the government intruded upon an area which was protected by the Constitution. The second was, if it had, did the intrusion involve a physical invasion which was constitutionally impermissible. Subsequent case law tried to determine if a search interfered with a "constitutionally protected area." Under this analysis, even if the case involved a constitutionally protected area, there had to be a physical intrusion or trespass of that area for a Fourth Amendment violation to exist. If there was no intrusion, the Fourth Amendment was not implicated and, thus, not violated. Wiretaps were not considered a Fourth Amendment violation because they involved no physical intrusion of a protected area.

In his opinion in *Olmstead*, Chief Justice Taft mentioned that Congress had the power to make electronic interception of phone conversations a violation of the law. Congress exerted that power in 1934 when it passed the Federal Communications Act. In the case of *Nardone v. United States* (1937)[8] the Court ruled that not only did the law make wiretapping by private individuals illegal it also made it illegal for federal officers to do so without a warrant. The Court found that evidence that was gathered by federal officers through a violation of the law could not be admitted into federal courts.

In *Katz v. United States* (1967)[9] the Court reexamined the issue as to whether a physical trespass of a constitutionally protected area was required to trigger the Fourth Amendment. This was an important question because technology was increasingly allowing intrusion into people's lives without physical trespass. *Katz* came before the Court due to the efforts of officers who bugged a phone booth that Katz used in his gambling business. The bug was placed on top of a phone booth that government agents knew was used by Katz. The bug did not physically intrude into the booth, but was capable of overhearing conversations in the booth. When the recorded conversation was introduced at trial, Katz objected to no avail and ended up being convicted.

On *certiorari* the Court in an 8-1 decision overruled the fifty year old precedent established in *Olmstead v. United States* by declaring that a conversation which was gained through electronic surveillance of a phone booth without a warrant violated the Fourth Amendment. The Court rejected the government's argument that because a public phone booth was not a constitutionally protected area no search had taken place under the Fourth Amendment. Justice Potter Stewart's majority opinion noted that "the correct solution of Fourth Amendment problems is not necessarily promoted by incantation of the phrase 'constitutionally protected area.'"[10] Justice Stewart wrote:

> The trespass doctrine [from *Olmstead*] can no longer be regarded as controlling. The government's activities in electronically listening to and recording the petitioner's words violated the privacy upon which he justifiably relied while

using the telephone booth and thus constituted a "search and seizure" within the meaning of the Fourth Amendment.[11]

Justice Stewart further noted: "[W]hat a person knowingly exposes to the public, even in his own home or office, is not a subject of Fourth Amendment protection. . . . But what he seeks to preserve as private, even in an area accessible to the public, may be constitutionally protected."[12] The Court explained that, even though Katz could be seen in the phone booth, the fact that he shut the door meant that he expected privacy and sought to keep the uninvited ear from overhearing the conversation. The Court went on and ruled that future use of electronic surveillance such as this would be *per se* unreasonable unless accompanied by a warrant unless the circumstances fit into one of the established exceptions to the need for a warrant. No exceptions fit this case.

Justice Stewart's majority opinion provided little analysis as to how later courts should determine when a person's individual privacy should be protected against governmental intrusion under the Fourth Amendment. Justice John Harlan's concurring opinion in *Katz* has proven to be more influential to later courts which have applied *Katz* to other factual situations. Justice Harlan reasoned that the Fourth Amendment would provide a person protection from unreasonable search and seizure when two requirements were met: "first that a person have exhibited an actual (subjective) expectation of privacy and, second, that the expectation be one that society is prepared to recognize as 'reasonable.'"[13] Beyond this statement, Justice Harlan left open the precise methods by which the Court should in future cases determine when a person had developed an expectation of privacy or how it would be determined if society would recognize that expectation as reasonable.

The Warren Court willingly rejected past precedent and used *Katz* to enlarge the protections of the Fourth Amendment by changing the basis of its analysis from a concern with location, the determination as to whether something was a constitutionally protected area, to one of privacy. Melvin Gutterman has stated that *Katz* was a declaration "that a privacy value-oriented analysis should replace" the *Olmstead* trespass analysis.[14] *Katz*'s change in approach gave the Fourth Amendment the ability to protect not just property, but also information and conversations from governmental intrusion. After *Katz*, what a person communicated could be protected by the Fourth Amendment, not just the place where it was spoken. Under *Katz*, if a privacy interest is involved in a search and the situation does not fit into one of the exceptions to the warrant requirement, then a warrant is required for the search.

Anthony Amsterdam and others agree that the decision in *Katz* was meant to expand the boundaries of the Fourth Amendment, but point out that it has not lived up to this potential.[15] The influential language used by Justice Harlan's concurring opinion has proven to be a double-edged sword and its reasoning has allowed later courts to limit the protections of the Fourth Amendment. This is because in order to successfully invoke the protections of the Fourth Amendment a person not only has to have a personal expectation of privacy, society also has to respect that expectation. This exercise of power has again placed the Court in the position of determining if a search is reasonable. Unlike the general reasonableness approach discussed in Chapter 5, however, the Court is not considering whether the search itself was reasonable. Instead, the Court is asking whether society is willing to find an individual's claim that they have an expectation of privacy to be reasonable. The determination as to whether society should respect such an expectation is supposedly objective, but without a standardized method of determining what personal expectations of privacy society is willing to accept the conclusion has been dependent on the shifting social and political views of the members of the Court.

Another concern from Justice Harlan's test is that if it only protects those expectations of privacy that society finds reasonable it might be possible for the government to take steps to limit any expectation of privacy that citizens could possibly hold. Phyllis Bookspan points out that if one took this principle to its extreme, "the government could defeat any subjective expectation of privacy simply by broadcasting on television every half-hour its intention to place all citizens under comprehensive electronic surveillance."[16] The Supreme Court, however, is aware of this weakness and in *Smith v. Maryland* (1979) noted:

> In such circumstances, where an individual's subjective expectations had been 'conditioned' by influences alien to well-recognized Fourth Amendment freedoms, those subjective expectations obviously could play no meaningful role in ascertaining what the scope of Fourth Amendment protection was.[17]

One year after *Katz* was decided Congress passed the Omnibus Crime Control and Safe Streets Act of 1968. It set standards for governmental wiretapping and bugging. The act made it a crime for an individual to directly, or arrange for someone else, to wiretap or eavesdrop on a phone conversation with any type of mechanical or electronic device. One exception to the blanket rule was when one of the parties to the conversation had given prior consent to an interception of the communication. It also forbade the use of illegally intercepted communications from being used in courts. The law did have a provision which allowed law enforcement officers to obtain warrants to intercept communications through the use of electronic surveillance devices. Warrants had to precede intercepting communications except in cases involving national security or organized crime where law enforcement had 48 hours to act before they had to secure a warrant. If the warrant was not forthcoming, any evidence gathered could not be used. The warrants had to state the name of the person who was targeted and the place where the conversations would be held. They also had to state the law enforcement agency that was responsible for the warrant and the time period in which eavesdropping would take place. The maximum time that the law allowed warrants to be issued for was thirty days. It also stated that individuals who were targeted had to be notified of the warrant within ninety days of the warrant being issued.

In the years after *Katz* was decided the Court was firm in its view that intercepting phone conversations required a search warrant. An example of this can be found in the case of *United States v. United States District Court for the Eastern District of Michigan* (1972).[18] In this case the Nixon Administration was concerned about the activities of members of the New Left and the anti-war movement. In its efforts to keep informed about their movements the administration infiltrated various domestic groups and engaged in warrantless wiretaps. Three defendants were charged with conspiring to destroy, and one of them with destroying, Government property. The defendants filed a pretrial motion for disclosure of electronic surveillance information. In response, the United States revealed that it did not have a warrant, but the Attorney General had approved the wiretaps for the purpose of protecting the nation from domestic organizations that were trying to attack and subvert the government. The government further claimed that the surveillance was lawful as a reasonable exercise of presidential power to protect national security. The district court and the court of appeals ruled that the government's actions had violated the Fourth Amendment. The Supreme Court then granted *certiorari*.

In a unanimous decision, opinion by Justice Lewis Powell, the Court rejected the government's argument. Justice Powell showed concern that the use of warrantless wiretaps in the name of national security might have a negative impact on the exercise of First Amendment rights to dissent against the government. For that reason, the Court was uneasy about giving the government unchecked power to decide which groups could have their communications intercepted without judicial oversight. He noted that individuals conducting ongoing investigations are often so focused on their quarry that they tend to bypass constitutional safeguards and concerns about privacy. Justice Powell was further concerned that the government's claim of national security was too vague. The Court ruled that the president could not use national security as an excuse to bypass the need to have a warrant before intercepting phone conversations. This was because the Court did not believe that the government should be in a position to "deter vigorous citizen dissent and discussion of Government action in private conversations."[19]

Despite early statements that the Court would be firm in its protection of individual privacy, the application of *Katz* has given the government ample opportunities to search and seize materials without violating the Fourth Amendment. The rest of this chapter examines the methods by which *Katz* has been used to limit the protections of the Fourth Amendment.

The Open Fields Doctrine after *Katz*

After *Katz* was decided there was some debate as to whether it would cause the Court to change the open fields doctrine that had come out of *Hester v. United States* (1924)[20] due to the open fields doctrine's partial reliance on the discredited "constitutionally protected areas" analysis. In *Hester v. United States* it had been decided that open fields did not deserve the "special protection accorded by the Fourth Amendment to the people in their 'persons, houses, papers, and effects.'"[21] Due to its statement that "the Fourth Amendment protects people, not places,"[22] the *Katz* decision had the potential to allow for Fourth Amendment protection of open fields if a person had a reasonable expectation of privacy in their field. Justice John Harlan had tried to fend off any change in the open field doctrine in his concurring opinion in *Katz* by noting that as far as he was concerned *Katz* did not alter the open fields doctrine, but the Court examined the possibility in 1984.

The opportunity to rule on a post-*Katz* open fields case came in *Oliver v. United States* (1984).[23] *Oliver* came to the Court after Kentucky State Police received an anonymous tip that Oliver was cultivating marijuana on his farm. Despite the fact that there was no indication of reliability in the tip, the police decided to investigate. Without getting a warrant or permission from Oliver, the state police entered Oliver's land, drove past his house down a private road, and continued past several "no trespassing" signs. When officers came upon a metal gate with a "no trespassing" sign on it that blocked their vehicle, they got out of their car, slipped through a gap in the fence, and continued on a dirt path past a barn and truck camper. At that time a man yelled at them to go no further. When they identified themselves as police, the man disappeared and the officers resumed their search, following the path over a mile through a wooded area to a field of marijuana. The field was surrounded by woods, fences, and an embankment. After the discovery, Oliver was arrested. Prior to trial the marijuana was suppressed because the district court ruled that Oliver's actions had created a reasonable expectation of privacy in the field. The Court of Appeals for the Sixth Circuit reversed the order and declared that the open fields exception survived *Katz* intact. The Supreme Court granted *certiorari* to determine the effect that *Katz* had upon the open fields exception to the warrant requirement.

The Court reached a 6-3 decision with the majority opinion written by Justice Lewis Powell. The Court decided against examining the subjective expectations of privacy that individuals might have in open fields. The Court explained that the test for the legitimacy of privacy expectation claims resulting from *Katz* was not whether a person tried to conceal behavior they considered to be private. The proper test was "whether the government's intrusion infringes upon the personal and societal values protected by the Fourth Amendment."[24] The Court then listed several factors which could be considered in determining if the values of the Fourth Amendment would create a recognizable privacy interest. These included the intent of the Framers, the ways in which the area under consideration was used, and whether the area is one which our societal values believe deserve protection from governmental intrusion. Justice Powell then reasoned that the Fourth Amendment was not meant to protect open fields from governmental inspection because they do not provide the proper setting for an individual's intimate activities when compared with the specific places which were protected in the Fourth Amendment. The Court believed the factual circumstances in individual cases created by such activities as the height of fences, the existence of locked gates, or "no trespassing" signs would create endless problems for resolving those cases. It believed that creating a case-by-case approach would prove to be unworkable. According to Justice Powell, "The ad-hoc approach not only makes it difficult for the policeman to discern the scope of his authority . . . it also creates a danger that constitutional rights will be arbitrarily and inequitably enforced."[25] The Court therefore dropped the first component of the test expounded by Justice Harlan's concurring opinion in *Katz* by refusing to consider if the individual had an expectation of privacy in their activities. In what may seem odd, due to the Court's concern that a case-by-case analysis of open fields may result in constitutional rights being arbitrarily enforced, the Court swept away any hope of Fourth Amendment protection in open fields by establishing a bright line rule that there was no legitimate expectation of privacy in open fields beyond the curtilage. As has often been true in post-*Katz* cases, the Court in *Oliver* found that a person's conduct was not entitled to any protection by the Fourth Amendment because an individual "has no legitimate expectation that open fields will remain free from warrantless intrusion by government officers."[26] In making this decision the Court gave government officials a broader right to enter a person's property that is posted for trespassing than private individuals would have.

In *Oliver* the Court did rule that the curtilage remained protected under the Fourth Amendment. The only explanation of what constituted the curtilage in *Oliver*, however, was that it was the "area immediately surrounding the home."[27] This left open questions as to what exactly constitutes the curtilage. The Court provided some guidance as to how to determine the extent of the curtilage in *United States v. Dunn* (1987).[28] *Dunn* came to the Court as a result of a warrantless search by law enforcement officials of the barn at Dunn's ranch. Having traced drug making supplies to Dunn's ranch through the use of electronic beepers and aerial photography, officers crossed a perimeter fence and walked through an open field to get to the barn which was located about fifty yards from a fence which surrounded the home. Officers then used flashlights to see in the barn where they discovered an illicit drug laboratory. When the case reached the Supreme Court, it had to determine if the barn was within the curtilage of the home and thus protected by the Fourth Amendment. The Court ruled that the barn was outside the curtilage. In doing so, it advanced four factors which it said were relevant to determining the extent of the curtilage. The factors to be considered were: (1) the proximity of the area under dispute to the home; (2) whether the area is within an enclosure that surrounds the home; (3) the types of uses for which the area was used; and (4) the steps that the resident has taken to protect the privacy of the area from passing people.[29]

It was hoped that giving the lower courts guidance as to what constitutes curtilage would create some consistency in this area of law. Two reasons have stopped this development from taking place. The first is the Court's own statement that the factors should not be used as "a finely tuned formula" which could be "mechanically applied" in every case.[30] The second reason is that the final factor the Court noted focuses Fourth Amendment analysis on whether an individual had a reasonable expectation of privacy which requires a case-by-case application of precedent. The application of *Dunn* has, therefore, according to Vanessa Rownaghi, resulted in, "a series of case-by-case analyses revealing an utter lack of consistency and uniformity as to what determinatively resolves the question" of what constitutes curtilage.[31]

Limiting the Definition of a Search under *Katz*

When the Court examines whether government actions trigger Fourth Amendment protection under *Katz*, the Court is again placed in the position of determining what is an unreasonable search versus a reasonable search. That is because the decision in *Katz* has brought before the Court a series of cases which feature one central question. That being under what circumstances does governmental activity infringe upon a reasonable expectation of privacy and thus constitute a search under the Fourth Amendment. This is a critical question because if the Court finds that governmental activity does constitute a search under the Fourth Amendment, then a warrant is normally required. If there is no reasonable expectation of privacy, then the Fourth Amendment provides no protection from the activity and the government is free to act as it pleases because its actions are seen as reasonable. In answering the question as to whether a search has taken place under the Fourth Amendment the Burger and Rehnquist Courts, unlike the Warren Court, have primarily used *Katz* to limit the protections of the Fourth Amendment.

There were two primary methods by which the Burger and Rehnquist Courts used the reasoning in *Katz* to narrow the Fourth Amendment. The first was through a finding that society was not willing to respect personal expectations of privacy, thus, making those expectations unreasonable. A second was by concentrating on the nature or purpose of the initial intrusion rather than the subjective expectations of privacy. The results of both methods of limiting the protections of the Fourth Amendment are the same. If a governmental action does not constitute a search under the *Katz* framework, the Fourth Amendment is not applicable and governmental actions are assumed to pass the reasonableness test.

Assumption of Risk

In a variety of instances, the Supreme Court has refused to use the *Katz* framework to provide Fourth Amendment protection from interference with an individual's privacy. This is especially true when the Court believes that a person has knowingly exposed their activities to others. As is so often true of Fourth Amendment law, the Warren Court decided a lead case in this area which was then further developed by the Burger Court. The Warren Court case of *Hoffa v. United States* (1966)[32] predated *Katz* by two years. In that case James Hoffa argued that governmental use of an undercover informant who testified against Hoffa and co-defendants violated their Fourth Amendment rights. The Court disagreed because it believed the Fourth Amendment only protected the security a person relied on when they placed themselves or their property in a constitutionally protected area. It did not, however, protect a misplaced belief that another person will not reveal their wrongdoing.

After *Katz,* the Court's approach changed from an examination of constitutionally protected areas to that of whether the person has a legitimate expectation of privacy, but the result has remained the same. In similar types of cases, the Court has continued to rule that individuals cannot have a reasonable expectation of privacy when they have assumed a risk in providing information to a third party. One such case was *United States v. White* (1971)[33] when the Court, via Justice Byron White's majority opinion, made it clear that the Court was going to apply Justice Harlan's concurring opinion in *Katz* to determine if the government violated the Fourth Amendment in its gathering of evidence. In *White* the government used an informant who was electronically wired for sound to gather evidence against White who claimed that such an action violated the Fourth Amendment. The Court found that that evidence was admissible and framed the issue in the following way:

> Our problem is not what the privacy expectations of particular defendants in particular situations may be or the extent to which they have in fact relied on the discretion of their companions. Very probably, individual defendants neither know nor suspect that their colleagues have gone or will go to the police or are carrying recorders or transmitters. Otherwise, conversation would cease and our problem with these encounters would be nonexistent or far different from those now before us. Our problem, in terms of the principles announced in *Katz*, is what expectations of privacy are constitutionally "justifiable" . . . [and] what expectations the Fourth Amendment will protect in the absence of a warrant.[34]

The Court went on to find that society would not be willing to respect any expectation of privacy that a person had in this circumstance because the person had willingly had a conversation with the informant. As a result, the bugging of an informant did not constitute a search under the Fourth Amendment and law enforcement was given a green light to continue such practices. Realizing that the Court's decision removed it from future oversight of this method of gathering evidence, Justice Harlan objected to such a use of his concurring opinion from *Katz*. He criticized the Court stating, "it is too easy to forget . . . that the issue here is whether to interpose a search warrant procedure between law enforcement agencies engaging in electronic eavesdropping and the public generally."[35]

Another example of the Court limiting the protections of the Fourth Amendment because a person had assumed a risk may be found in *United States v. Miller* (1976).[36] In that case, the Court ruled that people do not have a privacy interests in their bank records. The Court concentrated on *Katz's* statements that what "a person knowingly exposes to the public . . . is not a subject of Fourth Amendment protections" and reasoned that financial information that is a part of a commercial transaction is voluntarily provided by bank customers to the bank staff.[37] In addition, the existence of federal laws and regulations establish the possibility that banks will have to turn the customer's banking records over to the government. As a result, "the depositor takes the risk, in revealing his affairs to another, that the information will be conveyed by that person to the Government."[38]

Another example involving the assumption of risk may be found in *Smith v. Maryland* (1979)[39] when the Court considered the governmental use of a pen register which recorded for law enforcement officials the numbers of all the local phone calls which were made by Smith. Smith was a suspect in a robbery of a home and making obscene phone calls to the same address. Police, without a warrant, had the phone company put a pen register on Smith's phone which recorded all the outgoing phone numbers he called. The police then discovered that he had called the victim's home and used that information to get a warrant to search and find evidence at Smith's house. Smith argued on appeal that use of the pen register constituted a search without a warrant.

In *Smith* the Court in a 5-4 decision reaffirmed the precedent from *Katz*. Despite this, Justice Harry Blackmun, speaking for the Court, ruled there is no legitimate expectation of privacy in the telephone numbers that a person dials. The Court believed that it was doubtful that anyone would have a justifiable expectation of privacy in the phone numbers they dialed. This was because individuals should realize that by calling a phone number they have "voluntarily conveyed numerical information to the telephone company and 'exposed' that information to its equipment in the ordinary course of business."[40] Furthermore, even if an individual did have a personal expectation of privacy in the phone numbers they used, society would not be willing to respect the expectation. This was because "in these circumstances, petitioner assumed the risk that the information would be divulged to the police."[41] As a result, because it is not considered a search, law enforcement officials do not violate the Fourth Amendment when they use a pen register and track all the phone numbers that an individual dials without getting a warrant. The majority admitted that *Smith* had similarities to *Katz* where the conversation had to go through the phone company to be conveyed. *Smith* was distinguished, however, because the Court found that the use of a pen register was far less intrusive than intercepting the entire conversation.

Justice Stewart's dissenting opinion complained that citizens did have a reasonable expectation of privacy in the phone numbers that they dialed. This was true not because "such a list might in some sense be incriminating, but because it easily could reveal the identities of the persons and the places called, and thus reveal the most intimate details of a person's life."[42]

Miller and *Smith* added a new component, the assumption of risk, to the *Katz* precedent. When the Court examines a person's assumption of risk it takes into consideration the possibility that information may be exposed to others to determine whether the privacy interests must be respected. The more likely it is that the information will be exposed by the government or private activity the more difficult it will be for the Court to conclude that there is an objective expectation of privacy in the behavior. As a result, if a person assumed some risk that their personal business would become known to others, they could not have a *legitimate* expectation of privacy in their activities.

Public Exposure

A person also takes on an assumption of risk when they have a conversation with another person. The Court has thus reasoned that the use of information against a third party wherein one of the parties to a conversation consents to electronic surveillance by the government does not constitute a violation of the Fourth Amendment.[43] From the Court's perspective either party to the conversation could repeat the conversation to others and electronic surveillance does nothing more than lead to an accurate account of what a person willingly said in a conversation.

The Burger and Rehnquist Courts were less inclined than the Warren Court to find that society would find an individual's expectations of privacy to be reasonable. Building off of the limited expectation of privacy that a person has when they assumed risk by sharing information with others the Court has also limited the protections of the Fourth Amendment when a person has in any way exposed their activities to the public. An example of this trend is provided by *California v. Ciraolo* (1986).[44] In *Ciraolo* police got an anonymous tip that Ciraolo was growing marijuana in his backyard. They were unable to observe the yard because it was shielded by a 6-foot outer and 10-foot inner fence. Working off a desire to see in the backyard a police officer who was trained in air surveillance flew over Ciraolo's home at 1,000 feet and took pictures of the marijuana. This provided the probable cause necessary to get a search warrant. When the warrant was served police discovered seventy-three marijuana plants in Ciraolo's backyard. At trial Ciraolo sought to suppress the marijuana because he believed the aerial surveillance, without a warrant, had violated the Fourth Amendment.

On *certiorari*, applying the framework of *Katz*, Chief Justice Warren Burger spoke for a majority of five justices. He found that there was no violation. While Chief Justice Burger found that Ciraolo clearly had a subjective intent to maintain his privacy due to his ten foot fence, he went on to quote *Katz* and state that the Fourth Amendment only applies when a person has a "constitutionally protected reasonable expectation of privacy."[45] The critical question was whether Ciraolo's expectation of privacy was indeed reasonable from society's perspective. In deciding this question the Court examined three issues. These issues were the place of the surveillance, the degree of governmental intrusion, and the purpose behind the intrusion. Chief Justice Burger admitted that the area under question was within the curtilage of the house, an area normally protected under the Fourth Amendment, and that Ciraolo had an expectation of privacy due to the fences surrounding the yard. Chief Justice Burger then ignored Justice Stewart's statement in *Katz* that what a person tries to preserve as private, even in an area accessible to the public, might be constitutionally protected. Instead, Chief Justice Burger quoted *Katz* and stated "What a person knowingly exposes to the public, even in his own home or office, is not a subject of Fourth Amendment protection."[46] Taking this as the lesson to be learned from *Katz* Chief Justice Burger added:

> The Fourth Amendment protection of the home has never been extended to require law enforcement officers to shield their eyes when passing by a home on public thoroughfares. Nor does the mere fact that an individual has taken measures to restrict some views of his activities preclude an officer's observations from a public vantage point where he has a right to be and which renders the activities clearly visible.[47]

The Chief Justice then examined the level of the governmental intrusion. He wrote that there was no need for a warrant to conduct aerial surveillance since private and commercial flights in the public airways are common and "Any member of the public flying in this airspace who glanced down could have seen everything that these officers observed."[48] In a statement that seemed to hark back to the trespass doctrine contained in the *Olmstead* reasoning, Chief Justice Burger also noted that the actions of these officers had been "physically nonintrusive."[49]

Chief Justice Burger then distinguished the object of the search in *Katz*, interpersonal conversations, from that in *Ciraolo*, cultivation of illicit drugs. He reasoned that protecting the privacy of interpersonal communications involves a more important constitutional issue than does the desire to keep secret the cultivation of marijuana in a back yard. As a result, he found that the rule designed to protect conversations from invasion by new forms of surveillance, "does not translate readily into a rule of constitutional dimensions that one who grows illicit drugs in his backyard is 'entitled to assume' his unlawful conduct will not be observed by a passing aircraft."[50]

In *Ciraolo*, Justices William Brennan, Thurgood Marshall, and Harry Blackmun joined a dissent written by Justice Lewis Powell which complained that the majority had not faithfully followed the precedent established in *Katz*. Justice Powell did not believe that the public would be willing "to force individuals to bear the risk of this type of warrantless police intrusion into their residential areas."[51]

In the companion case to *Ciraolo, Dow Chemical Co. v. United States* (1986),[52] the Court had to examine whether aerial surveillance and the use of a high precision aerial mapping camera violated the Fourth Amendment when the defendant had protected the ground level views of an industrial complex from being photographed through elaborate security measures. The case came about when Dow Chemical Company discovered the Environmental Protection Agency (EPA) had conducted aerial surveillance of one of its plants without informing Dow and Dow sought an injunction to stop further surveillance. The district court applied *Katz* and found that Dow had a reasonable expectation of privacy due to its desire to be able to maintain trade secret protections and granted the injunction. The court of appeals reversed and ruled that Dow's property was closer to an open field than to a home or the curtilage surrounding a home and thus carried no expectation of privacy.

In a 5-4 decision the Court in *Dow* found no violation of the Fourth Amendment. As with *Ciraolo* the Court analyzed three factors: the location of the surveillance, the level of intrusion, and the object of the surveillance. Chief Justice Burger's majority opinion accepted the court of appeal's idea that the location of the surveillance was not a specially protected area because "the intimate activities associated with family privacy and the home and its curtilage simply do not reach the outdoor areas or spaces between structures and buildings of a manufacturing plant."[53] In doing so, the Court distinguished between the covered buildings and offices which had a greater expectation of privacy because they protected intimate activities and open areas which could not. The Court pointed out that the use of aerial surveillance and photographing of the plant did not require the government to engage in a physical entry of the location under surveillance. It was noted that the technology used to gather evidence only enhanced the government's natural senses in its surveillance abilities, thereby limiting the level of intrusion. The camera, which was powerful enough to identify wires as small as a half inch in diameter, did not create new methods of surveillance. Furthermore, the Court believed photos which came about through use of the camera were "not so revealing of intimate details as to raise constitutional concerns."[54] On top of these reasons, the Court believed that the object of the government's activities was simply to gain information regarding the layout of the Dow facility and did not raise the same types of privacy concerns that would have arisen if the government sought to identify chemical formulas or secret documents. The intimate details analysis first enunciated in *Dow* grew in importance in future cases and changed the focus of the constitutionality of a search from how and where the search was conducted to an examination of the particular subject matter searched as revealed.[55]

Justices Brennan, Marshall, and Blackmun again dissented in an opinion written by Justice Powell. Justice Powell argued that even though the Court failed to overrule *Katz*, its decision did not reflect the values of the precedent.

Justice Powell further believed that society would have been willing to find that Dow Chemical had a reasonable expectation of privacy.

The Court reinforced the *Ciraolo* and *Dow* decisions in *Florida v. Riley* (1989).[56] *Riley* came to the Court after police in Florida suspected that Riley was growing marijuana in his greenhouse which was located ten to twenty feet behind his mobile home. Riley's yard was posted with a "Do Not Enter" sign. The police were thwarted in investigating their suspicions because a clear view of the greenhouse interior was obstructed from all sides. Police, therefore, used a helicopter flying at 400 feet in elevation to peer into the two panels of the roof of the greenhouse which were not obstructed. Based on the observations of an officer, a warrant was issued and police found marijuana in the greenhouse. Riley successfully challenged the warrant at trial claiming that the helicopter observation constituted an illegal search. The court of appeals reversed, but the Florida Supreme Court reinstated the motion to suppress at which time the state sought and was granted *certiorari*.

The Court split 5-4 and in a plurality opinion written by Justice Byron White it held that there was no search under the Fourth Amendment despite ruling that the greenhouse was in the curtilage and that Riley had taken sufficient precautions to establish his subjective expectation of privacy. The reason that the use of the helicopter was deemed not to be a search was that the helicopter stayed within the navigable airspace that Federal Aviation Administration (FAA) regulations provide for helicopters. As in *Ciraolo* the Court ruled that having a subjective expectation of privacy from ground level surveillance does not protect a person from possible surveillance from the air. The Court declared that "the police may see what may be seen 'from a public vantage point where they have a right to be.'"[57] By failing to cover the entire roof of the greenhouse Riley had knowingly exposed the contents to the police and exempted police efforts to view it from Fourth Amendment scrutiny. The plurality further noted Riley had not demonstrated that "the helicopter interfered with respondent's normal use of the greenhouse or of other parts of the curtilage."[58] Furthermore, through the use of the helicopter "no intimate details connected with the use of home or curtilage were observed."[59]

Justice O'Connor's concurrence thought that the plurality had put too much emphasis on the fact that the helicopter had not violated any regulations of the FAA because the purpose of those regulations was to establish safety standards not to protect people against unreasonable search and seizure. She believed that *Ciraolo* provided better guidance and the Court needed to concentrate on whether "there is considerable public use of airspace at altitudes of 400 feet and above."[60] She further believed that it was Riley's burden to prove that his privacy expectations had been intruded upon by the helicopter by demonstrating that the helicopter used by police had occupied airspace that was rarely used and thus could not be considered public airspace. Lacking such a demonstration, the police had a right to use a helicopter within public airspace.

The application of *Ciraolo*, *Dow*, and *Riley* mean that unless a person takes precautions to protect their curtilage from aerial surveillance it will not be protected under the Fourth Amendment as long as government officials fly at a legal altitude. Due to the Court's view that in these cases the defendants had knowingly exposed their activities to the public, the Court ignored the fact that technology was used to gather the evidence. Instead, the Court emphasized that police had engaged in behavior that members of the public might also engage in and therefore the behavior could not offend any reasonable expectation of privacy. In his dissent in *Riley* Justice Brennan pointed out that in using this test, your constitutional protections only extend to that protection you would have from the worst of your prying neighbors regardless of "however infrequently anyone would in fact do so."[61] Justice Brennan also wondered what the plurality in *Riley* meant by "intimate details" and why they were thought to be so important since the Fourth Amendment makes no mention of the need for activities to be intimate to be protected.

Another example of how the Court has limited the application of *Katz* by finding that a defendant knowingly exposed his activities is *California v. Greenwood* (1988).[62] In *Greenwood* the Court had to decide whether garbage which had been set out to be collected was protected by the Fourth Amendment. In this case police directed the garbage collector to pick up Greenwood's garbage for them and then subjected it to a search. That search gave them the probable cause necessary to get a warrant which when served turned up hashish and cocaine. Greenwood argued that the probable cause upon which the warrant was based was discovered through a violation of the Fourth Amendment. His claim was upheld by the trial court, the court of appeals affirmed, and the California Supreme Court denied review. The state was then granted *certiorari* before the United States Supreme Court.

Speaking for a 6-2 majority, Justice White found that garbage which had been set out for collection was granted no constitutional protection. Justice White applied *Katz* and pointed out that even though Greenwood may have had an expectation of privacy in his garbage, society was not prepared to accept that expectation as objectively reasonable. Justice White relied on *Smith v. Maryland* (1979) and *Ciraolo* and emphasized that Greenwood had knowingly exposed his garbage to others so it could not be subject to Fourth Amendment protection. Justice White then went on to note that not only had Greenwood purposely left out his trash to be hauled away by a third party, it was also "common knowledge that plastic garbage bags left on or at the side of a public street are readily accessible to animals, children, scavengers, snoops, and other members of the public."[63] The Court further noted that police should not have to avert their attention from an object that is readily accessible to members of the public.

In dissent Justice Brennan joined by Justice Marshall also relied on *Katz* and also found the societal expectations prong to be critical. Justice Brennan pointed out that in his view individuals had an expectation of privacy in closed containers and that the Fourth Amendment did not distinguish between worthy and unworthy containers. To Brennan even containers which were discarded carried this expectation of privacy. Justice Brennan believed that society would be willing to respect this expectation of privacy. Justice Brennan reached this conclusion by pointing to a number of studies which demonstrated how much you could learn about a person and their habits by doing an analysis of their garbage. He further pointed out that individual members of society are repulsed when they see others scavenging through garbage and that many communities have passed ordinances which make it illegal to do so. To Justice Brennan that was a clear indication that a society believes that it is reasonable to have an expectation of privacy in garbage. Despite the fact that it was possible for individuals to scavenge through the garbage of others, society did not respect such activity. Justice Brennan further argued that simply because a person gave possession of their garbage to others, they did not lose their privacy interest in the object. In this way, Justice Brennan analogized that garbage was similar to mail in that you gave up a possessory interest, but not a privacy interest.

Emerging Technologies and *Katz*

In other emerging technology cases the outcome of a case involving surveillance and the admissibility of evidence has been dependent on the Court's view as to whether the technology involved merely enhanced the ability of law enforcement to observe what was already visible or exceeded that by providing new depths of surveillance.[64] The Court has long held that technologies which allowed law enforcement to more clearly see do not violate the Fourth Amendment. Examples would include use of flashlights and search lights.[65] As technologies have changed, the Court has been confronted with new challenges.

In *United States v. Knotts* (1983)[66] the Court ruled that governmental use of an electronic beeper which was attached to a container of chloroform allowing the government to track the suspect's movements did not constitute a search. In *Knotts*, police suspected some chloroform was going to be taken to an illicit drug lab so they attached an electronic beeper. The beeper transmitted radio signals at a set frequency, but did not broadcast conversations or sounds. When the chloroform was sold police engaged in visual and electronic surveillance. During transportation of the chloroform, they lost visual and electronic contact with the vehicle. The chloroform was relocated an hour later at a cabin owned by Knotts when a helicopter used by law enforcement officials picked up a signal from the electronic beeper. This and other information gained through visual surveillance of the cabin was used to get a warrant which was served to gather a variety of evidence that Knotts was involved in the manufacture of amphetamine and methamphetamine. Prior to his conviction, Knotts sought to have the evidence suppressed by arguing that the use of the beeper violated the Fourth Amendment. Knotts did not raise the question as to whether the installation of the beeper violated the Fourth Amendment. The court of appeals ruled in Knotts' favor and the government was granted *certiorari*.

The Court in a 5-4 decision, majority opinion by Justice Rehnquist, held that the use of the beeper constituted no search or seizure within the meaning of the Fourth Amendment. This was because the beeper primarily allowed the police to better follow a vehicle on public roads. The Court noted that it had long held that persons in automobiles had a lesser expectation of privacy. Furthermore, individuals could not have a legitimate expectation of privacy on such roads. Therefore, use of an electronic beeper provided police with no more information than they would have had if they relied on traditional forms of surveillance for following someone on the road. Justice Rehnquist explained that "Nothing in the Fourth Amendment prohibited the police from augmenting the sensory faculties bestowed upon them at birth with such enhancement as science and technology afforded them in this case."[67] In effect, the beeper simply enhanced the ability of the police to perform visual surveillance. Justice Rehnquist added, "Admittedly, because of the failure of the visual surveillance, the beeper enabled the law enforcement officials in this case to ascertain the ultimate resting place of the chloroform when they would not have been able to do so had they relied solely on their naked eyes. But scientific enhancement of this sort raises no constitutional issues which visual surveillance would not also raise."[68] In essence, since the Fourth Amendment did not apply to instances of pure visual surveillance on public roads, it did not in this case either. The Court ruled no additional constitutional issues were raised because police acquired information from the beeper after they lost track of the chloroform than if they had kept visual contact with the container.

United States v. Karo (1984)[69] is instructive for a case in which the Court believed that technology went beyond the enhancement of natural senses and gave excessive surveillance abilities to law enforcement. The facts in *Karo* begin like those in *Knotts*. The government placed a beeper in a container of ether which it believed would be used in the production of illicit drugs. In *Karo* the beeper was monitored for over five months as Drug Enforcement Administration (DEA) agents used the beeper to trace the transportation of the container as it traveled through three private houses, two rented lockers, a driveway of another home, and finally to a fifth house. Only through the monitoring of the beeper were agents capable of tracking the movements of the ether until it and other evidence were seized through the use of a warrant. At trial, Karo sought to unsuccessfully have the evidence suppressed and when convicted appealed. The Court of Appeals for the Tenth Circuit ruled in favor of Karo and the government was then granted *certiorari*.

In *Karo* the Court, in a majority opinion by Justice White, first examined the installation of the beeper into the can of ether and found that because neither the ether nor the can into which the beeper was installed belonged to the defendants at the time it was placed there, installation was okay. This was because at the time, "by no stretch of the imagination could it be said that respondents had any legitimate expectation of privacy in it."[70] The Court then noted that the transfer of the container with the beeper created a potential for an invasion of privacy. Nevertheless the Court stated "the mere transfer to Karo of a can containing an unmonitored beeper infringed no privacy interest. It conveyed no information that Karo wished to keep private, for it conveyed no information at all."[71] Furthermore, installation of the beeper had not created a meaningful interference with Karo's possession of the property. So at that point the Fourth Amendment was not implicated in the case because there had not been a search.

The Court moved on to explain that unlike *Knotts* where the beeper only provided police with information which could have been gained through normal surveillance, the beeper in *Karo* allowed the government to exceed the information they could have gained through normal surveillance. This was because even though the use of the beeper was "less intrusive than a full-scale search it does reveal a critical fact about the interior of the premises that the Government is extremely interested in knowing and that it could not have otherwise obtained without a warrant."[72] The beeper in *Karo* was used to gain information about private locations, homes and storage lockers, whereas in *Knotts* it had been used to gain information about public locations, the highways. Private location monitoring, the Court held, does constitute a search and is unlawful unless authorized by a warrant. The Court did note that warrants for beepers would not be problematic in meeting the particularity principle for warrants since, despite not knowing where the beeper may take law enforcement officials, "it will still be possible to describe the object into which the beeper is to be placed, the circumstances that led agents to wish to install the beeper, and the length of time for which the beeper surveillance is requested."[73]

In *Karo* the Court emphasized the traditional role that the Fourth Amendment has played in protecting homes from governmental intrusion and the presumption that such intrusions be monitored through the warrant process. Despite the fact that the beeper did not provide a wide variety of information about the interior of a home, the Court reasoned, "The beeper tells the agent that a particular article is actually located at a particular time in the private residence and is in the possession of the person or persons whose residence is being watched."[74] The Court further noted it would still have been a constitutional violation if law enforcement officials had visually observed the ether container being delivered to a home and then at a later time relied on the beeper for confirmation that the ether was still at the location. This was because the beeper established whether the article remained on the premises. The Court then drew a distinction between electronic monitoring of a general vicinity such as had happened in *Knotts*, which was acceptable, and of a private location, which was not acceptable. It concluded that "Indiscriminate monitoring of property that has been withdrawn from public view would present far too serious a threat to privacy interests in the home to escape entirely some sort of Fourth Amendment oversight."[75] Despite all of its reasoning which found that private location monitoring through use of an electronic beeper did violate the Fourth Amendment, the Court allowed use of all the evidence in *Karo* because it found that the warrant that was issued could have been supported by independent probable cause.

Not all members of the Court have been happy with the way the precedent from *Katz v. United States* has been applied. Justices Brennan and Marshall consistently complained about how *Katz* was applied during their tenure on the Burger and Rehnquist Courts. While they supported the framework of *Katz* as conceptualized by Justice Harlan's concurring opinion, they believed that society was more tolerant of individual expectations of privacy than the bloc of more conservative justices in the majority. As a result, they were much more likely to find individual expectations of privacy to be reasonable and, thus, protected by the Fourth Amendment.

For years the conservative wing of the Court had been satisfied with co-opting Harlan's approach in *Katz* to produce results that enhanced law enforcement efforts to gather evidence. More recently, however, attacks on the *Katz* precedent have come from the most conservative justices on the Court. *Minnesota v. Carter* (1998)[76] provides an example when Justice Scalia, in a concurring opinion, joined by Justice Thomas, complained that there was no support in the text of the Constitution for the *Katz* precedent. Furthermore, Justice Scalia believed *Katz* was not very helpful in ascertaining when government conduct constitutes a search and resulted in a situation in which judges and justices could self-indulgently determine when a person's privacy expectations are reasonable.

Despite his unhappiness with the *Katz* framework, *Kyllo v. United States* (2001)[77] demonstrates that Justice Scalia has applied it when it could be used as a vehicle for results he desired. In *Kyllo* the Court had to determine whether police use of a thermal imagery device to gather evidence about what was going on inside of a person's home violated the Fourth Amendment when it was done without a warrant. Thermal imagery devices detect infrared radiation and convert it to an image which tells the relative warmth of the image. *Kyllo* came to the Court after police, who suspected Kyllo of growing marijuana in his house, used a thermal imager to determine that Kyllo's house and garage were warmer than his neighbor's. Based on this and other information, police then applied for and were issued a search warrant with which they found marijuana being grown at Kyllo's house. At trial, Kyllo argued unsuccessfully that use of the thermal imager was a search under the Fourth Amendment. Kyllo was convicted and eventually was granted *certiorari*.

Speaking for a 5-4 Court, Justice Scalia's majority opinion reaffirmed his belief that in past cases the precedent from *Katz* had made it difficult to determine what constituted a search under the Fourth Amendment. In this case, however, he argued that the difficulty did not exist since the search of a home was involved. In the home, according to Justice Scalia, there is a high expectation of privacy and it is acknowledged to be reasonable. Justice Scalia traced these strong expectations of privacy in the home to the common law that existed at the time of the ratification of the Fourth Amendment. The majority believed that the use of the thermal imager which allowed police to gain knowledge about the interior of a home intruded on the reasonable expectation of privacy that people have in their homes. This was because the use of the thermal imager gave police the ability "to explore details of the home that would previously have been unknowable without physical intrusion."[78]

The dissenters in an opinion by Justice Stevens also relied on *Katz*, but emphasized that Kyllo had knowingly exposed the heat emanating from his house to the public and therefore lost any protection by the Fourth Amendment. They believed that since the thermal imager had not been able to tell the police exactly what was going on behind the walls of Kyllo's house it was a passive form of surveillance which did not give police the direct information about a person that police would have with an actual police presence inside the home. For the dissent off-the-wall technologies such as those used here should be acceptable, while through-the-wall technologies which provide intimate details concerning exactly what is going in a house should not be.

While seemingly extending protection from electronic surveillance, Justice Scalia's majority opinion, as had the opinions in *Katz*, also created openings for future Courts to allow wider use of technology without violating the Fourth Amendment. This is because Justice Scalia states, "obtaining by sense-enhancing technology any information regarding the interior of the home that could not otherwise have been obtained without physical intrusion into a constitutionally protected area constitutes a search—at least where (as here) the technology in question is not in general public use."[79] This assertion that the Fourth Amendment will not protect people's expectation of privacy once a surveillance device is in general public use has been called the Walmart test and been criticized by a number of scholars.[80] Another problem with the decision in *Kyllo* is that it backs away from a concern with privacy as established in *Katz* in favor of a concern with the location searched which is closer to the *Olmstead* precedent. Justice Scalia's opinion in *Kyllo* clearly explained that in "the home, our cases show, *all* details are intimate details."[81] Under its analysis it is clear that the interior of the house is fully protected by the Fourth Amendment, but other locations are not granted such broad protection.

The Nature of the Intrusion and *Katz*

A final method by which post-Warren Courts have diminished the protections of the Fourth Amendment in their interpretation of *Katz* has been to concentrate on the nature of the intrusion rather than on the individual's expectation of privacy. When the Court concentrates on the nature of the intrusion it examines what is the purpose of the government's action. In doing so, the Court has ruled that government actions which merely confirm the presence of contraband goods, such as drugs, are not a search under the Fourth Amendment. This is because no one has a *legitimate* expectation of privacy in illegal drugs. Movement in this direction was made possible by the Court's decisions narrowing the scope of standing in Fourth Amendment cases. By changing the focus in determinations concerning when a person had standing to challenge an unconstitutional search or seizure away from whether a person had a reasonable expectation of privacy to one concerned with whether it was a legitimate expectation of privacy the stage was set to narrow the scope of the protections of the Fourth Amendment. *United States v. Place* (1983)[82] provides an example. In *Place* agents working for the DEA temporarily seized a suitcase without a warrant to allow a dog to sniff it for possible drugs. Although there was no probable cause, the police did have articulable suspicions. Relying on *Terry v. Ohio* (1968)[83] the majority ruled that personal property could be briefly seized for the purpose of pursuing a limited investigation when reasonable suspicion existed. The problem in this particular case was that the agent's detention of Place's luggage for a period ninety minutes went beyond the brief period allowed under *Terry*. Therefore, there was a constitutional violation. Despite the fact that the parties had not raised or argued the question, Justice Sandra Day O'Connor stated in her majority opinion that even though there is a reasonable expectation of privacy in a person's luggage, a canine sniff is not a search under the Fourth Amendment. This was because canine sniffs are less intrusive than a search since they do not require the opening of luggage or examination of the contents. In addition, a sniff was also less intrusive because it only disclosed whether there were contraband items in the form of narcotics contained in the suitcase. Justice O'Connor noted that she was "aware of no other investigative procedure that is so limited both in the manner in which the information is obtained and in the content of the information revealed by the procedure."[84] Despite the fact that police did not have the prerequisite probable cause needed for a broader search, the Court reasoned that the limited intrusion by a dog was acceptable because it stops individuals from the embarrassment and inconvenience inherent in broader searches.

The application of *Katz* to dog sniffs in *Place* does weaken the framework that Justice Stewart had created in *Katz*. It does so because in *Katz* Justice Stewart focused on the extent to which a person tried to increase their expectation of privacy, thus creating a reasonable expectation of privacy. It would be assumed that placing items in luggage would create an expectation of privacy. The *Place* reasoning permits a minimum level of intrusion before governmental actions will even be considered to be a search and then ties that level of intrusion to the nature of the item of the search. Thus, if the purpose of the search is contraband, there is a lesser or no expectation of privacy which has to be respected. This scenario contradicts the purpose of the Fourth Amendment which was to stop arbitrary intrusions into personal privacy. It also weakens *Katz* by concentrating not on an expectation of privacy that a person may have in their luggage, but, instead, on the lack of a physical intrusion. This necessity for a physical intrusion to exist prior to the Fourth Amendment playing a role in the quest for evidence is reminiscent of the trespass doctrine of *Olmstead*, not *Katz*.

One of the problems with the decision in *Place* is that by deciding that use of drug sniffing dogs is outside of the protections of the Fourth Amendment, the Court seemingly conceded its ability to provide oversight of the use of such procedures. As a result, police were given the impression that they had been granted carte blanche to use drug dogs in all scenarios, regardless of whether reasonable suspicion existed. This turned out not to be true in *City of Indianapolis v. Edmonds* (2000)[85] when the Court overturned a drug check point which relied on drug dogs to indicate if vehicles should be searched. Rather than ruling that this was an inappropriate use of drug sniffing dogs, the Court held that when police were primarily engaged in crime-control purposes, as they were, some quantum of individualized suspicion was necessary to justify a stop.

The rationale of *Place* was more fully developed in *United States v. Jacobsen.*[86] *Jacobsen* came to the Court after Federal Express employees damaged a box with a forklift. The employees then sought to inventory the contents of the damaged box. In doing so they found a tube inside made out of silver duct tape. Inside the tube they found plastic bags filled with white powder. The employees then put the plastic bags back into the silver tubes, replaced the tube into the original box, and called the DEA. When federal agents arrived the box was repacked, but still open. The agents then pulled out the plastic bags from the silver tubes, and conducted a field test of the white powder which proved to be cocaine. An agent then rewrapped the package and got a warrant to search the residence to which it was addressed and arrested Jacobsen, the occupant. At trial Jacobsen objected to the admission of the cocaine, arguing that the field test was an enlargement of the original private search.

When *Jacobsen* came before the Court, it stated that warrantless searches of effects are presumptively unreasonable because containers "which can support a reasonable expectation of privacy may not be searched, even on probable cause, without a warrant."[87] The Court then noted that since the original opening of the box was not done by government agents there was no constitutional violation at that point. Reopening of the package by government agents gained them no information that was not already available. Furthermore, because the package had already been opened the assumption of risk principle came into play. As seen previously in *Smith* and *Miller*, when a person assumes a risk by giving others access to information, there can be no reasonable expectation of privacy. If the person decides to share the information gained with the authorities, then those contents are treated like items in plain view. The Court noted, "It is well settled that when an individual reveals private information to another, he assumes the risk that his confidant will reveal that information to the authorities and if that occurs the Fourth Amendment does not prohibit governmental use of that information."[88] As a result, once the agents were told about the package, Jacobsen's expectation of privacy evaporated. When it came time to conduct the field test for cocaine, the Court drew a difference between a reasonable expectation of privacy and a legitimate one. Normally, reasonable expectations of privacy are to be honored and subject to regulation under the Fourth Amendment. However, even when a person has a reasonable expectation of privacy in an article, such as Place's suitcase, it may not be a legitimate expectation and thus deserve the protection of the Fourth Amendment. The Court expanded on *Place* and found that a "chemical test that merely discloses whether or not a particular substance is cocaine does not compromise any legitimate interest in privacy."[89] The Court reasoned that the field test only revealed one piece of information to the agents, that being whether the substance was cocaine. Due to Congress having declared the possession of cocaine illegal, individuals could claim no legitimate expectation of privacy in its possession. As a result, the actions of the government, which only informed it whether the substance was cocaine, did not constitute a search under the Fourth Amendment.

Justice Brennan with Marshall dissented in *Jacobsen* pointing out several problems they believed existed in the majority's opinion. These included narrowing the definition of a search and thereby limiting the Court's opportunity to require police to act reasonably and shifting the focus from the context of police action in a search to the product of the search. Justice Brennan argued that the Court should have ruled that governmental procedures, like canine sniffs, which were minimally intrusive searches should be judged by the standard of reasonableness as established in the *Terry v. Ohio* (1968) precedent.

In *Illinois v. Caballes* (2005)[90] the Court used its decisions in *Place* and *Jacobsen* to allow police to conduct canine sniffs for controlled substances in traffic stops. *Caballes* came to the Court after an Illinois state trooper stopped Caballes for going 71 mph in a 65 speed zone. While stopped another state trooper who was in the vicinity arrived with a drug-detecting dog. He circled Caballes' vehicle with the dog and got a positive response from the dog to the trunk of the vehicle. The trunk was searched and marijuana was found. Caballes was convicted, but the Illinois Supreme Court overturned the conviction by ruling that the dog sniff had violated *Terry v. Ohio* (1968) because although the original stop for speeding was justified, the dog sniff was an unreasonable enlargement of the scope of the speeding investigation which justified the stop. The Supreme Court then granted *certiorari*.

In a 6-2 decision the Court ruled that use of a drug-detecting dog under these circumstances did not violate the Fourth Amendment. In the majority opinion Justice Stevens forcefully stated, "Official conduct that does not 'compromise any legitimate interest in privacy' is not a search subject to the Fourth Amendment."[91] Justice Stevens noted that the original stop had been based on the probable cause of the traffic violation. Furthermore, the duration of the stop was justified by the speeding violation and the standard operating procedures associated with that stop. Justice Stevens went on to demonstrate that the Court's precedents had consistently held that there could be no legitimate privacy interest in contraband. Therefore, "the use of a well-trained narcotics-detecting dog—one that 'does not expose noncontraband items that otherwise would remain hidden from public view'—during a lawful traffic stop, generally does not implicate legitimate privacy interests."[92] Justices David Souter and Ruth Bader Ginsburg had separate dissents in which they explained their worries that by removing drug dog sniffs from the protections of the Fourth Amendment, the government could establish intrusive programs that resulted in people on sidewalks, and vehicles in parking lots being subject to random sniff searches.

In *Place* the Court decided that legitimate expectations of privacy cannot exist in contraband items. In doing so it implied that the Fourth Amendment only protects the innocent, a qualification that is not found in the text of the amendment. It causes one to wonder how far the Court may want to extend this precedent. If the Court is willing to extend this view to its natural conclusion, the result of *Place*, *Jacobsen*, and *Caballes* is that defendants charged with possession of narcotics should not have standing to raise Fourth Amendment challenges. This is because they cannot have legitimate expectations of privacy in illicit drugs and the methods used to find such drugs are not to be considered searches under the Fourth Amendment.

Conclusion

The decision in *Katz v. United States* provides another example by which the Warren Court tried to broaden the Fourth Amendment, but used language which later Courts relied on to limit the protections of the Fourth Amendment. Justice Potter Stewart's opinion in *Katz* declaring that the Constitution protects people, not places, makes it clear that the Court was trying to expand the protections of the Fourth Amendment beyond a literal interpretation of the words. The Court sought to insure that the Fourth Amendment would protect zones of privacy around the individual. The essential holding of *Katz* still stands and it is still a violation of the Fourth Amendment for law enforcement officers to intercept an electronic communication without a warrant. Despite this, Justice John Harlan's concurring opinion has been more influential in later cases as the Court has applied *Katz*. Justice Harlan instructed the Court to ask two questions regarding whether an activity was protected by the Fourth amendment. Those were: (1) did the person have an actual expectation of privacy in their activity and (2) was that expectation one that society would recognize as reasonable.

Although the Burger and Rehnquist Courts did not overrule *Katz*, they did constrain its interpretation and limit its application. The application of *Katz* has proven to have the flexibility necessary to allow courts interpreting it to enhance or diminish the protections of the Fourth Amendment as they see fit. The cases in which post-Warren Courts have applied the reasoning and language of *Katz* have enhanced the area of permissible governmental activity under the Fourth Amendment using two primary methods. The first is by diminishing the broad number of areas of subjective expectation of privacy that individuals have by ruling that it is not reasonable to have society respect those expectations. The Court has found a number of reasons to explain why it is not reasonable for society to respect the subjective expectation of privacy that an individual may have. A first has been to declare that the individual took on an assumption of risk by exposing others to their actions. *United States v. Miller* and how the Court views a person's bank records provides an example. The Court has also found that society would not be willing to respect a person's subjective expectation of privacy when the emerging technology under scrutiny merely enhances, but does not exceed the government's ability to observe what is already visible. An example is *California v. Ciraolo* and aerial surveillance. The Court has also examined the nature of the intrusion and held that surveillance techniques that do not reveal intimate details of a person's life do not interfere with a person's subjective expectation of privacy. This is illustrated by *Dow Chemical Co. v. United States* and the use of highly detailed cameras. In all these scenarios it has become increasingly clear that the Court's view of the societal reasonableness prong of *Katz* is quite narrow. Expectations of privacy will only be reasonable to the extent to which persons do not engage in public exposure of their activities to other people. For the Court, it does not matter how unlikely it is that a third party would actually engage in the same activity as law enforcement, the mere possibility is enough for society to no longer find a person's expectation of privacy to be reasonable. While the Court has placed some limitations on the extremes to which the government may try to discover evidence, such as the necessity of flying in legal airspace, it has given the government a great deal of latitude in trying to discover evidence.

The second method by which the framework from *Katz* has been used to enlarge the legitimacy of governmental activity is by linking the definition of whether a search occurred to the nature of the item that is the object of the search. By finding that there is no legitimate expectation of privacy in contraband items in cases such as *United States v. Place* and *United States v. Jacobsen*, the Court has limited the protections of the Fourth Amendment. The Court made this change in direction possible in *New Jersey v. T.L.O.* (1985)[93] when it declared, "the Fourth Amendment does not protect subjective expectations of privacy that are unreasonable or otherwise 'illegitimate.'"[94] The end result is that now under *Katz* a search occurs only when individuals have a reasonable *and* legitimate expectation of privacy in their activities. Therefore, inspections that merely determine if an item is contraband are not to be defined as a search.

Regardless of the method by which the Court has limited what constitutes a search under the Fourth Amendment, the result is the same. Removing judicial scrutiny in these areas leaves the government with considerable power to engage in search and seizures. It allows governmental actors to engage in techniques for the purpose of discovering criminal activity, but not be regulated by the Fourth Amendment. This situation may embolden the government to develop other methods of learning about the activities of its citizens which will be considered outside the protection of the Fourth Amendment. This area of Fourth Amendment jurisprudence demonstrates that the Burger and Rehnquist Courts were interested in going beyond enlarging the number of exceptions to the warrant requirement, they were also interested in creating exceptions to the Fourth Amendment itself.

Illustrative Case Reprise

The case of *Doe v. Renfrow* (1980) was not a typical Fourth Amendment case because the police were not successful in gathering any evidence from Denise Doe. As a result, there was no criminal trial and the search tactics were not challenged in a suppression hearing as being a violation of the Fourth Amendment. Instead, the case came to the courts because Denise Doe sought injunctive and declaratory relief and compensatory and punitive damages against school and police officials over their actions toward her under Title 42 U.S.C., section 1983 and 1985(3). The specific reason for the suit according to papers filed by Doe's attorney was that the whole school/police operation and practice was "unsupported by particularized facts, reasonable suspicion or probable cause to believe that any of the persons" subject to the canine drug investigation would possess controlled substances.[95] The complaint further objected that Diane was subjected to a strip search. Diane Doe sought $50,000 in actual damages and $50,000 in punitive damages plus declaratory and injunctive relief.

The trial court rejected Doe's claim that the mass detention of students violated the Fourth Amendment. The court ruled that this was a justified action given that it took place in a school. The court noted that, while in school, students are subject to the daily routine of class attendance and these restrictions are not a violation of the Fourth Amendment. The court emphasized that the purpose of the detention and the searches which followed was to help maintain an educational environment within the school. The court also rejected the use of drug dogs to do an initial inspection of the students for drugs as a violation of the Fourth Amendment. It stated, "the sniffing of a trained narcotic detecting canine is not a search. Since no search was performed up until the time the dogs alerted, no warrant was necessary for the initial observation by the school officials."[96] The court found that searches of clothing were acceptable since they followed a positive indication by the drug dogs which gave reasonable cause for the intrusion. When it came to the strip search the court had a different view and stated this court holds that "conducting a nude search of a student solely upon the continued alert of a trained drug-detecting canine is unreasonable."[97] Despite this, the case was thrown out on summary judgment because the judge ruled that the chief of police did not play a direct role in the strip search and could not be held liable. The school officials who were defendants were immune from liability arising out of the nude search because they were school officials who had acted "in good faith with a regard for the welfare and health of the plaintiff" within the course of their duties.[98] On top of this, the court added that the school officials had not acted with disregard for the Fourth Amendment because "the law in the area of student searches in public schools is obviously unsettled."[99]

On appeal the Court of Appeals for the Seventh Circuit accepted all of the district court's opinion as its own except for the grant of immunity to the school officials for the strip search. The court pointed out:

It does not require a constitutional scholar to conclude that a nude search of a thirteen-year-old child is an invasion of constitutional rights of some magnitude. More than that: it is a violation of any known principle of human decency. Apart from any constitutional readings and rulings, simple common sense would indicate that the conduct of the school officials in permitting such a nude search was not only unlawful but outrageous under "settled indisputable principles of law."[100]

In 1980 Doe filed for *certiorari* with the Supreme Court. The Supreme Court found the initial search of students through the use of drug sniffing dogs to be of so little consequence that it voted against granting *certiorari* to review the constitutionality of the practice.[101] In 1983 the Supreme Court took the opportunity, despite the fact that the issue had not been properly briefed or argued before the Court, to determine that dog sniffs did not constitute a search under the Fourth Amendment.[102]

In the years since *Mapp v. Ohio* was decided we have seen the protections of the Fourth Amendment and exclusionary rule limited in a number of ways by post-Warren Courts. They increased both the number of exceptions to the warrant rule and accepted a general reasonableness approach to the amendment. These courts also changed the foundation of the exclusionary rule from being a requirement of the Fourth Amendment to being a judicial remedy that should only be applied if it can act as a police deterrent. They also added a number of exceptions to the exclusionary rule. As this chapter demonstrates, another way they have limited the protections of the Fourth Amendment is by finding that society would not respect an individual's expectation of privacy as reasonable. With all these changes in the law since *Mapp* one can wonder if the Roberts Court will in the post-9/11 world act to expand or contract the protections of the Fourth Amendment. The final chapter examines the government reaction to the terrorist attacks of 9/11 and provides an analysis of the Fourth Amendment cases the Roberts Court has resolved thus far.

Notes

1. *Horton v. Goose Creek Independent School Dist.*, 690 F.2d. 470, 476 (1982).
2. *Irvine v. California*, 347 U.S. 128, 132 (1954).
3. *Doe v. Renfrow*, 475 F. Supp 1012 (1979).
4. Potter Stewart, "The Road to *Mapp v. Ohio* and Beyond: The Origins Development and Future of the Exclusionary Rule in Search-and-Seizure Cases," *Columbia Law Review* 83 (1983): 1397.
5. *Burdeau v. McDowell*, 256 U.S. 465 (1921), ruled that private individuals were not bound by the Fourth Amendment.
6. Phyllis T. Bookspan, "Reworking the Warrant Requirement: Resuscitating the Fourth Amendment," *Vanderbilt Law Review* 44 (1991): 495.
7. *Olmstead v. United States*, 277 U.S. 438 (1928).

8. *Nardone v. United States,* 302 U.S. 379 (1937).

9. *Katz v. United States,* 389 U.S. 347 (1967).

10. *Katz,* 389 U.S. at 350.

11. *Katz,* 389 U.S. at 353.

12. *Katz,* 389 U.S. at 351-352.

13. *Katz,* 389 U.S. at 361 (Harlan, J., concurring).

14. Melvin Gutterman, "A Formulation of the Value and Means Model of the Fourth Amendment in the Age of Technologically Enhanced Surveillance," *Syracuse Law Review* 39 (1988): 662.

15. Anthony Amsterdam, "Perspectives on the Fourth Amendment," *Minnesota Law Review* 58 (1974): 385; see also Scott E. Sundby, "'Everyman's' Fourth Amendment: Privacy or Mutual Trust Between Government and Citizen," *Columbia Law Review* 94 (1994): 1757-1758; Raymond Shih Ray Ku, "The Founder's Privacy: The Fourth Amendment and the Power of Technological Surveillance," *Minnesota Law Review* 86 (2002): 1346; and John B. Mitchell, "What Went Wrong with the Warren Court's Conception of the Fourth Amendment?," *New England Law Review* 27 (1992): 47-53.

16. Bookspan, "Reworking the Warrant Requirement: Resuscitating the Fourth Amendment," 490.

17. *Smith v. Maryland,* 442 U.S. 735, 740 (1979).

18. *United States v. United States District Court for the Eastern District of Michigan,* 407 U.S. 297 (1972).

19. *United States v. United States District Court for the Eastern District of Michigan,* 407 U.S. at 314.

20. *Hester v. United States,* 265 U.S. 57 (1924).

21. *Hester,* 265 U.S. at 58-59.

22. *Katz,* 389 U.S. at 351.

23. *Oliver v. United States,* 466 U.S. 170 (1984).

24. *Oliver,* 466 U.S. at 182.

25. *Oliver,* 466 U.S. at 181.

26. *Oliver,* 466 U.S. at 181.

27. *Oliver,* 466 U.S. at 197.

28. *United States v. Dunn,* 480 U.S. 294 (1987).

29. *United States v. Dunn,* 480 U.S. at 297-298.

30. *United States v. Dunn,* 480 U.S. at 301.

31. Vanessa Rownaghi, "Driving into Unreasonableness: The Driveway, the Curtilage, and Reasonable Expectations of Privacy," *Journal of Gender, Social Policy & Law* 11 (2003): 1176.

32. *Hoffa v. United States,* 385 U.S. 293 (1966).

33. *United States v. White,* 401 U.S. 745 (1971).

34. *United States v. White,* 401 U.S. at 751-752.

35. *United States v. White,* 401 U.S. at 789 (Harlan, J., dissenting).

36. *United States v. Miller,* 425 U.S. 435 (1976).

37. *United States v. Miller,* 425 U.S. at 442.

38. *United States v. Miller,* 425 U.S. at 443.

39. *Smith v. Maryland,* 442 U.S. 735 (1979).

40. *Smith,* 442 U.S. at 744.

41. *Smith,* 442 U.S. at 745.

42. *Smith*, 442 U.S. at 746 (Stewart, J., dissenting).

43. *United States v. White*, 401 U.S. 745 (1971).

44. *California v. Ciraolo*, 476 U.S. 207 (1986).

45. *California v. Ciraolo*, 476 U.S. at 213 (Harlan, J., concurring) (citing *Katz v. United States*, 389 U.S. 347, 360 (1967)).

46. *California v. Ciraolo*, 476 U.S. at 213 (citing *Katz v. United States*, 389 U.S. 347, 351 (1967)).

47. *California v. Ciraolo*, 476 U.S. at 213.

48. *California v. Ciraolo*, 476 U.S. at 213-214.

49. *California v. Ciraolo*, 476 U.S. at 214.

50. *California v. Ciraolo*, 476 U.S. at 214-15.

51. *California v. Ciraolo*, 476 U.S. at 225 (Stewart, J., dissenting).

52. *Dow Chemical Co. v. United States*, 476 U.S. 227 (1986).

53. *Dow Chemical Co.*, 476 U.S. at 236.

54. *Dow Chemical Co.*, 476 U.S. at 237-38.

55. Merrick D. Bernstein, "'Intimate Details': A Troubling New Fourth Amendment Standard for Government Surveillance Techniques," *Duke Law Journal* 46 (1996): 597.

56. *Florida v. Riley*, 488 U.S. 445 (1989).

57. *Florida v. Riley*, 488 U.S. at 449 (citing *California v. Ciraolo*, 476 U.S. 207, 213 (1986)).

58. *Florida v. Riley*, 488 U.S. at 452.

59. *Florida v. Riley*, 488 U.S. at 452.

60. *Florida v. Riley*, 488 U.S. at 455 (O'Connor J., concurring).

61. *Florida v. Riley*, 488 U.S. at 457 (Brennan J., dissenting).

62. *California v. Greenwood*, 486 U.S. 35 (1988).

63. *California v. Greenwood*, 486 U.S. at 40.

64. For a comprehensive overview of the Court's decisions in the area of electronic surveillance see Clifford Fishman and Anne McKenna, *Wiretapping and Electronic Eavesdropping* (Rochester: Westgroup, 2nd ed., 1995).

65. *United States v. Lee*, 274 U.S. 559 (1927).

66. *United States v. Knotts*, 460 U.S. 276 (1983).

67. *United States v. Knotts*, 460 U.S. at 282.

68. *United States v. Knotts*, 460 U.S. at 285.

69. *United States v. Karo*, 468 U.S. 705 (1984).

70. *United States v. Karo*, 468 U.S. at 711.

71. *United States v. Karo*, 468 U.S. at 712.

72. *United States v. Karo*, 468 U.S. at 715.

73. *United States v. Karo*, 468 U.S. at 718.

74. *United States v. Karo*, 468 U.S. at 715.

75. *United States v. Karo*, 468 U.S. at 733.

76. *Minnesota v. Carter*, 525 U.S. 83 (1998).

77. *Kyllo v. United States*, 533 U.S. 27 (2001).

78. *Kyllo*, 533 U.S. at 40.

79. *Kyllo*, 533 U.S. at 34.

80. See, Christopher Slobgin, "Peeping Techno-Toms and the Fourth Amendment: Seeing Through *Kyllo*'s Rules Governing Technological Surveillance," *Minnesota Law Review* 86 (2002): 1393-1437; Andrew Riggs Dunlap, "Fixing the Fourth Amendment with Trade Secrets Law: A Response to *Kyllo v. United States*," *Georgetown Law Review* 90 (2002): 2190.

81. *Kyllo*, 533 U.S. at 37 (emphasis in original).
82. *United States v. Place*, 462 U.S. 696 (1983).
83. *Terry v. Ohio*, 392 U.S. 1 (1968).
84. *United States v. Place*, 462 U.S. 696, 708 (1983).
85. *City of Indianapolis v. Edmonds*, 531 U.S. 32 (2000).
86. *United States v. Jacobsen*, 466 U.S. 109 (1984).
87. *United States v. Jacobsen*, 466 U.S. at 120.
88. *United States v. Jacobsen*, 466 U.S. at 117.
89. *United States v. Jacobsen*, 466 U.S. at 123.
90. *Illinois v. Caballes*, 543 U.S. 405 (2005).
91. *Illinois v. Caballes*, 543 U.S. at 408.
92. *Illinois v. Caballes*, 543 U.S. at 409.
93. *New Jersey v. T.L.O.*, 469 U.S. 325 (1985).
94. *New Jersey v. T.L.O.*, 469 U.S. at 338.
95. *Doe v. Renfrow*, 631 F.2d 91, 92 (1980).
96. *Doe v. Renfrow*, 475 F. Supp 1012, 1019 (1979).
97. *Doe v. Renfrow*, 475 F. Supp at 1024.
98. *Doe v. Renfrow*, 475 F. Supp at 1029.
99. *Doe v. Renfrow*, 475 F. Supp at 1029.
100. *Doe v. Renfrow*, 631 F.2d 91, 92-93 (1980).
101. *Doe v. Renfrow*, 451 U.S. 1022 (1981).
102. *United States v. Place*, 462 U.S. 696 (1983).

Chapter 8
The Future of the Fourth Amendment

The Bill of Rights in general and the fourth amendment in particular are profoundly anti-government documents. They deny to government—worse yet, to
democratic government—desired means, efficient means, and means that must
inevitably appear from time to time throughout the course of centuries to be absolutely necessary means, for government to obtain legitimate and laudable objectives.[1]

[T]he art of being a judge, if there is such an art, comes in announcing clear
rules in the context of . . . infinitely varied cases, rules that can be understood
and observed by conscientious government officials.[2]

Illustrative Case

Jose Padilla was born in Brooklyn, New York on October 18, 1970. Padilla is
not your typical American. Padilla became a gang member and in 1983 was
convicted of murder and remained incarcerated until he turned eighteen. He was
convicted on a handgun charge in 1991 and again sent to prison. After being
released from prison on the gun charge, Padilla converted to Islam. It was his
activities after his conversion to Islam that again brought Padilla to the attention
of the government. He moved to Egypt in 1998 and between 1999 and 2000
traveled to several countries in the Middle East and Southwest Asia. In 2002 two
sources told the government that Jose Padilla had approached members of al
Qaeda with a plot to set off bombs in the United States. One source was a man
named Abu Zubaida who was identified as a top al Qaeda operative. Zubaida
later claimed that his statements were a result of torture while in U.S. custody.
According to Deputy Attorney General James Comey, Padilla originally contacted al Qaeda leaders about a plot involving his plans to set off a nuclear bomb

253

that he had purportedly learned to build off the internet. The bomb was to be detonated in a city within the United States. The leaders of al Qaeda believed that such an attack was too ambitious and suggested that Padilla build a simpler device, a dirty bomb which would use traditional explosives to disperse radioactive material.

On May 8, 2002 Padilla was arrested at O'Hare International Airport as he returned from a trip to Pakistan. Padilla's original arrest was for the purpose of being a "material witness" to the attacks of September 11, 2001. The material witness warrant was issued by the United States District Court for the Southern District of New York, in connection with a grand jury investigation into the September 11 attacks. While he was being held in New York, Padilla had access to an attorney. He was held as a material witness until June 8, 2002 when Attorney General John Ashcroft held a press conference and announced the Padilla was being declared an "enemy combatant" by President George Walker Bush for his role in a plot to plant a dirty bomb somewhere in the United States. Padilla differed from other individuals who had been declared enemy combatants in two ways. First, he was an American citizen and second he was not captured on a battlefield. The government argued, however, that "In a time of war, an enemy combatant is subject to capture and detention wherever found, whether on a battlefield or elsewhere abroad or within the United States."[3] When Padilla was declared an enemy combatant he was moved to a military brig in South Carolina. There he was held captive by the Department of Defense. While being held at the brig, Padilla was placed in isolation from other prisoners and denied access to a lawyer for three and a half years. The government argued that Padilla could be denied an attorney because there were no criminal charges brought against him and he was an enemy combatant.

While Padilla was being held in New York he consulted with an attorney, Donna Newman. Three days after he was declared an enemy combatant she initiated *habeas corpus* proceedings to try to free him. In those proceedings, the government submitted an unsealed declaration by Michael H. Mobbs, special advisor to the Under Secretary of Defense for Policy. The Mobbs Declaration set forth the information the President received before he designated Padilla as an enemy combatant. According to the information, while Jose Padilla had been traveling in the Middle East and Southwest Asia he had been in contact with known members and leaders of al Qaeda. Furthermore, when he was in Afghanistan in 2001, he became involved with a plan to build and set off a dirty bomb within the United States. His purpose in traveling to Pakistan was to receive training on explosives from al Qaeda. While in Pakistan he was instructed to return to the United States to conduct reconnaissance and/or plan other attacks on behalf of al Qaeda. Despite Padilla's activities, the government did not allege that Padilla was a member of al Qaeda. The government also offered sealed information explaining in cryptic terms the sources that had been used in gathering the information about Padilla and the circumstantial evidence which corroborated the allegations.

On December 4, 2002, Judge Michael Mukasey ruled on the *habeas* petition.[4] Judge Mukasey first ruled that the proper parties had brought and were
responding in the case. He then found that both statutes and the Constitution
allowed the president to declare American citizens to be enemy combatants and
detain them. He ruled that the government did have to provide evidence to support President Bush's declaration that Padilla was an enemy combatant. He also
ruled that Padilla had to be given a chance to respond to the government's evidence that he was an enemy combatant. Judge Mukasey did not believe that Padilla had a right to counsel under the Sixth Amendment because that right applied only to criminal prosecutions and Padilla had not yet been charged with a
crime. Despite this, Judge Mukasey did believe that since Padilla had a right to
present facts and contest the evidence presented by the government, he did have
a right to consult with counsel. He then ordered the parties to devise a method
by which Padilla could consult with his attorney. The government opted not to
follow the ruling and instead appealed the decision to the U.S. Court of Appeals
for the Second Circuit.

The Second Circuit ruled on December 13, 2003.[5] It first found that both the
district court and it had jurisdiction in the case. The Court never reached a decision on the primary issues concerning access to counsel, standard of review for
evidence against a declared enemy combatant, and burden of proof required to
hold a person as an enemy combatant because its ruling made those issues moot.
Instead of examining those issues, the court ruled that the president did not have
sole authority under Article II of the Constitution in his role as commander-in-
chief to declare American citizens to be enemy combatants. The court also
found that Congress had never given to the president the power to detain American citizens on U.S. soil as enemy combatants. The court believed that the president's power in this area needed to be guided by the Non-Detention Act which
Congress had passed and which prohibited the president from detaining American citizens in the U.S. without trials. The court further noted that it did not believe that the congressional Authorization for Use of Military Force of 2001
(AUMF), which justified the war on terrorism, altered Congress' intentions in
the Non-Detention Act. As a result, because the president had exerted power
where Congress had specifically denied it to him, his use of that power could not
be supported by law or the Constitution.

The government sought and received *certiorari* from the Supreme Court.
The only exception to the ban on access to lawyers for Padilla during this
process was that Padilla was granted brief, monitored visits with an attorney
while the Supreme Court was considering his case. During the visits the attorneys were not allowed to ask Padilla about the conditions of his confinement.
Between the time that the Court heard oral argument and when the decision was
announced Deputy Attorney General James Comey held a press conference on
June 1, 2004. In it he explained that not only had Padilla sought to plant a dirty
bomb somewhere in the United States, he also had considered plans to find high-

rise apartment buildings that used natural gas. He contemplated renting a couple of apartments in those buildings and creating gas leaks in the apartment filling them with natural gas for the purpose of blowing up the entire building. Comey also claimed "the night before Jose Padilla left on his mission to the United States, he was hosted at a farewell dinner by the mastermind of September the 11th and the coordinator of those attacks."[6]

The Court announced its decision on June 28, 2004.[7] In its resolution of the case the Supreme Court divided 5-4 and evaded answering the important questions as to whether Padilla was properly being detained under the laws and Constitution of the United States. The majority opinion written by Chief Justice William Rehnquist declared that both the district court and the court of appeals had lacked jurisdiction in the case. The Court found that Padilla's petition for *habeas corpus* had been brought before the wrong court. Because Padilla was being held in a military brig in South Carolina the proper party to the case was the individual who was physically in charge of Padilla at that facility and a district court in New York could not order Padilla set free. Likewise, the second circuit could not hear the case on appeal. As a result, the decisions of those two courts were not enforceable and if Padilla wanted to gain his freedom he would have to file a petition of *habeas corpus* in the proper court.

After the Supreme Court's decision, Padilla's attorneys began the process all over again using the proper district court in South Carolina. At the original hearing on the issue the government did not make use of the Mobbs Declaration. Instead, it relied on the Rapp Declaration which was prepared by Jeffery Rapp, a Bush administration official. Interestingly, the Rapp Declaration made no mention of Padilla's plan to explode a dirty bomb. On February 28, 2005 District Court Judge Henry Floyd granted Padilla's petition for *habeas corpus*.[8] In doing so, he found that the AMUF did not grant the president the power to detain American citizens in America as enemy combatants. On appeal to the Fourth Circuit of the Court of Appeals, the decision of the district court was reversed on September 9, 2005.[9] The Fourth Circuit believed that the AMUF did authorize the president to detain Americans who had been declared enemy combatants within the United States.

Padilla's attorneys sought to have the Supreme Court grant *certiorari* when the case took an interesting turn. On Nov. 22, 2005, a mere six days before passage of the deadline to file arguments with the Supreme Court to defend the administration's detention of Padilla, the Bush administration decided to abandon the enemy combatant status of Padilla. At that point the government decided to bring criminal charges against Padilla and court proceedings began in a Florida district court. Padilla and two coconspirators Ahmad Amin Hassoun, a computer programmer of Palestinian descent, and Kifah Wael Jayyousi, a public school administrator who came from Jordan, were charged with conspiracy to murder, kidnap, and maim people in a foreign country; conspiracy to provide material support for terrorists; and providing material support for terrorists. No mention was made in the indictment of the allegations that Padilla had planned to set off a dirty bomb or any other type of attack inside the United States.

Prior to trial, the defense moved to have Padilla declared incompetent to stand trial. Padilla's attorneys claimed that while being held by the military Padilla had been subjected to a variety of abuses including being confined to a nine by seven foot cell in isolation of other prisoners. According to his attorneys, Padilla was also subject to sleep deprivation, extreme noise, bound in contorted positions and the extremes of intense light or complete darkness. They claimed he was also given drugs meant to break his will. The government denied that Padilla was subject to harsh treatment and explained that Padilla's treatment and detention by the military involved classified information that could not be disclosed in open court. Due to the government's desire to either keep their treatment of Padilla classified or the actual conditions of detainment a secret, when the trial began the government did not introduce any statements that Padilla made during his confinement as evidence.

During the three month trial the most damning evidence presented against Padilla was an application to join al Qaeda which had Padilla's fingerprints on it. A covert CIA officer testified that the application form was given to him in Afghanistan. When tested for fingerprints the government discovered a match for Jose Padilla. Padilla's attorney argued that his client may have handled the document at one time or another, but the prints were inconsistent with those of someone who would have actually filled out the document. The government also introduced intercepts of 70 phone conversations. On seven of the conversations Padilla and his co-defendants allegedly talked in code about plans to travel overseas to fight with Islamic militants.

Padilla's lawyers argued that the defendant's phone calls and activities in the Middle East could be explained by the fact that they were involved in humanitarian missions for persecuted Muslims in Bosnia, Chechnya, Lebanon, Somalia and other places. The defense believed that the evidence against Padilla was so weak that it decided not to call any witnesses on Padilla's behalf. The assumption was that the burden of proving the charges "beyond a reasonable doubt" lay with the prosecution, and that this burden had not been met.

On Aug. 17, 2007 Jose Padilla and his two coconspirators were found guilty of conspiracy to murder, kidnap and maim people overseas and of providing material support to terrorist groups. The government asked the court to impose a life sentence for Padilla. On January 22, 2007 Jose Padilla was sentenced to 17 years and 4 months in prison. At the sentencing Judge Marcia Cooke explained her sentence by stating, "There is no evidence that these defendants personally maimed, kidnapped or killed anyone in the United States or elsewhere. There was never a plot to overthrow the United States government."[10] Judge Cooke also gave Padilla credit for time served for the three and a half years he spent in a naval brig in South Carolina. Jose Padilla is currently serving his sentence.

The ordeal of Jose Padilla illustrates a number of interesting questions regarding the power of the government in the post-9/11 world. During the continuing war on terrorism how much power will be given to the government to combat threats to the nation? Under what conditions can a person be seized and detained under the Constitution? Answers to these questions are important because in countless court filings, internal memos and testimony before Congress, the Bush administration claimed that there were no limits to a president's power to conduct war. As a result, President Bush authorized harsh interrogation techniques that have bordered on torture and imprisoning citizens and non-citizens for as long as deemed necessary. In the administration's view, the president's war power trumps any restrictions written into laws enacted by Congress or treaties signed and ratified during previous administrations. Far reaching powers have also been claimed in regards to the government's power to search and seize in its investigations of possible terrorism. This chapter begins with an examination of the new tools the government has created to combat crime and terrorism. It also examines evolving methods of gathering evidence and analyzes how the Court is likely to rule on their usage by the government. It then examines the emerging Fourth Amendment jurisprudence of the Roberts Court and ends by discussing the future of the Fourth Amendment.

The USA Patriot Act

Throughout American history when the country has been threatened by new perceived dangers the government has sought to meet those threats head on. The tactics selected by the government to combat those threats have often tested our understanding of what is seen as a legal search and seizure according to the Fourth Amendment. In the last century we saw the government ask the Court to broaden its powers to search and seize in order to try to meet dangers which it believed threatened the American way of life. Examples of perceived threats included dissenters in World War I, bootleggers during the Prohibition Era, the red scare of the 1920s, McCarthyism during the Cold War, the demonstrators and radicalism during the Vietnam War, and drug use since the 1980s. Based on governmental efforts to expand the powers to search and seize to combat past threats it should not come as a surprise that following September 11, 2001 the government quickly took steps to broaden its powers to meet the new threats. Attorney General John Ashcroft declared it was time for a "fundamentally different approach to law enforcement."[11] The new approach approved by Attorney General Ashcroft included guidelines authorizing government agents to make suspicionless visits to any place or attend any event open to the public, including religious services and online communities, for the purpose of advancing an investigation. One limitation that Attorney General Ashcroft sought to impose on federal agents was that they should not maintain "files on individuals solely for the purpose of monitoring activities protected by the First Amendment."[12]

The most prominent government attempt to aid the fight against terrorism which impacts interest protected by the Fourth Amendment has been passage of the United and Strengthening America by Providing Appropriate Tools Required to Intercept and Obstruct Terrorism (USA Patriot) Act. The USA Patriot Act was passed on October 26, 2001 a mere 45 days after the attacks of September 11. The legislation was fast tracked and did not go through the extensive congressional hearings or floor debates which are required of most pieces of legislation. The law which primarily consisted of amendments and modifications of existing laws covers 16 broad topics and includes 161 separate sections. The multiple purposes were as follows. First, it sought to give the federal government more power to track and intercept communications for the purposes of law enforcement and foreign intelligence gathering. Second, it gave the Department of Treasury more regulatory powers over financial institutions in the United States in order to combat corruption caused by foreign money laundering. Third, it sought to ensure that America's borders would be secure against foreign terrorists. Fourth, it expanded and redefined the crimes of domestic and international terrorism, providing new penalties and more efficient procedures for removing the threat from our society. Many of the provisions of the law had a sunset provision which expired on December 31, 2005, but Congress reauthorized most of the provisions on March 9, 2006.

The USA Patriot Act sought to make it easier for federal officials to track and gather communications to deter terrorism. The problem that many civil libertarians see for the Fourth Amendment is that these methods may involve searches and seizures which go beyond what the Constitution allows. There are several portions of the USA Patriot Act that have been most troubling to civil libertarians. The first concern is that Title II of the USA Patriot Act increases the government's power to engage in electronic surveillance and the ability to share the information gained with a multitude of law enforcement agencies. This is accomplished by blurring the line between intelligence gathering and law enforcement. As has been shown in earlier chapters, both the Fourth Amendment and the Omnibus Crime Control Act require probable cause that a crime has actually been committed before a warrant to interpret electronic communications can be granted. Intelligence investigations, on the other hand, may be initiated based on the Foreign Intelligence Surveillance Act (FISA). They can be started on a showing of the different standard that there is probable cause to believe that a person is an agent of a foreign power, no suspected criminal activity is required. The language of FISA does not require a person to be a spy before they can become a target of a FISA investigation. According to Stephen Schulhofer, "Foreign nationals from friendly countries who do nothing to conceal their activities nonethelsss qualify as 'foreign agents' subject to broad FISA surveillance simply because they have ties to *legitimate* foreign organizations, and the 'foreign intelligence information' that a FISA probe can seek to obtain broadly includes any information that relates to the foreign affairs of the United States."[13]

Requests for a warrant based on FISA go to a special FISA court developed for FISA for consideration. The FISA Court is made up of seven district court judges who are appointed by the Chief Justice of the United States for the sole purpose of determining if FISA warrants shall be issued. The USA Patriot Act changed FISA's language so that warrants could be issued if foreign intelligence gathering or an antiterrorist investigation was a significant purpose behind the investigation. It no longer has to be the primary purpose.[14] This provision could provide the government with an excuse to open investigations on anyone it believes is disruptive of the government's goals and may be advancing the interest of another nation. This for all intents and purposes lessens the probable cause standard that has been needed for criminal investigations. This is because under the USA Patriot Act any information which is gathered under a FISA warrant can be shared with law enforcement agencies which, if they sought a wiretap warrant, would be required to demonstrate a showing of probable cause.

Not only does the USA Patriot Act make electronic surveillance warrants easier to obtain, it also places few limitations on the warrants. FISA warrants do not have to specify particular things to be seized. Section 206 of the USA Patriot Act, which was not reauthorized and will expire on December 31, 2009, allows for roving wiretaps. As a result, a single warrant allows the government to track a person's communication activities regardless of what phone, computer, or other communication device they might be using. Issuance of a surveillance warrant allows homes and places of business to be placed under video surveillance. The government may also search all the internet sources that a person accesses and the government does not have to notify the target of the investigation that they were ever under investigation. Section 213 of the act allows the government to conduct sneak and peek searches in all criminal cases. Sneak and peek warrants can be justified when the court issuing the warrant believes there is reasonable cause to believe that informing the party against whom the warrant is served would cause adverse results. Under these warrants the government can sneak into a residence or business for which they have a warrant, observe what is there, take pictures, examine anything on the computer, then leave, and not inform anyone about the intrusion. Under the Reauthorization Act of 2005 the government may delay giving notice of a search for thirty days extendable to ninety days if the facts can justify such a delay.

As originally passed Title II of the USA Patriot Act in Section 215 also amended FISA to allow the government to search and seize "any tangible things" by giving the FBI power to trigger nondiscretionary judicial orders which could be used to seize tangible items such as books, records, papers, and documents in investigations meant to protect the country against international terrorism or clandestine international intelligence activities. The law stated that citizens should not be investigated "solely on the basis of activities protected by the First Amendment."[15] Investigations could, however, be started without reasonable suspicion. Furthermore, when a request was made for records the party served was forbidden from disclosing that the request was made or that items were given over to the government. The types of records involved include business, medical, and educational. Beyond the new powers which were granted by the USA Patriot Act to the government to access records on individuals suspected of terrorism, many private businesses after 9/11 gave the government access to their private data records.[16] The Reauthorization Act of 2005 changed section 215 of the law in several ways. The first was that it removed control over this power from the FBI and placed it in the sole hands of upper level Justice Department officials. It also provided for judicial oversight of the process by requiring a judge to find a showing of facts that provide reasonable grounds to believe that tangible items which are sought are relevant to an authorized investigation. The order must also adhere to the particularity requirement of the Fourth Amendment and explain exactly what tangible things the government seeks. Those who are served such orders now have the ability to challenge the order and may inform their attorneys of the order so that they can gain legal advice.

Under Section 505 of the USA Patriot Act the government can get many of the same types of records that it can access through Section 215, without having to use the FISA Court. This section allows the government to issue "national security letters" to gain access to business records and documents. The records that can be gained through a national security letter include telephone, financial, consumer, and transactional records. National security letters can be issued by FBI field supervisors who need not get approval from prosecutors, judges, or grand juries. There is no requirement that the FBI have specific or articulable reasons supporting the issuing of a letter. The FBI only has to certify that the information sought "is relevant to an authorized investigation to protect against international terrorism or clandestine intelligence activities."[17] A person who is served a national security letter is barred from informing anyone but their attorney about the letter. The information collected by the government is subjected to data mining in order to try to isolate patterns of behavior which may be indicative of terrorist activity. The Reauthorization Act of 2005 provided better oversight of Section 505. It allows a person who is served a national security letter to challenge both the letter and the nondisclosure order in a U.S. district court. It also clarified that libraries were not to be subject to such letters when performing their traditional functions.

Section 216 of the USA Patriot Act allows the government to automatically get judicial orders, without a showing of probable cause, to set up pen registers and trap and trace devices anywhere in the country whenever the information would be relevant to an ongoing criminal investigation. Pen registers give the government access to all the phone numbers and thus the identity of individuals called by suspects. Trap and trace devices give the government the same information about a person's internet and e-mail activities. The law does forbid using pen registers and trap devices to gain information about the content of conversations or communications.

Beyond the changes in the government's power to engage in search and seizures, the USA Patriot Act also broadly defined domestic terrorism. According

to Section 802 of the USA Patriot Act, domestic terrorism is defined to include
activities that:
  (A) Involve acts dangerous to human life that are a violation of the criminal
      laws of the United States or any state;
  (B) appear to be intended-
      (i) to intimidate or coerce a civilian population;
      (ii) to influence the policy of a government by intimidation or coercion; or
      (iii) to affect the conduct of a government by mass destruction, assassina-
      tion, or kidnapping; and
  (C) occur primarily within the territorial jurisdiction of the United States.

The New Surveillance Tools

New threats to the liberty and privacy of citizens will not just come from
changes in the law. They will also come from a variety of new technologies and
surveillance methods, some of which are still being developed, which present
issues which are currently unsettled by the Fourth Amendment. There are two
sides to the emerging forms of surveillance, data collection and data collation.
Both harbor their own dangers and may invoke Fourth Amendment scrutiny.
Data collection refers to how the government gets information. As technology
advances new forms of gaining information about citizens become available
with every passing year. Many of these methods could not have been imagined
by the Congress which proposed the Fourth Amendment. Data collation refers to
what the government does once it has the information or how it uses the information. David Lyon has explained the importance of collation of information
stating, "Today, the most important means of surveillance reside in computer
power, which allows collected data to be stored, matched, retrieved, processed,
marketed, and circulated."[18] The hope with many of the technologies being developed is that it will result in data which can be collated to detect crimes and
identify suspects. Some day it is hoped this information may also allow the government to develop profiles in order to predict and stop future criminal behavior.
     The technology already exists in a number of areas for the government to
enlarge its surveillance of the activities of American citizens. One of the technologies is biometrics. Biometrics is a method of identifying people based on
physical features. Biometric identification consists of two parts. The first is a
device which is capable of using algorithms to measure some physical feature of
the human body and reducing that measurement to a series of numbers to give it
an identity. The second is placing that identity measurement into a data base
which can be sorted and retrieved at a later time. Fingerprints are a form of biometric identification. While fingerprints have long been used in criminal investigations it was only recently that a system was developed that made their use
easy. The Automated Fingerprint Identification System created in the 1980s
created an efficient system of using computer scanning of fingerprints and mea-

suring them with special purpose algorithms to give each set its own identity. The system then collates the data to look for matches. Due to the difficulty of scanning, some biometric measures will only be helpful at identifying people at close range. Uses of such measures may include deciding who should have access to a building or identifying a suspect after arrest. These biometric measures include retina prints, iris prints, palm prints, and voice recognition. One example of this type of biometric measure being used may be found in the Cook County Jail in Illinois. The system requires inmates going from the jail to court to submit to a retinal scan on their way out and back to the jail.

Other biometric identifiers may be more helpful to law enforcement in identifying individuals from a distance. They also have an advantage for law enforcement in that they can be used without a person's knowledge. These measures include facial recognition, silhouette, and gait prints. An example of their use is the 2001 Super Bowl where unbeknownst to everyone who walked through the ticket turnstiles each person was subjected to a biometric face scan by law enforcement and then compared to faces on a watch list. The faceFinder equipment used at the Super Bowl is also used by numerous state governments for the purpose of comparing license photos against known photos of people wanted for crimes.

Another form of biometric identification is DNA. DNA measures pattern of deoxyribonucleic acid that exists in every cell of the human body. Due to the time it takes to get the results of a DNA tests, this is not a quick form of identification. When human biological samples are left at a crime scene, DNA has proven its effectiveness at identifying to whom it belongs. Currently, a number of states and the federal government collect DNA from all felons, while other states collect DNA samples from all people accused of crimes.[19] The FBI collects the samples taken and places it into its Combined DNA System (CODIS) which can be searched by law enforcement agencies throughout the country. Civil libertarians worry about the use of DNA because the information contained in a DNA sample carries much more than just a person's identity. Because DNA also carries a great deal of medical information some organizations question whether the government should be able to collect DNA unless there are tighter restrictions on its use.[20]

One method of surveillance which has been gaining in popularity is closed circuit television (CCTV) and video recorders. The private sector has long relied on CCTV as a method of providing security for buildings and businesses. Some governments have decided that CCTV is also a good method of providing security for society in general. The cameras are getting less expensive and can be as small as a box of matches. The most common law enforcement use of CCTV in America has probably been to catch individuals who run stop lights. The cameras are set to take a picture of the vehicle and license plate when such an event occurs thus providing the evidence to convict the person of the traffic offense.

Placement of cameras in high crime areas for general surveillance purposes has increased in America, but is far behind Great Britain which has over 300,000 CCTV installed for this purpose. The widespread use of CCTV together with a biometric program based on facial recognition which would inform police when a known criminal or suspect was identified could be of great assistance to law enforcement.

Closely related to CCTV is acoustical surveillance. Acoustical surveillance requires more technology than CCTV. It is a wide scale monitoring system that uses telecommunications and data processing to allow the operator to triangulate, categorize, and permanently record any sounds that they desire. Redwood City, California bought an acoustical surveillance system known as ShotSpotter to detect gunshots after testing it in 1995. The system uses eight microphones to monitor a one mile area that was known for firearms use. When a gun is fired the system can determine within 15 yards from where the shot came. Police are then notified. The system is accurate enough to distinguish gunshots from other sounds like car doors, hammering, trains, etc. If there is a series of gunshots, the system can determine if they were all fired in the same place or from a moving vehicle. It can also inform the police which direction the vehicle was moving.

Cell phones allow another method to determine the location of a person. When a cell phone is in use or set to receive calls it must communicate the user's location to a base station. The better the cell phone, the more precisely a person's location is revealed. The Federal Communications Commission (FCC) requires that cell phones be accurate to within 400 feet. The FCC also requires companies which provide cell phone service to provide to law enforcement agencies which have wiretap warrants the location of a person at the beginning and end of a cell phone call. Cell phones can also provide a history of the movements of a person who carries a cell phone. This is easy to do when the cell phone location is archived and saved.

Another method which can be used to identify and keep tabs on the movement of people and goods is through the use of Radio Frequency Identification Devices (RFID). A common use of RFID has been in Automatic Vehicle Identification (AVI). AVI is a system used on toll roads by individuals who elect to use E-Z Pass. As with other RFID, the system relies on a tiny transponder which has the capacity to send a unique signal with a built in serial number to an instrument which is capable of reading the signal. In the case of E-Z Pass the transponder is built into the pass a person puts on their car. The transponder relies on a lithium battery with a ten year lifespan and sends out a signal that identifies the serial number assigned to the owner of the vehicle. As the vehicle goes past toll booths the transponder informs the central computer what tolls are due. AVI also has the capacity to keep track of miles covered per hour between toll booths and could easily be set to send out tickets to any driver who goes over the speed limit. AVI could also tell law enforcement if a particular vehicle was on a stretch of road between two toll booths, as well as provide a history of their past movements on toll roads. Other RFID systems use a small silicon chip which requires no batteries so they have an indefinite life span and are stimulated by low level radio signals. RFID tags can be made as small as a grain of rice and can be placed on labels and pets. One nightclub in Barcelona, Spain has even implanted RFID chips under the skin of its patrons' arms so they can be identified when they come to the club and be admitted.[21]

Today almost any personal transaction involving money will probably be traceable unless cash is always used. Even if a person elected to use only cash, they might not be able to do so without attracting the attention of the government. For the purpose of stopping money laundering the law requires banks to report large deposits, withdrawls, and transfers. Normally, the amount required to trigger such a report is $10,000, but in neighborhoods which are considered to be high drug zones, the amount can be as low as $750.[22] Not only may the government trace financial transactions, the technology to monitor every type of electronic communication including phone, e-mail, internet activity and fax, also exists. The United States and its allies have developed a worldwide spying system capable of capturing all forms of electronic communications known as "Echelon." The system has the capacity to intercept and collate all forms of electronics communication. Once a communication is intercepted Echelon has the capacity to run a voiceprint recognition program to determine if the voice is on a watch list and if so it informs governmental agencies of the call for purposes of closer monitoring. Communications that use the printed word and e-mail can be run through a dictionary program that can recognize interesting words and phrases and flag them for further inspection

While it remains illegal for the United States government to use Echelon to examine the content of domestic communications without a warrant, there has been pressure to change the status quo during the era of terrorism. One example is by the National Security Agency's (NSA) domestic spying measure which was originally approved by President George Walker Bush through a secret order in 2002 and approved by Congress in July of 2008. The program has allowed the government to monitor the electronic communications between foreign nationals and U.S. citizens without first seeking a warrant. The government has emphasized the need to be able to move with speed in these situations and argued that the FISA court was too slow in approving warrants to allow the interception of the communications. The program also allowed the NSA to contact private communication providers in order to get records of calls made from phone numbers found in laptops and cell phones that had been discovered in al Qaeda hideouts. These new numbers then led to the collection of other phone numbers which were sometimes two or three calls removed from the original number. According to *USA Today* by May of 2006 the NSA had collected billions of phone records on Americans with the goal "to create a database of every call ever made" for the purpose of entering them into a data mining program which looks for suspicious call patterns that might be linked to terrorist behavior.[23]

The future of the Fourth Amendment will also be challenged by some investigative technologies which the Supreme Court has not yet ruled on. One high tech tool that is being developed to help law enforcement is the concealed weapon detector. The technology has been compared to giving police Superman's "x-ray vision."[24] Concealed weapon detectors using a technology known as passive millimeter wave imaging rely on natural emissions of radiation from the body and cause no harm to the individual. Because all objects have different temperatures they emit a different spectrum of electromagnetic radiation. These emissions can then be read on a screen to allow officers to see the shape of objects which are scanned. In a scan the body outline appears in a light gray color while the shapes of objects are shown in a darker shade. The technology has the capacity to show the form of any object which is liquid, powder, metal, plastic, or ceramic. These devices have the capacity to reveal objects through a variety of things such as clothing, wood, plaster, and other common building materials. Devices are small enough to be mounted in a police car or even held in a person's hand. For the officer on the street it has the advantage of scanning suspicious persons for weapons before they are stopped. It could also be used to scan the interior of a building for the same purpose.

Government use of gas chromatography and mass spectrometry may also provide helpful evidence of criminal activity. The government currently uses a device known as the "Sentor" to analyze dust particles taken from the bodies of people who are suspected of drug smuggling.[25] The device which easily fits into a person's hand is pointed at a suspect and then turned on causing it to vacuum the dust off the suspect. The dust sample is then placed in a gas chromatography machine that heats it a high speed to determine its chemical compounds and indicate whether there are any drug traces on the person. If a person tests positive for drugs, they are then normally subjected to a more thorough search.

Global positioning system technology (GPS) gives law enforcement the technology to follow the movement of individuals of interest who have been tagged with transmitters. GPS uses a group of 24 satellites to calculate position by comparing time signals in between a minimum of four satellites which can receive a signal from any place on earth.[26] It allows for real time tracking of anything with a GPS transmitter. Consumer applications include General Motors' OnStar system and the Garmin Nuvi mapping system. A law enforcement application is to plant transmitters on items to be tracked. Another use would be to require individuals under court supervision to either wear a tracking bracelet or even imbed a transmitter under their skin so that their movements could be tracked. In the future, by adding a device which causes pain if the subject goes too close to an area which is supposed to be off limits to the individual, such as a school in the case of a pedophile, the system could deliver the ability to both track and control an individual.

One area of concern for the Fourth Amendment that comes from new and old technological sources is what will be done with all the information gained. How the information is collated and used may also challenge our understanding of the Fourth Amendment. After the attacks of September 11, 2001, the government has shown a great deal of interest in preventing terrorism before it happens. This has caused increased activity in statistical analysis and modeling to try to uncover hidden patterns of behavior that may be indicative of terrorist activities. Manipulation of raw data in this way has been referred to as data mining, knowledge discovery, pattern-matching, and dataveillance.[27] Profiling individuals for special treatment based on predictive models presents several concerns. One is that investigations will be started based solely on individuals matching the model rather than any overt behavior on their part which would link them to criminal or terrorist actions. Another problem will be false positives when the data indicates that a person is dangerous and warrants investigation but either the data or model is wrong. An example can be found in the Transportation Security Administration's (TSA) no-fly list. The no-fly list in use collects personal information on an individual such as their name, address, birth date, and credit card number. It then compares this information with data from other government and commercial data bases. All of the information is then subjected to data mining to search for patterns in the person's behavior that may indicate a propensity for terrorist activities. The system then informs the TSA what level of security should be given to the person ranging from not allowing them to fly to no extra security measures. The system has in the past inaccurately indicated people as untrustworthy to fly. For example, Senator Ted Kennedy has been stopped and questioned because a terrorist suspect had used his name as an alias.[28]

All of these new forms of surveillance and technologies that allow the government to learn details about a person may play a large role in providing security against crimes and terrorism. The problem as Steven Hatfill, the doctor named as a person of interest in the Anthrax killings, found out is that the government can also use its power to destroy a person's life. For this reason the Supreme Court needs to give careful consideration to new challenges to the Fourth Amendment. It is always difficult predicting how the Supreme Court will interpret the Fourth Amendment based upon past behavior. In 1961 when *Mapp v. Ohio*[29] was decided by the Warren Court few observers probably believed that it would create an environment that would cause a weakening of the protections of the Fourth Amendment in the years following the decision. The same can easily be said of *Katz v. United States* (1967).[30] Despite the difficulty of predicting how the Court will act in the future based on its past behavior, a review of how the Court has interpreted the Fourth Amendment since *Mapp* can provide insights into how the Court will probably deal with new governmental methods of investigation and surveillance.

Based on how the Supreme Court has been interpreting the Fourth Amendment there are two related questions as to whether these new surveillance methods and technologies will violate the Constitution. The first is whether they even trigger the protections of the Fourth Amendment. Due to the Court's limiting of the coverage of the Fourth Amendment since *Katz* was decided, some of

the new surveillance methods should present little problem for the courts to rule
that they do not trigger the protections found in the Fourth Amendment. Surveillance methods that fit this category should include closed circuit television, even
when it is combined with facial biometrics, radio frequency identification devices and acoustical surveillance. There are multiple reasons why these surveillance
methods probably will not qualify for Fourth Amendment protection. The first
is, unlike the use of thermal imaging that the Court found unconstitutional in
Kyllo v. United States (2001),[31] the technology used to gather information by
these methods is not sense enhancing. The technologies simply allow the government to better capture those things which it can already see and hear. Furthermore, the technologies are, for the most part, readily available to the public
and in widespread public use. As in the case of *United States v. Knotts*,[32] when
the Court allowed use of an electronic beeper for tracking purposes, the technology leads to no information that would not be available to police if they conducted surveillance of the entire community themselves. The fact that the behavior caught by these forms of surveillance is public behavior also limits its
ability to trigger Fourth Amendment protections. The Court has made it clear
since *California v. Ciraolo* (1986),[33] when it allowed aerial surveillance, that if
the government has a right to be somewhere and can observe illegal conduct
there is no Fourth Amendment violation. For all these reasons the courts will
likely find that society would not find as reasonable any expectation of privacy
against the use of the mentioned technologies.

Several of the surveillance methods are also likely to be found to not trigger
the protections of the Fourth Amendment, but more analysis is needed. These
are methods involving technologies that allow law enforcement to learn about
the location of a person. They include the tracking of cell phones and use of
global positioning systems. The reason that these two technologies present a
more difficult answer as to whether use of them will be regulated by the Fourth
Amendment is that they can be used to track people out of public places and into
their homes. Thus, rather than being analogous to *Knotts* they may be closer in
their use to *United States v. Karo* (1984)[34] and *Kyllo*. In both cases the Court
ruled that use of technology was a violation of the Fourth Amendment if it provided information about the interior of a home that would not otherwise be
available to the government. Tracking the location of a person through either
their cell phone or a GPS transmitter hidden on them or their property certainly
has the potential of providing law enforcement agents with the location of a person while in their home. For that reason, we must examine a different category
of cases to determine if police may use such technologies without triggering the
amendment. One answer may be provided by examining cases which have involved technologies when a person has assumed some risk that a third party will
divulge private information such as *United States v. Miller* (1976)[35] and *Smith v.
Maryland* (1979).[36] In both cases the Court refused to give Fourth Amendment
protection to activities if an individual had either directly or indirectly given
information to another person because the individual had assumed the risk that
the other person would share the information. In the case of cell phones, the

Court could easily rule that a person gives up any expectation of privacy in their location through phone use because that information has to be shared with the phone service carrier so there are no protections granted by the Fourth Amendment. The same result could be reached in cases involving GPS if a person relies on a third party to provide service such as with OnStar. If the government plants a GPS transmitter on a person or their property and traces it to their home, the case should be fully analogous to *Karo* and should invoke the protections of the Fourth Amendment.

The interception of electronic communications through phones and the internet remains regulated by law, but what if it wasn't? The fact is that individuals must assume some risk when they work with phone companies and internet providers. Counter balancing this reason not to place interception of electronic communications and financial records under the control of the amendment are a number of other considerations. Interception of communications definitely gives the government access to private information which is not available to the general public and would not otherwise be available to it. The government has recognized the sensitive nature of this information and sought by law to insure that the information is not available to the general public. This information is of a communicative nature which was also true of the discussion overheard in the case of *Katz v. United States* which the Court ruled required a warrant to seize due to the protections of the Fourth Amendment. The communication often travels from one person's home to another. It also cannot be discovered through traditional methods of surveillance. For all of these reasons, one would think that government interception of such communications and records will continue to invoke the protections of the Fourth Amendment.

The question as to whether use of gas chromatography and mass spectrometry will meet the threshold for triggering the Fourth Amendment is complicated. The processes are sense enhancing technologies that are capable of gaining private information that the government would not otherwise be able to acquire. The technology is not readily available at this time and is not in general public use. In that way the processes are very similar to the use of thermal imagers which the Supreme Court said did trigger the protections of the Fourth Amendment in *Kyllo*. The analogy is not complete for two reasons. Although these devices may be used in a home they are primarily used by border agents to determine if persons crossing borders are involved in drug smuggling. Due to decisions such as *United States v. Flores-Montano* (2004)[37] borders do not carry the same level of protection from the Fourth Amendment as homes. Furthermore, the Court has ruled in *United States v. Place* (1983)[38] and *United States v. Jacobsen* (1984)[39] that individuals do not have a legitimate expectation of privacy in the drugs which these devices are meant to detect. Further complicating whether use of the device should trigger the Fourth Amendment is that they can also indicate a person has been in contact with drugs they are authorized to use thus providing the government with information about a medical condition a person might not want to reveal to the government. Millimeter technology presents similar problems. The use of the technology is not generally available but provides law enforcement with a fantastic tool, the ability to know if a person is armed. However, it also gives them more private information about what a person may have concealed on their body or in their home. Another problem with using these devices to secretly conduct a search for weapons is that not all weapons are a criminal violation. The answer as to whether use of these devices will be regulated may depend on where they are used and how much significance courts give to the fact that they can expose private information which is not related to possession of contraband items to which nobody has a legitimate expectation of privacy. The court may, therefore, decide cases involving these technologies on a case-by-case basis.

DNA collection from persons accused of crimes will probably raise no Fourth Amendment issues when used for purposes of identification of a person or investigation of unsolved crimes. Fingerprints have been used for these dual purposes for years and have never been successfully challenged as a violation of the Fourth Amendment. Questions about using DNA for purposes not associated with identification or investigation may raise Fourth Amendment concerns due to the great variety of private information it conveys which would not be available to the government by other means. As with the case of other information it may not be the gathering of DNA that violates the Constitution, it may be how it is used.

Data mining for the purposes of creating criminal and terrorist profiles has been on the increase. The USA Patriot Act gives the government new methods of gathering and sharing information among different law enforcement agencies. This information is being analyzed more than ever before in hopes of finding patterns which will be able to predict criminal behavior. The Supreme Court has not yet taken a definitive position as to whether stops based on matching such profiles violate the Fourth Amendment. In *United States v. Sokolow* (1989)[40] the Court reviewed a stop based on the suspect matching six characteristics of a drug courier profile. It ruled that in such situations the legality of the stop will be determined by the totality of the circumstances and found that the particular stop in that case was indeed reasonable based on the officer's suspicions. It would seem then that future profiles may be acceptable as long as enough behavior is exhibited to lead law enforcement to have reasonable suspicions of criminal activity. Of course, ideas concerning what is reasonable can be highly dependent on who is hearing the case.

The Roberts Court and the Future of the Fourth Amendment

The Supreme Court in the last twenty-five years has shown a great willingness to apply the reasonableness approach in interpreting the Fourth Amendment.

Under this standard the Fourth Amendment only forbids unreasonable searches and seizures, but all reasonable searches and seizures are allowed. This approach balances the intrusion that government actions have on the privacy expectation of an individual against the goals that the government is trying to accomplish. The decisions are often driven by two factors, the facts of the case and the justices who hear it. With increasing fears of crime and terrorism the Court may in the post-9/11 world be willing to draw a different balance in Fourth Amendment cases than in earlier times.

The Court under the leadership of Chief Justice John Roberts, who was appointed by President George Walker Bush in 2005, is inheriting a Fourth Amendment that looks very different than the one that existed at the end of the Warren Court. The Burger and Rehnquist Courts' interpretation of the Fourth Amendment allowed the government to engage in a broader array of searches and seizures than had the Warren Court. This demonstrates that the meaning of the Fourth Amendment can change depending on who is on the Court. The Roberts Court will have added pressure placed on it to broaden the government's power to search and seize because it will be interpreting the Fourth Amendment in an era in which the deadly reality of terrorism is well understood. In its first three terms the Roberts Court ruled on ten cases involving the Fourth Amendment. An analysis of these cases may provide some insight into the future direction of the Fourth Amendment.

One case resolved by the Roberts Court settles an interesting legal issue, but probably isn't too helpful in trying to discover possible future trends. That case is *United States v. Grubbs* (2006).[41] The issue involved whether anticipatory search warrants violate the Fourth Amendment. Anticipatory search warrants may be issued but cannot be served until an event named in the warrant takes place. The event must be something other than the mere passage of time. In *Grubbs* the triggering event was the controlled delivery of some child pornography that Grubbs had ordered. When the warrant was executed, it lacked the affidavit that explained the triggering event so Grubbs challenged the warrant. On *certiorari*, a unanimous Court in an opinion by Justice Antonin Scalia ruled that anticipatory warrants did not violate the Fourth Amendment. This was because they met the Fourth Amendment requirement of being based on probable cause that evidence would be found at the time that the warrant was executed. The majority also believed that even though the affidavit which explained the triggering event was missing the warrant did not violate the particularity clause of the Fourth Amendment. This was because the words of the amendment do not require describing in a particular way the conditions required to execute the warrant.

The rest of the Fourth Amendment cases settled by the Roberts Court do demonstrate what seems to be a couple of themes in its approach to the Fourth Amendment. These are the use of the reasonableness approach to interpret the amendment and victories for the government's position. Regardless of whether it ruled in favor of or against the government's position, the Roberts Court has used the reasonableness approach in all of its cases that have dealt specifically with the Fourth Amendment, except *Grubbs*, which involved a search warrant. In the vast majority of cases the Roberts Court has ruled in favor of the government position. We turn our attention to these cases first. These cases include: *Scott v. Harris* (2007);[42] *Brigham City, Utah v. Stuart* (2006);[43] *County of Los Angeles v. Rettele* (2007);[44] and *Virginia v. Moore* (2008).[45] In all these cases the Court has framed the legal issue as one involving whether the police had acted reasonably given the circumstances in which they found themselves

In *Scott v. Harris*, the Court settled a Title 42 U.S.C., section 1983 claim brought by Victor Harris against Timothy Scott. Harris had fled officers in his vehicle and led them on a high speed chase. Scott, a deputy, ended the chase by using the front bumper of his vehicle to push Harris' vehicle off the road. When that happened it caused Harris' vehicle to crash and he was injured leaving him a quadriplegic. Harris then brought suit against Scott claiming that Scott had used excessive force against him resulting in an unreasonable seizure. The lower courts denied Scott a summary judgment based on his claim of qualified immunity. The case then came to the Supreme Court on *certiorari*. The Court in an 8-0 vote overturned the lower court. The opinion by Justice Scalia explained that in cases of qualified immunity the threshold question that a court must answer is whether in the light most favorable to the party bringing the case do the facts demonstrate that the officer clearly violated a constitutional right. In answering this question the Court believed that the sequence of events captured on videotape of the chase was dispositive. The video clearly showed that Harris was the person who started the car chase and that it threatened injury to others who were on the roads. To determine whether Deputy Scott used excessive force to bring an end to the chase, the Court believed it was necessary to examine the reasonableness of his actions. This involved reaching a balance between the nature of the intrusion on a person's Fourth Amendment interests weighed against the governmental interest. In this case the governmental interests were substantial due to the danger that Harris' action presented to others. Furthermore, Harris had intentionally placed himself in the situation where Deputy Scott believed it was necessary to cause the accident. Therefore, the Court ruled that Scott's actions were reasonable, even though it placed Harris at risk of injury, given the need for Scott to bring an end to the chase.

In *Brigham City, Utah v. Stuart* the Court had to determine if police officers had acted reasonably under the Fourth Amendment when they entered a home without a warrant. Police were called to a residence because there was a loud party going on at 3 a.m. When police arrived at the residence they say two juveniles drinking in the backyard. They also heard people shouting in the home. Through windows and a screen door they saw four adults and a juvenile arguing in the house. The juvenile then hit one of the adults in the face causing him to have to spit blood into the sink. The police then opened the door and announced their presence, but no one noticed due to the distractions of the argument. The officers then entered the kitchen where the people were and again announced their presence. When the inhabitants finally realized the police were there the argument ceased. Three of the adults were arrested on charges of delinquency of a minor, disorderly conduct, and intoxication. At trial the defendants sought to have the evidence suppressed claiming that it violated the Fourth Amendment for the officers to enter the home without a warrant. The lower courts all agreed that there had been a Fourth Amendment violation. The Supreme Court then granted *certiorari*.

In a unanimous decision the Court decided that there was no constitutional violation in *Brigham City, Utah*. Chief Justice Roberts wrote for the Court. He started by reciting the warrant rule as it applies to homes stating "It is a 'basic principle of Fourth Amendment law that searches and seizures inside a home without a warrant are presumptively unreasonable.'"[46] Chief Justice Roberts continued and stated, "Nevertheless, because the ultimate touchstone of the Fourth Amendment is 'reasonableness,' the warrant requirement is subject to certain exceptions."[47] Chief Justice Roberts pointed out that one of the exceptions which had been clearly established was that of exigency when a person was in need of emergency aid, they were either seriously injured, or threatened with such an injury. The original entry into the house was reasonable given that, due to the argument, no one in the house would have heard them knock. The officers did not simply barge into the house, they first announced their entry. The entry was made all the more reasonable due to the altercation which had taken place causing the possibility that someone needed assistance and there was a need to stop the violence. Based on all this, there was no constitutional violation. Furthermore, because the Court had rejected the need to examine the motivations of officers under such circumstances it did not matter if the officers entered the home for the purpose of making arrests, gathering evidence, assisting the injured, or preventing further violence. An examination of the facts of this case demonstrated that everything the officers did was reasonable.

The case of *County of Los Angeles v. Rettele* gave the Court another chance to examine the reasonableness of police behavior. In *Rettele*, which is the illustrative case in Chapter 5, the Court had to determine if officers had violated the Fourth Amendment when they served a warrant on a home which they believed belonged to suspects in an investigation, but in reality had been sold three months prior to the search. The officers who executed the warrant knew that all the suspects were African-Americans and were surprised that none of the residents of the home were. Despite this, the officers would not let two individuals in the home put clothes on before they were allowed to get out of bed. Humiliated by being forced to stand naked before the officers for a warrant that they believed should have never been issued, the residents sued the officers under Title 42 U.S.C., section 1983. The district court granted summary judgment to the defendants, but the Court of Appeals for the Ninth Circuit overruled finding that reasonable officers would have stopped the search upon finding that the residents were not African-American and would not have required them to stand naked before them. The Supreme Court then granted *certiorari*.

In a unanimous *per curiam* decision the Court ruled that the officers should have been granted summary judgment because there was no Fourth Amendment violation. The Court reasoned that the warrant was valid. The Court made it clear that, "In executing a search warrant officers may take reasonable action to secure the premises and to ensure their own safety and the efficacy of the search."[48] The test of reasonableness was, according to the Court, an objective one. Under this test, officers would have acted in an unreasonable manner if they used excessive force, caused unnecessary pain, or restricted a person's freedom longer than necessary. In this case, however, the officers acted reasonably in securing the house and making sure that no one in the house was armed and dangerous. The fact that residents were not the same race as the suspects did not matter because in our society it is not uncommon for people of different races to share a residency. Once the officer had secured the house, they did allow the residents to put their clothes on in a reasonable time. The Court found it unfortunate that innocent people did at times have to bear the costs in situations like this, but when there is a valid warrant officers must be able to act in a reasonable manner.

The final case in which the Roberts Court had to determine if an officer acted reasonably under the Fourth Amendment and it ruled in favor of the government position is *Virginia v. Moore*. In this case David Moore was stopped for driving on a suspended license which was a misdemeanor under Virginia law. Despite the fact that Virginia law only allowed the officer to issue a summons for the offence, Moore was arrested. He was then searched incident to that arrest and the officer found crack cocaine on him. Moore unsuccessfully moved to suppress the drugs arguing that the arrest and subsequent seizure violated the Fourth Amendment since Virginia law only allowed a summons to be issued. He was convicted. On appeal the Virginia Supreme Court reversed finding that because Virginia law did not allow an arrest in these circumstances, a search should never have been done because the Fourth Amendment does not allow searches incident to a citation.

On *certiorari* the Supreme Court in a unanimous decision overruled the Virginia Supreme Court. Justice Scalia wrote the majority opinion. After examining the statutes and common law that were in practice during the founding era, the Court found that there was no clear evidence that the Fourth Amendment was meant to incorporate the existing state laws. Since history provided no clear guidance on the issue, Justice Scalia stated, "That suggests, if anything, that founding-era citizens were skeptical of using the rules for search and seizure set by government actors as the index of reasonableness."[49] The opinion explained that when history does not provide conclusive guidance as to what are the requirements of the Fourth Amendment the Court uses the reasonableness standard. Justice Scalia then added, "In a long line of cases, we have said that when an officer has probable cause to believe a person committed even a minor crime in his presence, the balancing of private and public interests is not in doubt. The arrest is constitutionally reasonable."[50] This is because allowing an arrest based upon probable cause serves the interest that justifies seizing the person. These interests include making sure that the person appears to answer the charges, stopping them from continuing to violate the law, securing evidence, and allowing officers to complete an in-custody investigation. The mere fact that Virginia sought to impose a more restrictive seizure standard did not negate the standards set by the Fourth Amendment. The Court also believed that incorporating state standards for arrest into the Fourth Amendment would make the amendment too complex and result in the Constitution meaning different things in different jurisdictions. Since the arrest of Moore was based on probable cause that a crime was committed and did not violate the Fourth Amendment the subsequent search incident to that arrest was also acceptable under the amendment.

The Roberts Court also used the reasonableness approach to justify a blanket exception to the warrant rule in the case of *Samson v. California* (2006).[51] This case came about because the State of California made release of a person on parole contingent upon the person signing a form giving consent for searches and seizures by both parole and law enforcement officers with or without a warrant or probable cause. Donald Samson was on parole when a police officer saw him walking down the street. The officer thought that there was an outstanding warrant out on Samson so he was stopped. The officer learned that there was no warrant on Samson. Knowing that Samson was a parolee the officer decided to search him, discovering methamphetamine. The trial court refused to suppress the drugs and Samson was convicted. The decision was upheld on appeal so Samson sought and was granted *certiorari*.

In a 6-3 decision, with the majority opinion written by Justice Clarence Thomas, the Court upheld the decision of the California court. Justice Thomas explained that the legality of such a search under the Fourth Amendment was dependent on its reasonableness. Reasonableness was to be determined based on the totality of the circumstances. For Justice Thomas "Whether a search is reasonable is determined by assessing, on the one hand, the degree to which it intrudes upon an individual's privacy and, on the other hand, the degree to which it is needed for the promotion of legitimate governmental interests."[52] Rather than finding that this particular form of search fit into the "special needs" cases the Court had developed, Justice Thomas found that under the circumstances which Samson found himself this search was reasonable.[53] That was because he was a parolee and that status brought with it a lesser expectation of privacy than others in society would have. This was because parolees understand the conditions placed on them for the continuance of their freedom. To gain his freedom Samson signed a form recognizing these lesser expectations. Justice Thomas concluded that for parolees, due to the conditions of their release, there was no legitimate expectation of privacy. The reality of the situation is that parolees are still under the legal custody of the state which can set terms and conditions which the parolee must obey. On top of this, the regulations of the state serves important goals such as stopping recidivism, integrating felons back into the community, and protecting the community from future crimes. The achievement of these goals would only be frustrated by imposing a more stringent standard to initiate a search against a parolee. Therefore, due to the important government interests and the lack of legitimate privacy expectations of parolees, it was reasonable to have an exception to the warrant requirement of the Fourth Amendment in these circumstances and allow suspicionless searches of parolees.

The Roberts Court has also used the reasonableness approach to decide two cases in favor of individuals who thought their Fourth Amendment rights had been violated. The first was *Georgia v. Randolph* (2006).[54] *Randolph* began when police responded to a domestic dispute between a man and his wife at the Randolph house. While police were talking to the wife, Janet Randolph, she informed the police that many of their problems were due to her husband's cocaine problem. The police then sought and gained permission from Janet to search the residence. The husband, Scott Randolph, who was present, objected to the search and steadfastly refused to grant consent for the search. Despite this, the police entered the home and upon finding evidence of drug usage got a warrant which when served resulted in more drugs being found in the house. When Scott Randolph went to trial he objected to the use of the drugs found in both searches arguing that all of the evidence was found in violation of the Fourth Amendment. The trial court ruled that Mrs. Randolph had authority to give consent for the search and allowed the evidence resulting in the conviction of Scott Randolph. On appeal the Georgia Court of Appeals and Georgia Supreme Court ruled that the wife's consent to search was not valid in the face of Scott Randolph being present and denying officers permission to conduct a search. The Supreme Court granted *certiorari*.

The Court split 5-3 in its decision in *Randolph*. Justice David Souter wrote for the majority. Justice Souter noted that based on precedent the Fourth Amendment does allow for consent searches when police reasonably believe that all the persons who have common authority over a property are present and do not object to the search. In other circumstances, however, the reasonableness of a search depends on widely shared social expectations which are influenced by the law of property. Justice Souter then argued that just as no sensible person would enter the home of two individuals who shared possession of a property when one of the people objected, a reasonable police officer would also have to respect the right of one of the parties to deny permission to enter. This was especially true in light of the Fourth Amendment's special protection given to the home. The opinion then asserted that the Court's decision should not be taken to upset earlier precedents which allow police to enter such a residency when all those who have common authority over the property and are present have consented. These decisions were still good law even when there may be others who share that authority which are not present at the time of the request to search. Justice Souter also explained that as long as there was no evidence that the police did not purposely remove a person from a home who they believed would object to a consent search, searches could be completed based on the permission of those residents actually present. In this case it was clear, however, that Scott Randolph never gave consent for police to enter and search the premises and since there were no exigent circumstances that could justify a warrantless search the police had violated the Fourth Amendment.

Chief Justice Roberts wrote a dissenting opinion, joined by Justice Scalia, which promoted a much narrower view of the protections of the Fourth Amendment. Chief Justice Roberts argued that the Constitution protected privacy, not societal expectations, and that constitutional foundations should not be subject to shifting social expectations. He argued that if anyone who had common authority over a property gave consent for a search, any subsequent search was reasonable under the Fourth Amendment. That was because when a person lived with others they took on an assumption of risk that their co-tenants might give consent under such circumstances. Chief Justice Roberts thought the Court's rule would cause great hardship in domestic dispute cases when police would not be allowed to enter a home when an abusive husband denied police consent to enter. In another criticism of the Court's decision he complained that it didn't really protect a person's privacy interests unless they were present when the police requested consent to search. This complaint, of course, seems hollow because Chief Justice Roberts was granting no protection for co-tenants whether they were at home or not. Justice Scalia added a separate dissent which said that a review of the history of property law that the Court referred to in the majority opinion showed any person with co-authority over a property could have granted consent for a search. Justice Thomas also gave a dissent in which he argued that based on the Court's decision in *Coolidge v. New Hampshire* (1971)[55] there was no violation of the Fourth Amendment when a wife voluntarily turned in evidence against her husband.

A final case in which the Roberts Court used the reasonableness approach to the Fourth Amendment and ruled against the government's position was *Brendlin v. California* (2007).[56] Bruce Brendlin was a passenger in a car which was stopped for the sole purpose of a registration check. The officer who made the stop had no reason to believe that the vehicle had violated any law. During the stop an officer recognized Bruce Brendlin as a parole violator and after verifying the information arrested him and subjected him, the car, and the driver to a search finding paraphernalia related to the manufacture of methamphetamine. Brendlin unsuccessfully moved to suppress the evidence at trial and was then convicted. On appeal the California Court of Appeals ruled that there was a Fourth Amendment violation, but the California Supreme Court overturned its decision. Brendlin then sought and received *certiorari*.

In a unanimous decision written by Justice Souter the Court overturned Brendlin's conviction and held that when a person is a passenger in a vehicle which is stopped by law enforcement officers, the person is seized for Fourth Amendment purposes and thus has standing to challenge the basis of the stop.

The Court explained that to determine whether a person is seized under the Fourth Amendment it was necessary to examine whether a reasonable person would believe themselves to be seized. One way of determining this was to ask whether a person would feel free to terminate the encounter. In a very practical decision which was reflective of the reality on the streets the Court concluded that when a vehicle is pulled over by the police no reasonable person would feel that they were free to leave, regardless of whether they were the driver or a passenger. Justice Souter found that when an officer stops a car it is implied that they are acting under the law and everyone in the vehicle will be subject to close scrutiny and, due to safety concerns, the officer will not allow individuals in the vehicle to move around freely during the stop. Illegal stops of a vehicle not predicated on any legal basis which result in evidence found on a passenger will, therefore, give the passenger standing to challenge the admission of the evidence at trial.

In *Wallace v. Kato* (2007)[57] the Roberts Court decided an issue that is closely related to the Fourth Amendment. The issue was when the time frame starts for the statute of limitations to file a federal lawsuit under Title 42 U.S.C., section 1983. In this case a fifteen year-old, Andre Wallace, was arrested without a warrant in January of 1994. Based upon incriminating statements made at the time of the arrest a conviction for first degree murder was gained in 1996. The appeal process for the murder conviction began and in August of 2001 a state appeals court ruled that the arrest violated the Fourth Amendment and the statements should have been suppressed at trial and reversed and remanded the case. On April 10, 2002 the state decided not to press charges a second time. Wallace then brought suit against the officers who had arrested him. The Supreme Court ruled, however, that the two year statute of limitations began on the date of his original trial, not when the judicial proceedings ended. The Court seemed unbothered by the fact that at the time that the statute of limitations would have ended Wallace did not yet have a ruling from the state courts that his Fourth Amendment rights had been violated.

In isolation the *Wallace* case may not have a large impact on the overall power of the government to engage in search and seizures, but if the Court were to dramatically change the role of the exclusionary rule in our society, then Title 42 U.S.C., section 1983 suits may become one of the primary deterrents against violations of the Fourth Amendment. The chances for such a future may have increased due to the Roberts Court decision in *Hudson v. Michigan* (2006).[58] In this case four members of the Roberts Court seemed to be signaling that they were willing to reexamine the appropriateness of the exclusionary rule in our constitutional system. The *Hudson* case came to the Court after police served a valid warrant on Booker Hudson's home and discovered the drugs and weapons which were described in the warrant. Despite the warrant describing narcotics and weapons to be seized, the officers who secured the warrant did not receive permission to bypass the knock and announce rule. The problem that created the legal issue which worked its way up the Supreme Court was that when police executed the warrant they only gave Hudson a matter of seconds between the announcement of their presence and breaking into the residence. Hudson moved to suppress the evidence found in his home because the police had violated the Fourth Amendment's knock and announce rule. The state admitted that the police had violated the knock and announce rule, but the Michigan Court of Appeals on interlocutory review found that suppression was inappropriate under these circumstances. When the Michigan Supreme Court refused to review the decision, Hudson was convicted and then began the appeals process again. After the state courts upheld his conviction he was granted *certiorari* by the Supreme Court.

The Supreme Court in a 5-4 decision in *Hudson* created an exception to the exclusionary rule for evidence found in violation of the knock and announce rule of the Fourth Amendment. Justice Scalia wrote the opinion for the Court and clarified that because the state admitted that the search violated the knock and announce rule the only issue left was the appropriate remedy. Justice Scalia made it clear that the Court now views the exclusionary rule differently than when it decided *Mapp v. Ohio* by stating that the Court no longer accepted the "expansive dicta in *Mapp*" which required all evidence illegally seized to be excluded.[59] Scalia declared that the Court had rejected the idea that evidence had to be suppressed every time the Fourth Amendment was violated in favor of only applying the rule when its deterrent effect was greater than its cost to society.

In finding that the application of the exclusionary rule was unnecessary in this case Justice Scalia's opinion relied on several lines of reasoning which modified the Court's earlier exclusionary rule decisions. He first found that the violation of the Fourth Amendment which took place in this case, avoidance of the knock and announce rule, was not the but for cause of the evidence being found. Instead, it was clear that the reason for this evidence being found was the valid warrant. Justice Scalia next explained that even if the violation of the knock and announce rule was the but for cause of the discovery of the evidence exclusion would not be necessary. This was because the evidence was so attenuated that exclusion was unnecessary. Justice Scalia reasoned that the purposes behind the knock and announce rule, the protection of persons, property, and individual dignity, which can be threatened by the sudden entrance of an individual in the home, were different than the purpose of the Fourth Amendment. That purpose was preventing the government from searching and seizing items in an arbitrary manner. The knock and announce rule was never meant to limit the government's ability to seize evidence described in a valid warrant. Justice Scalia then noted that because the interests protected by the knock and announce rule have nothing to do with deterring the illegal invasion of privacy which lies at the heart of the Fourth Amendment, the exclusionary rule was inapplicable because admission of the evidence did not interfere with the purposes of the knock and announce rule.

Justice Scalia also explained that exclusion was inappropriate because the social costs of applying the rule to this factual scenario would be too high. These costs included the possibility that dangerous criminals would be released, increased litigation rates, and officers delaying entry into homes for which they had valid warrants giving criminals adequate time to either destroy evidence or resist the warrant through violent means. Weighing against these social costs was the deterrent benefit of the exclusionary rule. In this situation the deterrent effect was minimal because the evidence would be found through the warrant any way. On top of this, police could legitimately bypass the knock and announce rule when there was a risk that evidence would be destroyed or that police would be met with violence in the location where the warrant was served. Under those conditions, waiting to serve the warrant raised the social costs of the exclusionary rule even higher.

According to Justice Scalia, automatically requiring exclusion "would be forcing the public today to pay for the sins and inadequacies of a legal regime that existed almost half a century ago" when *Mapp* was decided.[60] Justice Scalia explained that in this day and age there were a variety of forms of deterrence available which could help to preserve the knock and announce rule that carry fewer social costs than the exclusionary rule. The other viable forms of deterrence which Justice Scalia referred to included civil suits brought through Title 42 U.S.C., section 1983 and the increasing professionalism of police departments which emphasize internal police discipline. In the last part of his opinion Justice Scalia relied on three cases, *Segura v. United States,* (1984)[61] *New York v. Harris* (1990),[62] and *United States v. Ramirez* (1998)[63] to demonstrate that that simply because law enforcement had used an impermissible manner of entry to conduct a search, it did not automatically trigger the exclusionary rule.

Justice Anthony Kennedy wrote a concurring opinion to explain that while he agreed with the result and most of the reasoning of the majority opinion he wanted it known that he did not think the last three cases in Justice Scalia's opinion were applicable. He also sought to clarify two things. First, knock and announce violations of the Fourth Amendment were serious and should not be treated as if they were trivial. Second, the decision in no way threatened the "continued operation of the exclusionary rule, as settled and defined by our precedents."[64]

Justice Stephen Breyer wrote a dissenting opinion which had the support of Justices John Paul Stevens, David Souter, and Ruth Bader Ginsburg. The opinion started with a statement that the Court's decision "represents a significant departure" from precedent.[65] He then went on to point out that in the past the Court had made it clear that violations of the knock and announce rule violated the Fourth Amendment. It was clear that going back to *Weeks* and *Mapp* constitutional violations require suppression of the evidence gained. Justice Breyer then questioned whether the alternative forms of deterrence noted by the Court would be effective. He also believed that the Court had exaggerated the social costs to the exclusionary rule by calling them substantial when, in fact, they would be the same as in all cases of excluded evidence. He believed that the way the majority had framed the costs in this case was "an argument against the Fourth Amendment's exclusionary principle itself."[66]

The final result of the Court's decision in *Hudson* is that there is now a blanket exception that evidence found through a violation of the knock and announce rule when serving a warrant will not be subject to the exclusionary rule. In effect, even though the knock and announce rule is still required by the Fourth Amendment, violations no longer matter. It is largely reminiscent of the Court's decision in *Wolf v. Colorado* (1949)[67] in which the Court incorporated the Fourth Amendment, but not the exclusionary rule. As a result of *Wolf,* if a state did not have an exclusionary rule of its own, its law enforcement officers could openly violate the Fourth Amendment as long as their behavior did not shock the conscience of the Court. Under *Hudson* the same situation will be true for both state and federal law enforcement officers when there is a violation of the knock and announce rule. *Wolf* also began a period in which the Court followed a fragmented model of government. According to the fragmented model, the courts should serve as a neutral forum for evidence to be brought forward at trial. The judge should, therefore, not consider the source of the evidence, even when gained through constitutional violation, because a fair trial can only be held by considering all available evidence. The fragmented model sees the constitutional violation as a distinct and separate stage from the admission of the evidence at trial and believes that suppression of the evidence cannot correct the government's constitutional violation of a person's right. The Court's decision in *Hudson* makes it clear that a majority of the members of the Roberts Court are following the lead of the Burger and Rehnquist Courts in their adherence to a fragmented model of government and the exclusionary rule.

The broader ramifications of *Hudson* are not yet known, but it is clear from the perspectives of each of the opinions written that the Court is taking a fresh look at the merits of the exclusionary rule. Justice Scalia and the majority see no reason why they should be bound by *Mapp* which they see as ancient history and decided in a period of history which may no longer be applicable. Justice Kennedy who agreed with almost the entire majority opinion found it necessary, nevertheless, to write a concurrence indicating that the majority opinion does not disturb the current operation of the exclusionary rule. Likewise, the dissenters clearly believe that Justices Antonin Scalia, Clarence Thomas, Samuel Alito, and Chief Justice John Roberts have targeted the rule for disposal.

In the post 9/11 era, the Court may decide that crime and terrorism present such a great danger to American society that it may not be necessary to rely on past interpretations of the Fourth Amendment to determine how much power the government should have to search and seize. The Court may decide that in order to prevent future acts of crime and terrorism and capture those who do commit such acts changes will be necessary in how the Fourth Amendment is interpreted. Based on the cases decided thus far by the Roberts Court there are two primary areas in Fourth Amendment jurisprudence that bear watching. The first area of jurisprudence to watch is how broadly the Roberts Court will apply the reasonableness approach in future cases. Despite endorsing the traditional approach to the Fourth Amendment and its emphasis on warrants for home searches in *Brigham City, Utah*, it is clear that the reasonableness approach is the preferred method of Fourth Amendment interpretation for the Roberts Court. The Court has relied on that approach in every case involving a strict Fourth Amendment issue when a warrant was not directly involved. In future cases it will be interesting to see whether the Roberts Court will see crime and terrorism as such a great threat to the nation that the Court will find use of bolder methods to stop crime and terrorism as reasonable under the Fourth Amendment.

In determining the reasonableness of a search and or seizure the Court has resolved only two cases in which the government's position did not win. The first was *Georgia v. Randolph* where the Court in a 5-3 decision ruled that police must have the consent of all parties present prior to searching a home without a warrant. For civil libertarians it was victory, but a narrow one and one which will not have broad ramifications. This is because the Court made it quite clear that if a person was not present, as long as the police had not purposely lured them away to conduct a search, they had no authority to stop a consent search. Thus, officers will find ways around the precedent of *Randolph*. In the second case which resulted in a loss for government interests, *Brendlin v. California*, the Court made a commonsense application of reasonableness. It found that when police stop a vehicle, for purposes of the Fourth Amendment, everyone in that vehicle has been seized because no one would reasonably believe they were free to leave unhindered by the police. Therefore, if the stop violated the Fourth Amendment everyone in the car has standing to challenge the evidence as a result of the stop.

In every other case the Roberts Court has decided using the reasonableness approach, they have ruled in favor of the government. In doing so, they have enlarged the power of the government to engage in searches and seizures. In *Samson,* for example, the Court decided that a whole class of citizens, parolees, have no legitimate expectation of privacy in their lives and may therefore be subject to suspicionless searches at any time. In *Brigham City, Utah v. Stuart* the Court found it reasonable to allow police to enter a home when there was an exigent circumstance caused by fight regardless of whether their purpose was to provide aid or to gather evidence. In *Virginia v. Moore* the Court decided to allow evidence to be used at trial which was found incident to an unlawful arrest because the Court believed that all arrests based on probable cause that a law was broken are reasonable, even when the arrest violates state law. The pattern seems clear that the Roberts Court, thus far, is interested in protecting the power of the government to maintain law and order within society.

Closely related to the issue of how the Court will interpret the Fourth Amendment in the post-9/11 world is what will be the Court's view of the exclusionary rule. Will the fear of crime and terrorism give rise to a new balance in the cost/benefit analysis? We have already seen in *Hudson* that some members of the Court are willing to draw a new balance. In that case the Court found that if a constitutional violation does not protect the interests of the Fourth Amendment, exclusion of any evidence gathered is not required. Reacting to *Hudson*, David Moran has pointed out that none of the interests "protected by the Fourth Amendment is about preventing the government from seizing one's contraband or criminal evidence."[68] As a result, it could be reasoned that because the primary purpose of the Fourth Amendment is to limit the power of the government to arbitrarily interfere in the lives of citizens, then the admission of contraband evidence found in violation of the Fourth Amendment does not create a new harm to the Fourth Amendment and should therefore be admissible. Ever since the decision in *United States v. Calandra*, (1974)[69] the Court has emphasized a fragmented model of government in which it has believed that the costs of the exclusionary rule are so high that it is acceptable for the courts to make use of evidence which is indeed illegally gathered by another branch of the government. The Court in *Hudson* not only accepted this view, but questioned the very continuance of the exclusionary rule by hinting that other forms of deterrence might better serve the interests of the community due to the substantial costs of exclusion. Discussing the potential for a change in the Court's approach to the exclusionary rule after *Hudson,* Morgan Cloud has written of Justice Scalia's opinion in *Hudson* that what makes it so striking is that, "It resurrects arguments questioning the very legitimacy of the exclusionary rule."[70]

The question may well be asked, does the Roberts Court have the desire to say no to government attempts to gather evidence in bolder and bolder ways. Based on a review of the Fourth Amendment cases the Roberts Court decided in its first term, John Castiglione stated "Going forward, challenges to government action in the Fourth Amendment context will have a high hurdle to overcome, because the presumption exists among at least five members of the Court that the governmental interest in law enforcement (specifically crime prevention and evidence gathering) will usually trump the individual's interest in privacy."[71] In the years to come we shouldn't expect leadership on the Roberts Court to limit the power of the government to engage in search and seizures to come from the youngest members of the Court. Chief Justice Roberts and Justices Alito and Thomas are all consistent conservative voices who are not likely to use the Fourth Amendment to narrow the government's power to search and seize. Their votes, along with Justice Scalia's, provides a solid bloc of four votes which will usually support the government's power to search and seize and to rule against an expansive view of the exclusionary rule. The voices on the Court which most often resist broadening the power of the government to search and seize are Justice Stevens, the oldest member of the Court, and Justices Souter, Ginsberg, and Breyer. It must be said, however, that members of this group do not present as cohesive of a bloc on Fourth Amendment issues as does the conservative wing. This is best demonstrated by the fact that in six of the ten cases decided by the Roberts Court, the Court has been unanimous and the Court found in favor of governmental actions in five of those cases.

As was true in the *Hudson* case, the direction of the Court's Fourth Amendment jurisprudence when there are close cases will temporarily hinge on the votes of Justice Kennedy. He is in a unique position to decide whether the government's power will be expanded or be held in check. The future of the exclusionary rule will also be dependent on his position. Looking beyond the justices who currently serve on the Court it is always hard to predict what will happen to any area of constitutional law and the Fourth Amendment is not different. Change in any direction is possible, but it must be said that with a solid conservative base of relatively young justices, it would take a number of appointments to substantially change the direction that Fourth Amendment jurisprudence has taken since the end of the Warren Court. That direction has, of course, been one of enhancing the power of the government to search and seize and limiting the role of the exclusionary rule. Beyond the personal predilections of its members regarding the appropriate power of the government to engage in search and seizure, the amendment's future will also be dependent on the Court's willingness to adhere to precedent.

Stare Decisis and Protection of the Principles of the Fourth Amendment

Not all courts respect precedent equally. For some Courts, if the justices believe that the Constitution has been improperly interpreted, there is little apprehension at overruling precedents. The Warren Court was such a Court. It inherited a Fourth Amendment jurisprudence that it believed failed, in some ways, to advance the principle of the amendment. When given the opportunity, the Warren Court did not shy away from overruling precedent. The most forceful example is, of course, *Mapp v. Ohio* in which the Court overruled the decision in *Wolf v. Colorado* not to incorporate the exclusionary rule. The Court also broadened the protections of the Fourth Amendment by overruling *Olmstead v. United States* in *Katz v. United States* and ruling that the Fourth Amendment was flexible enough to provide protection for persons against forms of electronic surveillance. The Warren Court also disliked the decision in *Frank v. Maryland* (1959)[72] that governmental inspectors could enter a person's property and not be subject to Fourth Amendment limitations so it was overruled in *Camara v. Municipal Court* (1967).[73] All of these examples demonstrate that when the Warren Court objected to earlier Court interpretations of the Fourth Amendment it openly rejected the interpretations, failed to apply *stare decisis*, and overruled precedent.

One could ask with all the changes in Fourth Amendment law since *Mapp v. Ohio* why hasn't any major decision of the Warren Court been overruled. After all, many changes have been made in Fourth Amendment jurisprudence since the Court incorporated the exclusionary rule in *Mapp*. The large number of split decisions and the curves in the road since *Mapp* clearly demonstrates that using *stare decisis* to resolve cases is not as easy as following a mathematical formula.

It also shows that reasonable people will often reach different results when interpreting the Constitution. This is especially true when the Court is interpreting opinions which use broad, flexible language. Such language was often used by the Warren Court when it overruled precedent. The Warren Court's use of language allowed the Burger and Rehnquist Courts to claim that they followed *stare decisis* in Fourth Amendment cases because they refrained from overruling any major Fourth Amendment cases decided by the Warren Court. The problem for those trying to understand what constitutes an unreasonable search and seizure today is not that the Warren Court precedents aren't still in place. They are, the problem is that they just don't mean the same thing today as they did when they were decided. The post-Warren Courts have cited the precedents of the Warren Court, but emphasized other aspects of the opinions than did the Warren Court. In effect, they practiced a version of *stare decisis* in which these Courts have cited a case and then changed the precedent to one which was friendlier to governmental needs. The broad, flexible language used in the Warren Court opinions allowed later courts to legitimately use this type of cite and change approach to the precedents of the Warren Court. As a result, the language and reasoning relied upon by later courts often originated in the opinions of the Warren Court.

What the post-Warren Courts have done cannot be seen as illegitimate. These Courts did not use creativity or judicial license in the decisions they made to enhance the power of the government to search and seize. These Courts simply took advantage of the language used in Warren Court opinions and emphasized different aspects of the opinions than did the Warren Court. This allowed the post-Warren Courts to maintain the precedents, but change the meaning of the amendment and, thus, its protections. As a result, the original lesson from *Mapp* that the government should not be able to gain from violating the Fourth Amendment, becomes the government can benefit from Fourth Amendment violations if it would not serve to act as a deterrent to future constitutional violations. The lesson from *Katz v. United States* is no longer that the Fourth Amendment protects people, not places, from government interference. Instead, it becomes that Fourth Amendment rights are personal rights so any evidence gathered against a third person while the government violated the Fourth Amendment is admissible at trial. *Terry v. Ohio* (1968)[74] changes from a case which allowed a stop and frisk for the purpose of protecting the safety of officers when police have articulable suspicions that a person is involved in criminal activity and is armed and dangerous to a case which allows a person's baggage to be seized for investigative reasons when there is no safety threat. These changes in what the Fourth Amendment protects, as previous chapters demonstrate, go on and on.

It is clear that the precedents of the Supreme Court are not written in stone and the Court has shown a willingness to overrule itself when conditions are right. Deborah Hellman has summarized the conditions that the Court has stated should exist in order to overrule precedent as the following:

> [T]he judge ought to consider whether there has been substantial reliance on the old rule, whether the old rule was unworkable, whether intervening decisions or congressional enactments have rendered the old rule an anachronism, and whether circumstances have so changed as to eviscerate the justification for the old rule. Generally mere erroneousness of the old rule is not enough. At least one of the above additional factors is also required.[75]

One reason why Fourth Amendment law may lack precision today is that the Court has not found the old rule, the warrant rule, to be unsound in principle. Thus, the warrant rule still stands. The warrant rule has, however, been found by the Court to be unworkable in practice. This explains why the court has accepted a growing number of exceptions to the warrant rule. It also explains the Court's embrace of the reasonableness approach in *Camara, Terry* and their progeny. Likewise, the Court believes the principle behind the exclusionary rule that it is improper for the government to benefit when it violates the Constitution to be sound. Nevertheless, when this results in freeing individuals who are factually guilty, the Court has found the practice of the principle to result in too high of a price for society to pay in some situations. The line of cases applying *Mapp* and the narrowing of the exclusionary rule must be explained by a dislike of the practical implications of a broad interpretation of the Fourth Amendment and the exclusionary rule working together.

What is, perhaps, more problematic for understanding the evolution of the Fourth Amendment is that while the Post-Warren Courts have limited the protections of the Fourth Amendment and recast the prior precedents to be more in line with the desired outcomes of the justices, these Courts have failed to clarify the amendment's requirements. Instead, the changes have resulted in growing confusion as to what are the core principles behind the amendment and how those principles should be applied. Speaking in general about the Court's use of *stare decisis*, Ronald Krotoszynski, Jr. has noted that, "the erosion of stare decisis through devices such as perpetual dissent and 'cite-and-switch' has left the Supreme Court's members in a position to create an increasingly ad hoc, highly subjective jurisprudence that reflects little more than the ability of a contemporary group of five justices to find a sufficient common ground to join a result."[76] This description accurately reflects the Court's Fourth Amendment cases.

The Court's adoption of the reasonableness approach has often created consistency in the result of Fourth Amendment cases with the government's power to search and seize being expanded. The problem is that the very nature of the reasonableness approach lends itself to shifting majorities and ad hoc reasoning based on the particular facts of each case. This tendency of the Court to decide Fourth Amendment cases on an ad hoc reasonable basis has caused the Court's analysis in recent years to resemble the fundamental fairness standard that existed during the period between the decisions in *Wolf v. Colorado* and *Mapp v.*

Ohio. The primary difference might be that rather than asking if the method of gathering evidence violated those principles implicit to ordered liberty, the Court now asks whether the government's actions were reasonable. The case-by-case analysis as the Court concentrates on the minute facts of each case to determine whether there has been a violation of the Fourth Amendment is similar to the case-by-case analysis in its fundamental fairness approach. In a growing number of scenarios, despite clear evidence that the government has asserted its authority and interfered with the liberty of citizens, the Court seems unwilling to call a search a search and a seizure a seizure because it finds the action reasonable. The problem with this type of analysis is that, other than a gradual broadening of the government's search and seizure power, the reasonableness approach has brought little stability or predictive ability in the law. This leaves both citizens and law enforcement agents unsure about where the lines between legal and illegal government activity begins and ends.

Even though post-Warren Courts have not overruled the Warren Court's decisions, they have greatly modified Fourth Amendment law since *Mapp* was decided by not adhering to a strict application of *stare decisis*. The advantages of a system of law based on *stare decisis* have long been declared to be predictability, reliance on the law, promotion of equality, and efficiency in the administration of justice. The first advantage, predictability, results when a judge decides cases based on the rule of law that comes out of earlier decisions. Relying on earlier cases and the rule of law from those decisions develops stability in the way that individuals are treated under the law. This stability is important because it leads to predictability in the application of the law. In regards to the Fourth Amendment, predictability allows law enforcement officials to clearly understand what legal methods they can use to gather evidence and make arrests. When predictability in law exists, both police and citizens can have a strong sense as to what the law allows and can adjust their behavior to conform to the expectations established by the law.

For the last thirty years scholars have noted that Fourth Amendment law lacks consistency and predictability.[77] One reason that Fourth Amendment cases have been difficult to predict is that once the Court moved away from the traditional approach to Fourth Amendment jurisprudence and applied a reasonableness approach the results of a case were quite often dependent on the minute facts of the case which constantly change from case to case making it hard to predict future outcomes. Despite the reliance on factual considerations, it is becoming increasingly true that, while individual cases can still be tricky to predict, Fourth Amendment law is stabilizing in favor of enhancing governmental powers to search and seize. This has been done in several ways including limiting those activities which trigger Fourth Amendment scrutiny, use of the reasonableness approach to the Fourth Amendment, and narrowing those circumstances in which the Court deems exclusion to be necessary. It can also be seen through the continuing issuance of opinions which use broad, flexible language which may in the future allow even broader governmental authority to search and seize. An example may be seen in *Kyllo v. United States* when Justice Scalia announced in his majority opinion that citizens were only protected by sense-enhancing technologies that were not in general public use, thus giving a green light for governmental use of technologies that are in such use.

Even if the Court stopped placing so much emphasis on the facts of its Fourth Amendment cases, there is no guarantee that we would see increased predictability in Fourth Amendment cases. That is because the increasing use of the reasonableness approach makes the outcomes of cases dependent on the personal preferences of the justices, which are subject to change. Public pressures may develop which influence the justices to change the power of the government to search and seize. In the post-9/11 world it is likely that the Court will be subject to societal and governmental pressures to change Fourth Amendment law to combat increasing fears of crime and terrorism.

The lack of clarity in the law which can lead to predictability also has a negative impact on the ability of *stare decisis* to achieve the other advantages that come from the application of precedent. Once the law becomes predictable another advantage that comes out of the practice of *stare decisis* is that individuals can develop reliance on the law. For the Fourth Amendment this would mean that observant citizens should be able to adjust their behavior and stay within the lines established by the courts and not be subject to government invasion of their privacy due to the protections of the Fourth Amendment. Likewise, law enforcement officials could also rely on the rules developed by the courts to insure that the methods by which they gather evidence are legal and the results admissible at trial. If there was enough clarity in Fourth Amendment law so that citizens and police could rely upon it, there would be few Fourth Amendment cases that would reach the Supreme Court. This has not happened. Prior to the decision in *Mapp v. Ohio* in 1961 the Court had only heard ninety-six Fourth Amendment cases. Since *Mapp,* the Court has decided over 300 Fourth Amendment cases and the Supreme Court continues to grant *certiorari* in Fourth Amendment cases.[78] Furthermore, as the Fourth Amendment now stands it is impossible for a person who understands Fourth Amendment law to rely on the precedents now in place and be assured that the government will not arbitrarily interfere in their lives. This is because the Court has allowed for suspicionless searches and seizures in a variety of circumstances.[79]

When courts consistently apply the law it also creates another benefit for the society. That is equality of treatment before the law. Equality of treatment would exist if the principles of the Fourth Amendment were evenly applied in all cases regardless of who is the suspect, of what they are accused, or to what organizations they may belong. The Supreme Court has not purposely tried to make rules concerning the application of the Fourth Amendment that will work to the disadvantage of certain individuals, groups, or organizations within society. Despite this, the application of the Court's precedents like *Terry v. Ohio* have given so much deference to police officers in determining who will be subject to investigative stops that claims have been made that the results are discriminatory and often based on race.[80] Others have made the claim that the Court has created a general exception to the Fourth Amendment for cases involving drugs.[81] While the Court can claim its decisions demonstrate equality of treatment because it has decided that all students who want to participate in after school activities will be treated the same by ruling that they can be subjected to suspicionless drug tests,[82] its commitment to equality of treatment can be questioned since it has been unwilling to hold persons who desire to run for public office to the same standard.[83]

A final advantage that comes from the use of *stare decisis* is that of efficiency in the administration of justice. Once a judge determines the facts of a case and recognizes similar factual patterns in earlier cases he or she should be able to quickly reach a decision in the current case before them. Proper following of precedent also makes the appeals process less likely, thus helping to bring each case to a close as efficiently as possible. As Justice Scalia has noted the Court has not reached a point where the Fourth Amendment is being developed in an efficient manner that has led to few appeals.[84] The Court's continuing granting of *certiorari* in Fourth Amendment cases also demonstrates that this area of law has not stabilized.

The question must be asked, if the Court has not achieved the advantages that *stare decisis* has traditionally been thought to accomplish with its Fourth Amendment decisions and citizens seem to be less free from arbitrary interference in their lives, why has the Supreme Court been so active in changing this area of law since the incorporation of the exclusionary rule? *Mapp v. Ohio* stands as the pivotal case in Fourth Amendment jurisprudence. Prior to *Mapp* the states that desired to do so effectively ignored the provisions of the Fourth Amendment by allowing illegally gathered evidence to be used. Once exclusion became a reality under *Mapp* it took more courage than the Supreme Court could muster to continue to apply the cardinal principle of the Fourth Amendment that all searches and seizures conducted without a warrant were per se unreasonable unless the facts fit into either the limited exceptions of consent, plain view, open fields, automobiles, or being incident to a lawful arrest. None of the post-Warren Courts had the fortitude to confront the large number of state violations of the Fourth Amendment and teach state governments to conform their behavior to the cardinal principle of the Fourth Amendment. In order to avoid exclusion of evidence and the release of individuals who were often factually guilty the Court has felt the need to modify the application of the Fourth Amendment and the exclusionary rule to allow for greater government authority to search and seize. This effort has taken the 54 words in the Fourth Amendment and turned them into a body of law that is extremely complicated. It has also, at times, removed the Fourth Amendment from its first principle, to protect citizens from arbitrary governmental interference in their lives.

The answer as to why the post-Warren Courts created so many changes in Fourth Amendment jurisprudence may be found in the Court's opinions and its hope of accomplishing goals it believed should take a higher priority than those associated with *stare decisis*. The goal that seems to be the priority of the Supreme Court since the collapse of the Warren Court has been the development of a flexible Fourth Amendment that is capable of protecting society from criminal activity in a reasonable manner. As the Court has stated, there is a high societal cost that must be paid when probative evidence is suppressed at trial. Exclusion has the effect of releasing individuals when the evidence points to their guilt. The post-Warren Courts have firmly believed that there is a lesser threat to individuals in society from the misdeeds of the government than from the misdeeds of criminals. It isn't that these Courts have not cared about violations of the law committed by the government. If that were the case, *Weeks v. United States* (1914)[85] and *Mapp v. Ohio* could have simply been overruled and the Courts could have turned a blind eye to all government violations of the Fourth Amendment. Instead, these Courts have sought to help the government in its crime control efforts by limiting what constituted a search, expanding the exceptions to the warrant rule, finding a wider variety of governmental search and seizure actions to be reasonable, and narrowing the application of the exclusionary rule. These Courts have also recognized that often the inability of government officials to follow the law was due to the complexities of the law the Court had developed, not the government's desire to flagrantly violate the law. Therefore, these Courts created more exceptions to the exclusionary rule and found that the government should not be penalized in those cases in which it had made honest mistakes in gathering evidence.[86] Individuals may disagree with the positions of the post-Warren Courts that we have more to fear from criminals than from an overbearing government, but that is the conclusion they reached. The correctness of that conclusion will continue to be debated on and off the Court and the Fourth Amendment will remain open to further interpretations and revisions as the composition of the Court and times in which we live change.

Notes

1. Anthony Amsterdam, "Perspectives on the Fourth Amendment," *Minnesota Law Review* 58 (1974): 353.

2. Potter Stewart, "The Road to *Mapp v. Ohio* and Beyond: The Origins, Development and Future of the Exclusionary Rule in Search and Seizure Cases," *Columbia Law Review* 83 (1983): 1393.

3. Louis Fisher, "The Federal Courts and Terrorism," in *Exploring Judicial Politics*, ed. Mark C. Miller (New York: Oxford University Press, 2009), 261.

4. *Padilla ex. Rel. Newman v. Bush*, 233 F. Supp. 2d 564 (2002).

5. *Padilla v. Rumsfeld*, 352 F.3d 695 (2003).

6. Karen Branch-Briscoe, "Padilla targeted high-rises, U.S. says 'Combatant' case is detailed," *St. Louis Post-Dispatch*, June 2, 2004.

7. *Padilla v. Rumsfeld*, 542 U.S. 426 (2004).

8. *Padilla v. Hanft*, 389 F.Supp. 2d 678 (2005).

9. *Padilla v. Hanft*, 423 F.3d 386 (2005).

10. Kirk Semple, "Padilla Gets 17-Year Term For Role in Conspiracy," *New York Times*, January 23, 2008, 14.

11. http://www.usdoj.gov/archive/ag/speeches/2002/080702eighthcircuitjudgesag-remarks.htm (26 Oct. 2008).

12. http://www.ignet.gov/pande/standards/prgexhibitg.pdf (26 Oct. 2008).

13. Stephen Schulhofer, *Rethinking the Patriot Act: Keeping America Safe and Free* (New York: The Century Foundation Press, 2005), 33.

14. Section 215 of the USA Patriot Act, 115 Stat. 272, 291, amending 50 U.S.C. 1804(a)(7)(B).

15. Section 215 of the USA Patriot Act, 115 Stat. 287.

16. Seth F. Kreimer, "Watching the Watchers: Surveillance, Transparency, and Political Freedom in the War on Terror," *University of Pennsylvania Journal of Constitutional Law* 7 (2004): 157.

17. Section 505(a)(3)(B) of the USA Patriot Act.

18. David Lyon, *Surveillance Society: Monitoring Everyday Life* (Philadelphia: Open University Press, 2001), 2.

19. Simson Garfinkel, *Database Nation: The Death of Privacy in the 21st Century* (Sebastopol, CA: O'Reilly & Associates, 2000), 53.

20. http://www.aslme.org/dna_04/description.php (26 Oct. 2008).

21. Harry Henderson, *Privacy in the Information Age* (New York: Facts on File, 2006), 128.

22. A. Michael Froomkin, "Symposium: Cyberspace and Privacy A New Legal Paradigm," *Stanford Law Review* 52 (2000): 1474.

23. Leslie Cauley, "NSA has Massive Database of American's Phone Calls; 3 Telecoms Help Government Collect Billions of Domestic Records," *USA Today*, May 11, 2006, p. 1A.

24. Laura B. Riley, "Comment, Concealed Weapon Detectors and the Fourth Amendment: The Constitutionality of Remote Enhanced Searches," *University of California, Los Angeles Law Review*, 45 (1997): 283.

25. Richard S. Julie, "High-Tech Surveillance Tools and the Fourth Amendment: Reasonable Expectations of Privacy in the technological Age," *American Criminal Law Review* 37 (2000): 137.

26. Mark Monmonier, *Spying With Maps: Surveillance Technologies and the Future of Privacy* (Chicago: University of Chicago Press, 2002), 14.

27. Daniel J. Steinbock, "Data Matching, Data Mining, and Due Process," *Georgia Law Review* 40 (2005): 13.

28. Keith L. Alexander, "A Common Name Can Be a Curse," *The Washington Post,* October 12, 2004: E01.

29. *Mapp v. Ohio*, 367 U.S. 643 (1961).

30. *Katz v. United States*, 389 U.S. 347 (1967).

31. *Kyllo v. United States*, 533 U.S. 27 (2001).

32. *United States v. Knotts*, 460 U.S. 276 (1983).

33. *California v. Ciraolo*, 476 U.S. 207 (1986).

34. *United States v. Karo*, 468 U.S. 705 (1984).

35. *United States v. Miller*, 425 U.S. 435 (1976).

36. *Smith v. Maryland*, 442 U.S. 735 (1979).

37. *United States v. Flores-Montano*, 541 U.S. 149 (2004).
38. *United States v. Place*, 462 U.S. 696 (1983).
39. *United States v. Jacobsen*, 466 U.S. 109 (1984).
40. *United States v. Sokolow*, 490 U.S. 1 (1989).
41. *United States v. Grubbs*, 547 U.S. 90 (2006).
42. *Scott v. Harris*, 127 S. Ct. 1769 (2007).
43. *Brigham City, Utah v. Stuart*, 547 U.S. 398 (2006).
44. *County of Los Angeles v. Rettele*, 127 S. Ct. 1989 (2007).
45. *Virginia v. Moore*, 128 S. Ct. 1598 (2008).
46. *Brigham City, Utah v. Stuart*, 547 U.S. 398, 403 (2006) (quoting *Groh v. Ramirez*, 540 U.S. 551, 559 [2004]).
47. *Brigham City, Utah*, 547 U.S. at 403.
48. *County of Los Angeles v. Rettele*, 127 S. Ct. 1989, 1992 (2007).
49. *Virginia v. Moore*, 128 S. Ct. 1598, 1603 (2008).
50. *Virginia v. Moore*, 128 S. Ct. at 1605.
51. *Samson v. California*, 547 U.S 843 (2006).
52. *Samson*, 547 U.S. at 848.
53. For a discussion of the special needs test see Chapter 5.
54. *Georgia v. Randolph*, 547 U.S. 103 (2006).
55. *Coolidge v. New Hampshire*, 403 U.S. 443 (1971).
56. *Brendlin v. California*, 127 S. Ct. 2400 (2007).
57. *Wallace v. Kato*, 549 U.S. 384 (2007).
58. *Hudson v. Michigan*, 547 U.S. 586 (2006).
59. *Hudson*, 547 U.S. at 591.
60. *Hudson v. Michigan*, 547 U.S. at 597.
61. *Segura v. United States*, 468 U.S. 796 (1984).
62. *New York v. Harris*, 495 U.S. 796 (1990).
63. *United States v. Ramirez*, 523 U.S. 65 (1998).
64. *Hudson*, 547 U.S. at 603 (Kennedy, J., concurring).
65. *Hudson*, 547 U.S. at 605 (Breyer, J., dissenting).
66. *Hudson*, 547 U.S. at 614 (Breyer, J., dissenting).
67. *Wolf v. Colorado*, 338 U.S. 25 (1949).
68. David A. Moran, "The End of the Exclusionary Rule, Among Other Things: The Roberts Court takes on the Fourth Amendment," *Cato Supreme Court Review* (2005-2006): 301.
69. *United States v. Calandra*, 414 U.S. 338 (1974).
70. Morgan Cloud, "Rights Without Remedies: The Court that Cried '*Wolf*,'" *Mississippi Law Journal* 77 (2007): 468.
71. John D. Castigilione, "*Hudson* and *Samson*: The Roberts Court Confronts Privacy, Dignity and the Fourth Amendment," *Louisiana Law Review* 68 (2007): 116.
72. *Frank v. Maryland*, 359 U.S. 360 (1959).
73. *Camara v. Municipal Court*, 387 U.S. 523 (1967).
74. *Terry v. Ohio*, 392 U.S. 1 (1968).
75. Deborah Hellman, "The Importance of Appearing Principled," *Arizona Law Review* 37 (1995): 1112-13.
76. Ronald J. Krotoszynski, Jr., "An Epitaphios for Neutral Principles in Constitutional Law: *Bush v. Gore* and the Emerging Jurisprudence of Oprah!," *Georgetown Law Review* 90 (2002): 2117-18.
77. See, Stephen A. Saltzburg, "A Symposium on the Legacy of the Rehnquist Court: The Fourth Amendment: Internal Revenue Code or Body of Principles,?" *George*

Washington Law Review 74 (2006): 956; Craig M. Bradley, "Two Models of the Fourth Amendments," *Michigan Law Review* 83 (1985): 1468; Phillip A. Hubbart, *Making Sense of Search and Seizure Law: A Fourth Amendment Handbook* (Durahm, NC: Carolina Academic Press, 2006), xvii; and Lloyd L. Weinreb, "Generalities of the Fourth Amendment," *University of Chicago Law Review*, 42 (1974): 49.

78. Between 1999 and 2008 the Supreme Court has granted *certiorari* to between 1 and 7 cases each term. The average number has been 4 cases per term.

79. Examples include drunk driving checkpoints, *Michigan Department of State Police v. Sitz*, 496 U.S. 444 (1990); participating in after school activities, *Board of Education v. Earls*, 536 U.S. 822 (2002) and government employment, *National Treasury Employees Union v. Von Raab*, 489 U.S. 656 (1989).

80. Omar Saleem, "The Age of Unreason: The impact of Reasonableness, Increased Police Force, and Colorblindness on *Terry* 'Stop and Frisk,'" *Oklahoma Law Review* 50 (1997): 451-493; Tracey Maclin, "*Terry v. Ohio's* Fourth Amendment Legacy: Black Men and Police Discretion," *St. John's Law Review* 72 (1998): 1271-1321.

81. Steven Wisotsky, "Crackdown: The Emerging 'Drug Exception' to the Bill of Rights," *Hastings Law Review* 38 (1987): 889-926.

82. *Board of Education v. Earls*, 536 U.S. 822 (2002).

83. *Chandler v. Miller*, 520 U.S. 305 (1997).

84. Antonin Scalia, "The Rule of Law as a Law of Rules," *University of Chicago Law Review* 56 (1989): 1186.

85. *Weeks v. United States*, 232 U.S. 383 (1914).

86. *United States v. Leon*, 468 U.S. 897 (1984).

Bibliography

Adams, James A. "The Supreme Court's Improbable Justifications for Restriction of Citizen's Fourth Amendment Privacy Expectations in Automobiles," *Drake Law Review* 47 (1999): 833-851.

Agati, Andrew. "The Plain Feel Doctrine of *Minnesota v. Dickerson*: Creating an Illusion," *Case Western Reserve Law Review* 45 (1995): 927-956.

Aizenstein, Neal I. "Fourth Amendment—Searches by Public School Officials Valid on 'Reasonable Grounds': *New Jersey v. T.L.O.*, 105 S. Ct. 733 (1985)," *Journal of Criminal Law and Criminology* 76 (1985): 898-932.

Amar, Akhil Reed. "Fourth Amendment First Principles," *Harvard Law Review* 107 (1994): 757-819.

___. "*Terry* and Fourth Amendment First Principles," *St. John's Law Review* 72 (1998): 1097-1131.

Ames, Joy L. "*Chandler v. Miller*: Redefining 'Special Needs' for Suspicionless Drug Testing Under the Fourth Amendment," *Akron Law Review* 31 (1997): 273-295.

Amsterdam, Anthony G. "Perspectives on the Fourth Amendment," *Minnesota Law Review* 58 (1974): 349-477.

Aswad, Evelyn M., David W. Balch, Katherine Butler Houlihan, Patrick Brown, and Brian M. Buroker. "Investigation and Police Practice: Warrantless Search and Seizures," *Georgetown Law Journal* 82 (1994): 622-697.

Bacigal, Ronald J. "Dodging a Bullet, But Opening Old Wounds in Fourth Amendment Jurisprudence," *Seton Hall Law Review* 16 (1986): 597-629.

Bandes, Susan. "Power, Privacy, and Thermal Imaging," *Minnesota Law Review* 86 (2002): 1379-1391.

Banks, Patrick. "Fourth and Fourteenth Amendments-Search and Seizure-Police Officers with Probable Cause to Search a Vehicle May Inspect a Passenger's Belongings found in the Vehicle that are Capable of Concealing the Object of the Search-*Wyoming v. Houghton*, 119 S.Ct. 1297 (1999)," *Seton Hall Constitutional Journal* 10 (2000): 534-575.

Beller, Amy B. "United States v. MacDonald: The Exigent Circumstances Exception and the Erosion of the Fourth Amendment," *Hofstra Law Review* 20 (1991): 407-428.

Belsky, Martin. H. *The Rehnquist Court: A Retrospective*, New York: Oxford University Press, 2002.

Bernstein, Merrick D. "'Intimate Details': A Troubling New Fourth Amendment Standard for Government Surveillance Techniques," *Duke Law Journal* 46 (1996): 575-610.

Bloom, Robert M. "Warrant Requirement—The Burger Court Approach," *University of Colorado Law Review* 53 (1982): 691-744.

___. "The Supreme Court and Its Purported Preference for Warrants," *Tennessee Law Review* 50 (1983): 231-270.

Bloom, Robert M. and Mark S. Brodin. *Criminal Procedure: Examples and Explanations*, 3rd edition, New York: Aspen Law and Business, 2000.

Bookspan, Phyllis T. "Reworking the Warrant Requirement: Resuscitating the Fourth Amendment," *Vanderbilt Law Review* 44 (1991): 473-530.

Bradley, Craig M. "The 'Good Faith Exception' Cases: Reasonable Exercises in Futility," *Indiana Law Journal* 60 (1984): 287-304.

___. "Two Models of the Fourth Amendment," *Michigan Law Review* 83 (1985): 1468-1501.

___. "Criminal Procedure in the Rehnquist Court: Has the Rehnquisition Begun?," *Indiana Law Journal* 62 (1989): 273-294.

___. "Criminal Law: The Court's 'Two Model' Approach to the Fourth Amendment: Carpe Diem!" *Journal of Criminal Law and Criminology* 84 (1993): 429-461.

Buckland, Laura J. "Informant's Tips and Probable Cause: The Demise of *Aguilar-Spinelli—Illinois v. Gates,* 103 S. Ct. 2317 (1983)," *Washington Law Review* 59 (1984): 635-651.

Buffaloe, Jennifer Y. "'Special Need' and the Fourth Amendment: An Exception Poised to Swallow the Warrant Preference Rule," *Harvard Civil Rights-Civil Liberties Law Review* 32 (1997): 529-564.

Burger, Warren E. "Who Will Watch the Watchman," *American University Law Review* 14 (1964): 1-23.

Burkhoff, John M. 1979. "The Court that Devoured The Fourth Amendment: The Triumph of an Inconsistent Exclusionary Doctrine," *Oregon Law Review* 58: 151-192.

___. "When is a Search not a 'Search?' Fourth Amendment Doublethink," *Toledo Law Review* 15 (1984): 515-559.

Burnett, Robert J. "Comment: Random Police-Citizen Encounters: When is a Seizure a Seizure?" *Duquesne Law Review* 33 (1995): 283-307.

Butterfoss, Edwin J. "Bright Line Seizures: The need for Clarity in Determining when Fourth Amendment Activity Begins," *Journal of Criminal Law and Criminology* 79 (1988): 437-482.

Buxbaum, Edward. "*Florida v. Brady:* Can *Katz* Survive in Open Fields?," *American University Law Review* 329 (1983): 921-943.

Cameron, James Duke and Richard Lustiger. "The Exclusionary Rule: A Cost-Benefit Analysis," *Federal Rules Decisions* 101 (1984): 109-159.

Campbell, Michael. "Defining a Fourth Amendment Search: A Critique of the Supreme Court's Post-*Katz* Jurisprudence," *Washington Law Review* 61 (1986): 191-216.

Canon, Bradley C. "Ideology and Reality in the Debate Over the Exclusionary Rule: A Conservative Argument for its Retention," *South Texas Law Review* 23 (1982): 559-582

Cardozo, Benjamin N. *The Nature of the Judicial Process*, New Haven, CT: Yale University Press, 1921.

Castigilione, John D. "*Hudson* and *Samson*: The Roberts Court Confronts Privacy, Dignity and the Fourth Amendment," *Louisiana Law Review* 68 (2007) : 63-116.

Cauley, Leslie "NSA has Massive Database of American's Phone Calls; 3 Telecoms Help Government Collect Billions of Domestic Records," *USA Today*, May 11, 2006, p. 1A.

Christensen, Steven M. "*Colorado v. Bertine* Opens the Inventory Search to Containers," *Iowa Law Review* 73 (1988): 771-796.

Clancy, Thomas K. "The Role of Individualized Suspicion in Assessing the Reasonableness of Searches and Seizures," *University of Memphis Law Review* 25 (1994): 483-635.

___. "Protective Searches, Pat-Downs, or Frisks?: The Scope of the Permissible Intrusion to Ascertain if a Detained Person is Armed," *Marquette Law Review* 82 (1999): 491-533.

Cloud, Morgan. "Search and Seizure by the Numbers: The Drug Courier Profile and Judicial Review of Investigative Formulas," *Boston University Law Review* 65 (1985): 843-921.

___. "Rights Without Remedies: The Court that Cried '*Wolf,*'" *Mississippi Law Journal* 77 (2007): 467-505.

Clymer, Steven D. "Warrantless Vehicle Searches and the Fourth Amendment: The Burger Court Attacks the Exclusionary Rule," *Cornell Law Review* 68 (1982): 105-145.

Creamer, J. Shane. *The Law of Arrest, Search and Seizure*, 2nd ed., Philadelphia: W.B. Saunders Company, 1975.

Cunis, David W. "*California v. Greenwood*: Discarding the Traditional Approach to the Search and Seizure of Garbage," *Catholic University Law Review* 38 (1989): 543-569.

Davies, Thomas Y. "Denying a Right by Disregarding Doctrine: How *Illinois v. Rodriguez* Demeans Consent, Trivializes Fourth Amendment Reasonableness, and Exaggerates the Excusability of Police Error," *Tennessee Law Review* 59 (1991): 1-100.

___. "Denying a Right by Disregarding Doctrine: How *Illinois v. Rodriguez* Demeans Consent, Trivializes Fourth Amendment Reasonableness, and Exaggerates the Excusability of Police Error," *Tennessee Law Review* 59 (1991): 1-100.

___. "Recovering the Original Fourth Amendment," *Michigan Law Review* 98 (1999): 547-667.

Decker, John F. "Emergency Circumstances, Police Responses, and Fourth Amendment Restrictions," *Journal of Criminal Law and Criminology* 89 (1999): 433-533.

del Carmen, Rolando V. *Criminal Procedure Law and Practice*, 2nd ed. Pacific Grove: Brooks/Cole, 1991.

Dery, George M., III. "The Unwarranted Extension of the Good Faith Exception to Computers: An Examination of *Arizona v. Evans* and Its Impact on the Exclusionary Rule and the Structure of Fourth Amendment Litigation," *American Journal of Criminal Law* 23 (1995): 61-98.

___. "Are Politicians More Deserving of Privacy than Schoolchildren? How *Chandler v. Miller* exposed the Absurdities of Fourth Amendment 'Special Needs' Balancing," *Arizona Law Review* 40 (1998): 73-103.

Diffendal, Gretchan R. "Application of the Good-Faith Exception in Instances of a Predicate Illegal Search: 'Reasonable' Means Around the Exclusionary Rule?" *St. John's Law Review* 68 (1994): 217-239.

Dinger, Daniel R. and John S. Dinger. "Deceptive Drug Checkpoints and Individualized Suspicion: Can Law Enforcement Really Deceive Its Way into a Drug Trafficking Conviction?" *Idaho Law Review* 39 (2002): 1-56.

Dripps, Donald. "Living with *Leon*," *Yale Law Journal* 95 (1986): 906-948.

___. "Akhil Amar on Criminal Procedure and Constitutional Law: "Here I Go Down the Wrong Road Again," *North Carolina Law Review* 74 (1996): 1559-1639.

Dudley, Earl C., Jr. "*Terry v. Ohio*, the Warren Court and the Fourth Amendment: A Law Clerk's Perspective," *St. John's Law Review* 72 (1998): 891-903.

Dumbauld, Edward. *The Bill of Rights: And What It Means Today*, Norman: University of Oklahoma Press, 1957.

Dunlap, Andrew Riggs. "Fixing the Fourth Amendment with Trade Secret Law: A Response to *Kyllo v. United States*," *The Georgetown Law Review* 90 (2002): 2175-2205.

Eisenberg, Teryl Smith. "*Connecticut v. Mooney*: Can a Homeless Person Find Privacy Under a Bridge?," 13 (1993): 229-267.

Esseks, David Clark. "Errors in Good Faith: The *Leon* Exception Six Years Later," *Michigan Law Review* 89 (1990): 625-660.

Fallon, Richard H., Jr. "Stare Decisis and the Constitution: An Essay on Constitutional Methodology," *New York University Law Review* 76 (2001): 570-597.

Fink, Jennifer. 2000. "*People v. Ray*: The Fourth Amendment and the Community Caretaking Exception," *University of San Francisco Law Review* 35: 135-158.

Fisher, George S. "Search and Seizure, Third-party Consent: Rethinking Police Conduct and the Fourth Amendment," *Washington Law Review* 66 (1991): 189-208.

Fisher, Louis. "The Federal Courts and Terrorism," in *Exploring Judicial Politics*, ed. Mark C. Miller, New York: Oxford University Press, 2009, 256-273.

Fishman, Clifford S. "Electronic Tracking Devices and the Fourth Amendment: *Knotts*, *Karo* and the Questions Still Unanswered," *Catholic University Law Review* 34 (1985): 277-395.

Fishman, Clifford and Anne McKenna, *Wiretapping and Electronic Eavesdropping*, 2nd ed. Rochester: Westgroup, 1995.

Friedman, Michael J. "Another Stab at *Schneckloth*: The Problem of Limited Consent Searches and Plain View Searches," *Journal of Criminal Law and Criminology* 89 (1998): 313-346.

Froomkin, A. Michael. "Symposium: Cyberspace and Privacy: A New Legal Paradigm," *Stanford Law Review* 52 (2000): 1461-1543.

Gammon, Timothy E. "The Exclusionary Rule and the 1983-1984 Term," *Marquette Law Review* 68 (1984): 1-25.

Garfinkel, Simson. *Database Nation: The Death of Privacy in the 21st Century*, Sebastopol, CA: O'Reilly & Associates, 2000.

Gavenman, Jon. "*Florida v. Riley*: The Descent of Fourth Amendment Protections in Aerial Surveillance Cases," *Hastings Constitutional Law Quarterly* 17 (1990): 725-757.

Gee, Donald. "The Independent Source Exception to the Exclusionary Rule: The Burger Court's Attempted Common-Sense Approach and Resulting 'Cure-All' to Fourth Amendment Violations," *Howard Law Journal* 28 (1985): 1005-1049.

Gillespie, Daniel T. "Bright-Line Rules: Development of the Law of Search and Seizure During Traffic Stops," *Loyola University Chicago Law Journal* 31 (1999): 1-28.

Gioia, Stephanie. "*Knowles v. Iowa*: No 'Search Incident to Citation' Exception," *American Journal of Criminal Law* 26: (1998): 193-195.

Goddard, Jennifer M. "Note, The Destruction of Evidence Exception to the Knock-and-Announce Rule: A Call for the Protection of Fourth Amendment Rights," *Boston University Law Review* 75 (1995): 458-459.

Gottlieb, David J. "Drug Testing, Collective Suspicion, and a Fourth Amendment Out of Balance: A Reply to Professor Howard," *Kansas Journal of Law and Public Policy* 6 (1997): 27-36.

Gonzalez, Bryan T. "Making it Fit—The Good Faith Exception to the Exclusionary Rule: A Critical Examination of *Arizona v. Evans*," *Whittier Law Review* 17 (1996): 609-650.

Greenberg, Peter S. "The Balance of Interests Theory and the Fourth Amendment: A Selective Analysis of Supreme Court Action since *Camera* and *See*," *California Law Review* 61 (1973): 1011-1064.

Greenhalgh, William W. *The Fourth Amendment Handbook: A Chronological Survey of Supreme Court Decisions*, 2nd ed. Chicago: American Bar Association, 2003.

Greenhalgh, William W. and Mark Y. Jost. "In Defense of the 'Per Se' Rule: Justice Stewart's Struggle to Preserve the Fourth Amendment's Warrant Clause," *American Criminal Law Review* 31 (1994): 1013-1098.

Gunter, David. "The Plain View Doctrine and the Problem of Interpretation: The Case of *State v. Barnum*," *Oregon Law Review* 75 (1996): 577-607.

Gutterman, Melvin. "A Formulation of the Value and Means Models of the Fourth Amendment in the Age of Technologically Enhanced Surveillance," *Syracuse Law Review* 39 (1988): 647-735.

Haemmerle, Todd M. "*Florida v. Bostick*: The War on Drugs and Evolving Fourth Amendment Standards," *University of Toledo Law Review* 24 (1992): 253-268.

Hall, Hope Walker. "Sniffing out the Fourth Amendment: *United States v. Place*—Dog Sniffs—Ten Years Later," *Maine Law Review* 46 (1994): 151-188.

Hall, Kermit "The Warren Court in Historical Perspective," in *The Warren Court: A Retrospective*, ed. Bernard Schwartz, New York: Oxford University Press, 1996, 293-312.

Hall, Stephen E. "A Balancing Approach to the Constitutionality of Drug Courier Profiles," *University of Illinois Law Review* (1993): 1007-1036.

Hanson, Roger S. "The Common Carrier Drug Courier Profile: The Drug Interdiction Program and its Development in the Federal Courts," *Western State University Law Review* 18 (1991): 654-664.

Hardin, Charles W., Jr. "Searching Public Schools: *T.L.O.* and the Exclusionary Rule," *Ohio State Law Journal* 47 (1986): 1099-1114.

Harlow, John Michael. "*California v. Acevedo*: The Ominous March of a Loyal Foot Soldier," *Louisiana Law Review* 52 (1992): 1205-1266.

Harris, David A. "Frisking Every Suspect: The Withering of Terry," 28 *University of California-Davis Law Review* 1 (1994): 1-52.

___. "'Driving While Black' and All Other Traffic Offenses: The Supreme Court and Pretextual Traffic Stops," *Journal of Criminal Law and Criminology* 87 (1997): 544-582.

___. "*Terry* and the Fourth Amendment: Particularized Suspicion, Categorical Judgments: Supreme Court Rhetoric Versus Lower Court Reality Under *Terry v. Ohio*," *St. John's Law Review* 72 (1998): 975-1023.

___. "Car Wars: The Fourth Amendment's Death on the Highway," *George Washington Law Review* 66 (1998): 565.

Heffernan, William C. "Fourth Amendment Privacy Interests," *Journal of Criminal Law and Criminology* 92 (2001): 1-126.

Heffernan, William C. and Richard W. Lovely. "Evaluating the Fourth Amendment Exclusionary Rule: The Problem With the Law," *University of Michigan Journal of Law* 24 (1991): 311-369.

Hellman, Deborah. "The Importance of Appearing Principled," *Arizona Law Review* 37 (1995): 1108-1151.

Henderson, Harry. *Privacy in the Information Age*, New York: Facts on File, 2006.

Herdrich, Madeline A. *"California v. Greenwood*: The Trashing of Privacy," *American University Law Review* 38 (1998): 993-1020.

Hobart, Donald, J. Jr. *"Illinois v. Krull*: Extending the Fourth Amendment Exclusionary Rule 's Good Faith Exception to Warrantless Searches Authorized by Statute," *North Carolina Law Review* 66 (1988): 781-800.

Hoehl, Margaret Anne. "Usual Suspects Beware: 'Walk, Don't Run' Through Dangerous Neighborhoods," *University of Richmond Law Review* 35 (2001): 111-147.

Holly, Wayne D. "The Fourth Amendment Hangs in the Balance: Resurrecting the Warrant Requirement Through Strict Scrutiny," *New York School Journal of Human Rights* 13(1997): 531-587.

Honsinger, H. Paul. *"Katz* and Dogs: Canine Sniff Inspections and the Fourth Amendment," *Louisiana Law Review* 44 (1984): 1093-1107.

Hubbart, Phillip A. *Making Sense of Search and Seizure Law: A Fourth Amendment Handbook* (Durham: Carolina Academic Press, 2005).

Jackson, Darla W. "Protection of Privacy in the Search and Seizure of E-Mail: Is the United States Doomed to an Orwellian Future?" *Temple Environmental Law and Technology Journal* 17 (1999): 97-120.

Janzen, Ralph. *"United States v. Field*: Infrared Scans; Curbing Potential Privacy Invasions," *St. John's Law Review* 69 (1995): 633-647.

Johnson, Sheri Lynn. "Race and the Decision to Detain a Suspect," *Yale Law Journal* 93 (1983): 214-258.

Jones, Stepehn P. "Reasonable Expectations of Privacy: Searches, Seizures, and the Concept of Fourth Amendment Standing," *University of Memphis Law Review* 27 (1997): 907-985.

Joseph, Paul R. "The protective Sweep Doctrine: Protecting Arresting Officers from Attack by persons Other than the Arrestee," *Catholic University Law Review* 33 (1983): 95-145.

Josephson, Mark. "Supreme Court Review: Fourth Amendment—Must Police Knock and Announce themselves Before Kicking in the Door of a House?" *Journal of Criminal Law and Criminology* 86 (1996): 1229-1264.

Julie, Richard S. "High-Tech Surveillance Tools and the Fourth Amendment: Reasonable Expectations of Privacy in the Technological Age," *American Criminal Law Review* 37 (2000): 127-143.

Kamisar, Yale. *"Gates*, 'Probable Cause,' 'Good Faith,' and Beyond," *Iowa Law Review* 69 (1982): 551-615.

___. "Does (Did) (Should) the Exclusionary Rule Rest on a 'Principled Basis' Rather than an 'Empirical Proposition'?," *Creighton Law Review* 16 (1983): 565-667

___. "'Comprehensive Reprehensibility' and the Fourth Amendment Exclusionary Rule," *Michigan Law Review* 86 (1987): 1-50.

___. "The 'Police Practice' Phases of the Criminal Process and the Three Phases of the Burger Court," in *The Burger Years: Rights and Wrongs in the Supreme Court 1969-1986*, ed. Herman Schwartz, New York: Viking Penguin, 1987, 143-168.

___. "The Warren Court and Criminal Justice," in *The Warren Court: A Retrospective*, ed. Bernard Schwartz, New York: Oxford, 1996,116-158.

Kim, Brian. "Marijuana or Football (or the Future Farmers of America): *Board of Education v. Earls*, 122 S.Ct. 2559 (2002)," 26 (2003): 973-980.

King, Clayton E. 'Fourth Amendment—Toward Police Discretion in Determining the Scope of Administrative Searches: *Florida v. Wells*, 110 S. Ct. 1632 (1990)," *Journal of Criminal Law and Criminology* 81 (1991): 841-861.

Kreimer, Seth F. "Watching the Watchers: Surveillance, Transparency, and Political Freedom in the War on Terror," *University of Pennsylvania Journal of Constitutional Law* 7 (2004): 133-181.

Krotoszynski, Ronald J., Jr. "An Epitaphios for Neutral Principles in Constitutional Law: *Bush v. Gore* and the Emerging Jurisprudence of Oprah!," *Georgetown Law Journal* 90 (2002): 2087-2141.

Ku, Raymond Shih Ray "The Founder's Privacy: The Fourth Amendment and the Power of Technological Surveillance," *Minnesota Law Review* 86 (2002): 1325-1378.

Kulowiec, David J. "Determining the Reasonableness Length of a *Terry* Stop: United States v. Sharpe, 105 S.Ct. 1568 (1985)," *Journal of Criminal Law and Criminology* 76 (1985): 1003-10026.

LaFave, Wayne R. "Fourth Amendment Vagaries (Of Improbable Cause, Imperceptible Plain View, Notorious Privacy, and Balancing Askew)," *Journal of Criminal Law and Criminology*, 74 (1983): 1222.

___. "Being Frank About the Fourth: On Allen's 'Process of Factualization in the Search and Seizure Cases," *Michigan Law Review* 85 (1986): 427-480.

___. "'The Fourth Amendment Today'" A Bicentennial Appraisal," *Villanova Law Review* 32 (1987): 1061-1088.

___. "Computers, Urinals, and the Fourth Amendment: Confessions of a Patron Saint," *Michigan Law Review* 94 (1996): 2553-2589.

Landynski, Jacob W. *Search and Seizure and the Supreme Court: A Study in Constitutional Interpretation,* Baltimore: The Johns Hopkins Press, 1966.

___. "The Supreme Court's Search for Fourth Amendment Standards," *Connecticut Bar Journal* 45 (1971): 2-39.

___. "Reasonability and the Fourth Amendment: Comments," *Criminal Law Bulletin* 25 (1989): 51-56.

Larkosh, Daniel J. "The Shrinking Scope of Individual Privacy: Drug Cases Make Bad Law," *Suffolk University Law Review* 24 (1990): 1009-1042.

Lasson, Nelson B. *The History and Development of the Fourth Amendment to the United States Constitution,* Baltimore: The Johns Hopkins Press, 1937.

Lawerence, S. Bryan. "Curtilage or Open Fields: *Oliver v. United States* Gives Renewed Significance to the Concept of Curtilage in Fourth Amendment Analysis," *University of Pittsburgh Law Review* 46 (1985): 795-819.

Lazarus, Jason. "Vision Impossible? Imaging Devices—The New Police Technology and the Fourth Amendment," *Florida Law Review* 48 (1996): 299-335.

Lee, Thomas R. 1999. "Stare Decisis in Historical Perspective: From the Founding Era to the Rehnquist Court," *Vanderbilt Law Review* 52: 647-735.

Leonard, James. "Criminal Procedure—*Oliver v. United States*: The Open Fields Doctrine Survives *Katz*," *North Carolina Law Review* 63 (1985): 546-562.

Lerner, Craig S. "The Reasonableness of Probable Cause," *Texas Law Review* 81 (2003): 951-1029.

Leslie, Heather C. "*Ferguson v. City of Charleston*: A Limitation of the 'Special Needs' Doctrine," *Loyola Journal of Public Interest Law* 3 (2001): 93-104.

Levit, Janet Koven. "Pretextual Traffic Stops: *United States v. Whren* and the Death *Terry v. Ohio*," *Loyola University of Chicago Law Journal* 28 (1996): 145-187.

Lewis, Anthony "Earl Warren," in *The Warren Court: A Critical Analysis,* ed. Richard H. Sayler, Barry B. Boyer, and Robert E. Gooding, New York: Chelsea House, 1969, 1-31.

Lewis, Peter W. "Justice Stewart and Fourth Amendment Probable Cause: 'Swing Voter' or Participant in a 'New Majority,'" *Loyola Law Review* 22 (1976): 713-741.

Livingston, Debra. "Police, Community Caretaking, and the Fourth Amendment," *University of Chicago Legal Forum* 1998: 261-313.

Lochhead, George S. "Supreme Court Review: Fourth Amendment—Expanding the Scope of Automobile Consent Searches," *Journal of Criminal Law and Criminology* 82 (1992): 773-796.

Long, Carolyn N. *Mapp v. Ohio: Guarding Against Unreasonable Search and Seizures*, Lawrence: University Press of Kansas, 2006.

Lyon, David. *Surveillance Society: Monitoring Everyday Life*, Philadelphia: Open University Press, 2001.

Mabry, Cynthia R. "The Supreme Court Opens a Pandora's Box in the law of Warrantless Automobile Searches and Seizures—*United States v. Ross*," *Howard Law Journal* 26 (1983): 1231-1263.

Machado Zotti, Priscilla H. *Injustice for All: Mapp v. Ohio and the Fourth Amendment*, New York: Peter Lang Publishing, 2005.

Maclin, Tracey. "The Decline of the Right of Locomotion: The Fourth Amendment on the Streets," *Cornell Law Review* 75 (1990): 1258-1337.

___. "Justice Thurgood Marshall: Taking the Fourth Amendment Seriously," *Cornell Law Review* 77 (1992): 723-812.

___. "The Central Meaning of the Fourth Amendment," *William and Mary Law Review* 35 (1993): 197-249.

___. "The Complexity of the Fourth Amendment: A Historical Review," *Boston University Law Review* 77 (1997): 925-974.

___. "*Terry v. Ohio's* Fourth Amendment Legacy: Black Men and Police Discretion," *St. John's Law Review* 72 (1998): 1271-1321.

Magee, Robin K. "The Myth of the Good Cop and the Inadequacy of Fourth Amendment Remedies for Black Men: Contrasting Presumptions on Innocence and Guilt," *Capital University Law Review* 23 (1994): 151-169.

Malin, Jennifer L. "*Vernonia School District 47J v. Acton*: A Further Erosion of the Fourth Amendment," *Brooklyn Law Review* 62 (1996): 469-518.

Maltz, Earl. "The Nature of Precedent," *North Carolina Law Review* 66 (1988): 367-393.

Mansukhani, Sanuil H. "School Searches After *New Jersey v. T.L.O.*: Are There Any Limits?" *University of Louisville Journal of Family Law* 34 (1995/1996): 345-378.

Marshall, Elizabeth Phillips. "On Rollercoasters, Submarines, and Judicial Shipwrecks: Acoustic Separation and the Good Faith Exception to the Fourth Amendment Exclusionary Rule," *University of Illinois Law Review* 1989: 941-1017.

McCall, Madhavi M. and Michael A. McCall. "Chief Justice William Rehnquist: His Law-and-Order Legacy and Impact on Criminal Justice," *Akron Law Review* 39 (2006): 323-372.

McC. Mathias, Charles Jr. "The Exclusionary Rule Revisited," *Loyola Law Review* 28 (1982): 7-12.

McInnis, Thomas N. *The Christian Burial Case: An Introduction to Criminal and Judicial Procedure*. Westport, CT: Praeger Publishers, 2001.

McTaggart, David T. "Reciprocity on the Streets: Reflections on the Fourth Amendment and the Duty to Cooperate with the Police," *New York University Law Review* 76 (2001): 1233-1258.

Meares, Tracey L. "*Terry* and the Relevance of Politics," *St. John's Law Review* 72 (1998): 1343-1349.

Mitchell, John B. "What Went Wrong with the Warren Court's Conception of the Fourth Amendment?," *New England Law Review* 27 (1992): 47-53.

Monaghan, Henry Paul. "Stare Decisis and Constitutional Adjudication," *Columbia Law Review* 88 (1988): 723-773.

Monmonier, Mark. *Spying With Maps: Surveillance Technologies and the Future of Politics,* Chicago: University of Chicago Press, 2002.

Moran, David A. "The End of the Exclusionary Rule, Among Other Things: The Roberts Court takes on the Fourth Amendment," *Cato Supreme Court Review* (2005-06): 283-309.

Moran, Peter E. "Unprovoked Flight Upon Noticing Police Officers While Present in a High-Crime Area Are Relevant Factors Which Creates a Reasonable Suspicion to Justify a *Terry* Stop and Thus does not Violate the Fourth Amendment's Prohibition of Unreasonable Searches and Seizures," *Seton Hall Constitutional Law Journal* 11 (2001): 859-885.

Morgan, John S. "The Junking of the Fourth Amendment: *Illinois v. Krull* and *New York v. Burger,*" *Tulane Law Review* 63 (1988): 335-377.

Muller, Eric L. "Hang on to Your Hats! *Terry* into the Twenty-First Century," *St. John's Law Review* 72 (1998): 1141-1148.

Mulligan, Ann. "*City of Indianapolis v. Edmond*: The Constitutionality of Drug Interdiction Checkpoints," *Journal of Criminal Law and Criminology* 93 (2002): 227-257.

Naumann, Mary Elizabeth. "The Community Caretaker Doctrine: Yet Another Fourth Amendment Exception," *American Journal of Criminal Law* 26 (1999): 325-365.

Newman, Loren Keith. "*Horton v. California*: Searching for a Good Cause," *University of Miami Law Review* 46 (1991): 455-502.

Nuger, Kenneth. "The Special Needs Rationale: Creating a Chasm in Fourth Amendment Analysis," *Santa Clara Law Review* 32 (1992): 89-136.

Oliver, Wesley MacNeil. "With an Evil Eye and an Unequal Hand: Pretextual Stops and Doctrinal Remedies to Racial Profiling," *Tulane Law Review* 74 (2000): 1409-1481.

Pallitto, Robert M. and Williams G. Weaver. *Presidential Secrecy and the Law,* Baltimore: John Hopkins University Press, 2007.

Palmer, Joseph H. Jr. "Expanding the Good Faith Exception to the Exclusionary Rule: *Arizona v. Evans,*" *Creighton Law Review* 29 (1996): 903-937.

Peck, Adam Kennedy. "The Securing of the Premises Exception: A Search for the Proper Balance," *Vanderbilt Law Review* 38 (1985): 1589-1619.

Pollack, Kenneth H. "Stretching the Terry Doctrine to the Search for Evidence of Crime: Canine Sniffs, State Constitutions, and the Reasonable Suspicion Standard," *Vanderbilt Law Review* 47 (1994): 803-855.

Prince, Barbara J. "The Special Needs Exception to the Fourth Amendment and how it Applies to Government Drug Testing of Pregnant Women: The Supreme Court Clarifies Where the Lines are Drawn in *Ferguson v. City of Charleston,*" *Creighton Law Review* 35 (2002): 857-911.

Prynkiewiez, Peter C. "*California v. Acevedo*: The Court Establishes One Rule to Govern All Automobile Searches and Opens the Door to Another 'Frontal Assault' on the Warrant Requirement," *Notre Dame Law Review* 67 (1992): 1269-1286.

Ramerman, Ramsey. "Shut the Blinds and Lock the Doors—Is that Enough?: The Scope of Fourth Amendment Protection Outside One's Home," *Washington Law Review* 75 (2000): 281-312.

Rappaport, Stacey Paige. "Stop and Frisk—Police May Seize Nonthreatening Contraband Detected Through the Sense of Touch During a Protective Pat Down Search so Long as the Search Stays within the Bounds Marked by *Terry v. Ohio*—*Minnesota v. Dickerson,* 113 S. Ct. 2130 (1993)," *Seton Hall Law Review* 24 (1994): 2257-2319.

Raymond, Margaret. "Police Policing Police: Some Doubts," *St. John's Law Review* 72 (1998): 1255-1264.

Reich, Marissa. "*United States v. Drayton*: The Need for Bright-line Warnings during Consensual Bus Searches," *Journal of Criminal Law and Criminology* 93 (2003): 1057-1093.

Renick, Anderson M. "Orwellian Mischief: Extending the Good Faith Exception to the Exclusionary Rule: *Arizona v. Evans*," *Capital University Law Review* 25 (1996): 705-729.

Resendez, Madelyn Daley. "Police Discretion and the Redefinition of Reasonable Under the Fourth Amendment: *Maryland v. Wilson*, 519 U.S. 408 (1997)," *Southern Illinois University Law Journal* 23 (1998): 193-222.

Ricciardelli, Gino N. "Stretching the Good Faith Exception Beyond its Constitutional Limits: *Maryland v. Garrison*," *New England Law Review* 23 (1989): 853-885.

Riley, Laura B. "Comment, Concealed Weapon Detectors and the Fourth Amendment: The Constitutionality of Remote Enhanced Searches," *University of California, Los Angeles Law Review*, 45 (1997):281-336.

Ripans, John M. "*Michigan Department of State Police v. Sitz*: Sober Reflections on how the Supreme Court has blurred the Law of Suspicionless Seizures," *Georgia Law Review* 25 (1990): 199-225.

Ritchie, Tiffany R. "A Potential Casualty in the War on Drugs, the Fourth Amendment Survives a Threatening Attack: *Ferguson v. Charleston*, 532 U.S. 67 (2001)," *Southern Illinois University Law Journal* 27 (2002): 169-194.

Rogers, Brent A. "*Florida v. Wells*: The Supreme Court Bypasses an Opportunity to Protect Motorists from Abuses of Police Discretion," *Iowa Law Review* 77 (1991): 347-370.

Romero, Elsie. "Casenote: Fourth Amendment—Requiring Probable Cause for Searches and Seizures Under the Plain View Doctrine," *Journal of Criminal Law and Criminology* 78 (1998): 763-791.

Rownaghi, Vanessa. "Driving Into Unreasonableness: The Driveway, the Curtilage, and Reasonable Expectations of Privacy," 11 (2003): 1165-1198.

Rozzini, Jennifer. "Supreme Court Update on Reasonable Suspicion Analysis: A Review of the Supreme Court Decisions in *Illinois v. Wardlow* and *Florida v. J.L.*," *New Mexico Law Review* 31 (2001): 421-437.

Rutledge, Devallis. *The Search and Seizure Handbook for Law Officers*, Flagstaff, AZ: Flag Publishing Company, 1980.

Saleem, Omar. "The Age of Unreason: The Impact of Reasonableness, Increased Police Force, and Colorblindness on *Terry* 'Stop and Frisk,'" *Oklahoma Law Review* 50 (1997): 451-493.

Saltzburg, Stephen A. "Another Victim of Illegal Narcotics: The Fourth Amendment (As Illustrated in the Open Fields Doctrine)," *University of Pittsburgh Law Review* 48 (1986): 1-25.

___. "*Terry v. Ohio*: A Practically Perfect Doctrine," *St. John's Law Review* 72 (1998): 911-974.

___. "The Supreme Court, Criminal Procedure and Judicial Integrity," *American Criminal Law Review* 40 (2003): 133-158.

___. "A Symposium on the Legacy of the Rehnquist Court: The Fourth Amendment: Internal Revenue Code or Body of Principles,?" *George Washington Law Review* 74 (2006): 956-1018.

Saylor, Richard H., Barry B. Boyer and Robert E. Gooding, Jr. eds. *The Warren Court: A critical Analysis*, New York: Chelsea House, 1969.

Scalia, Antonin. "The Rule of Law as a Law of Rules," *University of Chicago Law Review* 56 (1989): 1175-1188.

Schulhofer, Stephen. *Rethinking the Patriot Act: Keeping America Safe and Free*, New York: The Century Foundation Press, 2005.

Schwartz, Bernard. *A History of the Supreme Court.* New York: Oxford University Press, 1993.

___. ed. *The Warren Court: A Retrospective*, New York: Oxford University Press, 1996.

Schwaratz, Herman. *The Burger Years Rights and Wrongs in the Supreme Court 1969-1986*, New York: Elisabeth Sifton Books, 1987.

Seamon, Richard H. "*Kyllo v. United States* and the Partial Ascendance of Justice Scalia's Fourth Amendment," 79 (2001): 1013-1033.

Serr, Brian J. "Great Expectations of Privacy: A New Model for Fourth Amendment Protection," *Minnesota Law Review* 73 (1989): 583-642.

Sharp, Darren K. "Drug testing and the Fourth Amendment: What Happened to Individualized Suspicion?" *Drake Law Review* 46 (1997): 149-172.

Shepard, Catherine A. "Search and Seizure: From *Carroll* to *Ross*, the Odyssey of the Automobile Exception," *Catholic University Law Review* 32 (1982): 221-260.

Shih Ray Ku, Raymond. "The Founder's Privacy: The Fourth Amendment and the Power of Technological Surveillance." *Minnesota Law Review* 86 (2002): 1325-1378.

Sickman, Linda M. "Supreme Court Review: Fourth Amendment—Limited Luggage Seizures Valid on Reasonable Suspicion: *United States v. Place*, 103 S. Ct. 2637 (1983)," *Journal of Criminal Law and Criminology* 74 (1983): 1225-1248.

Slobogin, Christopher. "The World Without a Fourth Amendment," *University of California Los Angles Law Review* 39 (1991): 1-107.

___. "Let's Not Bury *Terry*: A Call for Rejuvenation of the Proportionality Principle," *St. John's Law Review* 72 (1998): 1053-1095.

___. "Peeping Techno-Toms and the Fourth Amendment: Seeing Through *Kyllo's* Rules Governing Technological Surveillance," *Minnesota Law Review* 86 (2002): 1393-1437.

Sokolowoski, James. "Government Drug Testing: A Question of Reasonableness," *Vanderbilt Law Review* 43 (1990): 1343-1376.

Sorenson, Quin M. "Losing a Plain View of *Katz*: The Loss of a Reasonable Expectation of Privacy Under the Readily Available Standard," *Dickinson Law Review* 107 (2002): 179-207.

Stallings, Kurt. "Fishing Allowed: No Basis Required for Investigatory Stops on Inland Waters with Access to Open Sea—*United States v. Villamonte-Marquez*," *The Maritime Lawyer* 9 (1984): 137-152.

Steiker, Carol S. "Second Thoughts About First Principles," *Harvard Law Review* 107 (1994): 820-857.

Steinbock, Daniel J. "Data Matching, Data Mining, and Due Process," *Georgia Law Review* 40 (2005): 13.

Stelzner, Luis G. "The Fourth Amendment: The Reasonableness and Warrant Clauses," *New Mexico Law Review* 10 (1979): 33-49.

Stern, Barry Jeffrey. "Warrants Without Probable Cause," *Brooklyn Law Review* 59 (1994): 1385-1441.

Stewart, David J. "*Florida v. Riley*: The Emerging Standard for Aerial Surveillance of the Curtilage," *Vanderbilt Law Review* 43 (1990): 275-295.

Stewart, Potter. "The Road to *Mapp v. Ohio* and Beyond: The Origins, Development, and Future of the Exclusionary Rule in Search-and-Seizure Cases," *Columbia Law Review* 83 (1983): 1365-1404.

Storing, Herbert J. ed. *The Complete Anti-Federalist, 2 vol.,* Chicago: University of Chicago Press, 1981.

Stratton, Brent D. "The Attenuation Exception to the Exclusionary Rule: A Study in Attenuated Principle and Dissipated Logic," *Journal of Criminal Law and Criminology* 75 (1984).

Strauss, Mary. "Reconstructing Consent," *Journal of Criminal Law and Criminology* 92 (2001): 211-272.

Strauss, Rebecca. "We Can Do This the Easy Way or the Hard Way: The Use of Deceit to Induce Consent Searches," *Michigan Law Review* 100 (2002): 868-888.

Stuntz, William J. "The Substantive Origins of Criminal Procedure," *Yale Law Journal* 105 (1995): 393-447.

Sundby, Scott E. "A Return to Fourth Amendment Basics: Undoing the Mischief of *Camara* and *Terry,*" *Minnesota Law Review* 72 (1988): 383-448.

___. "Everyman's Fourth Amendment: Privacy or Mutual Trust Between Government and Citizen?," *Columbia Law Review* 94 (1994): 1751-1812.

___. "An Ode to Probable Cause: A Brief Response to Professors Amar, Slobogin," *St. John's Law Review* 72 (1998): 1133-1139.

Taylor, Telford. *Two Studies in Constitutional Interpretation: Search, Seizure and Surveillance and Fair Trial and Free Press,* Columbus: Ohio State University Press, 1969.

Thomas, George C, III. "When Constitutional Worlds Collide: Resurrecting the Framers' Bill of Rights and Criminal Procedure," *Michigan Law Review* 100 (2001): 145-233.

Torpy, Vincent G., Jr. "*United States v. Ross* and the Container Cases—Another Chapter in the Police Manuel on Search and Seizure," *Florida State University Law Review* 10 (1982): 471-496.

Traband, Rhett. "The *Acton* Case: The Supreme Court's Gradual Sacrifice of Privacy Rights on the Altar of the War on Drugs," *Dickinson Law Review* 100 (1995): 1-28.

Uviller, H. Richard. "Reasonability and the Fourth Amendment: A (Belated) Farewell to Justice Potter Stewart," *Criminal Law Bulletin* 25 (1989): 29-50.

Van Duizend, Richard, et. al., *The Search Warrant Process: Preconceptions, Perceptions, and Practices,* National Center for State Courts, 1984.

Wasserstrom, Silas J. "The Incredible Shrinking Fourth Amendment," *American Criminal Law Review* 21 (1984): 257-401.

___. "The Court's Turn Toward a General Reasonableness Interpretation of the Fourth Amendment," *American Criminal Law Review* 27 (1989): 119-148.

___. "The Fourth Amendment's Two Clauses," *American Criminal Law Review* 26 (1989): 1389-1396.

Wasserstrom, Silas and William J. Mertens. "The Exclusionary Rule on the Scaffold: But was it a Fair Trial?," *American Criminal Law Review* 22 (1984): 85-179.

Weinreb, Lloyd L. "Generalities of the Fourth Amendment," *University of Chicago Law Review,* 42 (1974): 49.

Weinstein, Jack B. and Mae C. Quinn. "*Terry,* Race, and Judicial Integrity: The Court and Suppression during the War on Drugs," *St. John's Law Review* 72 (1998): 1323-1341.

White, Edward G. *Earl Warren: A Public Life,* New York, Oxford University Press, 1982.

White, Elisa Masterson. "Good Faith, Big Brother, and You: The United States Supreme Court's Latest Good Faith Exception to the Fourth Amendment Exclusionary Rule. Arizona v. Evans, 115 S.Ct. 1185 (1995)," *University of Arkansas Law Journal* 18 (1996): 533-554.

Wieber, Michael C. "The Theory and Practice of *Illinois v. Rodriguez*: Why an Officer's Reasonable Belief About a Third Party's Authority to Consent Does Not Protect a Criminal Suspect's Rights," *Journal of Criminal Law and Criminology* 84 (1993): 604-641

Wilkins, Richard G. "Defining the 'Reasonable Expectation of Privacy': An Emerging Tripartite Analysis," *Vanderbilt Law Review* 40 (1987): 1077-1129.

Wilson, Bradford. "The Origins and Development of the Federal Rule of Exclusion," *Wake Forest Law Review* 18 (1982): 1073-1109.

Wisotsky, Steven. "Crackdown: The Emerging 'Drug Exception' to the Bill of Rights," *Hastings Law Review* 38 (1987): 889-926.

Wolcott, Alexander P. "Abandonment of the Two-Pronged *Aguilar-Spinelli* Test: *Illinois v. Gates*," *Cornell University Law Review* 70 (1985): 316-334.

Wray, John M. "The Inventory Search and the Arrestee's Privacy Expectation," *Indiana Law Journal* 59 (1983): 321-338.

Yarbrough, Tinsley E. *The Rehnquist Court and the Constitution*, New York: Oxford University Press, 2000.

Yatchak, Patrick S. "Breaching the Peace: the Trivialization of the Fourth Amendment Reasonableness Standard in the Wake of *Atwater v. City of Lago Vista*, 121 S. Ct. 1536 (2001)," *Hamline Law Review* 25 (2001): 329-372.

Zambelli, Carolyn J. "A Band-Aid for the Fourth Amendment: *Knowles v. Iowa* and the Supreme Court," *Connecticut Law Review* 31 (1999): 1217-1243.

Table of Cases

309

Index

315

About the Author

Thomas N. McInnis is professor of political science at the University of Central Arkansas. He teaches courses in American government, judicial systems, civil liberties, and constitutional law. He is the author of *The Christian Burial Case: An Introduction to Criminal and Judicial Procedure* (Westport, CT: Praeger, 2001) and numerous articles.